She's
turning
into

one of
Them!

Other *For Better or For Worse*® Collections

Never Wink at a Worried Woman
Striking a Chord
Reality Check
With This Ring
Family Business
Graduation: A Time for Change
The Big 5-0
Sunshine and Shadow
Middle Age Spread
Growing Like a Weed
Love Just Screws Everything Up
Starting from Scratch
"There Goes My Baby!"
Things Are Looking Up . . .
What, Me Pregnant?
If This Is a Lecture, How Long Will It Be?
Pushing 40
It's All Downhill from Here
Keep the Home Fries Burning
The Last Straw
Just One More Hug
"It Must Be Nice to Be Little"
Is This "One of Those Days," Daddy?
I've Got the One-More-Washload Blues . . .

Retrospectives

Suddenly Silver: 25 Years of For Better or For Worse®
All About April
The Lives Behind the Lines: 20 Years of For Better or For Worse®
Remembering Farley: A Tribute to the Life of Our Favorite Cartoon Dog
It's the Thought That Counts . . . Fifteenth Anniversary Collection
A Look Inside . . . For Better or For Worse®: The 10th Anniversary Collection

With Andie Parton

Wags and Kisses
Leaving Home
Graduation: Just the Beginning!
So You're Going to Be a Grandma!
I Love My Grandpa!

She's turning into **one of Them!**

A *For Better or For Worse*® Collection by Lynn Johnston

Andrews McMeel
Publishing, LLC

Kansas City

For Better or For Worse® is distributed by Universal Press Syndicate.

She's Turning Into One of Them copyright © 2006 by Lynn Johnston Productions, Inc. All rights reserved. Printed in the United States of America. No part of this book may be used or reproduced in any manner whatsoever without written permission except in the case of reprints in the context of reviews. For permission information, write Andrews McMeel Publishing, LLC, 4520 Main Street, Kansas City, Missouri 64111.

06 07 08 09 10 BBG 10 9 8 7 6 5 4 3 2 1

ISBN-13: 978-0-7407-5815-7
ISBN-10: 0-7407-5815-2

Library of Congress Control Number: 20069260005

www.andrewsmcmeel.com

www.FBorFW.com

──────── ATTENTION: SCHOOLS AND BUSINESSES ────────

Andrews McMeel books are available at quantity discounts with bulk purchase for educational, business, or sales promotional use. For information, please write to: Special Sales Department, Andrews McMeel Publishing, LLC, 4520 Main Street, Kansas City, Missouri 64111.

IN MEMORY OF
FRANK THOMAS

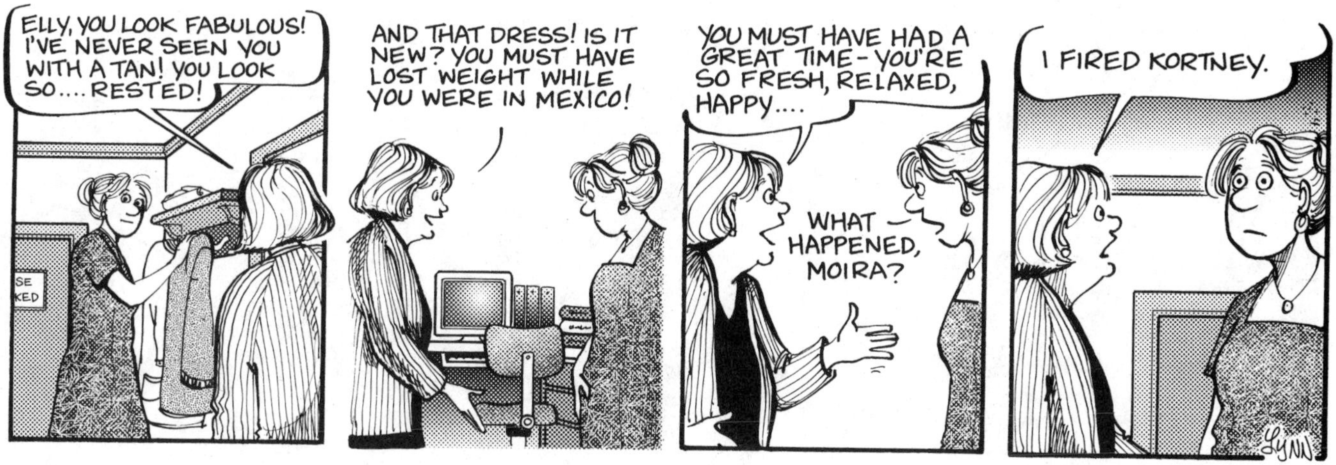
ELLY, YOU LOOK FABULOUS! I'VE NEVER SEEN YOU WITH A TAN! YOU LOOK SO.... RESTED!
AND THAT DRESS! IS IT NEW? YOU MUST HAVE LOST WEIGHT WHILE YOU WERE IN MEXICO!
YOU MUST HAVE HAD A GREAT TIME - YOU'RE SO FRESH, RELAXED, HAPPY....
WHAT HAPPENED, MOIRA?
I FIRED KORTNEY.

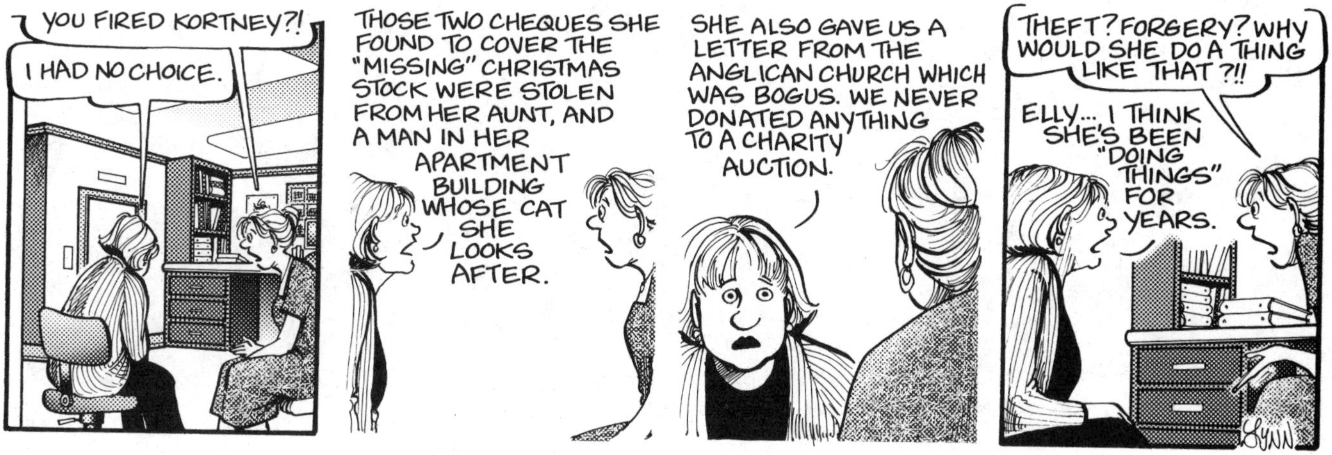
YOU FIRED KORTNEY?!
I HAD NO CHOICE.
THOSE TWO CHEQUES SHE FOUND TO COVER THE "MISSING" CHRISTMAS STOCK WERE STOLEN FROM HER AUNT, AND A MAN IN HER APARTMENT BUILDING WHOSE CAT SHE LOOKS AFTER.
SHE ALSO GAVE US A LETTER FROM THE ANGLICAN CHURCH WHICH WAS BOGUS. WE NEVER DONATED ANYTHING TO A CHARITY AUCTION.
THEFT? FORGERY? WHY WOULD SHE DO A THING LIKE THAT?!!
ELLY... I THINK SHE'S BEEN "DOING THINGS" FOR YEARS.

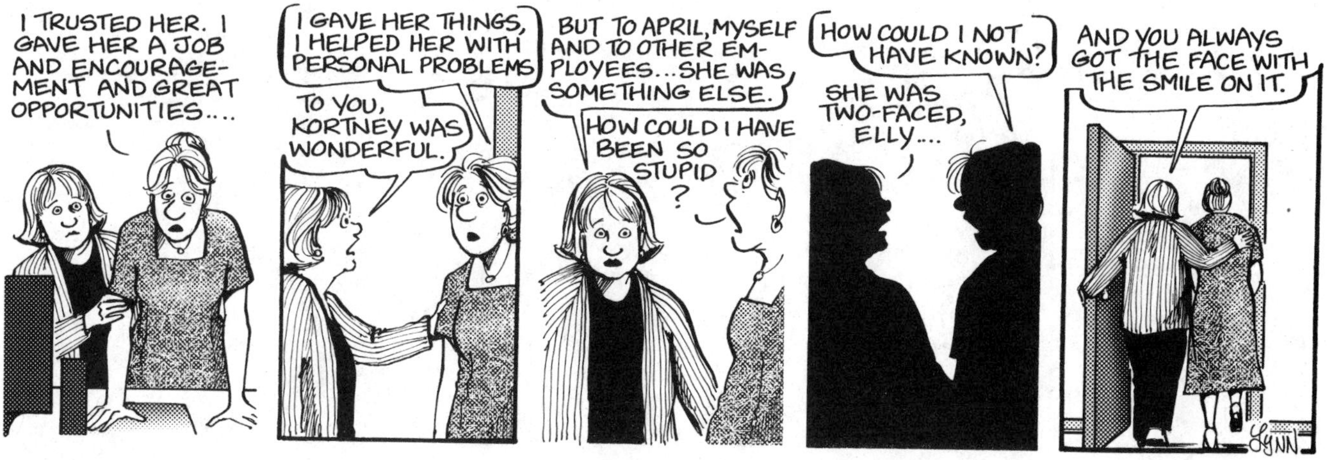
I TRUSTED HER. I GAVE HER A JOB AND ENCOURAGE-MENT AND GREAT OPPORTUNITIES....
I GAVE HER THINGS, I HELPED HER WITH PERSONAL PROBLEMS
TO YOU, KORTNEY WAS WONDERFUL.
BUT TO APRIL, MYSELF AND TO OTHER EM-PLOYEES...SHE WAS SOMETHING ELSE.
HOW COULD I HAVE BEEN SO STUPID ?
HOW COULD I NOT HAVE KNOWN?
SHE WAS TWO-FACED, ELLY....
AND YOU ALWAYS GOT THE FACE WITH THE SMILE ON IT.

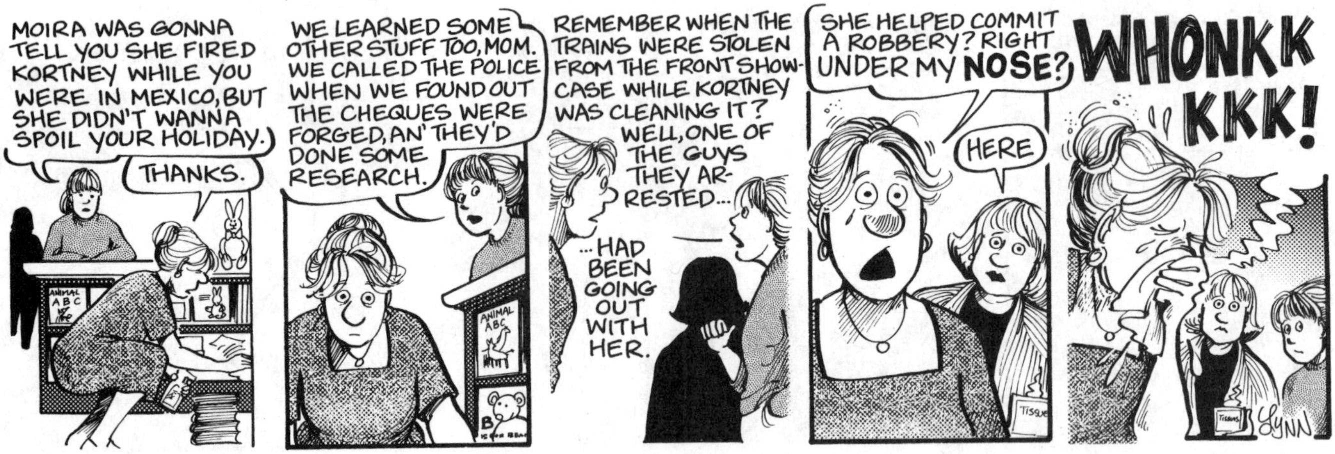
MOIRA WAS GONNA TELL YOU SHE FIRED KORTNEY WHILE YOU WERE IN MEXICO, BUT SHE DIDN'T WANNA SPOIL YOUR HOLIDAY.
THANKS.
WE LEARNED SOME OTHER STUFF TOO, MOM. WE CALLED THE POLICE WHEN WE FOUND OUT THE CHEQUES WERE FORGED, AN' THEY'D DONE SOME RESEARCH.
REMEMBER WHEN THE TRAINS WERE STOLEN FROM THE FRONT SHOW-CASE WHILE KORTNEY WAS CLEANING IT?
WELL, ONE OF THE GUYS THEY AR-RESTED...
...HAD BEEN GOING OUT WITH HER.
SHE HELPED COMMIT A ROBBERY? RIGHT UNDER MY NOSE?
HERE
WHONKK KKK!
LYNN

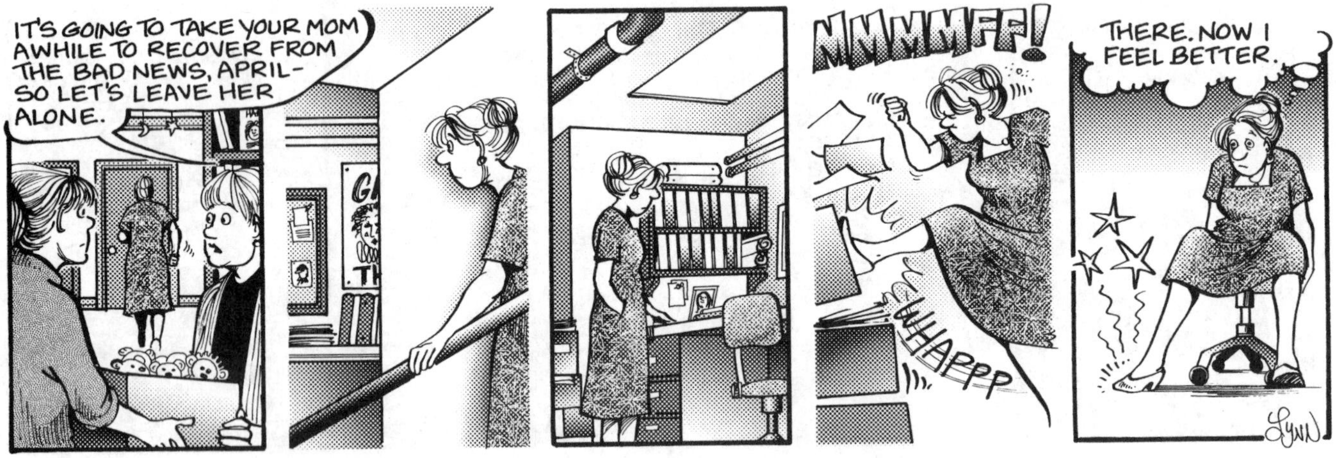
IT'S GOING TO TAKE YOUR MOM AWHILE TO RECOVER FROM THE BAD NEWS, APRIL-SO LET'S LEAVE HER ALONE.
NMMMMFF!
WHAPPP
THERE. NOW I FEEL BETTER.
LYNN

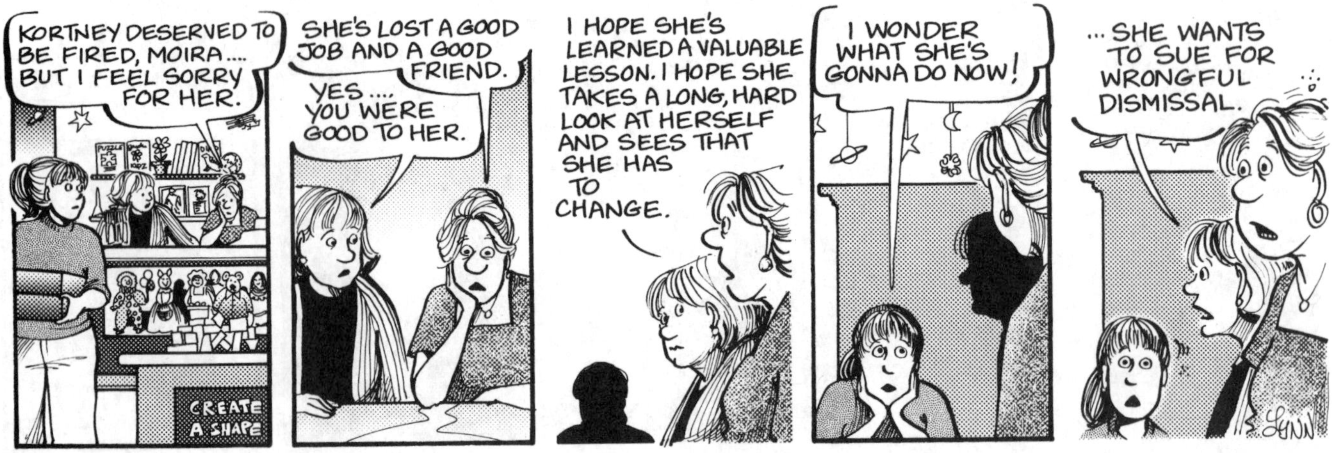
KORTNEY DESERVED TO BE FIRED, MOIRA.... BUT I FEEL SORRY FOR HER.
CREATE A SHAPE
SHE'S LOST A GOOD JOB AND A GOOD FRIEND.
YES.... YOU WERE GOOD TO HER.
I HOPE SHE'S LEARNED A VALUABLE LESSON. I HOPE SHE TAKES A LONG, HARD LOOK AT HERSELF AND SEES THAT SHE HAS TO CHANGE.
I WONDER WHAT SHE'S GONNA DO NOW!
...SHE WANTS TO SUE FOR WRONGFUL DISMISSAL.
LYNN

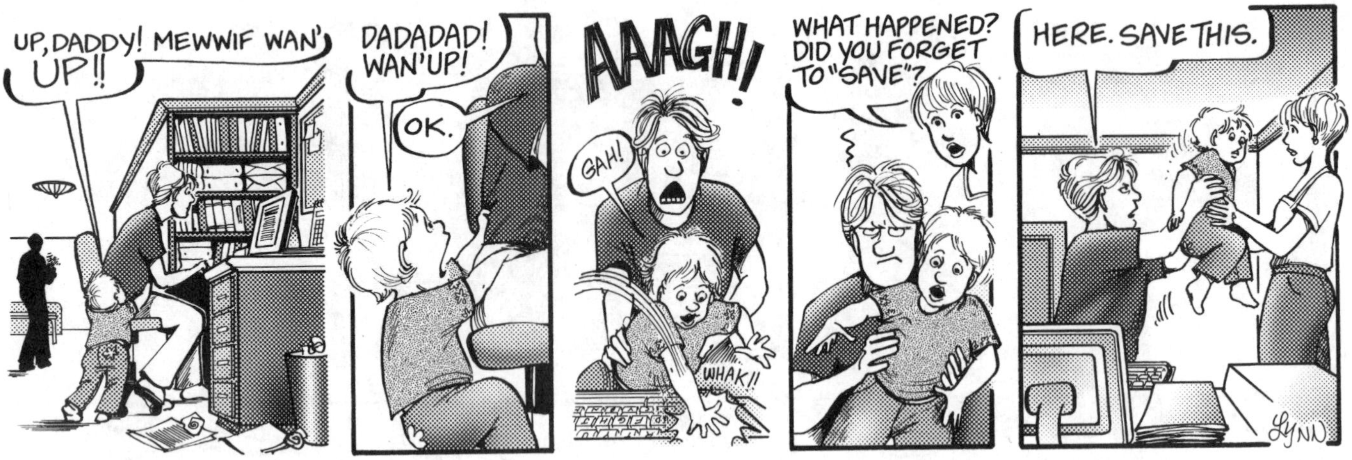
UP, DADDY! MEWWIF WAN' UP!!
DADADAD! WAN'UP!
OK.
AAAGH!
GAH!
WHAK!!
WHAT HAPPENED? DID YOU FORGET TO "SAVE"?
HERE. SAVE THIS.
LYNN

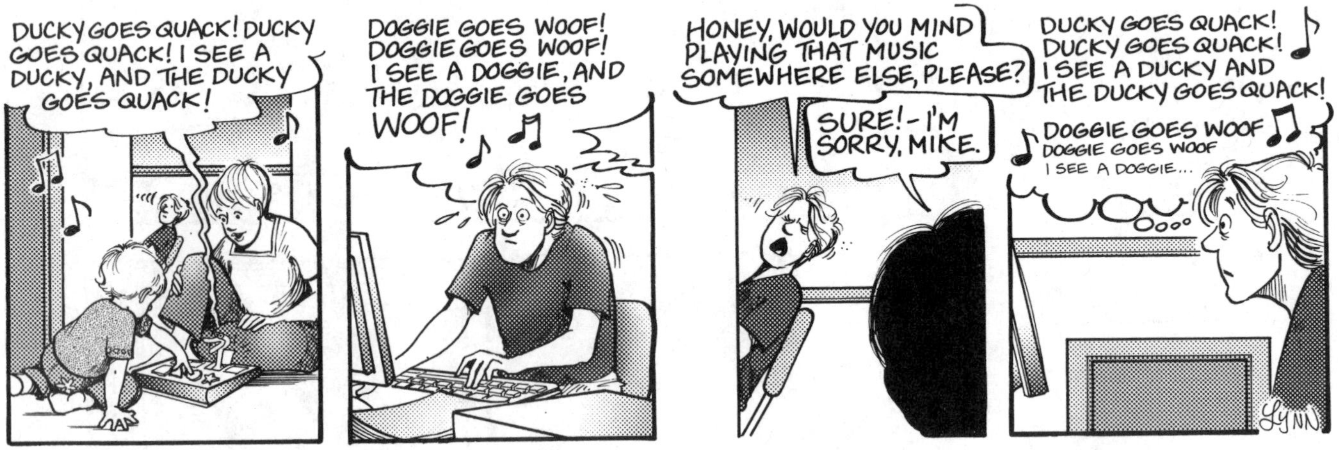
DUCKY GOES QUACK! DUCKY GOES QUACK! I SEE A DUCKY, AND THE DUCKY GOES QUACK!
DOGGIE GOES WOOF! DOGGIE GOES WOOF! I SEE A DOGGIE, AND THE DOGGIE GOES WOOF!
HONEY, WOULD YOU MIND PLAYING THAT MUSIC SOMEWHERE ELSE, PLEASE?
SURE! - I'M SORRY, MIKE.
DUCKY GOES QUACK! DUCKY GOES QUACK! I SEE A DUCKY AND THE DUCKY GOES QUACK!
DOGGIE GOES WOOF
DOGGIE GOES WOOF
I SEE A DOGGIE...
LYNN

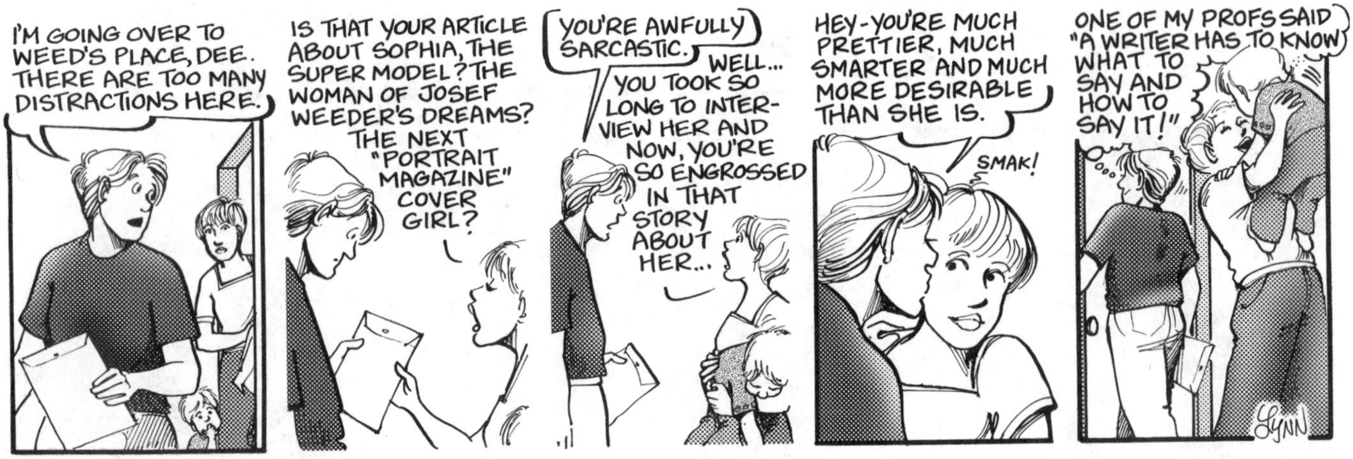
I'M GOING OVER TO WEED'S PLACE, DEE. THERE ARE TOO MANY DISTRACTIONS HERE.
IS THAT YOUR ARTICLE ABOUT SOPHIA, THE SUPER MODEL? THE WOMAN OF JOSEF WEEDER'S DREAMS? THE NEXT "PORTRAIT MAGAZINE" COVER GIRL?
YOU'RE AWFULLY SARCASTIC.
WELL... YOU TOOK SO LONG TO INTERVIEW HER AND NOW, YOU'RE SO ENGROSSED IN THAT STORY ABOUT HER...
HEY - YOU'RE MUCH PRETTIER, MUCH SMARTER AND MUCH MORE DESIRABLE THAN SHE IS.
SMAK!
ONE OF MY PROFS SAID "A WRITER HAS TO KNOW WHAT TO SAY AND HOW TO SAY IT!"
LYNN

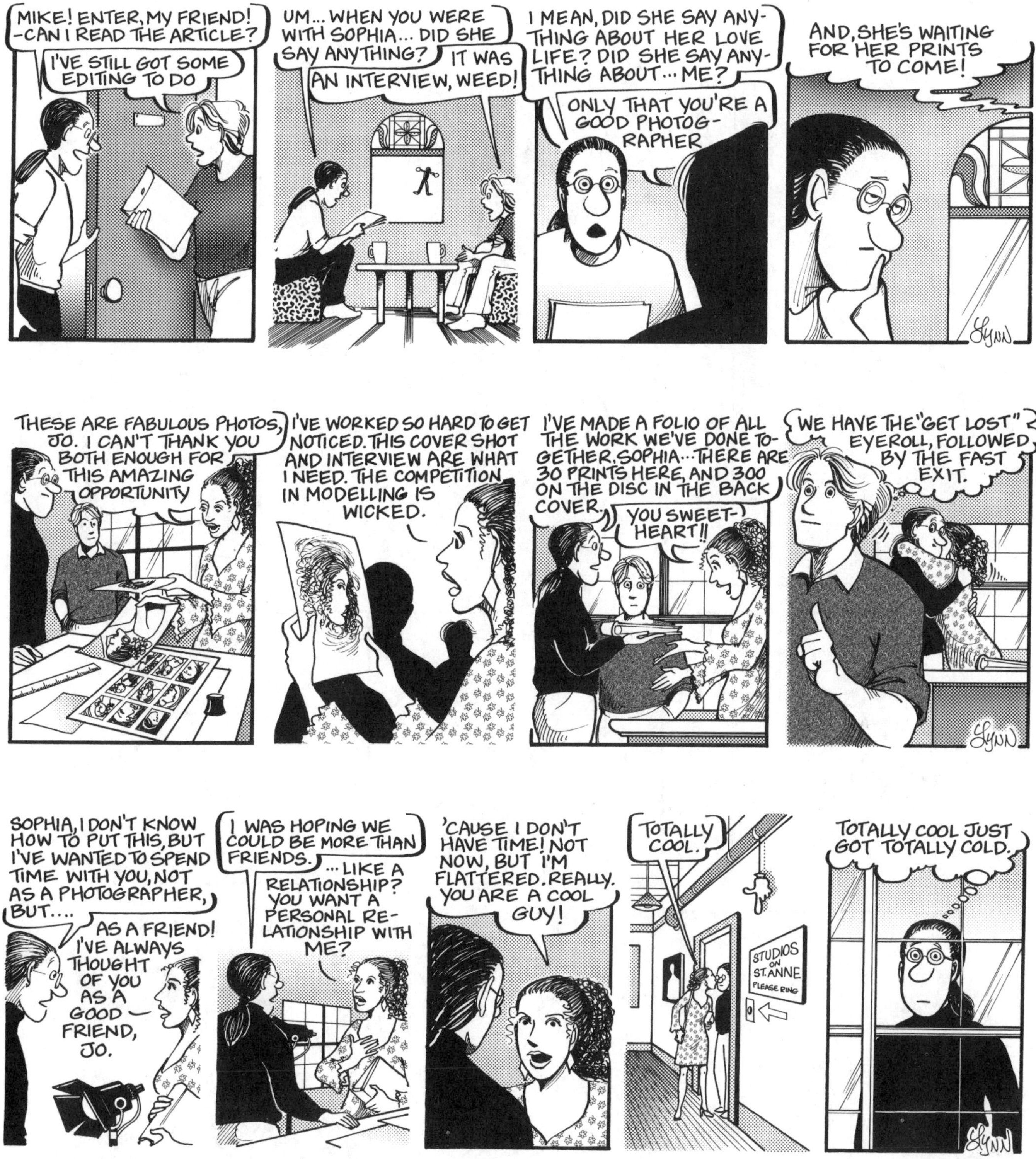
MIKE! ENTER, MY FRIEND! -CAN I READ THE ARTICLE?
I'VE STILL GOT SOME EDITING TO DO
UM... WHEN YOU WERE WITH SOPHIA... DID SHE SAY ANYTHING?
IT WAS AN INTERVIEW, WEED!
I MEAN, DID SHE SAY ANYTHING ABOUT HER LOVE LIFE? DID SHE SAY ANYTHING ABOUT... ME?
ONLY THAT YOU'RE A GOOD PHOTOGRAPHER
AND, SHE'S WAITING FOR HER PRINTS TO COME!
LYNN
THESE ARE FABULOUS PHOTOS, JO. I CAN'T THANK YOU BOTH ENOUGH FOR THIS AMAZING OPPORTUNITY
I'VE WORKED SO HARD TO GET NOTICED. THIS COVER SHOT AND INTERVIEW ARE WHAT I NEED. THE COMPETITION IN MODELLING IS WICKED.
I'VE MADE A FOLIO OF ALL THE WORK WE'VE DONE TOGETHER, SOPHIA... THERE ARE 30 PRINTS HERE, AND 300 ON THE DISC IN THE BACK COVER.
YOU SWEETHEART!!
WE HAVE THE "GET LOST" EYEROLL, FOLLOWED BY THE FAST EXIT.
LYNN
SOPHIA, I DON'T KNOW HOW TO PUT THIS, BUT I'VE WANTED TO SPEND TIME WITH YOU, NOT AS A PHOTOGRAPHER, BUT....
AS A FRIEND! I'VE ALWAYS THOUGHT OF YOU AS A GOOD FRIEND, JO.
I WAS HOPING WE COULD BE MORE THAN FRIENDS.
...LIKE A RELATIONSHIP? YOU WANT A PERSONAL RELATIONSHIP WITH ME?
'CAUSE I DON'T HAVE TIME! NOT NOW, BUT I'M FLATTERED. REALLY. YOU ARE A COOL GUY!
TOTALLY COOL.
STUDIOS ON ST. ANNE
PLEASE RING
TOTALLY COOL JUST GOT TOTALLY COLD.
LYNN

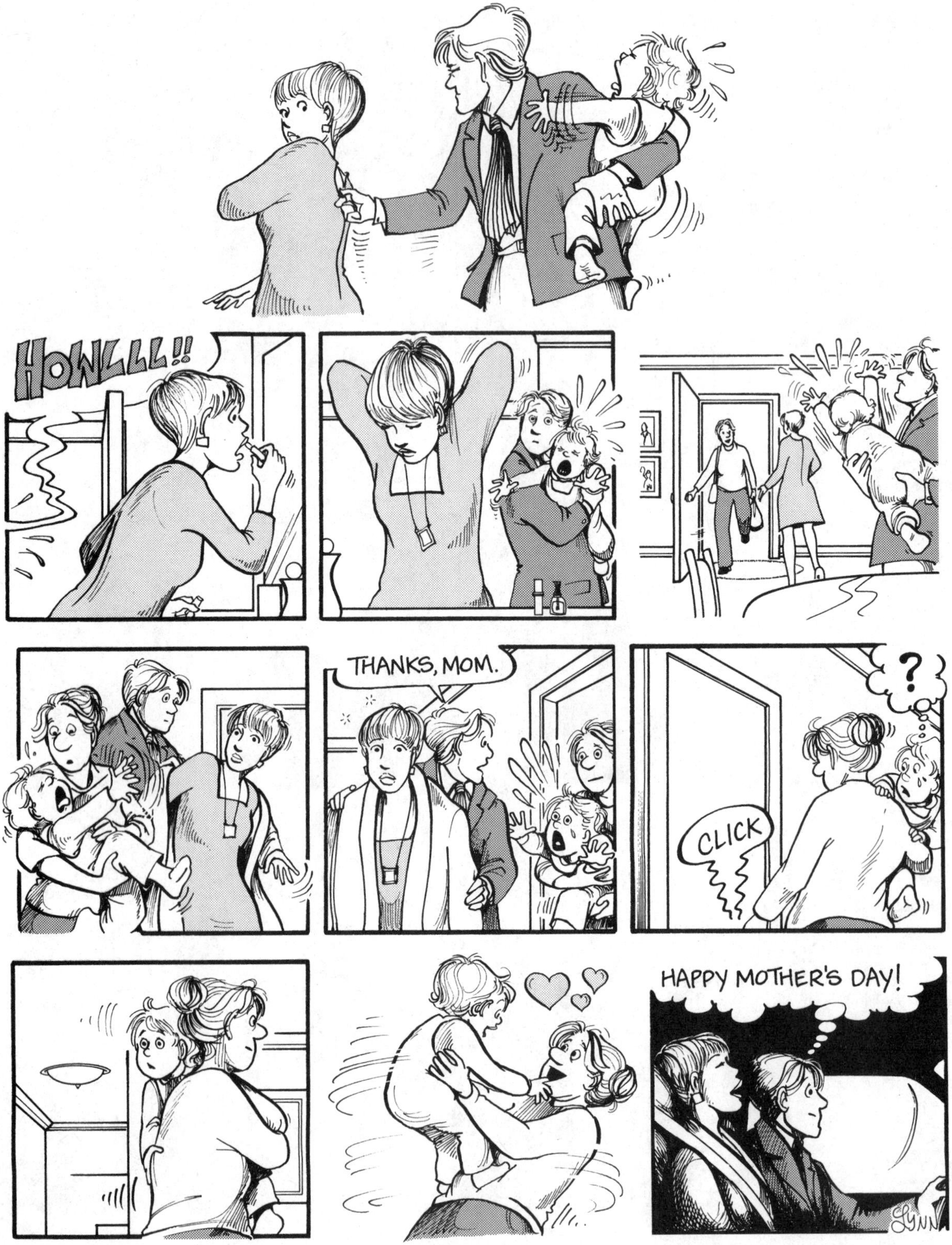
HOWLLL!!
THANKS, MOM.
?
CLICK
HAPPY MOTHER'S DAY!
LYNN

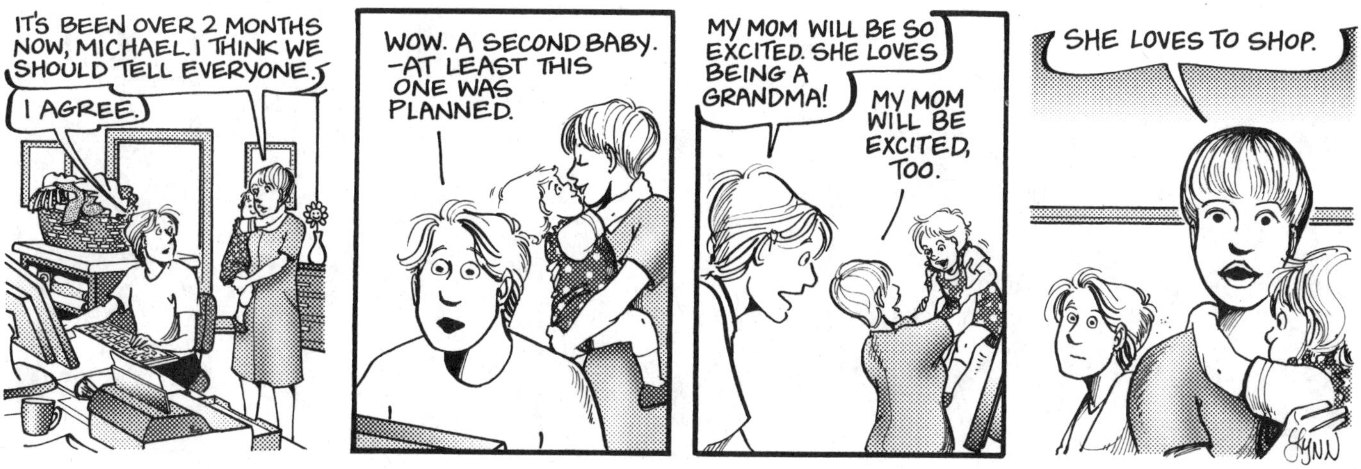
IT'S BEEN OVER 2 MONTHS NOW, MICHAEL. I THINK WE SHOULD TELL EVERYONE.
I AGREE.
WOW. A SECOND BABY. -AT LEAST THIS ONE WAS PLANNED.
MY MOM WILL BE SO EXCITED. SHE LOVES BEING A GRANDMA!
MY MOM WILL BE EXCITED, TOO.
SHE LOVES TO SHOP.
LYNN

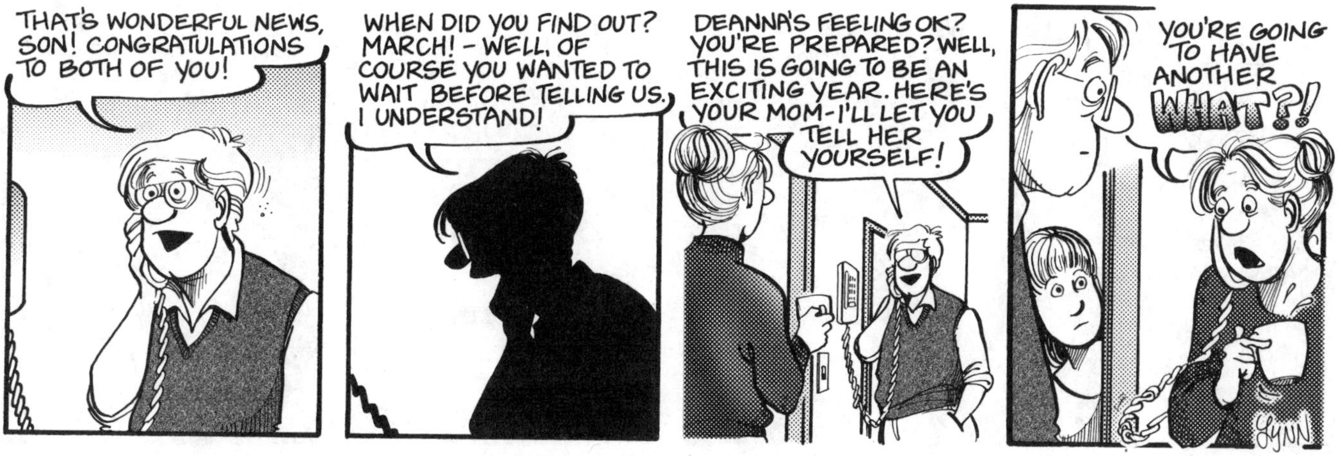
THAT'S WONDERFUL NEWS, SON! CONGRATULATIONS TO BOTH OF YOU!
WHEN DID YOU FIND OUT? MARCH! - WELL, OF COURSE YOU WANTED TO WAIT BEFORE TELLING US. I UNDERSTAND!
DEANNA'S FEELING OK? YOU'RE PREPARED? WELL, THIS IS GOING TO BE AN EXCITING YEAR. HERE'S YOUR MOM - I'LL LET YOU TELL HER YOURSELF!
YOU'RE GOING TO HAVE ANOTHER
WHAT?!
LYNN

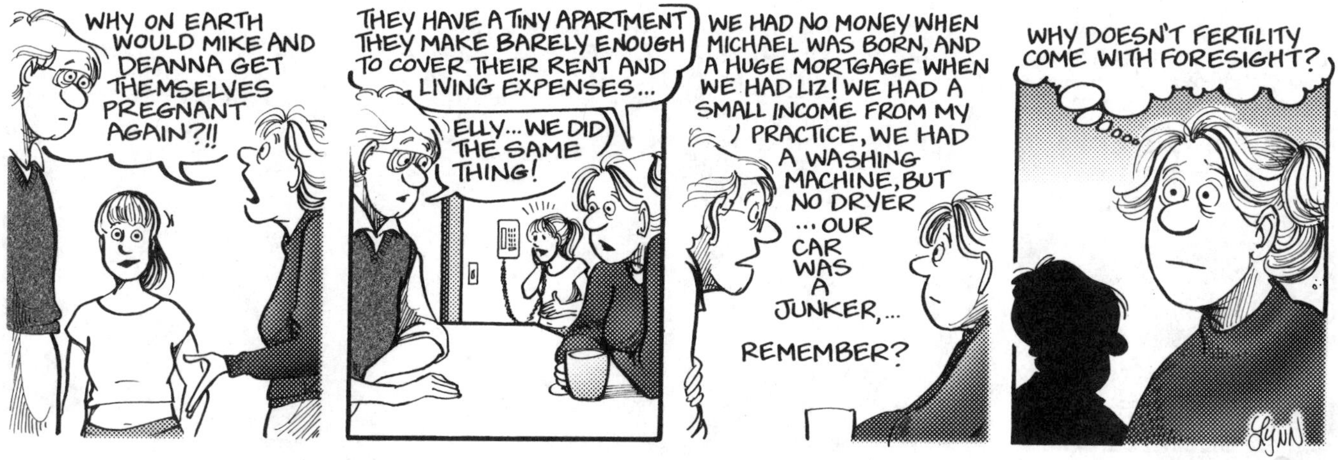
WHY ON EARTH WOULD MIKE AND DEANNA GET THEMSELVES PREGNANT AGAIN?!!
THEY HAVE A TINY APARTMENT THEY MAKE BARELY ENOUGH TO COVER THEIR RENT AND LIVING EXPENSES...
ELLY... WE DID THE SAME THING!
WE HAD NO MONEY WHEN MICHAEL WAS BORN, AND A HUGE MORTGAGE WHEN WE HAD LIZ! WE HAD A SMALL INCOME FROM MY PRACTICE, WE HAD A WASHING MACHINE, BUT NO DRYER ...OUR CAR WAS A JUNKER,...
REMEMBER?
WHY DOESN'T FERTILITY COME WITH FORESIGHT?
LYNN

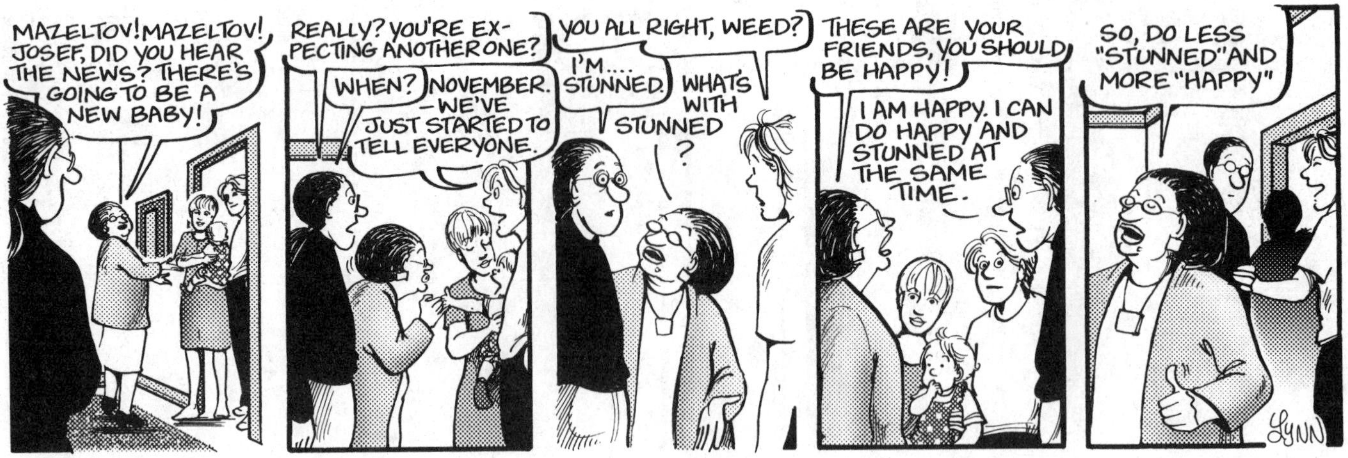
MAZELTOV! MAZELTOV! JOSEF, DID YOU HEAR THE NEWS? THERE'S GOING TO BE A NEW BABY!
REALLY? YOU'RE EXPECTING ANOTHER ONE?
WHEN?
NOVEMBER. —WE'VE JUST STARTED TO TELL EVERYONE.
YOU ALL RIGHT, WEED?
I'M.... STUNNED.
WHAT'S WITH STUNNED ?
THESE ARE YOUR FRIENDS, YOU SHOULD BE HAPPY!
I AM HAPPY. I CAN DO HAPPY AND STUNNED AT THE SAME TIME.
SO, DO LESS "STUNNED" AND MORE "HAPPY"
LYNN

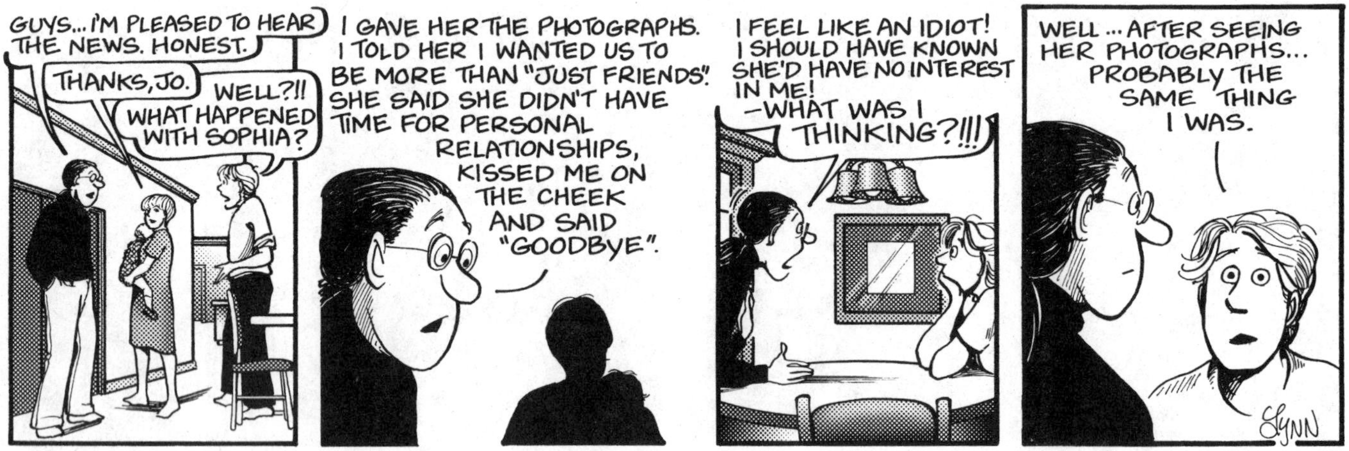
GUYS... I'M PLEASED TO HEAR THE NEWS. HONEST.
THANKS, JO.
WELL?!! WHAT HAPPENED WITH SOPHIA?
I GAVE HER THE PHOTOGRAPHS. I TOLD HER I WANTED US TO BE MORE THAN "JUST FRIENDS". SHE SAID SHE DIDN'T HAVE TIME FOR PERSONAL RELATIONSHIPS, KISSED ME ON THE CHEEK AND SAID "GOODBYE".
I FEEL LIKE AN IDIOT! I SHOULD HAVE KNOWN SHE'D HAVE NO INTEREST IN ME! —WHAT WAS I THINKING?!!!
WELL ... AFTER SEEING HER PHOTOGRAPHS... PROBABLY THE SAME THING I WAS.
LYNN

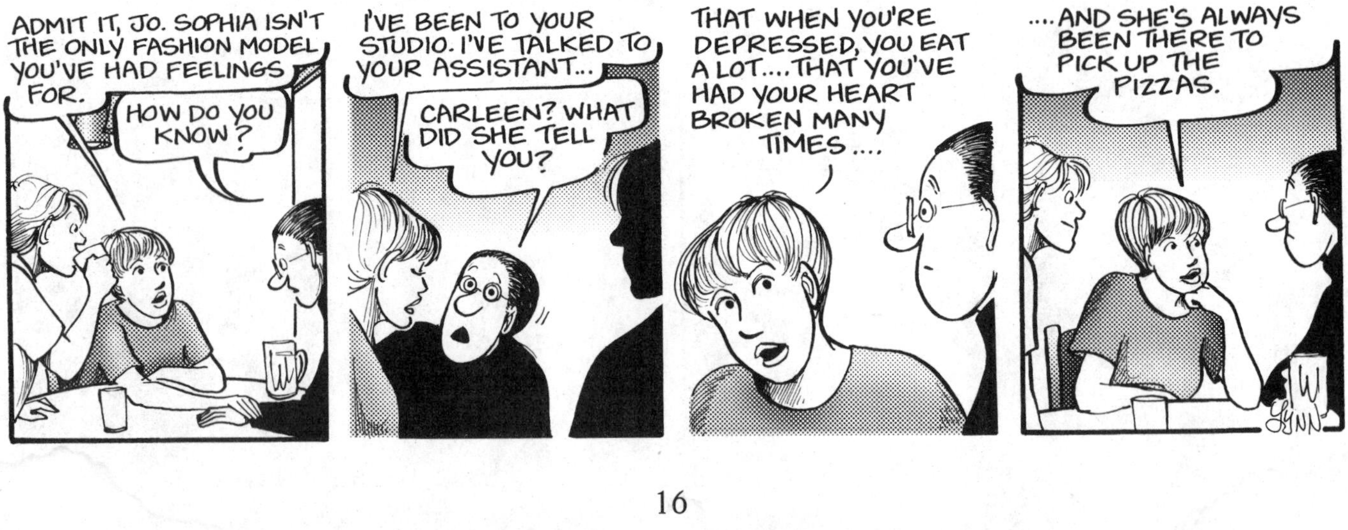
ADMIT IT, JO. SOPHIA ISN'T THE ONLY FASHION MODEL YOU'VE HAD FEELINGS FOR.
HOW DO YOU KNOW?
I'VE BEEN TO YOUR STUDIO. I'VE TALKED TO YOUR ASSISTANT...
CARLEEN? WHAT DID SHE TELL YOU?
THAT WHEN YOU'RE DEPRESSED, YOU EAT A LOT.... THAT YOU'VE HAD YOUR HEART BROKEN MANY TIMES....
....AND SHE'S ALWAYS BEEN THERE TO PICK UP THE PIZZAS.
LYNN

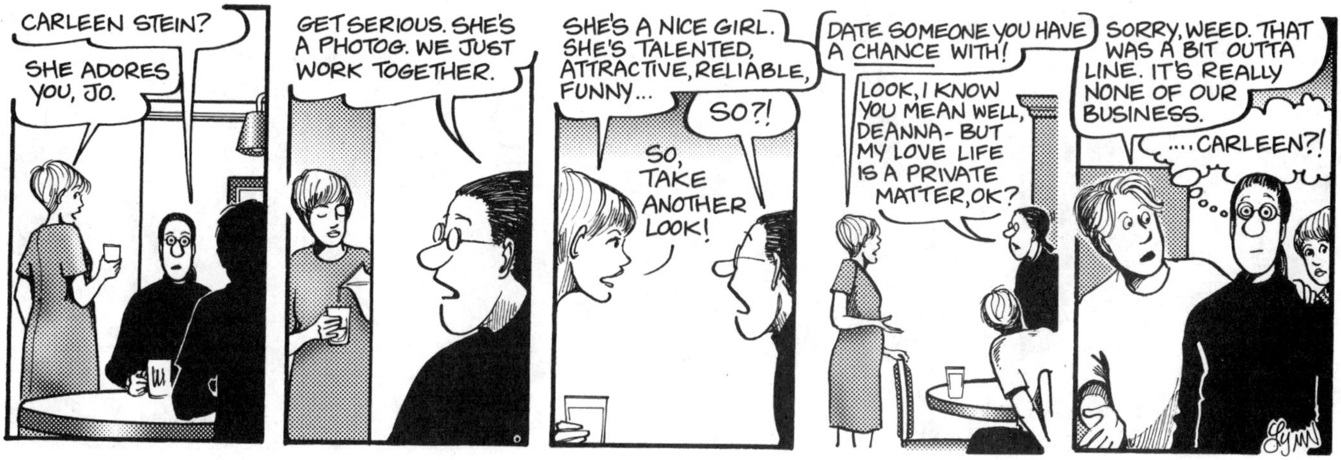
CARLEEN STEIN?
SHE ADORES YOU, JO.
GET SERIOUS. SHE'S A PHOTOG. WE JUST WORK TOGETHER.
SHE'S A NICE GIRL. SHE'S TALENTED, ATTRACTIVE, RELIABLE, FUNNY...
SO?!
SO, TAKE ANOTHER LOOK!
DATE SOMEONE YOU HAVE A CHANCE WITH!
LOOK, I KNOW YOU MEAN WELL, DEANNA- BUT MY LOVE LIFE IS A PRIVATE MATTER, OK?
SORRY, WEED. THAT WAS A BIT OUTTA LINE. IT'S REALLY NONE OF OUR BUSINESS.
....CARLEEN?!
LYNN

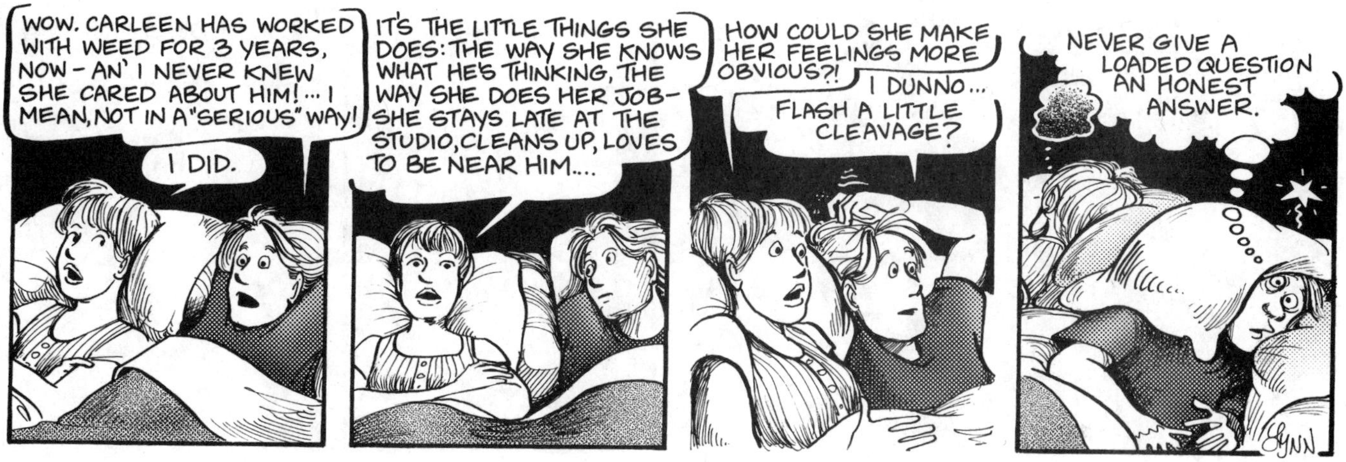
WOW. CARLEEN HAS WORKED WITH WEED FOR 3 YEARS, NOW - AN' I NEVER KNEW SHE CARED ABOUT HIM!... I MEAN, NOT IN A "SERIOUS" WAY!
I DID.
IT'S THE LITTLE THINGS SHE DOES: THE WAY SHE KNOWS WHAT HE'S THINKING, THE WAY SHE DOES HER JOB- SHE STAYS LATE AT THE STUDIO, CLEANS UP, LOVES TO BE NEAR HIM....
HOW COULD SHE MAKE HER FEELINGS MORE OBVIOUS?!
I DUNNO... FLASH A LITTLE CLEAVAGE?
NEVER GIVE A LOADED QUESTION AN HONEST ANSWER.
LYNN

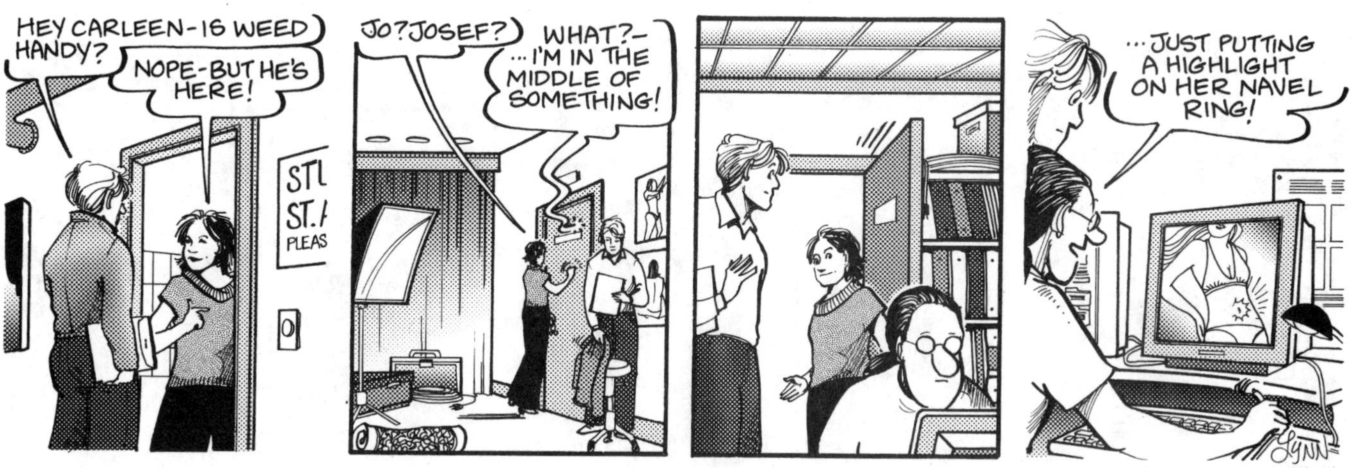
HEY CARLEEN- IS WEED HANDY?
NOPE- BUT HE'S HERE!
JO? JOSEF?
WHAT?- ... I'M IN THE MIDDLE OF SOMETHING!
...JUST PUTTING A HIGHLIGHT ON HER NAVEL RING!
LYNN

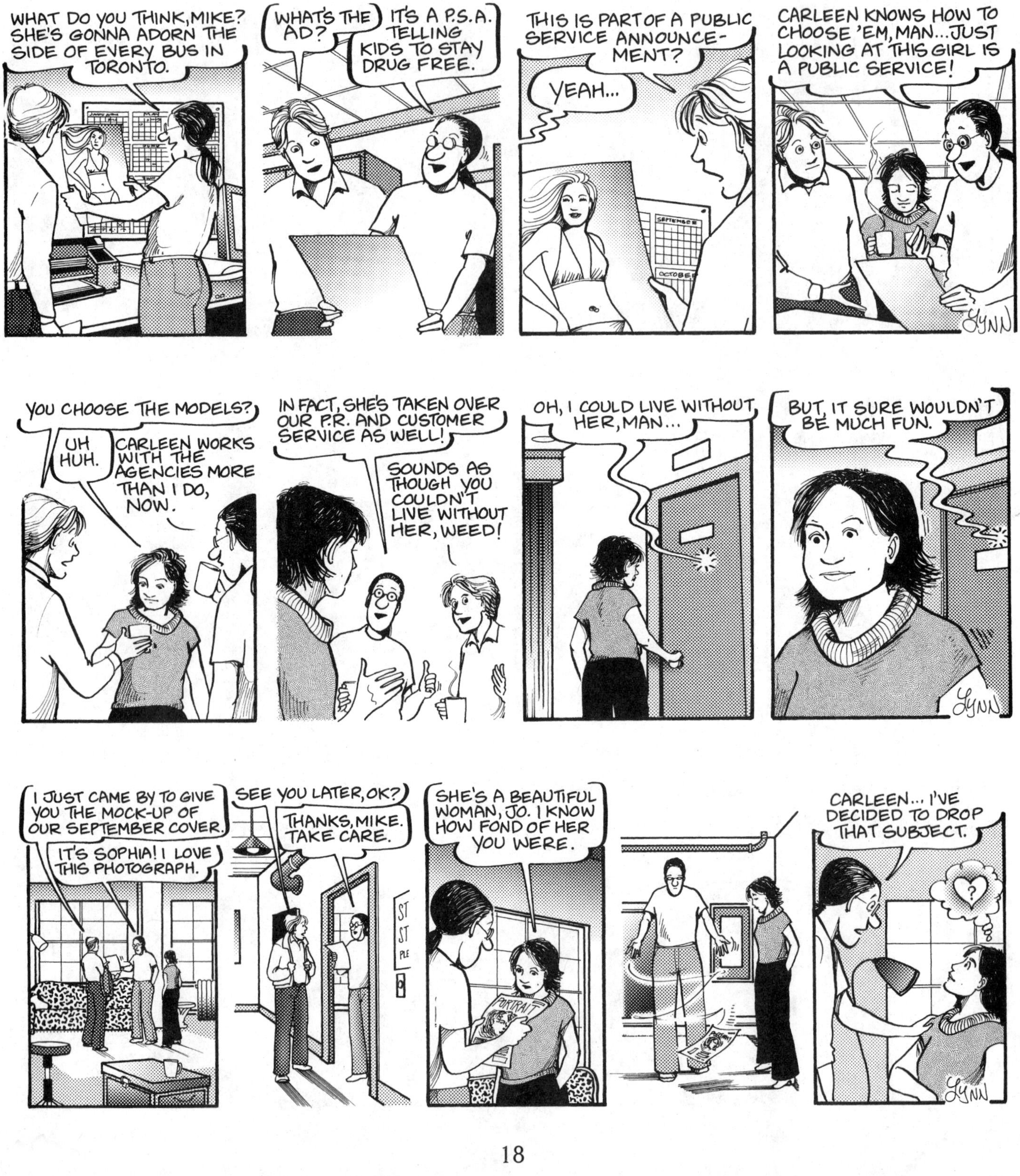
WHAT DO YOU THINK, MIKE? SHE'S GONNA ADORN THE SIDE OF EVERY BUS IN TORONTO.
WHAT'S THE AD?
IT'S A P.S.A. TELLING KIDS TO STAY DRUG FREE.
THIS IS PART OF A PUBLIC SERVICE ANNOUNCEMENT?
YEAH...
CARLEEN KNOWS HOW TO CHOOSE 'EM, MAN... JUST LOOKING AT THIS GIRL IS A PUBLIC SERVICE!
LYNN
YOU CHOOSE THE MODELS?
UH HUH.
CARLEEN WORKS WITH THE AGENCIES MORE THAN I DO, NOW.
IN FACT, SHE'S TAKEN OVER OUR P.R. AND CUSTOMER SERVICE AS WELL!
SOUNDS AS THOUGH YOU COULDN'T LIVE WITHOUT HER, WEED!
OH, I COULD LIVE WITHOUT HER, MAN...
BUT, IT SURE WOULDN'T BE MUCH FUN.
LYNN
I JUST CAME BY TO GIVE YOU THE MOCK-UP OF OUR SEPTEMBER COVER.
IT'S SOPHIA! I LOVE THIS PHOTOGRAPH.
SEE YOU LATER, OK?
THANKS, MIKE. TAKE CARE.
SHE'S A BEAUTIFUL WOMAN, JO. I KNOW HOW FOND OF HER YOU WERE.
PORTRAIT
CARLEEN... I'VE DECIDED TO DROP THAT SUBJECT.
LYNN

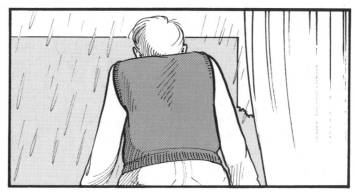

IRIS...LET'S GO FOR A WALK, NOW?

I WANT TO SMELL THE COOL, DAMP SOIL....

I WANT TO SEE CLEAR PEARLS OF WATER ON THE GRASS, THE LEAVES, THE FLOWERS!

I WANT TO FEEL THE WIND IN MY HAIR AND THE RAIN IN MY FACE!

OK....

....I'VE HAD ENOUGH.

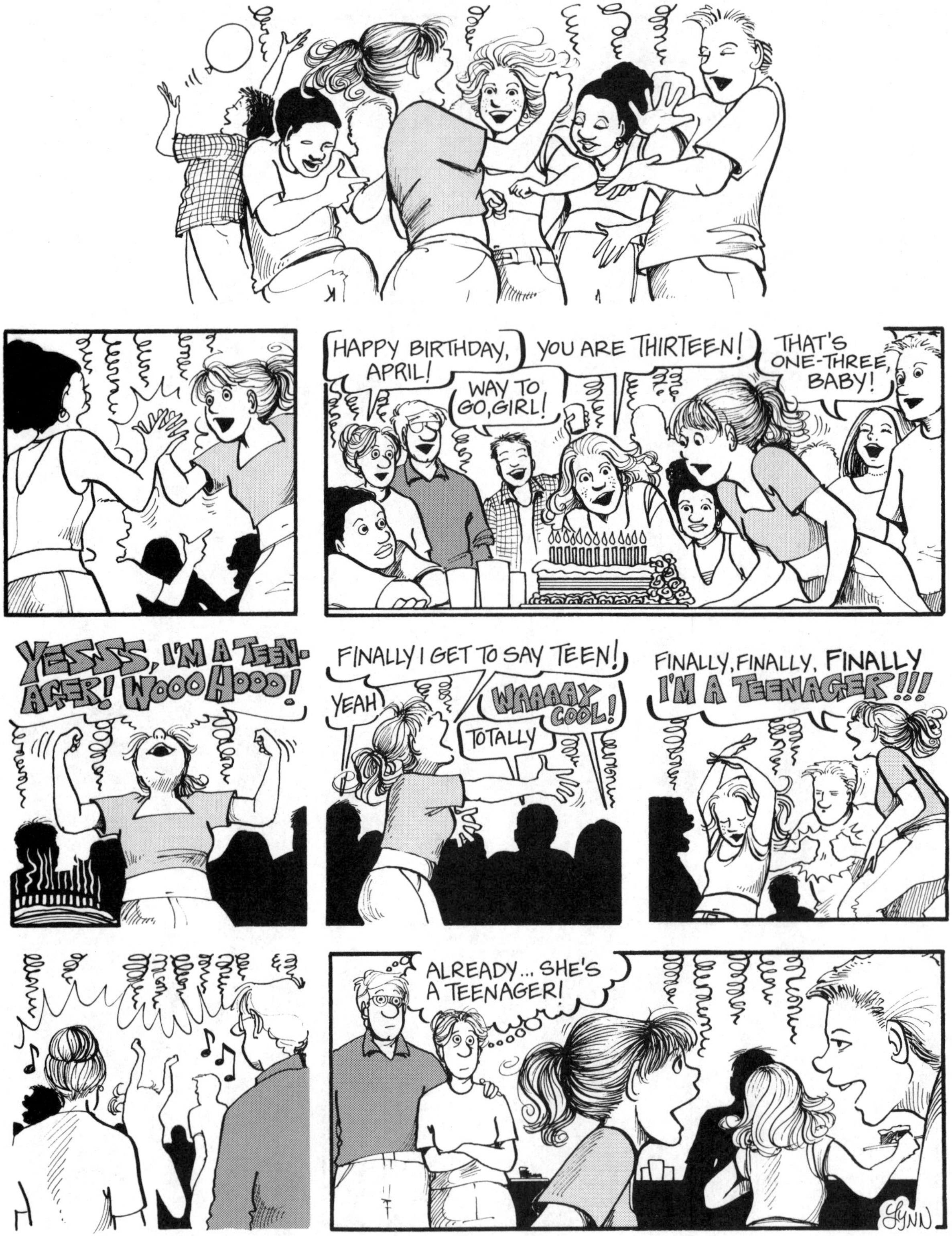
HAPPY BIRTHDAY, APRIL!
YOU ARE THIRTEEN!
WAY TO GO, GIRL!
THAT'S ONE-THREE, BABY!
YESSSS, I'M A TEEN-AGER! WOOOHOOO!
FINALLY I GET TO SAY TEEN!
YEAH
TOTALLY
WAAAAY COOL!
FINALLY, FINALLY, FINALLY I'M A TEENAGER!!!
ALREADY... SHE'S A TEENAGER!
LYNN

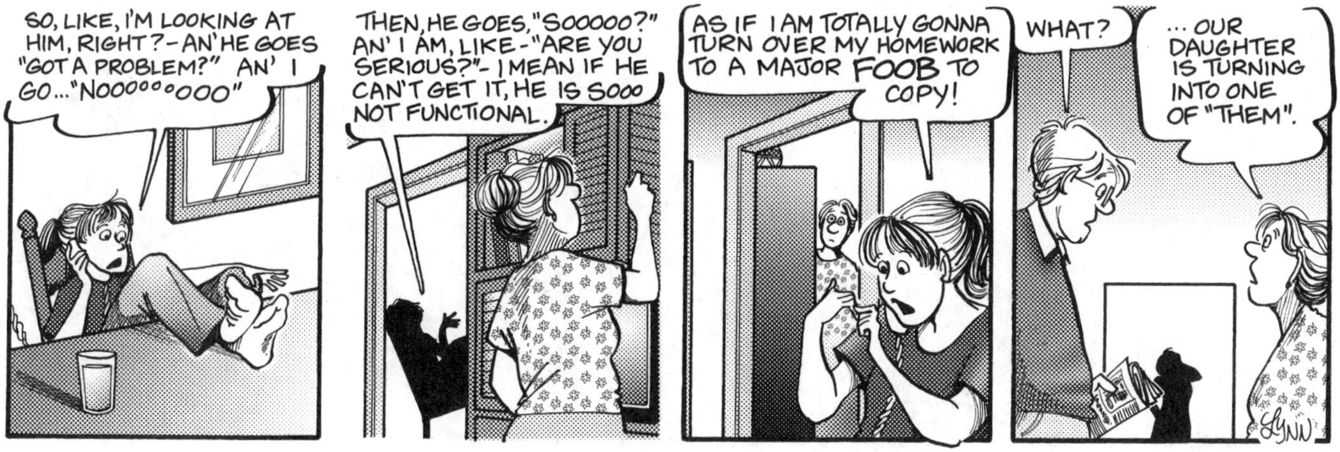
SO, LIKE, I'M LOOKING AT HIM, RIGHT?–AN' HE GOES "GOT A PROBLEM?" AN' I GO..."NOOOOOOOOO"
THEN, HE GOES, "SOOOOO?" AN' I AM, LIKE–"ARE YOU SERIOUS?"–I MEAN IF HE CAN'T GET IT, HE IS SOOO NOT FUNCTIONAL.
AS IF I AM TOTALLY GONNA TURN OVER MY HOMEWORK TO A MAJOR FOOB TO COPY!
WHAT?
...OUR DAUGHTER IS TURNING INTO ONE OF "THEM".
LYNN

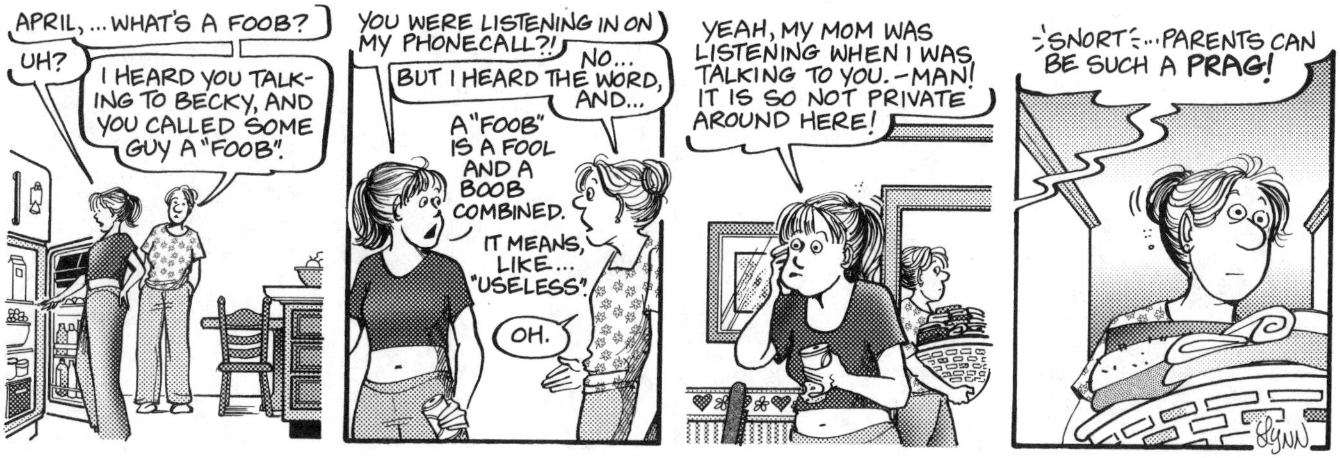
APRIL, ...WHAT'S A FOOB?
UH?
I HEARD YOU TALKING TO BECKY, AND YOU CALLED SOME GUY A "FOOB".
YOU WERE LISTENING IN ON MY PHONECALL?!
NO... BUT I HEARD THE WORD, AND...
A "FOOB" IS A FOOL AND A BOOB COMBINED.
IT MEANS, LIKE... "USELESS".
OH.
YEAH, MY MOM WAS LISTENING WHEN I WAS TALKING TO YOU.–MAN! IT IS SO NOT PRIVATE AROUND HERE!
SNORT ...PARENTS CAN BE SUCH A PRAG!
LYNN

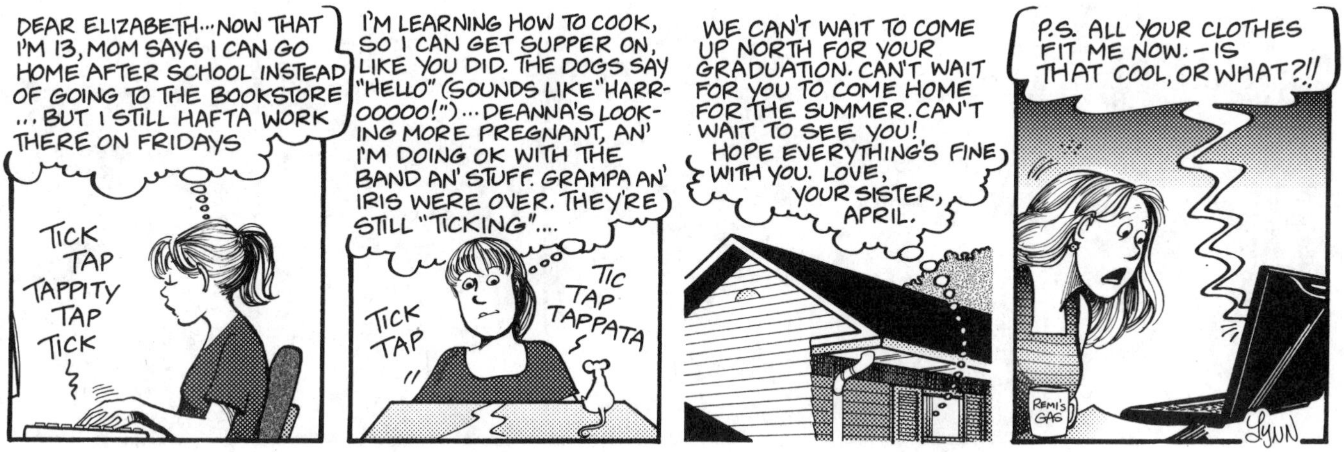
DEAR ELIZABETH...NOW THAT I'M 13, MOM SAYS I CAN GO HOME AFTER SCHOOL INSTEAD OF GOING TO THE BOOKSTORE ...BUT I STILL HAFTA WORK THERE ON FRIDAYS
TICK TAP TAPPITY TAP TICK
I'M LEARNING HOW TO COOK, SO I CAN GET SUPPER ON, LIKE YOU DID. THE DOGS SAY "HELLO" (SOUNDS LIKE "HARROOOOO!")...DEANNA'S LOOKING MORE PREGNANT, AN' I'M DOING OK WITH THE BAND AN' STUFF. GRAMPA AN' IRIS WERE OVER. THEY'RE STILL "TICKING"....
TICK TAP
TIC TAP TAPPATA
WE CAN'T WAIT TO COME UP NORTH FOR YOUR GRADUATION. CAN'T WAIT FOR YOU TO COME HOME FOR THE SUMMER. CAN'T WAIT TO SEE YOU! HOPE EVERYTHING'S FINE WITH YOU. LOVE, YOUR SISTER, APRIL.
P.S. ALL YOUR CLOTHES FIT ME NOW.–IS THAT COOL, OR WHAT?!!
REMI'S GAG
LYNN

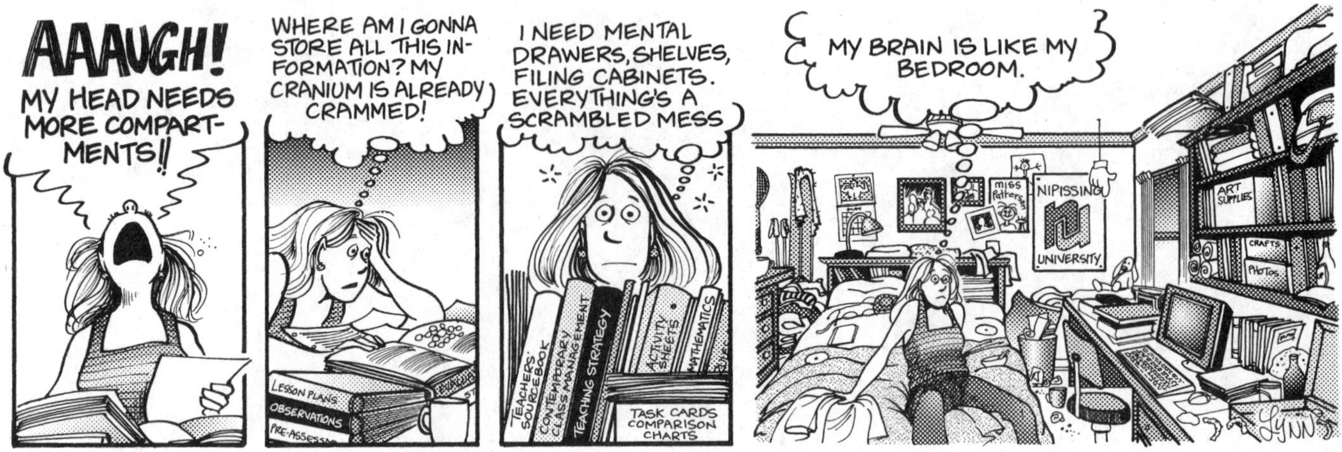
AAAUGH! MY HEAD NEEDS MORE COMPART-MENTS!!
WHERE AM I GONNA STORE ALL THIS IN-FORMATION? MY CRANIUM IS ALREADY CRAMMED!
LESSON PLANS
OBSERVATIONS
I NEED MENTAL DRAWERS, SHELVES, FILING CABINETS. EVERYTHING'S A SCRAMBLED MESS
TEACHERS' SOURCEBOOK
CONTEMPORARY CLASS MANAGEMENT
TEACHING STRATEGY
ACTIVITY SHEETS
MATHEMATICS
TASK CARDS COMPARISON CHARTS
MY BRAIN IS LIKE MY BEDROOM.
NIPISSING UNIVERSITY
ART SUPPLIES
CRAFTS
PHOTOS
LYNN

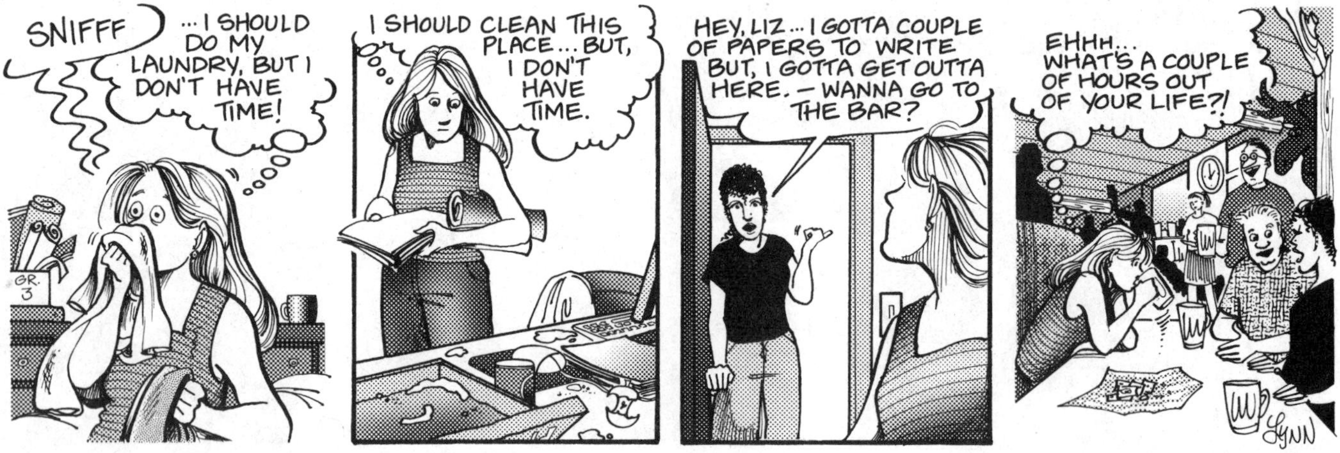
SNIFFF
...I SHOULD DO MY LAUNDRY, BUT I DON'T HAVE TIME!
GR. 3
I SHOULD CLEAN THIS PLACE... BUT, I DON'T HAVE TIME.
HEY, LIZ... I GOTTA COUPLE OF PAPERS TO WRITE BUT, I GOTTA GET OUTTA HERE. — WANNA GO TO THE BAR?
EHHH... WHAT'S A COUPLE OF HOURS OUT OF YOUR LIFE?!
LYNN

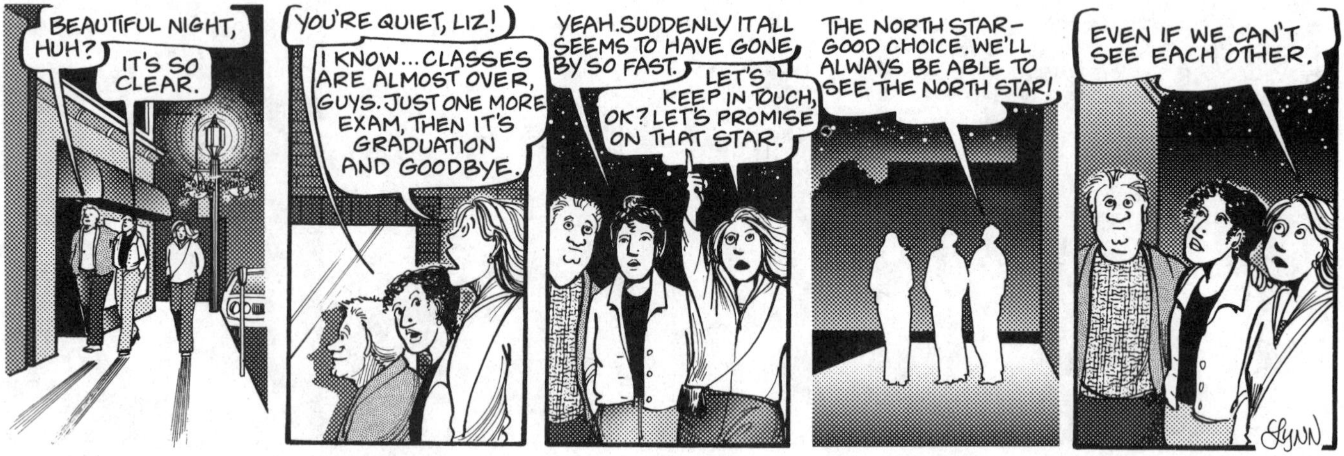
BEAUTIFUL NIGHT, HUH?
IT'S SO CLEAR.
YOU'RE QUIET, LIZ!
I KNOW... CLASSES ARE ALMOST OVER, GUYS. JUST ONE MORE EXAM, THEN IT'S GRADUATION AND GOODBYE.
YEAH. SUDDENLY IT ALL SEEMS TO HAVE GONE BY SO FAST.
LET'S KEEP IN TOUCH, OK? LET'S PROMISE ON THAT STAR.
THE NORTH STAR — GOOD CHOICE. WE'LL ALWAYS BE ABLE TO SEE THE NORTH STAR!
EVEN IF WE CAN'T SEE EACH OTHER.
LYNN

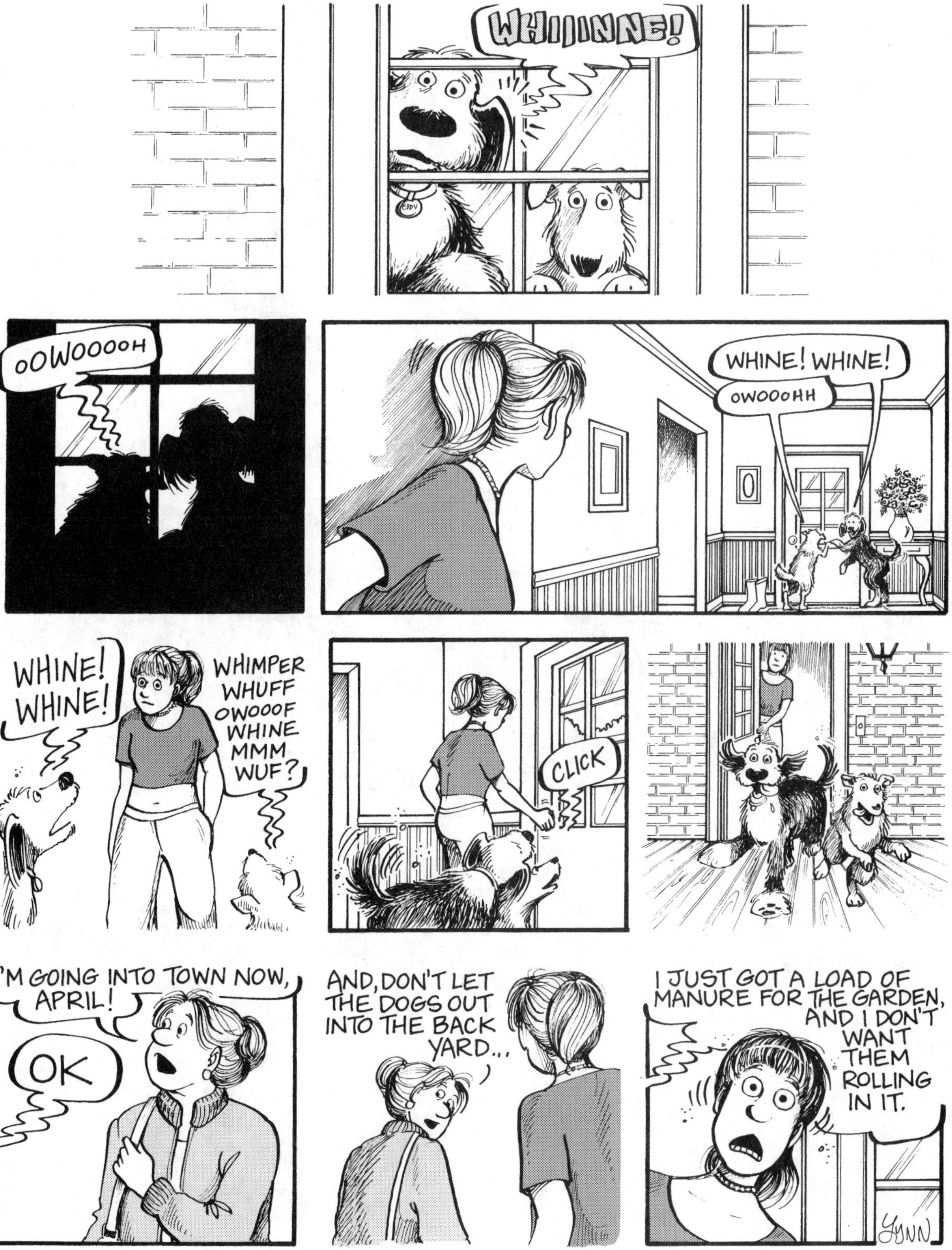
WHIIINNE!
OOWOOOOH
WHINE! WHINE!
OWOOOHH
WHINE! WHINE!
WHIMPER WHUFF OWOOOF WHINE MMM WUF?
CLICK
I'M GOING INTO TOWN NOW, APRIL!
OK
AND, DON'T LET THE DOGS OUT INTO THE BACK YARD...
I JUST GOT A LOAD OF MANURE FOR THE GARDEN, AND I DON'T WANT THEM ROLLING IN IT.
LYNN

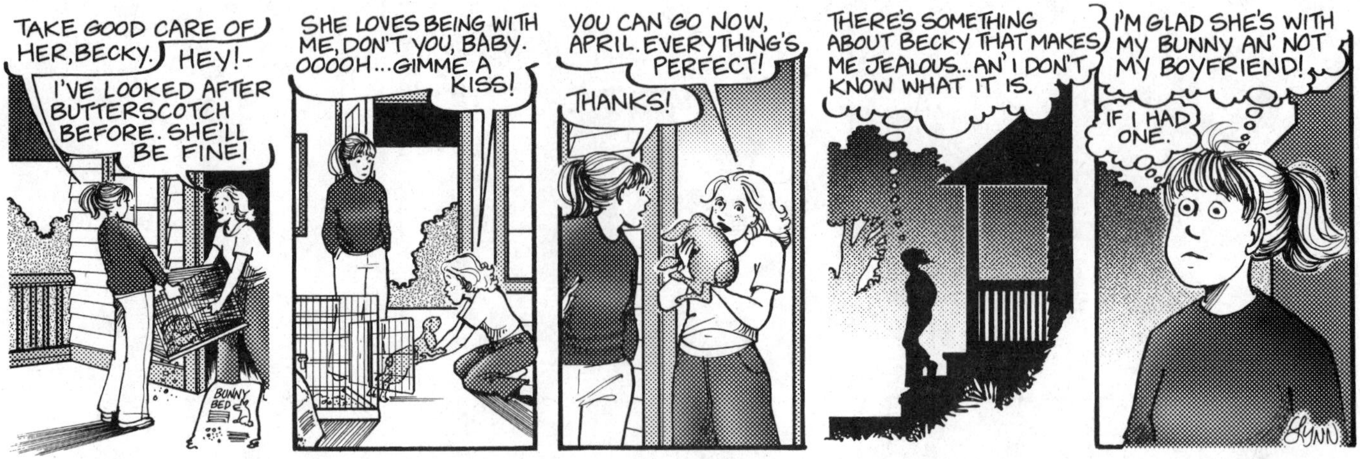
TAKE GOOD CARE OF HER, BECKY.
HEY!- I'VE LOOKED AFTER BUTTERSCOTCH BEFORE. SHE'LL BE FINE!
BUNNY BED
SHE LOVES BEING WITH ME, DON'T YOU, BABY. OOOOH... GIMME A KISS!
YOU CAN GO NOW, APRIL. EVERYTHING'S PERFECT!
THANKS!
THERE'S SOMETHING ABOUT BECKY THAT MAKES ME JEALOUS... AN' I DON'T KNOW WHAT IT IS.
I'M GLAD SHE'S WITH MY BUNNY AN' NOT MY BOYFRIEND!
IF I HAD ONE.
LYNN

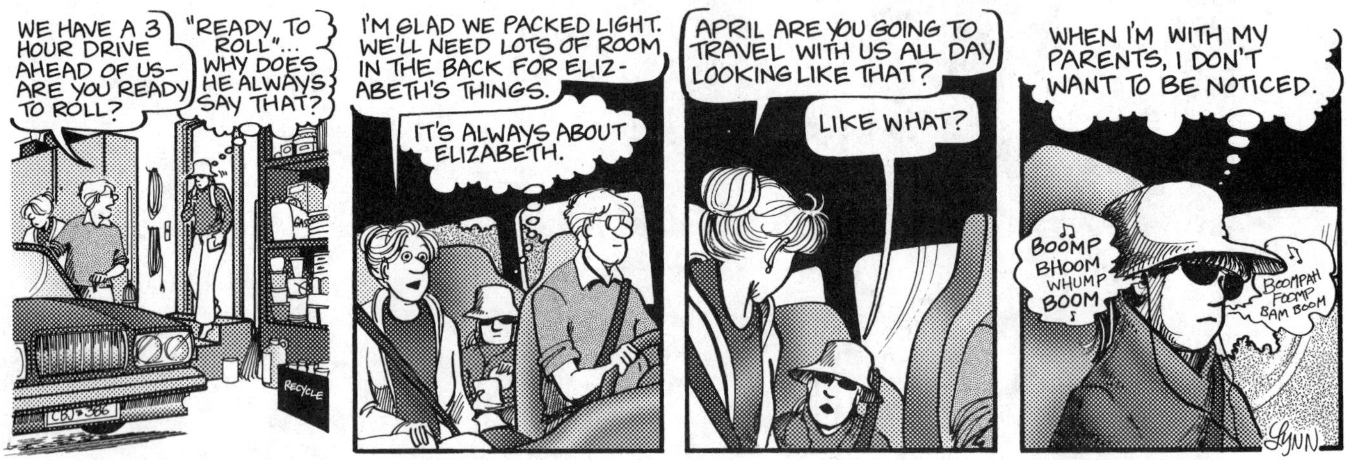
WE HAVE A 3 HOUR DRIVE AHEAD OF US- ARE YOU READY TO ROLL?
"READY TO ROLL"... WHY DOES HE ALWAYS SAY THAT?
RECYCLE
I'M GLAD WE PACKED LIGHT. WE'LL NEED LOTS OF ROOM IN THE BACK FOR ELIZ-ABETH'S THINGS.
IT'S ALWAYS ABOUT ELIZABETH.
APRIL ARE YOU GOING TO TRAVEL WITH US ALL DAY LOOKING LIKE THAT?
LIKE WHAT?
WHEN I'M WITH MY PARENTS, I DON'T WANT TO BE NOTICED.
BOOMP BHOOM WHUMP BOOM
BOOMPAH FOOMP BAM BOOM
LYNN

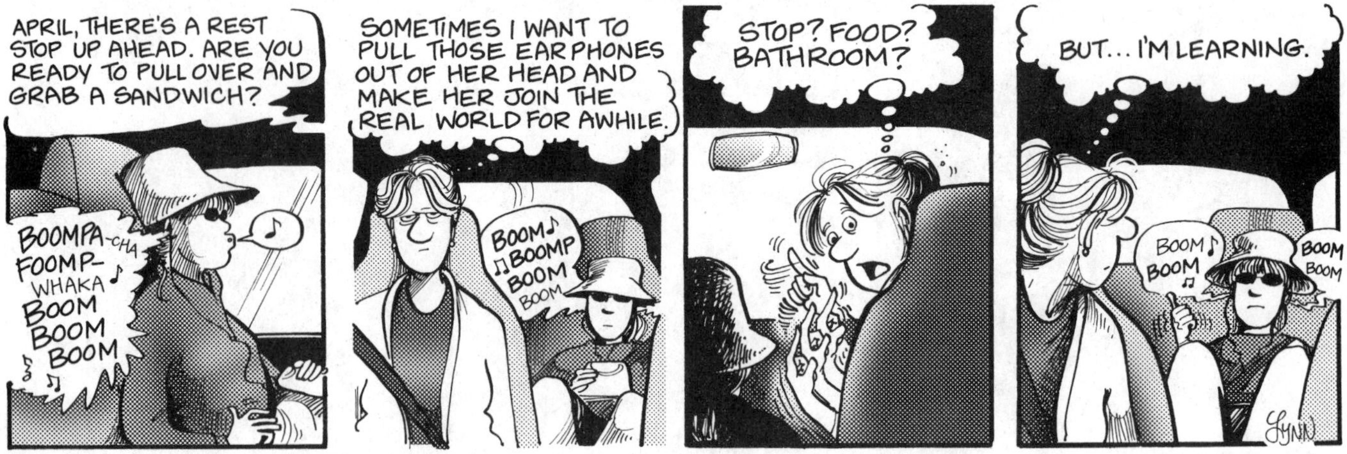
APRIL, THERE'S A REST STOP UP AHEAD. ARE YOU READY TO PULL OVER AND GRAB A SANDWICH?
BOOMPA-CHA FOOMP- WHAKA BOOM BOOM BOOM BOOM
SOMETIMES I WANT TO PULL THOSE EARPHONES OUT OF HER HEAD AND MAKE HER JOIN THE REAL WORLD FOR AWHILE.
BOOM BOOMP BOOM BOOM
STOP? FOOD? BATHROOM?
BUT... I'M LEARNING.
BOOM BOOM
BOOM BOOM
LYNN

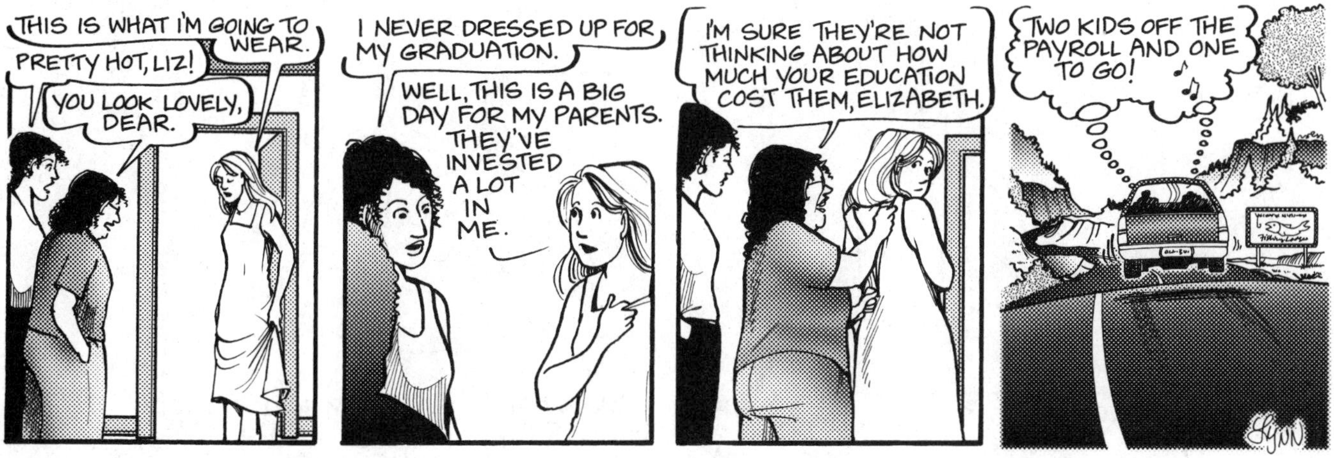
THIS IS WHAT I'M GOING TO WEAR.
PRETTY HOT, LIZ!
YOU LOOK LOVELY, DEAR.
I NEVER DRESSED UP FOR MY GRADUATION.
WELL, THIS IS A BIG DAY FOR MY PARENTS. THEY'VE INVESTED A LOT IN ME.
I'M SURE THEY'RE NOT THINKING ABOUT HOW MUCH YOUR EDUCATION COST THEM, ELIZABETH.
TWO KIDS OFF THE PAYROLL AND ONE TO GO!
LYNN

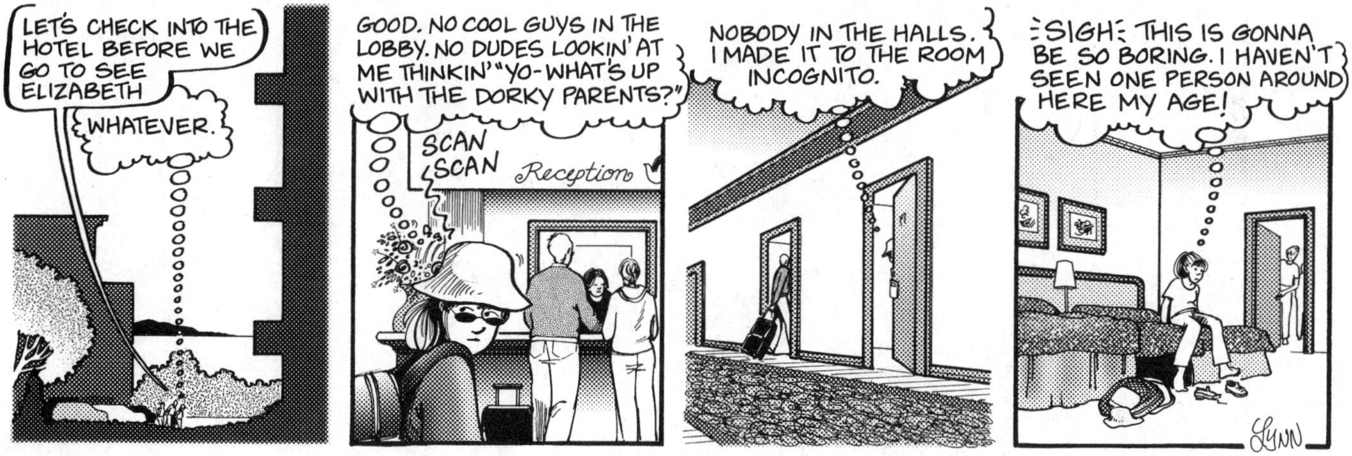
LET'S CHECK INTO THE HOTEL BEFORE WE GO TO SEE ELIZABETH
WHATEVER.
GOOD. NO COOL GUYS IN THE LOBBY. NO DUDES LOOKIN' AT ME THINKIN' "YO-WHAT'S UP WITH THE DORKY PARENTS?"
SCAN SCAN
Reception
NOBODY IN THE HALLS. I MADE IT TO THE ROOM INCOGNITO.
SIGH THIS IS GONNA BE SO BORING. I HAVEN'T SEEN ONE PERSON AROUND HERE MY AGE!
LYNN

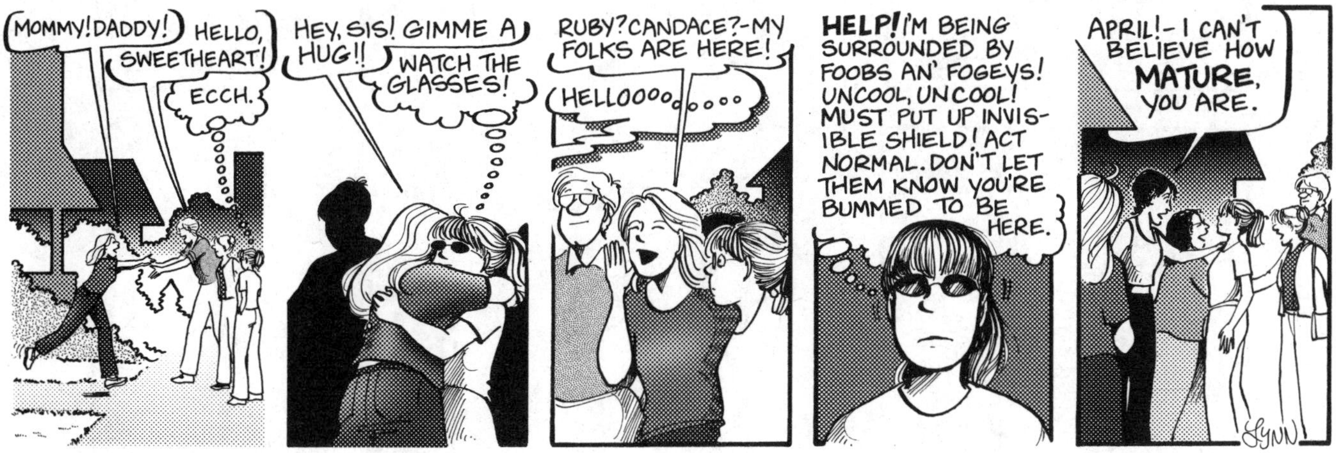
MOMMY! DADDY!
HELLO, SWEETHEART!
ECCH.
HEY, SIS! GIMME A HUG!!
WATCH THE GLASSES!
RUBY? CANDACE?-MY FOLKS ARE HERE!
HELLOOOOo....
HELP! I'M BEING SURROUNDED BY FOOBS AN' FOGEYS! UNCOOL, UNCOOL! MUST PUT UP INVISIBLE SHIELD! ACT NORMAL. DON'T LET THEM KNOW YOU'RE BUMMED TO BE HERE.
APRIL!- I CAN'T BELIEVE HOW MATURE, YOU ARE.
LYNN

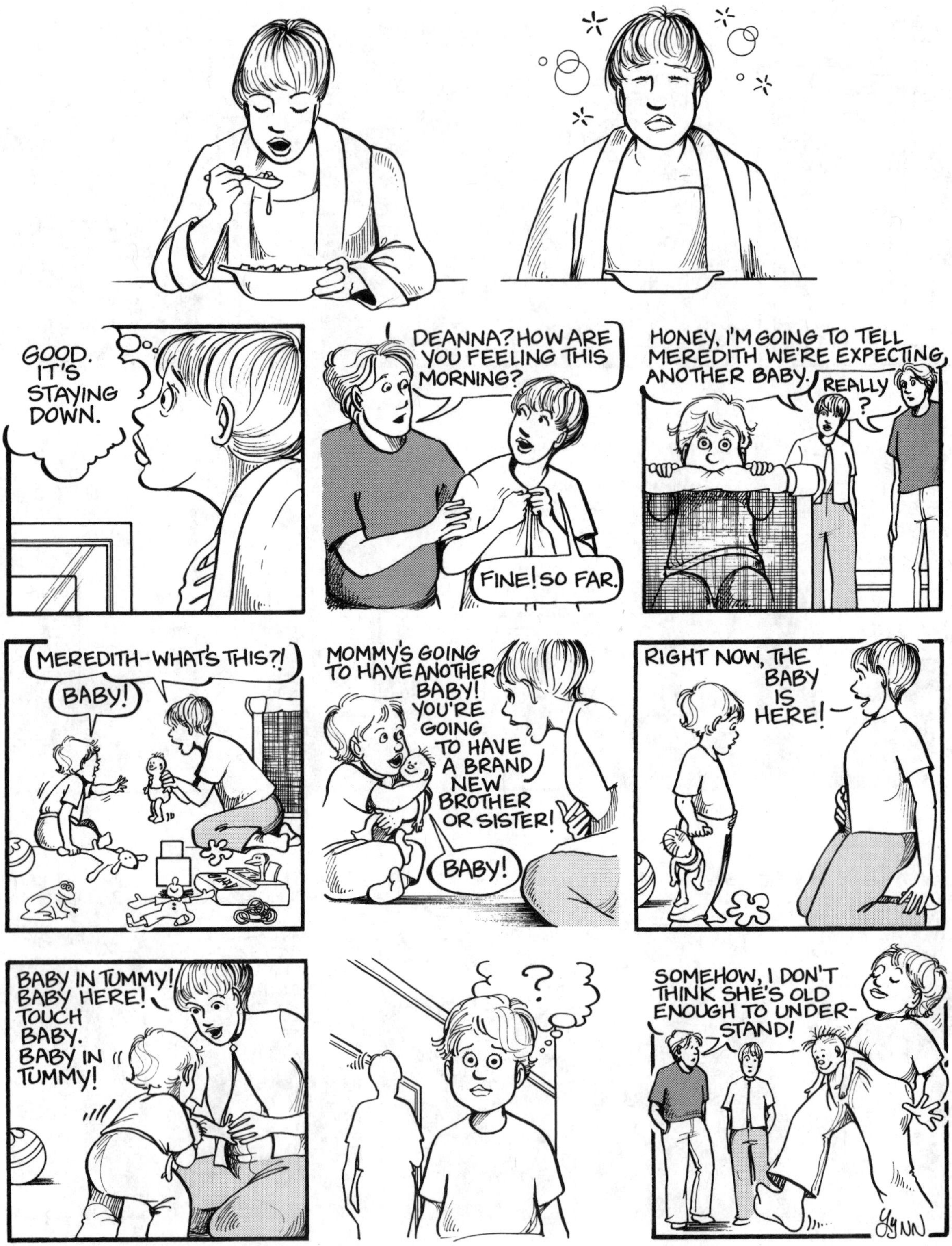
GOOD. IT'S STAYING DOWN.
DEANNA? HOW ARE YOU FEELING THIS MORNING?
FINE! SO FAR.
HONEY, I'M GOING TO TELL MEREDITH WE'RE EXPECTING ANOTHER BABY.
REALLY?
MEREDITH-WHAT'S THIS?!
BABY!
MOMMY'S GOING TO HAVE ANOTHER BABY! YOU'RE GOING TO HAVE A BRAND NEW BROTHER OR SISTER!
BABY!
RIGHT NOW, THE BABY IS HERE!
BABY IN TUMMY! BABY HERE! TOUCH BABY. BABY IN TUMMY!
?
SOMEHOW, I DON'T THINK SHE'S OLD ENOUGH TO UNDER-STAND!
LYNN

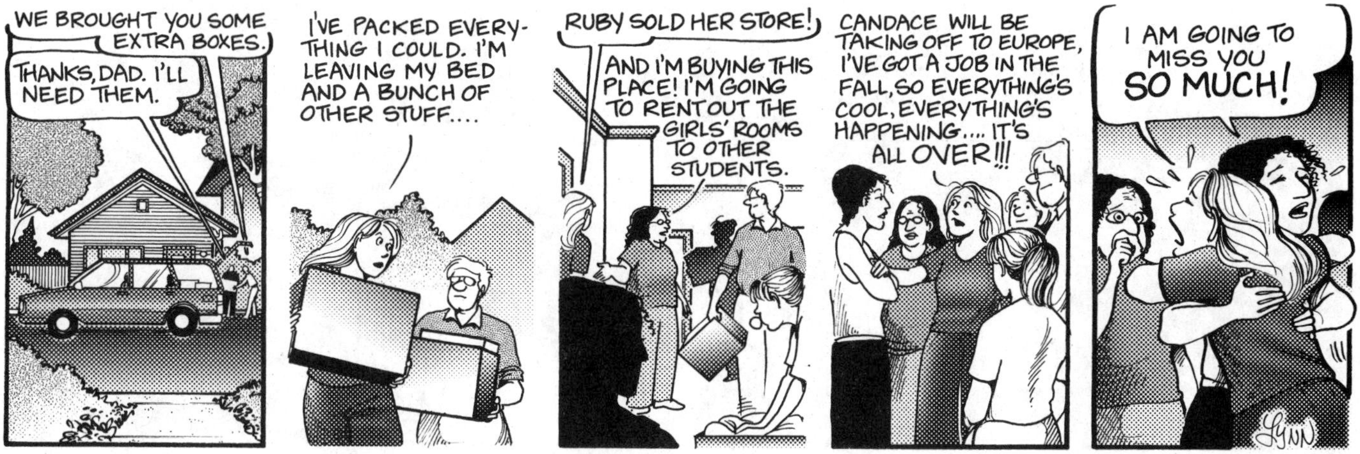
WE BROUGHT YOU SOME EXTRA BOXES.
THANKS, DAD. I'LL NEED THEM.
I'VE PACKED EVERYTHING I COULD. I'M LEAVING MY BED AND A BUNCH OF OTHER STUFF....
RUBY SOLD HER STORE!
AND I'M BUYING THIS PLACE! I'M GOING TO RENT OUT THE GIRLS' ROOMS TO OTHER STUDENTS.
CANDACE WILL BE TAKING OFF TO EUROPE, I'VE GOT A JOB IN THE FALL, SO EVERYTHING'S COOL, EVERYTHING'S HAPPENING.... IT'S ALL OVER!!!
I AM GOING TO MISS YOU SO MUCH!
LYNN

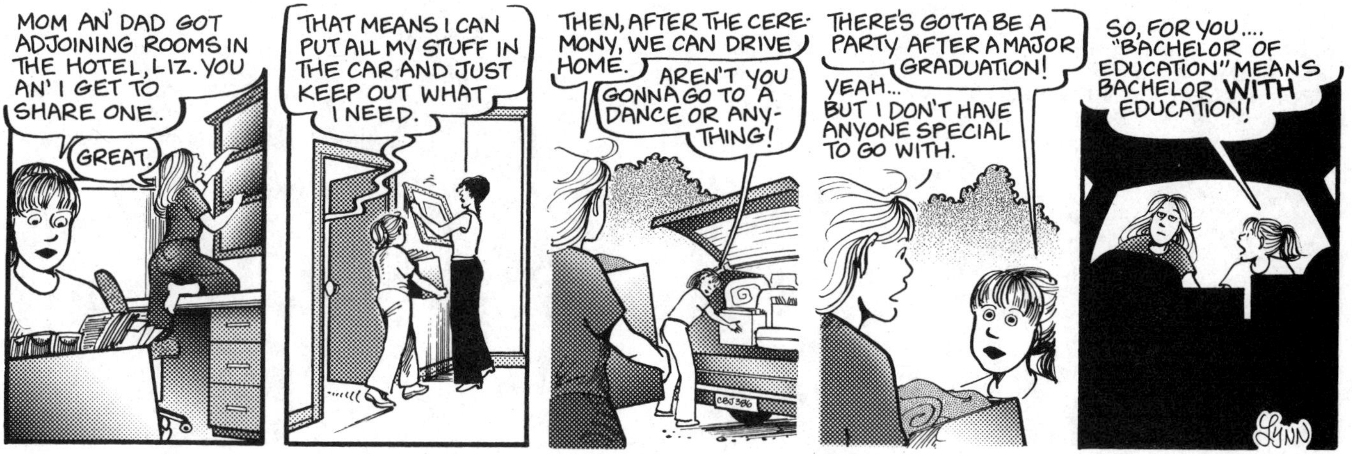
MOM AN' DAD GOT ADJOINING ROOMS IN THE HOTEL, LIZ. YOU AN' I GET TO SHARE ONE.
GREAT.
THAT MEANS I CAN PUT ALL MY STUFF IN THE CAR AND JUST KEEP OUT WHAT I NEED.
THEN, AFTER THE CEREMONY, WE CAN DRIVE HOME.
AREN'T YOU GONNA GO TO A DANCE OR ANYTHING?
THERE'S GOTTA BE A PARTY AFTER A MAJOR GRADUATION!
YEAH... BUT I DON'T HAVE ANYONE SPECIAL TO GO WITH.
SO, FOR YOU.... "BACHELOR OF EDUCATION" MEANS BACHELOR WITH EDUCATION!
LYNN

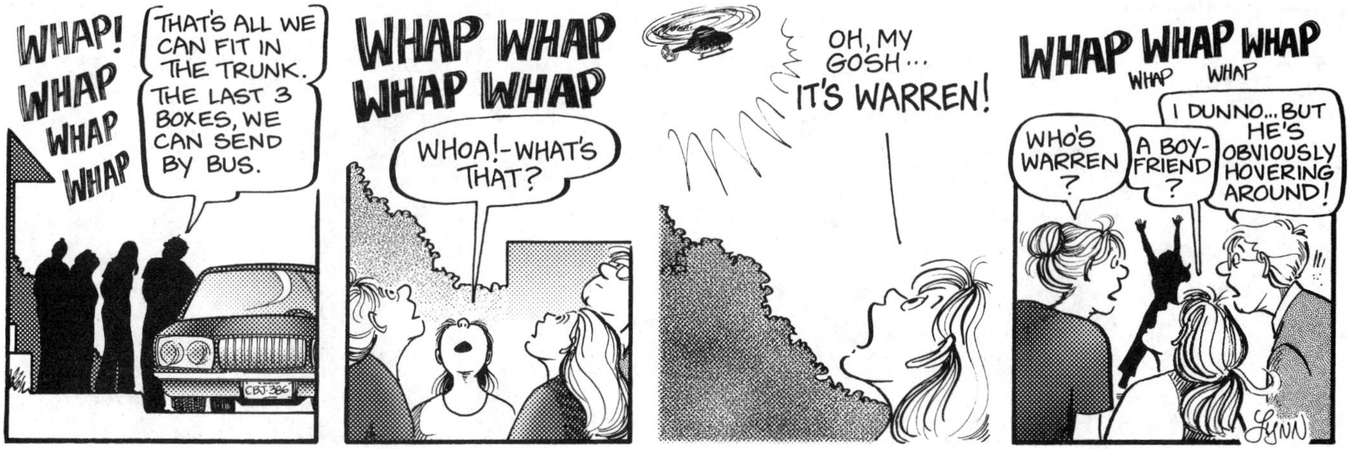
WHAP! WHAP WHAP WHAP
THAT'S ALL WE CAN FIT IN THE TRUNK. THE LAST 3 BOXES, WE CAN SEND BY BUS.
CBJ 386
WHAP WHAP WHAP WHAP
WHOA! - WHAT'S THAT?
OH, MY GOSH... IT'S WARREN!
WHAP WHAP WHAP WHAP WHAP
WHO'S WARREN?
A BOY-FRIEND?
I DUNNO... BUT HE'S OBVIOUSLY HOVERING AROUND!
LYNN

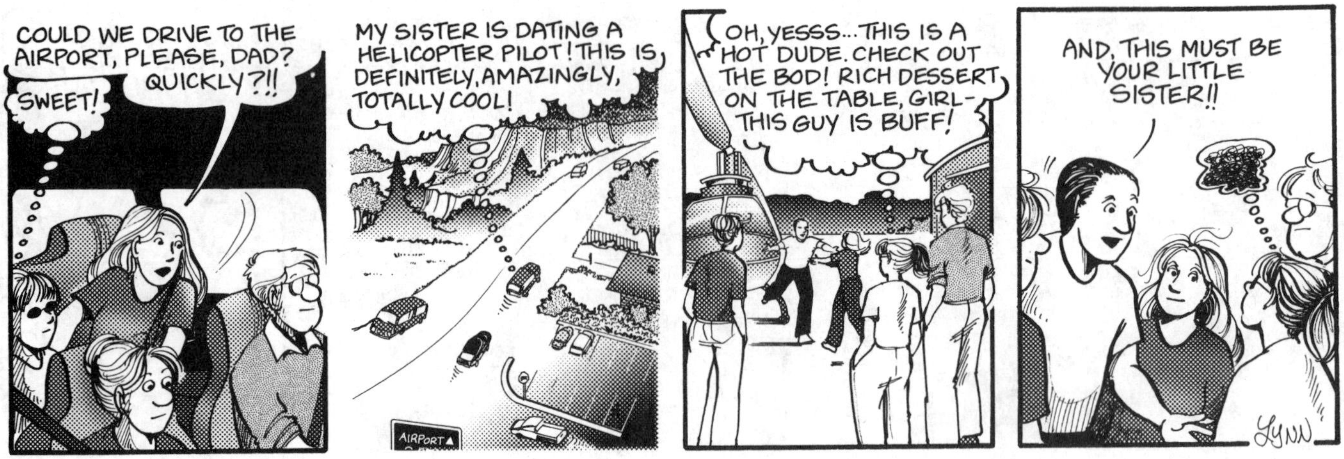
COULD WE DRIVE TO THE AIRPORT, PLEASE, DAD? QUICKLY?!!
SWEET!
MY SISTER IS DATING A HELICOPTER PILOT! THIS IS DEFINITELY, AMAZINGLY, TOTALLY COOL!
AIRPORT
OH, YESSS... THIS IS A HOT DUDE. CHECK OUT THE BOD! RICH DESSERT ON THE TABLE, GIRL- THIS GUY IS BUFF!
AND, THIS MUST BE YOUR LITTLE SISTER!!
LYNN

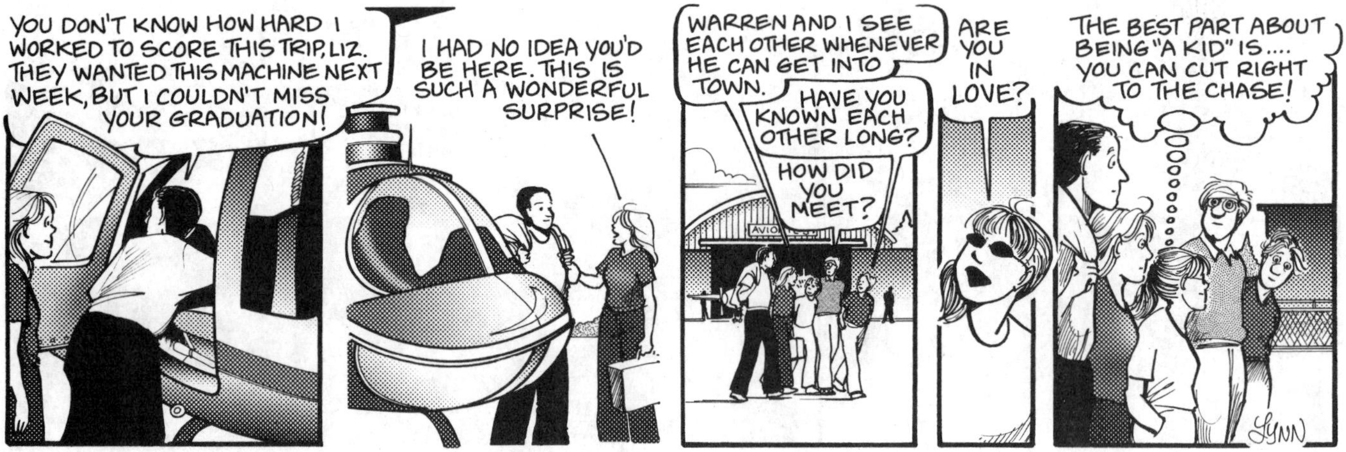
YOU DON'T KNOW HOW HARD I WORKED TO SCORE THIS TRIP, LIZ. THEY WANTED THIS MACHINE NEXT WEEK, BUT I COULDN'T MISS YOUR GRADUATION!
I HAD NO IDEA YOU'D BE HERE. THIS IS SUCH A WONDERFUL SURPRISE!
WARREN AND I SEE EACH OTHER WHENEVER HE CAN GET INTO TOWN.
HAVE YOU KNOWN EACH OTHER LONG?
HOW DID YOU MEET?
ARE YOU IN LOVE?
THE BEST PART ABOUT BEING "A KID" IS.... YOU CAN CUT RIGHT TO THE CHASE!
LYNN

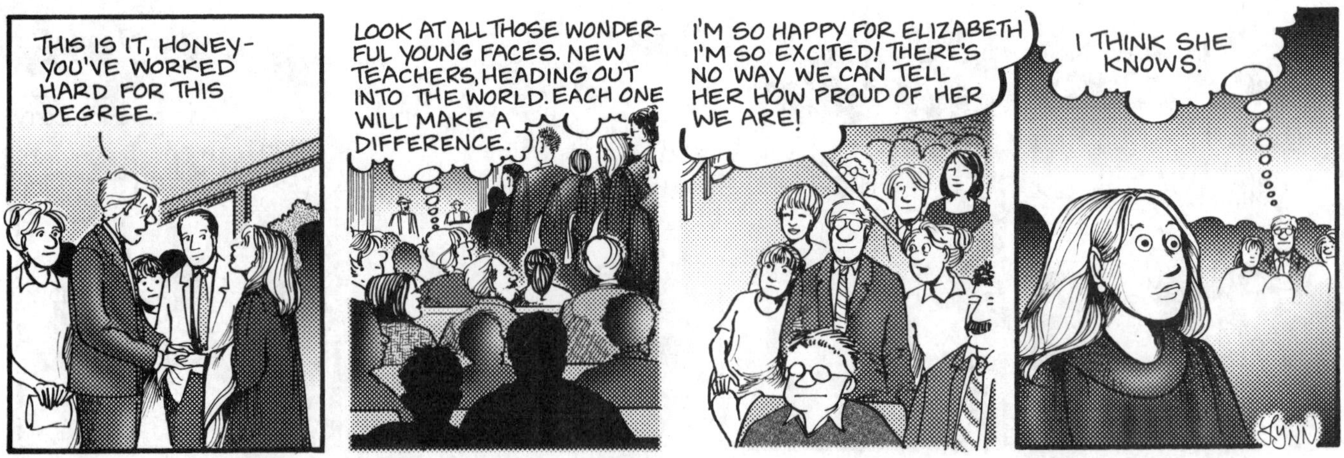
THIS IS IT, HONEY- YOU'VE WORKED HARD FOR THIS DEGREE.
LOOK AT ALL THOSE WONDERFUL YOUNG FACES. NEW TEACHERS, HEADING OUT INTO THE WORLD. EACH ONE WILL MAKE A DIFFERENCE.
I'M SO HAPPY FOR ELIZABETH I'M SO EXCITED! THERE'S NO WAY WE CAN TELL HER HOW PROUD OF HER WE ARE!
I THINK SHE KNOWS.
LYNN

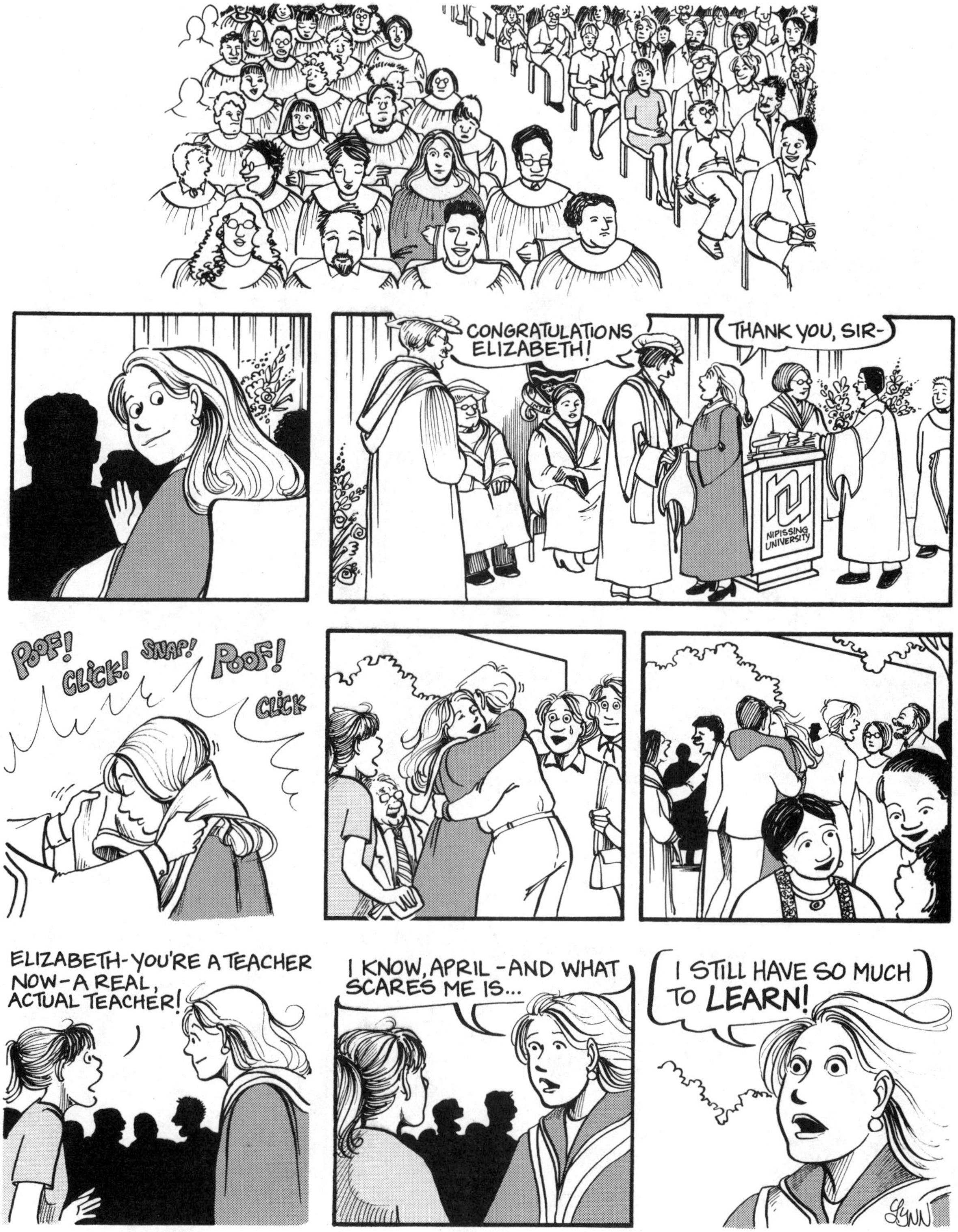
CONGRATULATIONS ELIZABETH!
THANK YOU, SIR-
NIPISSING UNIVERSITY
POOF!
CLICK!
SNAP!
POOF!
CLICK
ELIZABETH- YOU'RE A TEACHER NOW-A REAL, ACTUAL TEACHER!
I KNOW, APRIL -AND WHAT SCARES ME IS...
I STILL HAVE SO MUCH TO LEARN!
LYNN

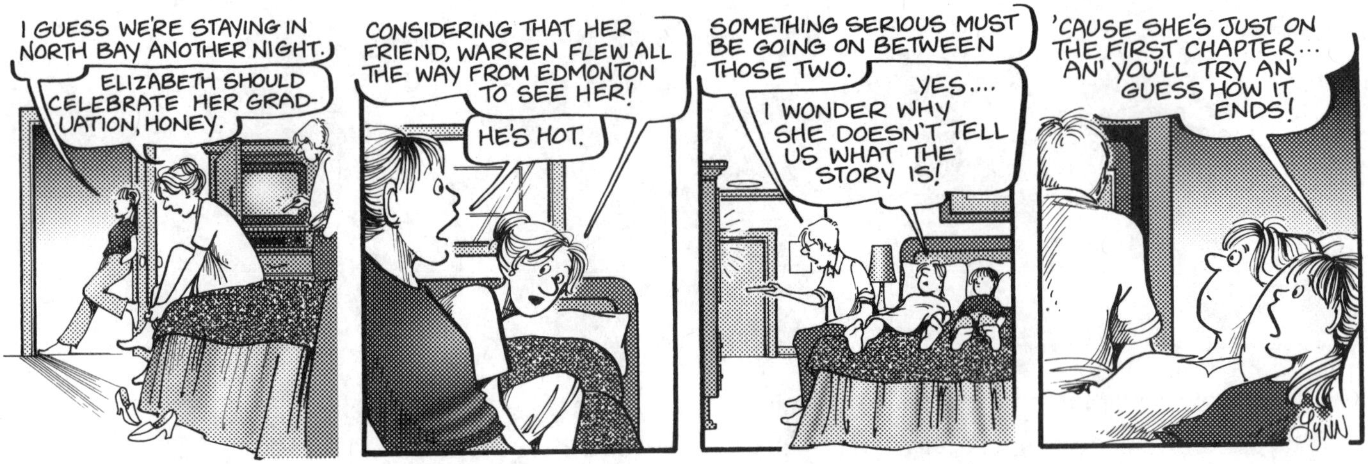
I GUESS WE'RE STAYING IN NORTH BAY ANOTHER NIGHT.
ELIZABETH SHOULD CELEBRATE HER GRADUATION, HONEY.
CONSIDERING THAT HER FRIEND, WARREN FLEW ALL THE WAY FROM EDMONTON TO SEE HER!
HE'S HOT.
SOMETHING SERIOUS MUST BE GOING ON BETWEEN THOSE TWO.
YES.... I WONDER WHY SHE DOESN'T TELL US WHAT THE STORY IS!
'CAUSE SHE'S JUST ON THE FIRST CHAPTER... AN' YOU'LL TRY AN' GUESS HOW IT ENDS!
LYNN

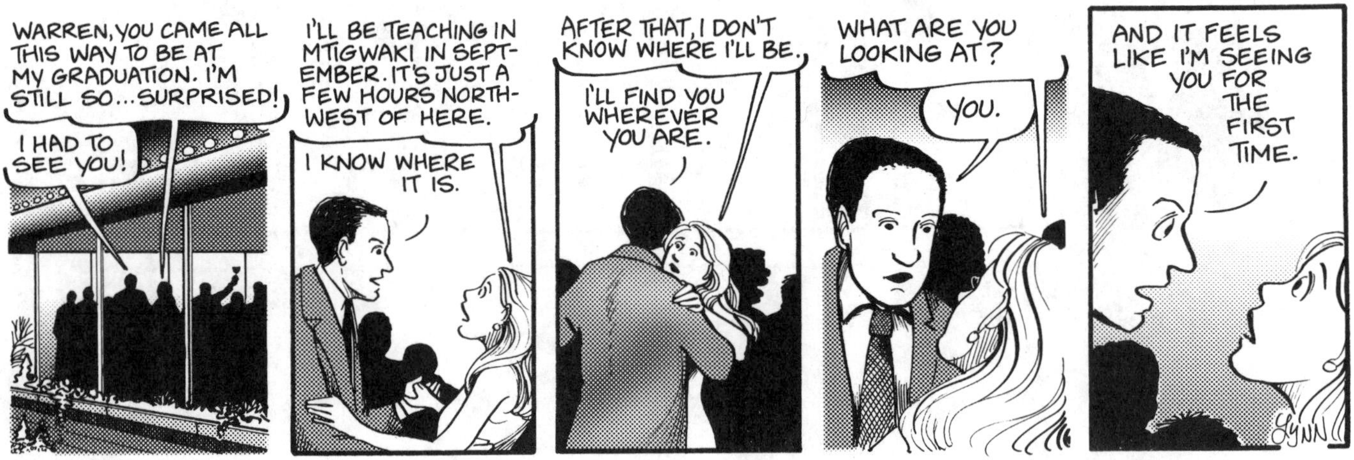
WARREN, YOU CAME ALL THIS WAY TO BE AT MY GRADUATION. I'M STILL SO... SURPRISED!
I HAD TO SEE YOU!
I'LL BE TEACHING IN MTIGWAKI IN SEPTEMBER. IT'S JUST A FEW HOURS NORTHWEST OF HERE.
I KNOW WHERE IT IS.
AFTER THAT, I DON'T KNOW WHERE I'LL BE.
I'LL FIND YOU WHEREVER YOU ARE.
WHAT ARE YOU LOOKING AT?
YOU.
AND IT FEELS LIKE I'M SEEING YOU FOR THE FIRST TIME.
LYNN

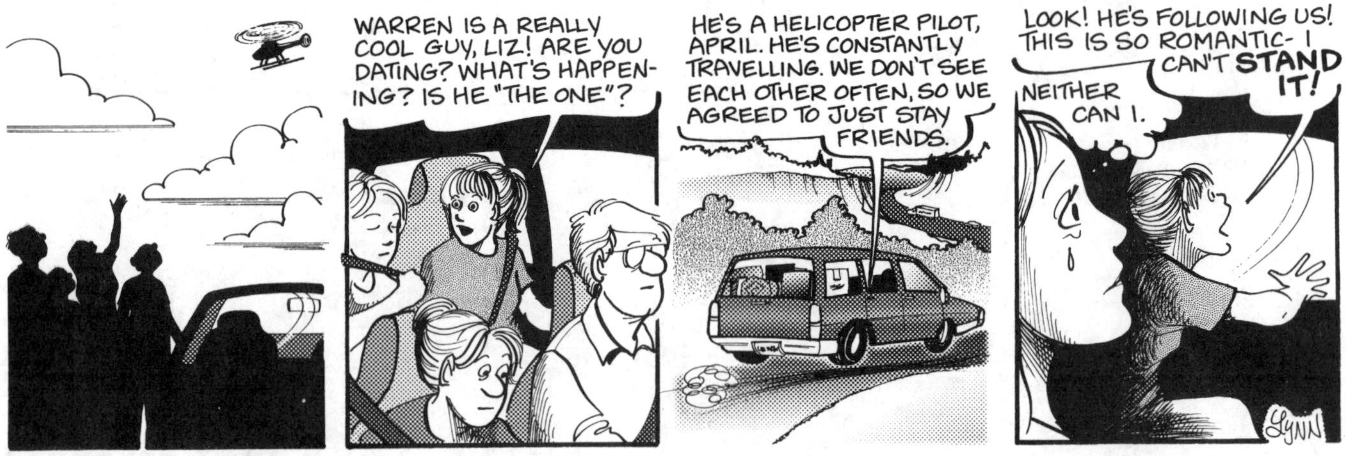
WARREN IS A REALLY COOL GUY, LIZ! ARE YOU DATING? WHAT'S HAPPENING? IS HE "THE ONE"?
HE'S A HELICOPTER PILOT, APRIL. HE'S CONSTANTLY TRAVELLING. WE DON'T SEE EACH OTHER OFTEN, SO WE AGREED TO JUST STAY FRIENDS.
LOOK! HE'S FOLLOWING US! THIS IS SO ROMANTIC- I CAN'T **STAND IT!**
NEITHER CAN I.
LYNN

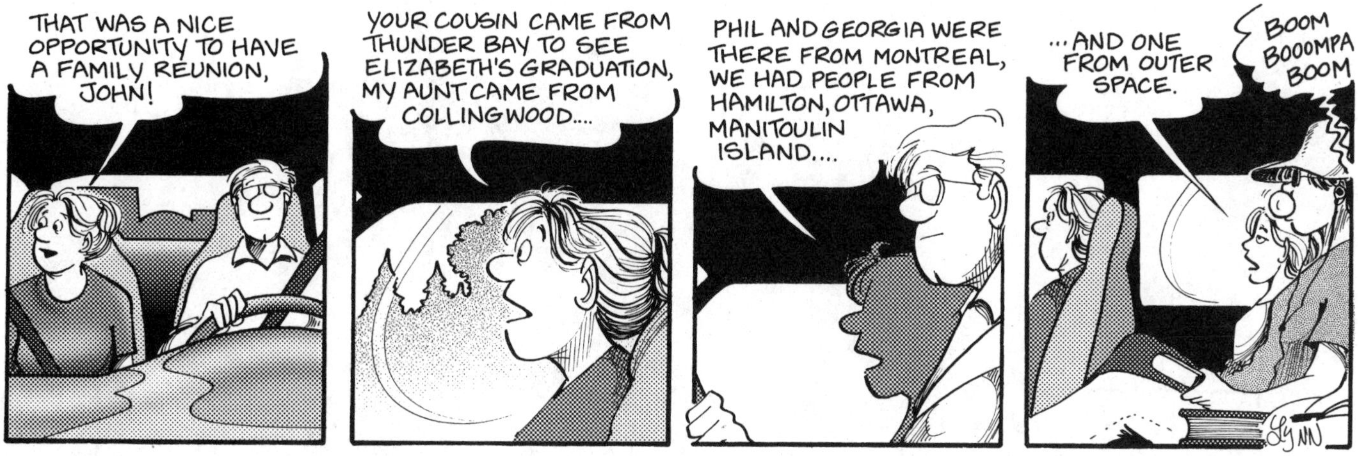
THAT WAS A NICE OPPORTUNITY TO HAVE A FAMILY REUNION, JOHN!
YOUR COUSIN CAME FROM THUNDER BAY TO SEE ELIZABETH'S GRADUATION, MY AUNT CAME FROM COLLINGWOOD....
PHIL AND GEORGIA WERE THERE FROM MONTREAL, WE HAD PEOPLE FROM HAMILTON, OTTAWA, MANITOULIN ISLAND....
...AND ONE FROM OUTER SPACE.
BOOM BOOOMPA BOOM

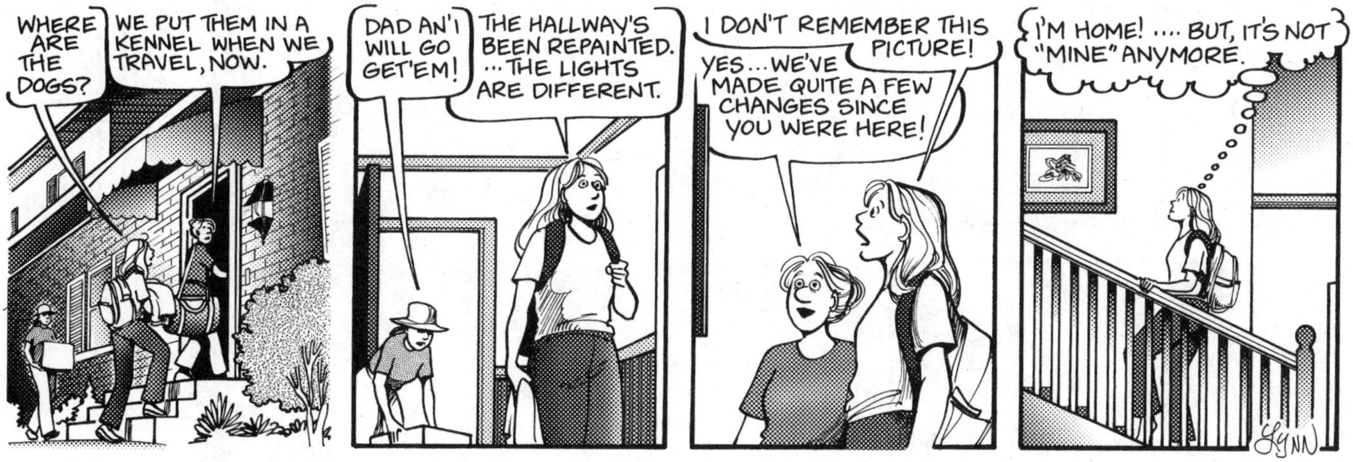
WHERE ARE THE DOGS?
WE PUT THEM IN A KENNEL WHEN WE TRAVEL, NOW.
DAD AN' I WILL GO GET'EM!
THE HALLWAY'S BEEN REPAINTED. ...THE LIGHTS ARE DIFFERENT.
I DON'T REMEMBER THIS PICTURE!
YES...WE'VE MADE QUITE A FEW CHANGES SINCE YOU WERE HERE!
I'M HOME! .... BUT, IT'S NOT "MINE" ANYMORE.

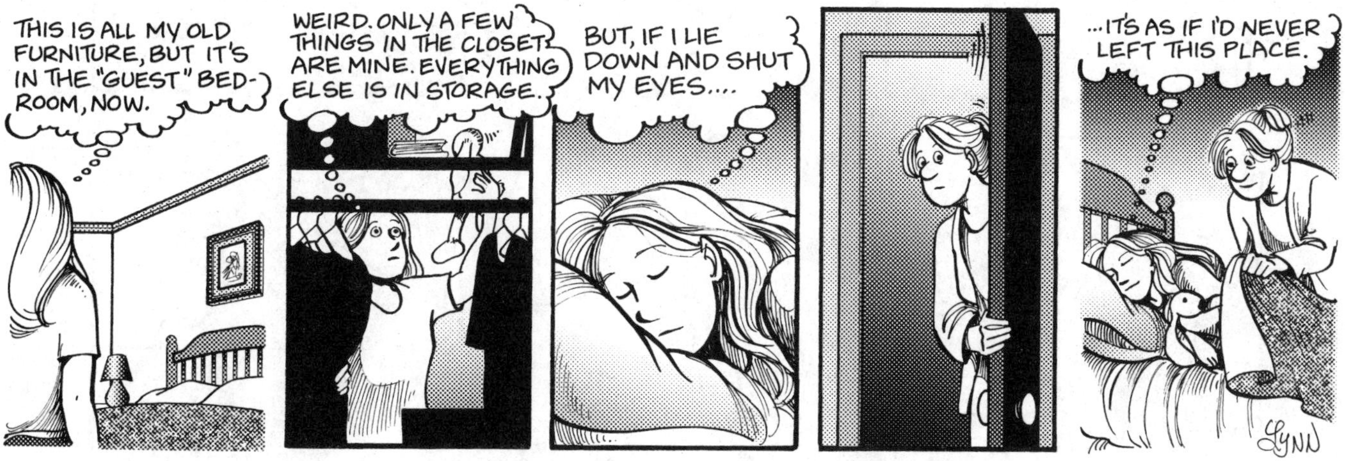
THIS IS ALL MY OLD FURNITURE, BUT IT'S IN THE "GUEST" BED-ROOM, NOW.
WEIRD. ONLY A FEW THINGS IN THE CLOSET ARE MINE. EVERYTHING ELSE IS IN STORAGE.
BUT, IF I LIE DOWN AND SHUT MY EYES....
...IT'S AS IF I'D NEVER LEFT THIS PLACE.

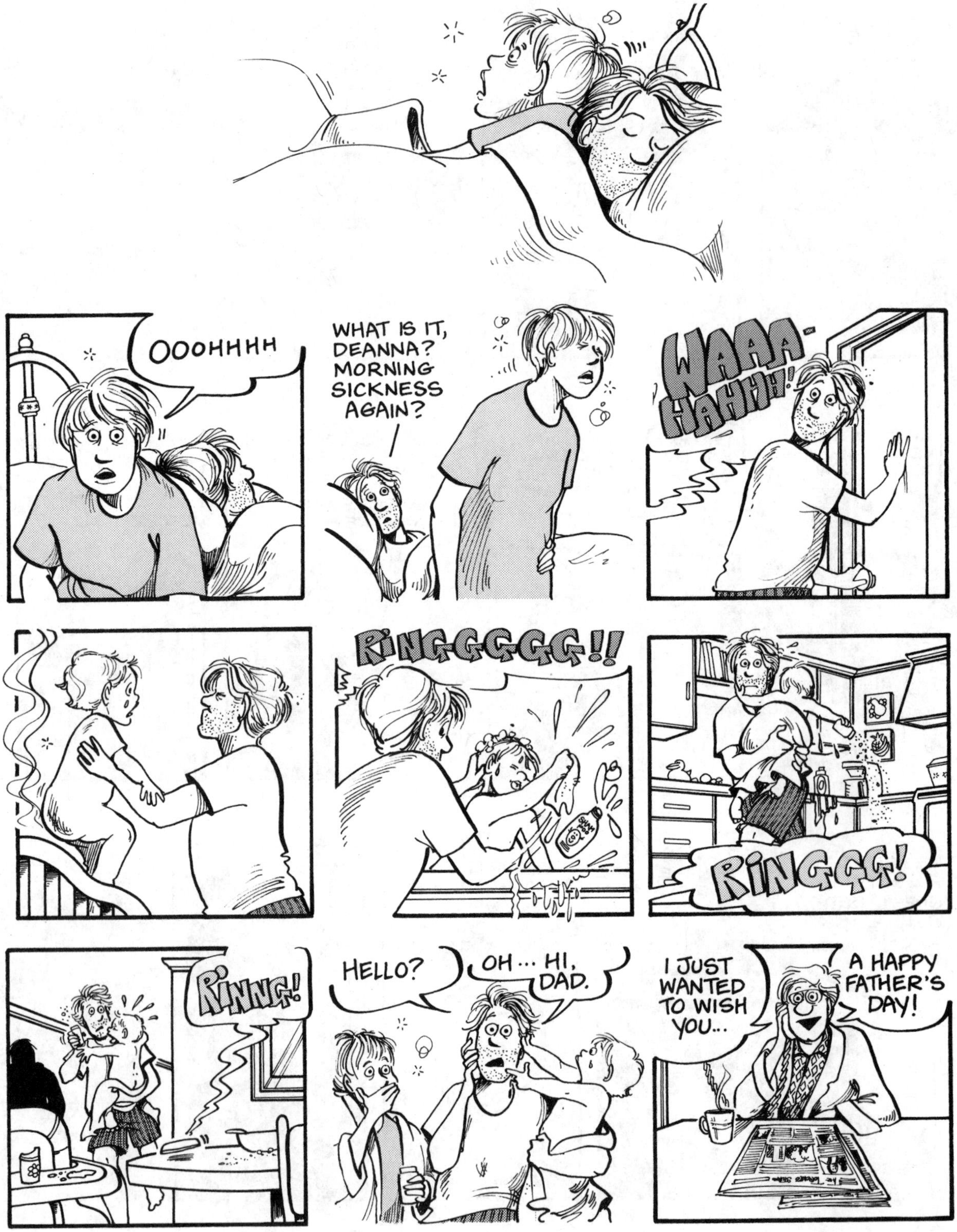
OOOHHHH
WHAT IS IT, DEANNA? MORNING SICKNESS AGAIN?
WAAA-HAHHH!
RINGGGGG!!
RINGGG!
RINNNG!
HELLO?
OH... HI, DAD.
I JUST WANTED TO WISH YOU...
A HAPPY FATHER'S DAY!

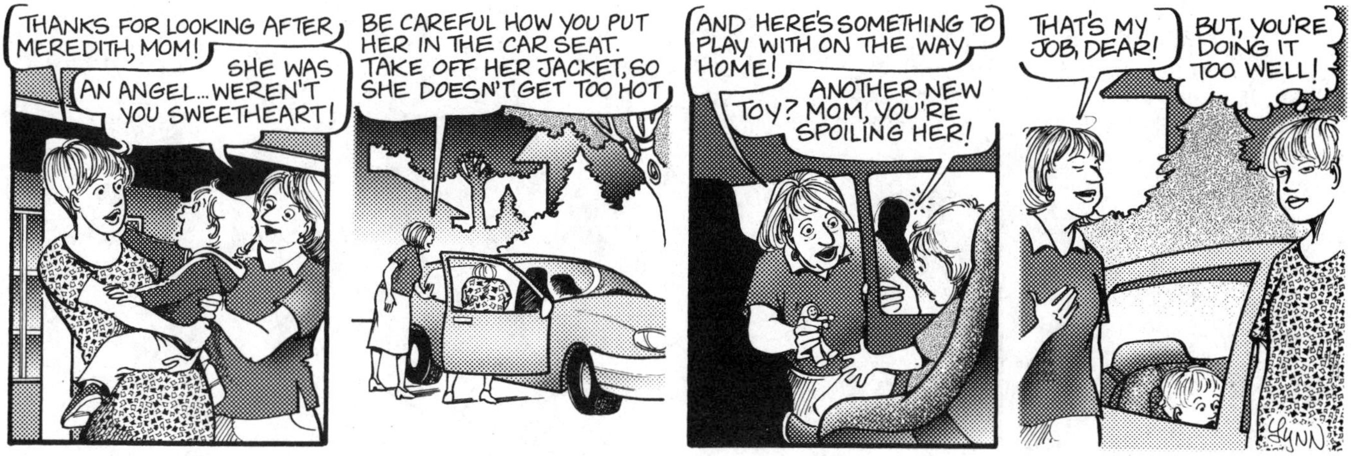
THANKS FOR LOOKING AFTER MEREDITH, MOM!
SHE WAS AN ANGEL...WEREN'T YOU SWEETHEART!
BE CAREFUL HOW YOU PUT HER IN THE CAR SEAT. TAKE OFF HER JACKET, SO SHE DOESN'T GET TOO HOT
AND HERE'S SOMETHING TO PLAY WITH ON THE WAY HOME!
ANOTHER NEW TOY? MOM, YOU'RE SPOILING HER!
THAT'S MY JOB, DEAR!
BUT, YOU'RE DOING IT TOO WELL!
LYNN

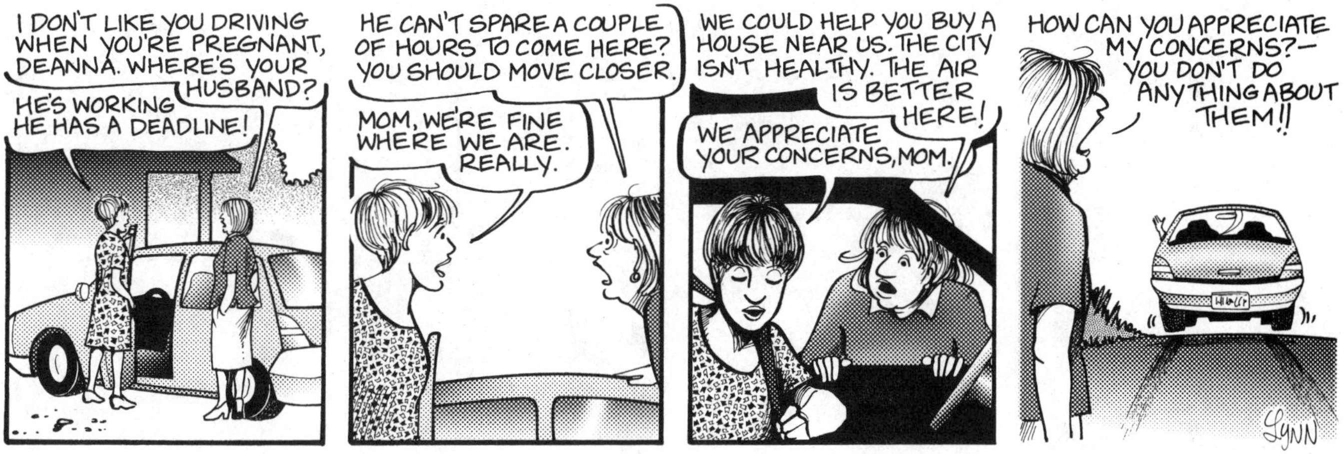
I DON'T LIKE YOU DRIVING WHEN YOU'RE PREGNANT, DEANNA. WHERE'S YOUR HUSBAND?
HE'S WORKING HE HAS A DEADLINE!
HE CAN'T SPARE A COUPLE OF HOURS TO COME HERE? YOU SHOULD MOVE CLOSER.
MOM, WE'RE FINE WHERE WE ARE. REALLY.
WE COULD HELP YOU BUY A HOUSE NEAR US. THE CITY ISN'T HEALTHY. THE AIR IS BETTER HERE!
WE APPRECIATE YOUR CONCERNS, MOM.
HOW CAN YOU APPRECIATE MY CONCERNS?— YOU DON'T DO ANYTHING ABOUT THEM!!
LYNN

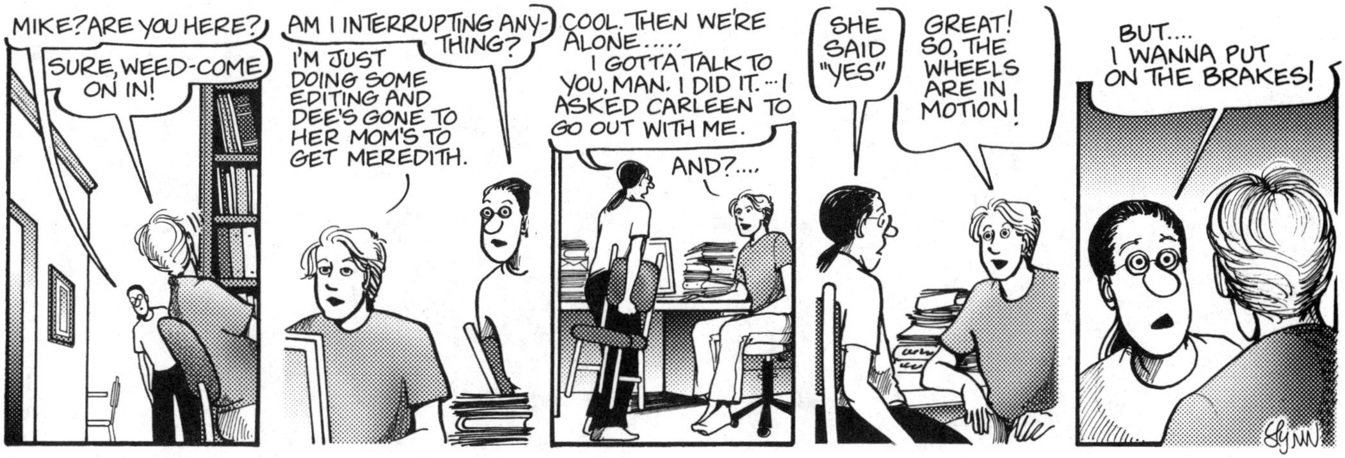
MIKE? ARE YOU HERE?
SURE, WEED-COME ON IN!
AM I INTERRUPTING ANY-THING?
I'M JUST DOING SOME EDITING AND DEE'S GONE TO HER MOM'S TO GET MEREDITH.
COOL. THEN WE'RE ALONE.....
I GOTTA TALK TO YOU, MAN. I DID IT....I ASKED CARLEEN TO GO OUT WITH ME.
AND?....
SHE SAID "YES"
GREAT! SO, THE WHEELS ARE IN MOTION!
BUT.... I WANNA PUT ON THE BRAKES!
LYNN

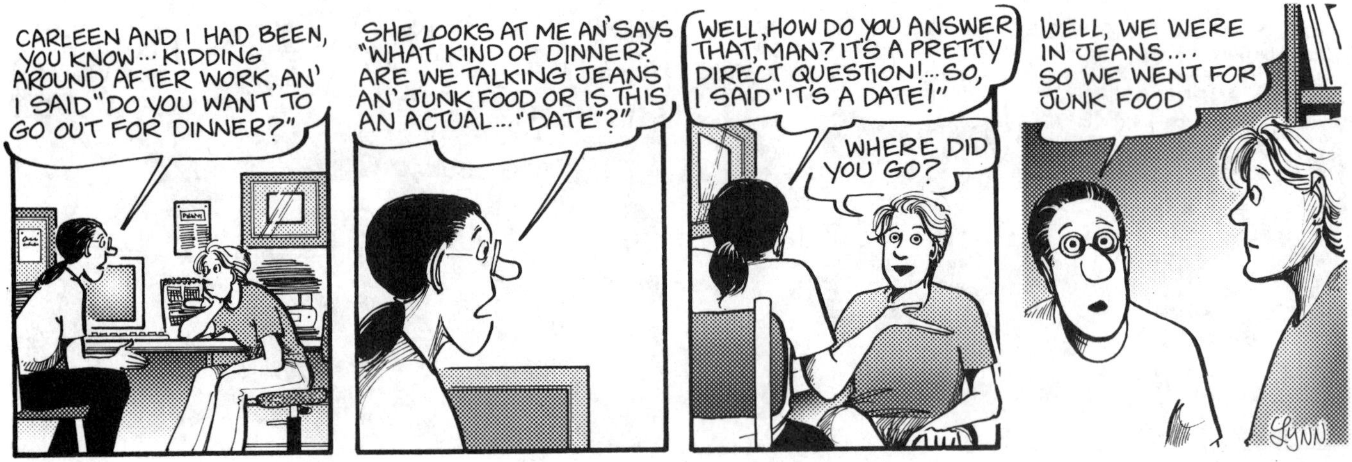
CARLEEN AND I HAD BEEN, YOU KNOW... KIDDING AROUND AFTER WORK, AN' I SAID "DO YOU WANT TO GO OUT FOR DINNER?"
SHE LOOKS AT ME AN' SAYS "WHAT KIND OF DINNER? ARE WE TALKING JEANS AN' JUNK FOOD OR IS THIS AN ACTUAL... "DATE"?"
WELL, HOW DO YOU ANSWER THAT, MAN? IT'S A PRETTY DIRECT QUESTION!... SO, I SAID "IT'S A DATE!"
WHERE DID YOU GO?
WELL, WE WERE IN JEANS.... SO WE WENT FOR JUNK FOOD
LYNN

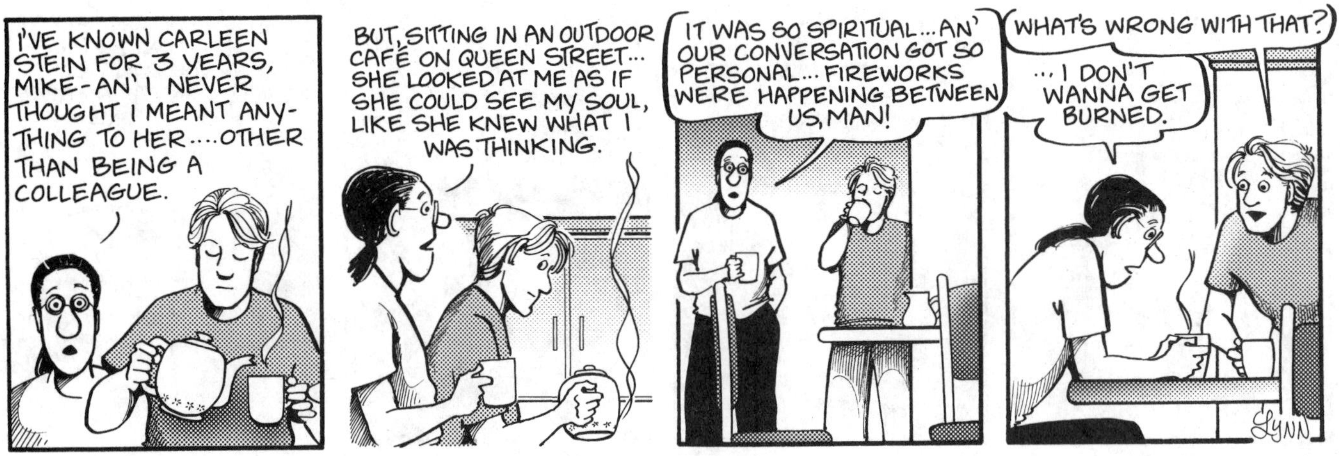
I'VE KNOWN CARLEEN STEIN FOR 3 YEARS, MIKE- AN' I NEVER THOUGHT I MEANT ANY-THING TO HER.... OTHER THAN BEING A COLLEAGUE.
BUT, SITTING IN AN OUTDOOR CAFÉ ON QUEEN STREET... SHE LOOKED AT ME AS IF SHE COULD SEE MY SOUL, LIKE SHE KNEW WHAT I WAS THINKING.
IT WAS SO SPIRITUAL... AN' OUR CONVERSATION GOT SO PERSONAL... FIREWORKS WERE HAPPENING BETWEEN US, MAN!
WHAT'S WRONG WITH THAT?
... I DON'T WANNA GET BURNED.
LYNN

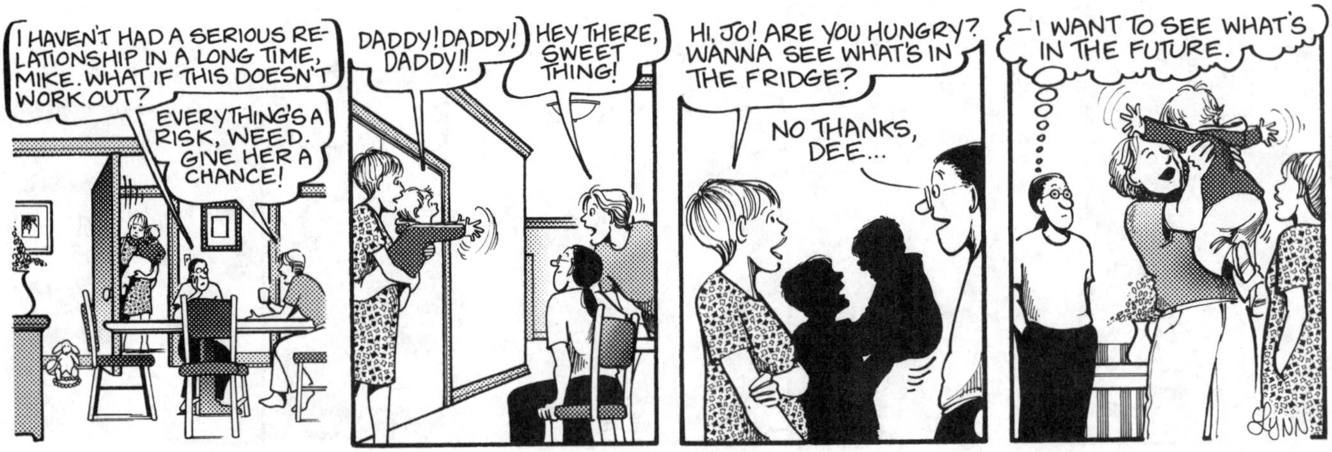
I HAVEN'T HAD A SERIOUS RE-LATIONSHIP IN A LONG TIME, MIKE. WHAT IF THIS DOESN'T WORK OUT?
EVERYTHING'S A RISK, WEED. GIVE HER A CHANCE!
DADDY! DADDY! DADDY!!
HEY THERE, SWEET THING!
HI, JO! ARE YOU HUNGRY? WANNA SEE WHAT'S IN THE FRIDGE?
NO THANKS, DEE...
—I WANT TO SEE WHAT'S IN THE FUTURE.
LYNN

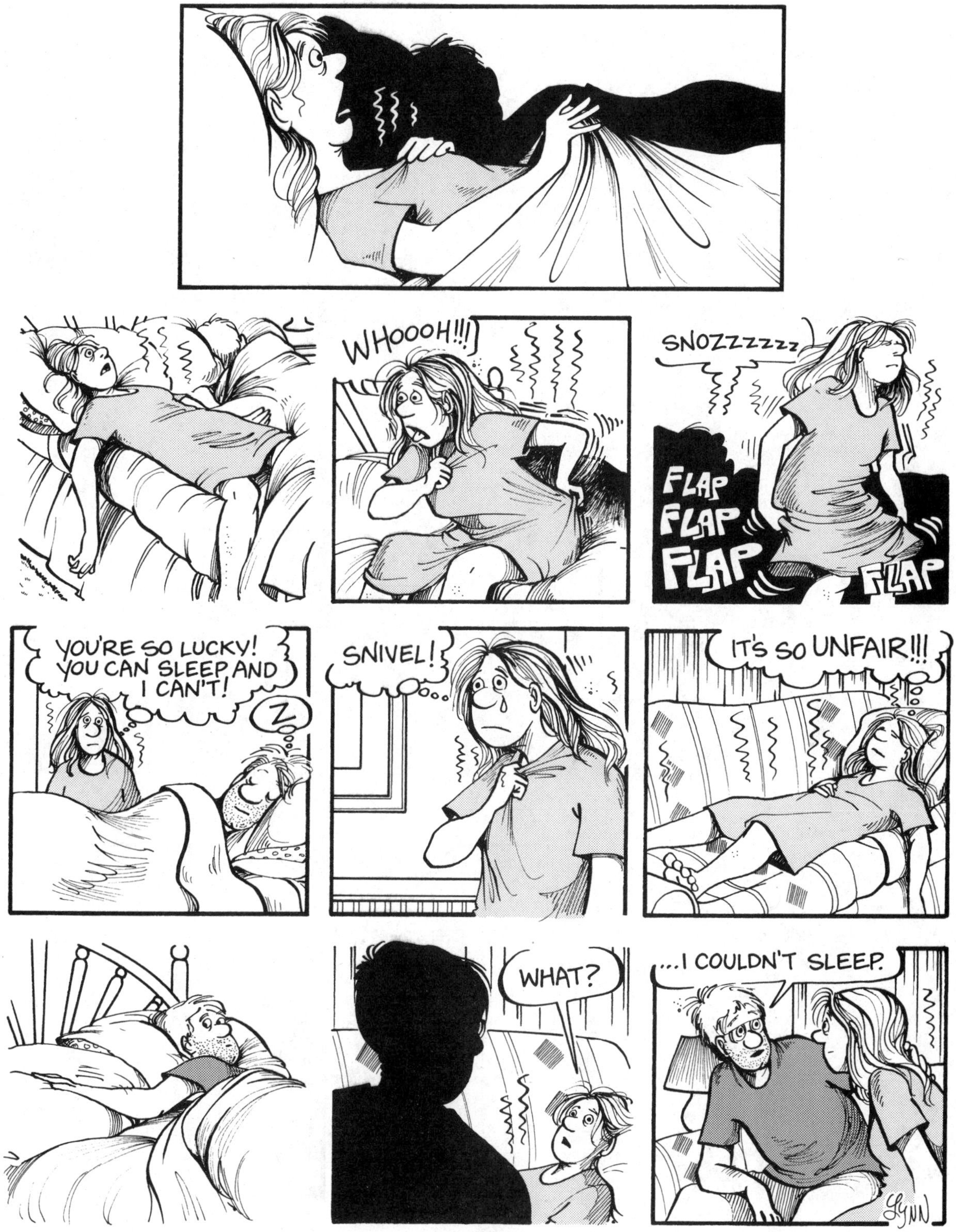
WHOOOH!!!
SNOZZZZZZZ
FLAP
FLAP
FLAP
FLAP
YOU'RE SO LUCKY! YOU CAN SLEEP AND I CAN'T!
Z
SNIVEL!
IT'S SO UNFAIR!!!
WHAT?
...I COULDN'T SLEEP.
LYNN

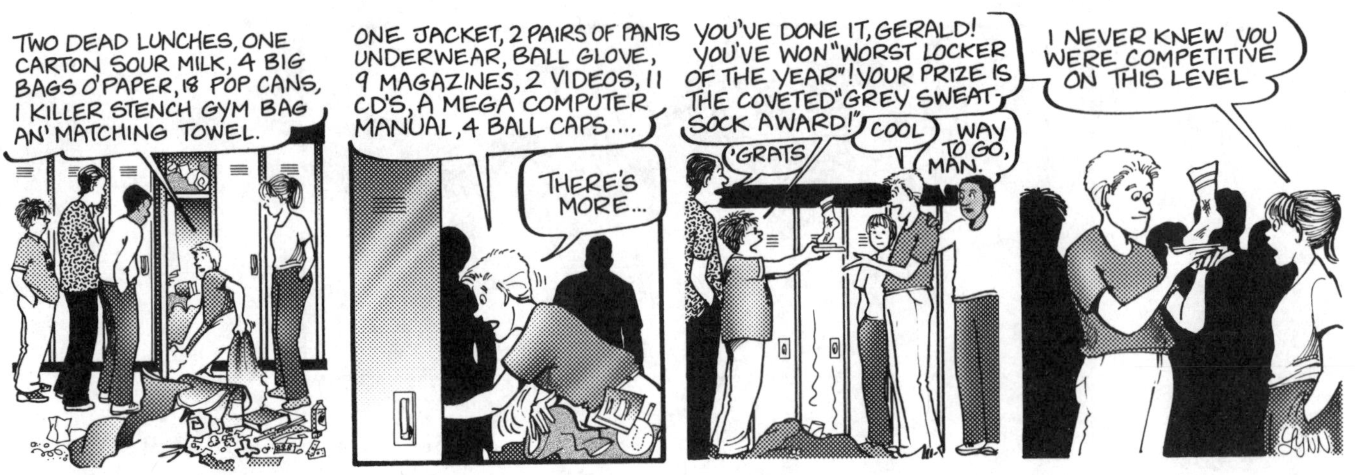
TWO DEAD LUNCHES, ONE CARTON SOUR MILK, 4 BIG BAGS O'PAPER, 18 POP CANS, 1 KILLER STENCH GYM BAG AN' MATCHING TOWEL.
ONE JACKET, 2 PAIRS OF PANTS UNDERWEAR, BALL GLOVE, 9 MAGAZINES, 2 VIDEOS, 11 CD'S, A MEGA COMPUTER MANUAL, 4 BALL CAPS....
THERE'S MORE...
YOU'VE DONE IT, GERALD! YOU'VE WON "WORST LOCKER OF THE YEAR"! YOUR PRIZE IS THE COVETED "GREY SWEAT-SOCK AWARD!"
'GRATS
COOL
WAY TO GO, MAN.
I NEVER KNEW YOU WERE COMPETITIVE ON THIS LEVEL
LYNN

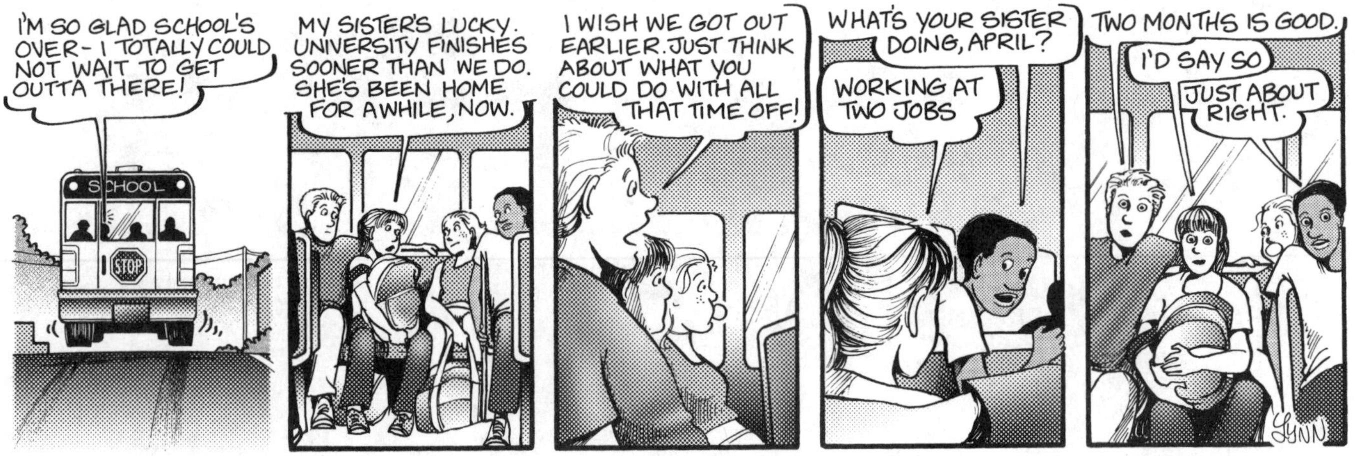
I'M SO GLAD SCHOOL'S OVER - I TOTALLY COULD NOT WAIT TO GET OUTTA THERE!
SCHOOL
STOP
MY SISTER'S LUCKY. UNIVERSITY FINISHES SOONER THAN WE DO. SHE'S BEEN HOME FOR AWHILE, NOW.
I WISH WE GOT OUT EARLIER. JUST THINK ABOUT WHAT YOU COULD DO WITH ALL THAT TIME OFF!
WHAT'S YOUR SISTER DOING, APRIL?
WORKING AT TWO JOBS
TWO MONTHS IS GOOD.
I'D SAY SO
JUST ABOUT RIGHT.
LYNN

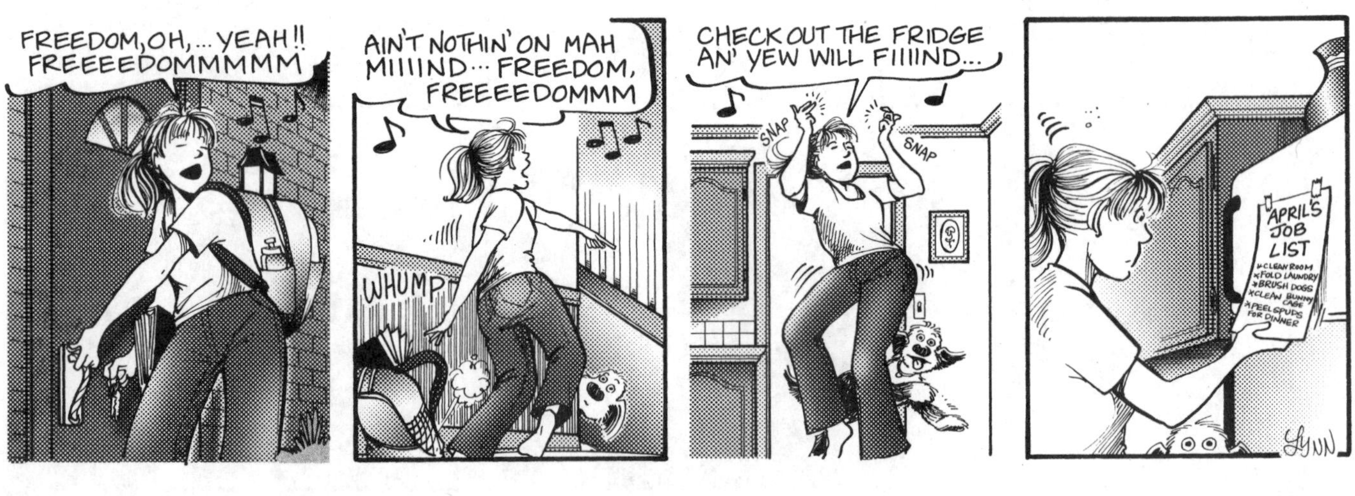
FREEDOM, OH, ... YEAH!! FREEEEDOMMMMM
AIN'T NOTHIN' ON MAH MIIIIND... FREEDOM, FREEEEDOMMM
WHUMP
CHECK OUT THE FRIDGE AN' YEW WILL FIIIIND...
SNAP
SNAP
APRIL'S JOB LIST
CLEAN ROOM
FOLD LAUNDRY
BRUSH DOGS
CLEAN BUNNY CAGE
PEEL SPUDS FOR DINNER
LYNN

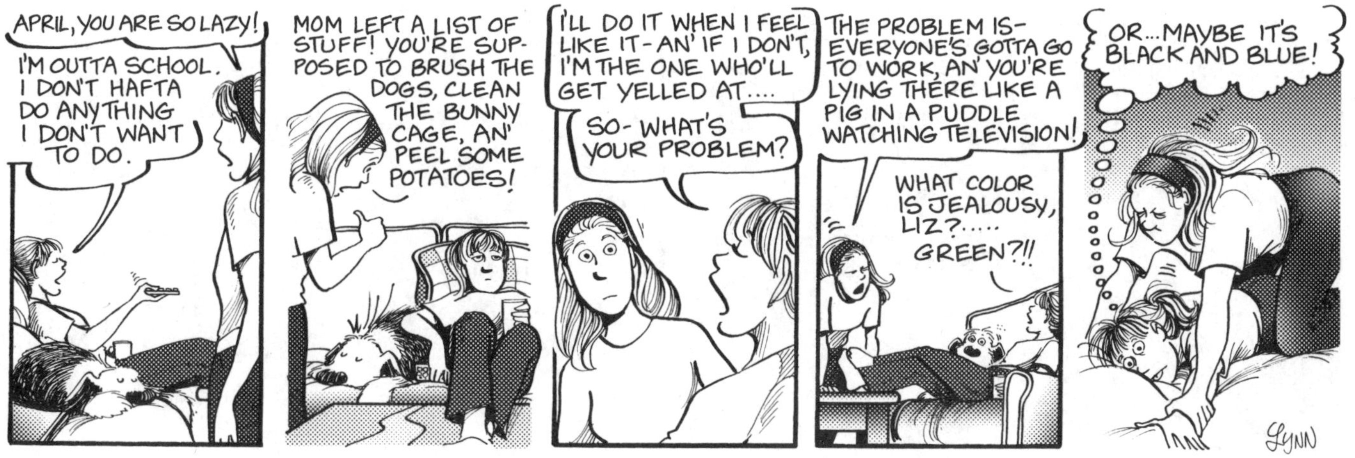
APRIL, YOU ARE SO LAZY!
I'M OUTTA SCHOOL. I DON'T HAFTA DO ANYTHING I DON'T WANT TO DO.
MOM LEFT A LIST OF STUFF! YOU'RE SUPPOSED TO BRUSH THE DOGS, CLEAN THE BUNNY CAGE, AN' PEEL SOME POTATOES!
I'LL DO IT WHEN I FEEL LIKE IT - AN' IF I DON'T, I'M THE ONE WHO'LL GET YELLED AT....
SO- WHAT'S YOUR PROBLEM?
THE PROBLEM IS- EVERYONE'S GOTTA GO TO WORK, AN' YOU'RE LYING THERE LIKE A PIG IN A PUDDLE WATCHING TELEVISION!
WHAT COLOR IS JEALOUSY, LIZ?..... GREEN?!!
OR...MAYBE IT'S BLACK AND BLUE!
LYNN

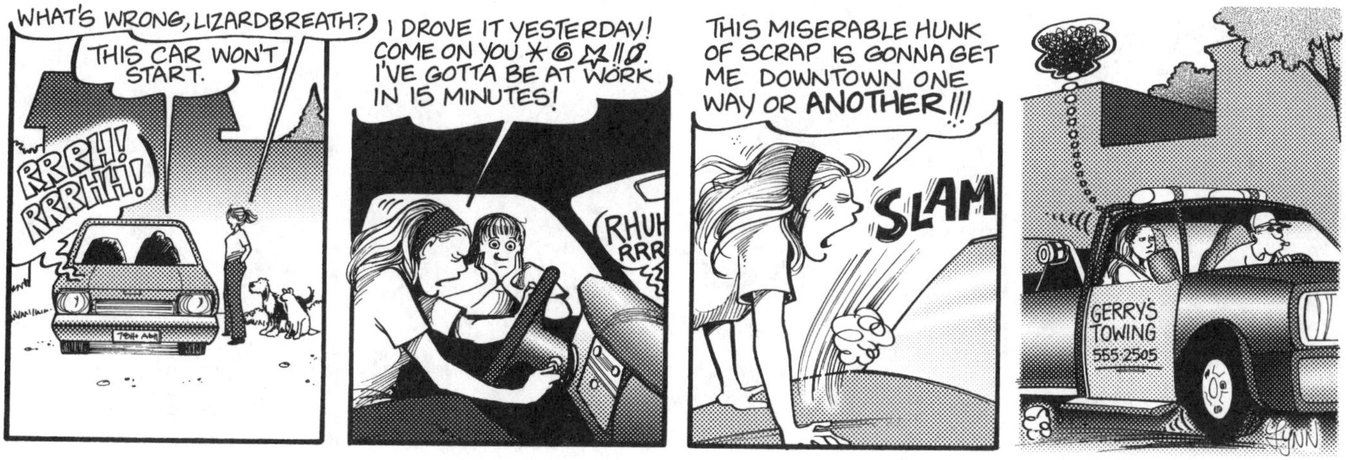
WHAT'S WRONG, LIZARDBREATH?
THIS CAR WON'T START.
RRRH! RRRHH!
I DROVE IT YESTERDAY! COME ON YOU
I'VE GOTTA BE AT WORK IN 15 MINUTES!
RHUH RRR
THIS MISERABLE HUNK OF SCRAP IS GONNA GET ME DOWNTOWN ONE WAY OR **ANOTHER**!!!
SLAM
GERRY'S TOWING 555-2505
LYNN

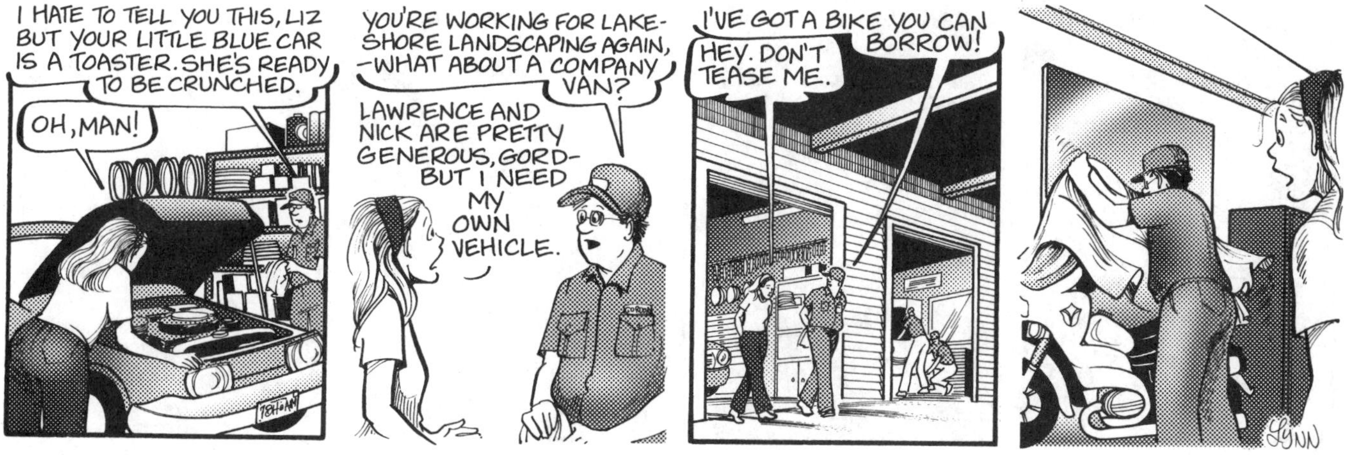
I HATE TO TELL YOU THIS, LIZ BUT YOUR LITTLE BLUE CAR IS A TOASTER. SHE'S READY TO BE CRUNCHED.
OH, MAN!
YOU'RE WORKING FOR LAKESHORE LANDSCAPING AGAIN, -WHAT ABOUT A COMPANY VAN?
LAWRENCE AND NICK ARE PRETTY GENEROUS, GORD- BUT I NEED MY OWN VEHICLE.
I'VE GOT A BIKE YOU CAN BORROW!
HEY. DON'T TEASE ME.
LYNN

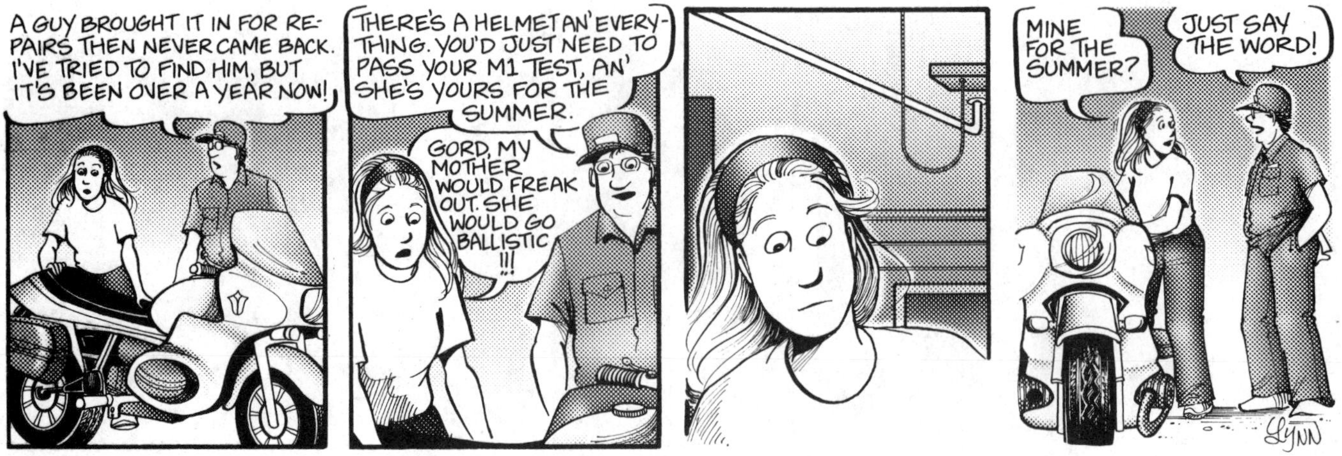
A GUY BROUGHT IT IN FOR REPAIRS THEN NEVER CAME BACK. I'VE TRIED TO FIND HIM, BUT IT'S BEEN OVER A YEAR NOW!
THERE'S A HELMET AN' EVERYTHING. YOU'D JUST NEED TO PASS YOUR M1 TEST, AN' SHE'S YOURS FOR THE SUMMER.
GORD, MY MOTHER WOULD FREAK OUT. SHE WOULD GO BALLISTIC!!!
MINE FOR THE SUMMER?
JUST SAY THE WORD!
LYNN

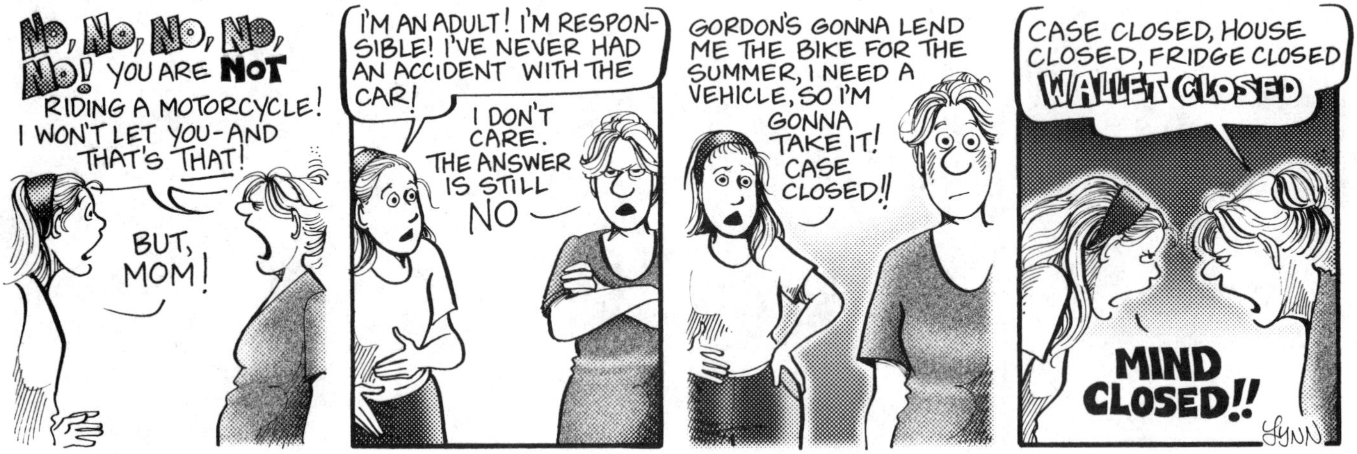
NO, NO, NO, NO, NO! YOU ARE NOT RIDING A MOTORCYCLE! I WON'T LET YOU-AND THAT'S THAT!
BUT, MOM!
I'M AN ADULT! I'M RESPONSIBLE! I'VE NEVER HAD AN ACCIDENT WITH THE CAR!
I DON'T CARE. THE ANSWER IS STILL NO
GORDON'S GONNA LEND ME THE BIKE FOR THE SUMMER, I NEED A VEHICLE, SO I'M GONNA TAKE IT! CASE CLOSED!!
CASE CLOSED, HOUSE CLOSED, FRIDGE CLOSED WALLET CLOSED
MIND CLOSED!!
LYNN

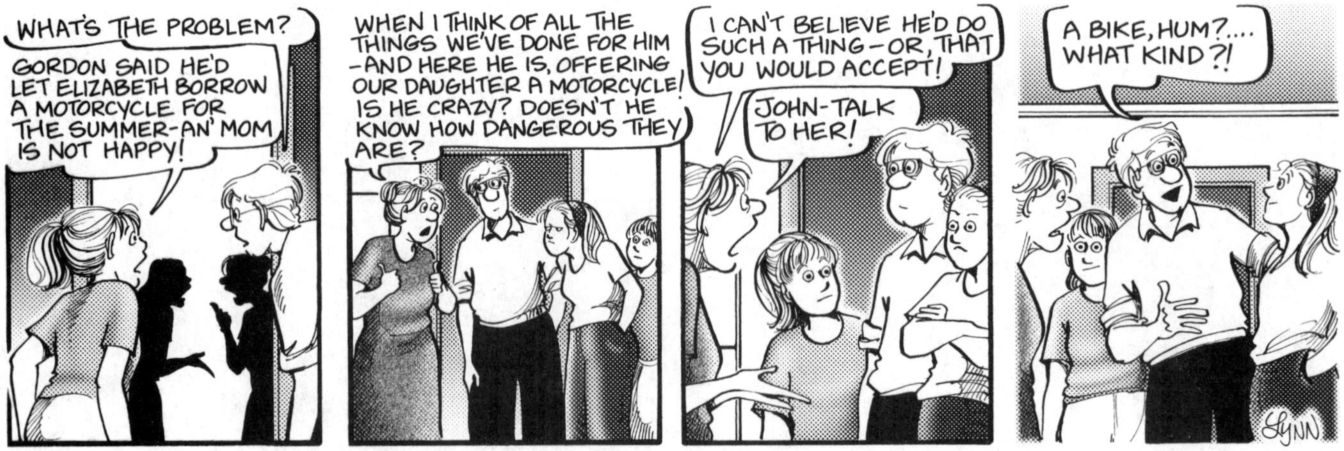
WHAT'S THE PROBLEM?
GORDON SAID HE'D LET ELIZABETH BORROW A MOTORCYCLE FOR THE SUMMER-AN' MOM IS NOT HAPPY!
WHEN I THINK OF ALL THE THINGS WE'VE DONE FOR HIM -AND HERE HE IS, OFFERING OUR DAUGHTER A MOTORCYCLE! IS HE CRAZY? DOESN'T HE KNOW HOW DANGEROUS THEY ARE?
I CAN'T BELIEVE HE'D DO SUCH A THING-OR, THAT YOU WOULD ACCEPT!
JOHN-TALK TO HER!
A BIKE, HUM?.... WHAT KIND?!
LYNN

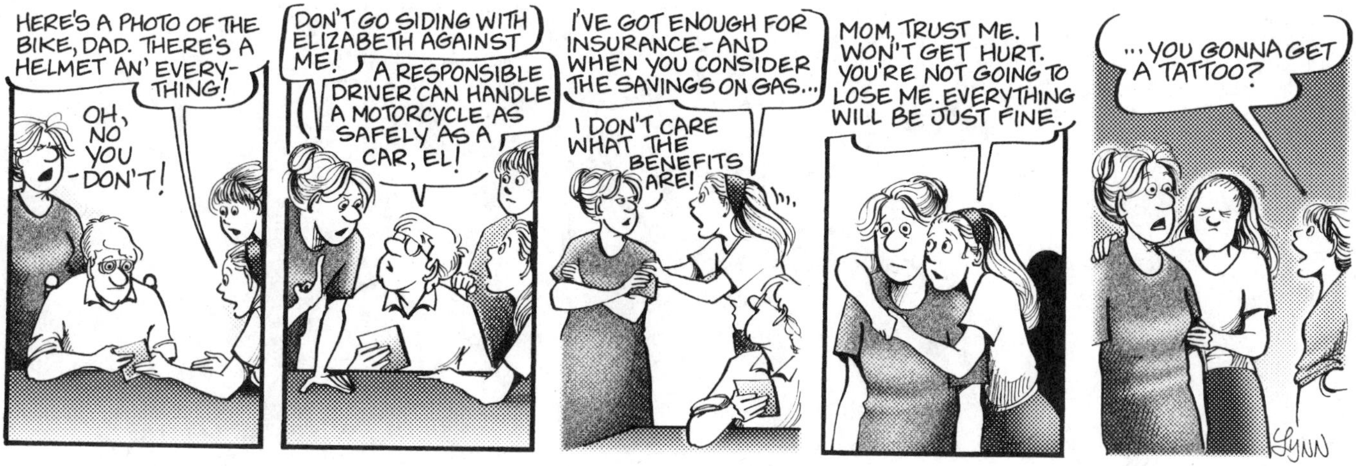
HERE'S A PHOTO OF THE BIKE, DAD. THERE'S A HELMET AN' EVERY-THING!
OH, NO YOU -DON'T!
DON'T GO SIDING WITH ELIZABETH AGAINST ME!
A RESPONSIBLE DRIVER CAN HANDLE A MOTORCYCLE AS SAFELY AS A CAR, EL!
I'VE GOT ENOUGH FOR INSURANCE - AND WHEN YOU CONSIDER THE SAVINGS ON GAS...
I DON'T CARE WHAT THE BENEFITS ARE!
MOM, TRUST ME. I WON'T GET HURT. YOU'RE NOT GOING TO LOSE ME. EVERYTHING WILL BE JUST FINE.
...YOU GONNA GET A TATTOO?
LYNN

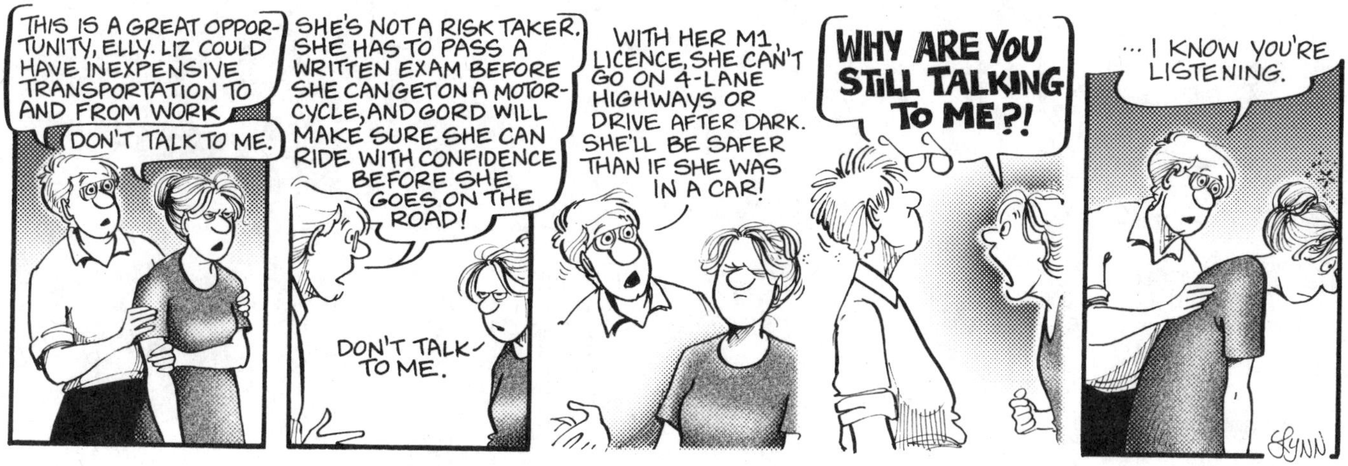
THIS IS A GREAT OPPOR-TUNITY, ELLY. LIZ COULD HAVE INEXPENSIVE TRANSPORTATION TO AND FROM WORK
DON'T TALK TO ME.
SHE'S NOT A RISK TAKER. SHE HAS TO PASS A WRITTEN EXAM BEFORE SHE CAN GET ON A MOTOR-CYCLE, AND GORD WILL MAKE SURE SHE CAN RIDE WITH CONFIDENCE BEFORE SHE GOES ON THE ROAD!
DON'T TALK TO ME.
WITH HER M1 LICENCE, SHE CAN'T GO ON 4-LANE HIGHWAYS OR DRIVE AFTER DARK. SHE'LL BE SAFER THAN IF SHE WAS IN A CAR!
WHY ARE YOU STILL TALKING TO ME?!
...I KNOW YOU'RE LISTENING.
LYNN

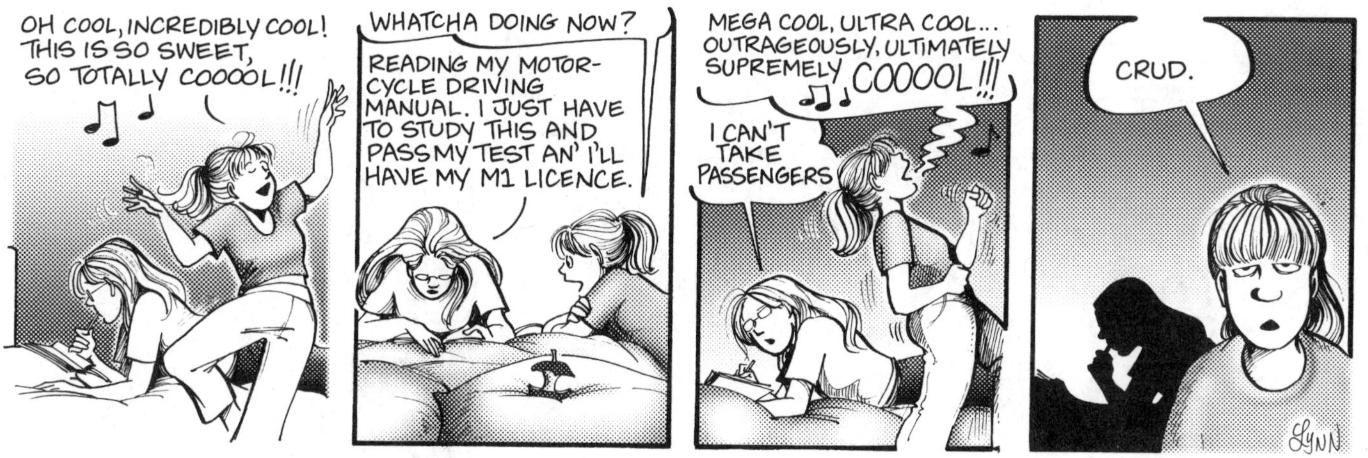
OH COOL, INCREDIBLY COOL! THIS IS SO SWEET, SO TOTALLY COOOOL!!!
WHATCHA DOING NOW?
READING MY MOTOR-CYCLE DRIVING MANUAL. I JUST HAVE TO STUDY THIS AND PASS MY TEST AN' I'LL HAVE MY M1 LICENCE.
MEGA COOL, ULTRA COOL... OUTRAGEOUSLY, ULTIMATELY SUPREMELY COOOOL!!!
I CAN'T TAKE PASSENGERS
CRUD.
LYNN

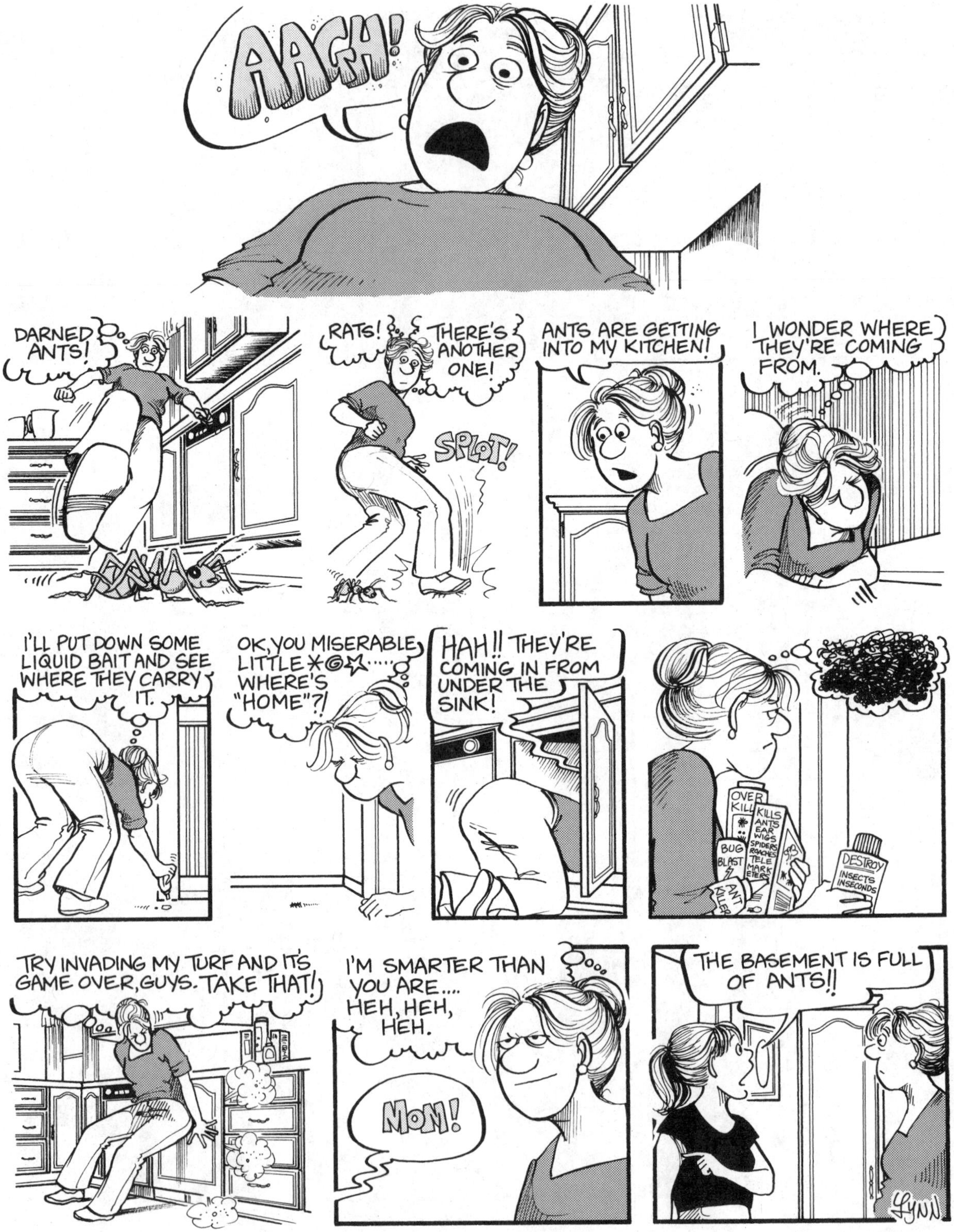
AAGH!
DARNED ANTS!
RATS!
THERE'S ANOTHER ONE!
SPLOT!
ANTS ARE GETTING INTO MY KITCHEN!
I WONDER WHERE THEY'RE COMING FROM.
I'LL PUT DOWN SOME LIQUID BAIT AND SEE WHERE THEY CARRY IT.
OK, YOU MISERABLE LITTLE *@☆..... WHERE'S "HOME"?!
HAH!! THEY'RE COMING IN FROM UNDER THE SINK!
OVER KILL
KILLS ANTS EARWIGS SPIDERS ROACHES TELEMARKETERS
BUG BLAST
ANT KILLER
DESTROY INSECTS IN SECONDS
TRY INVADING MY TURF AND IT'S GAME OVER, GUYS. TAKE THAT!
I'M SMARTER THAN YOU ARE.... HEH, HEH, HEH.
MOM!
THE BASEMENT IS FULL OF ANTS!!
LYNN

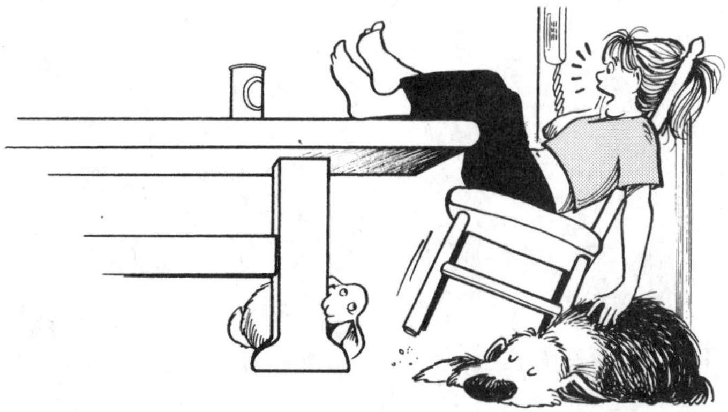

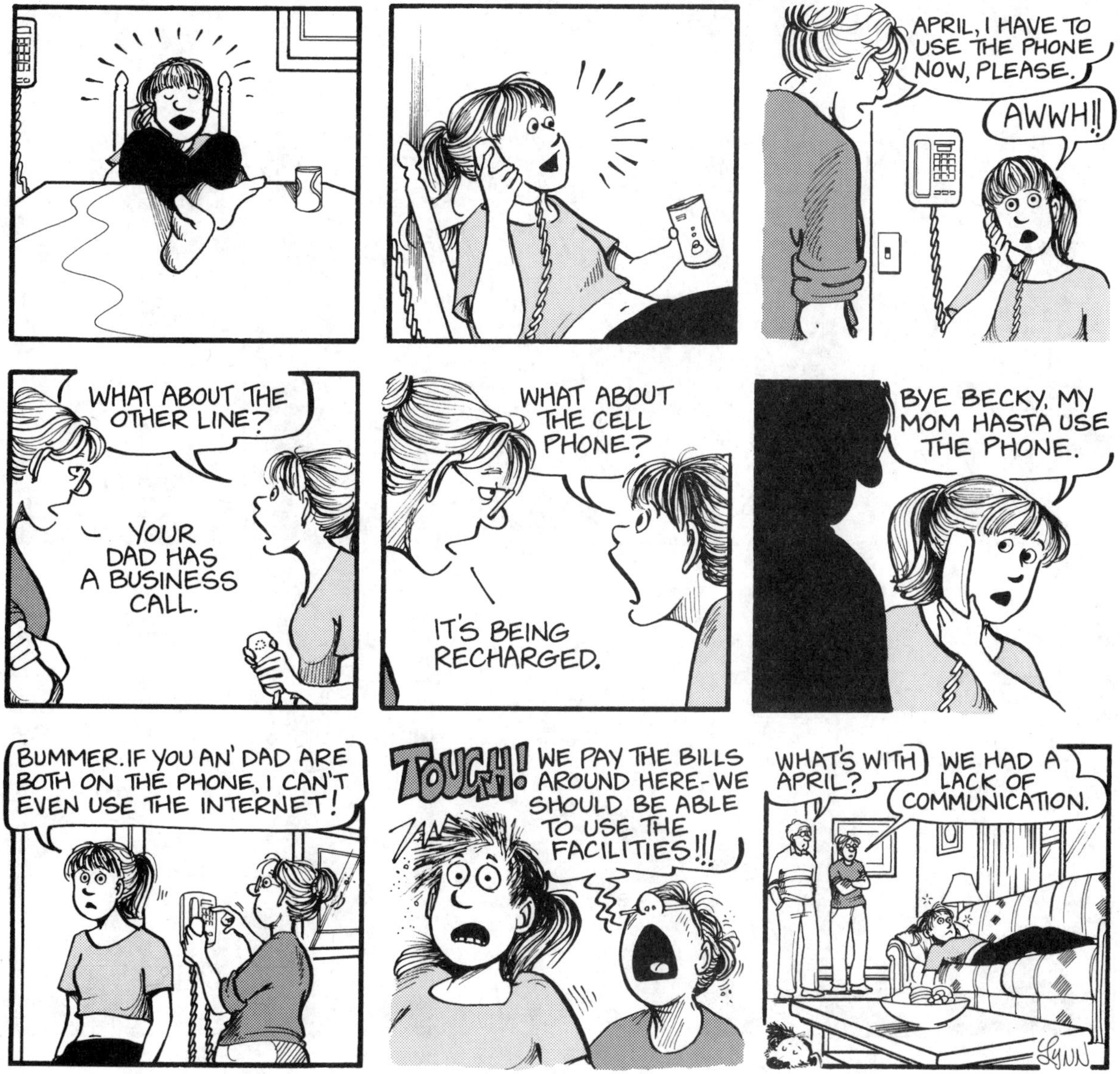
APRIL, I HAVE TO USE THE PHONE NOW, PLEASE.
AWWH!!
WHAT ABOUT THE OTHER LINE?
YOUR DAD HAS A BUSINESS CALL.
WHAT ABOUT THE CELL PHONE?
IT'S BEING RECHARGED.
BYE BECKY, MY MOM HASTA USE THE PHONE.
BUMMER. IF YOU AN' DAD ARE BOTH ON THE PHONE, I CAN'T EVEN USE THE INTERNET!
TOUGH!
WE PAY THE BILLS AROUND HERE- WE SHOULD BE ABLE TO USE THE FACILITIES!!!
WHAT'S WITH APRIL?
WE HAD A LACK OF COMMUNICATION.
LYNN

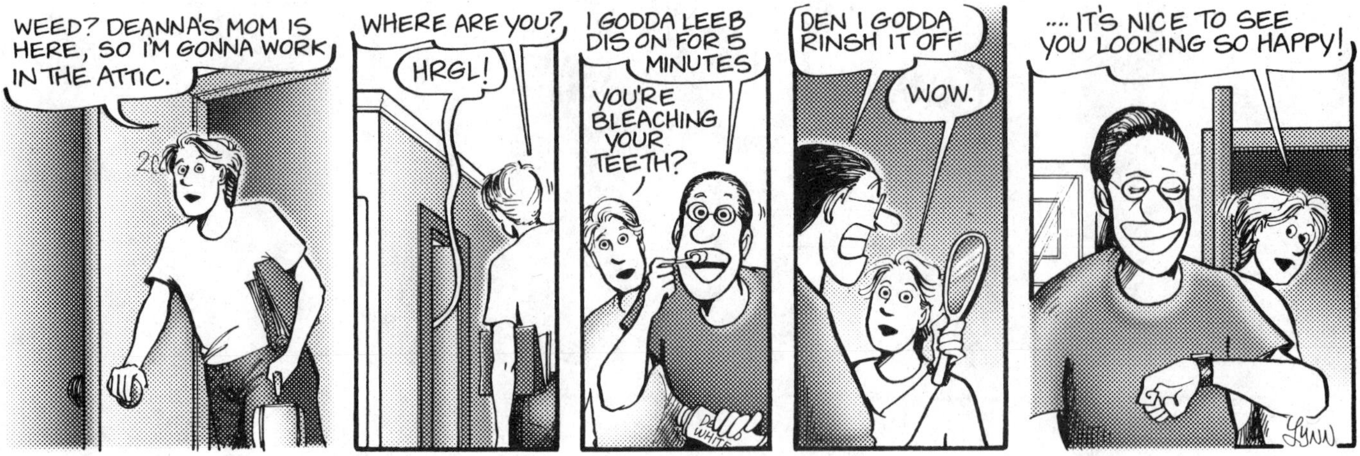
WEED? DEANNA'S MOM IS HERE, SO I'M GONNA WORK IN THE ATTIC.
WHERE ARE YOU?
HRGL!
I GODDA LEEB DIS ON FOR 5 MINUTES
YOU'RE BLEACHING YOUR TEETH?
DEN I GODDA RINSH IT OFF
WOW.
.... IT'S NICE TO SEE YOU LOOKING SO HAPPY!
LYNN

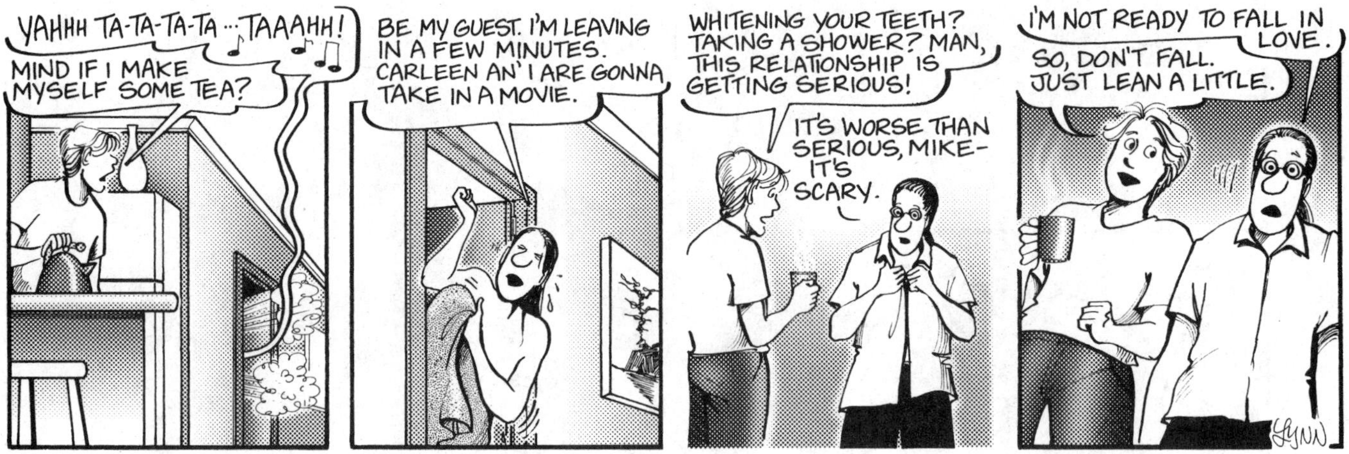
YAHHH TA-TA-TA-TA ... TAAAHH!
MIND IF I MAKE MYSELF SOME TEA?
BE MY GUEST. I'M LEAVING IN A FEW MINUTES. CARLEEN AN' I ARE GONNA TAKE IN A MOVIE.
WHITENING YOUR TEETH? TAKING A SHOWER? MAN, THIS RELATIONSHIP IS GETTING SERIOUS!
IT'S WORSE THAN SERIOUS, MIKE- IT'S SCARY.
I'M NOT READY TO FALL IN LOVE.
SO, DON'T FALL. JUST LEAN A LITTLE.
LYNN

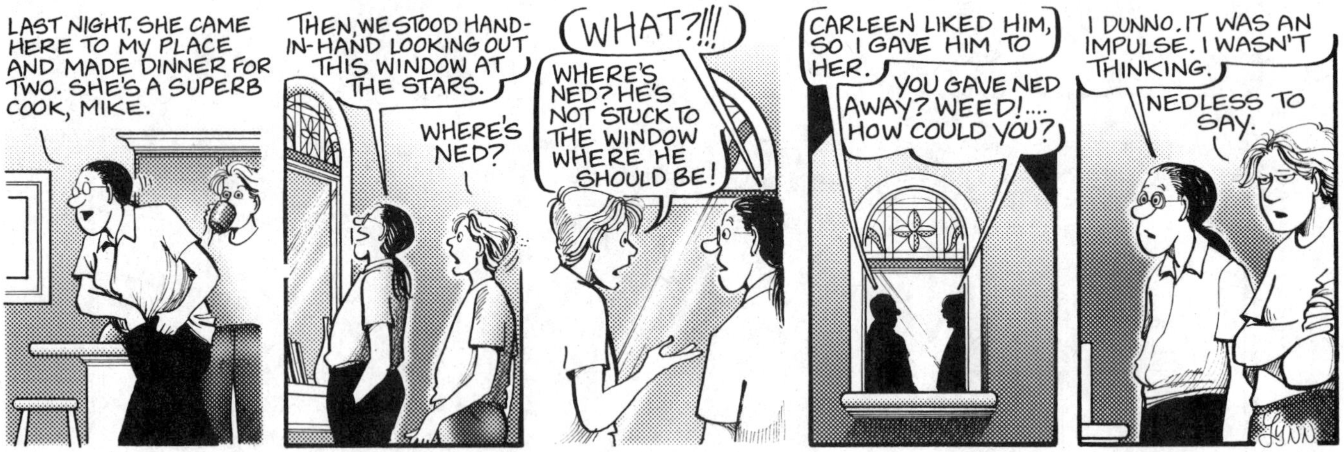
LAST NIGHT, SHE CAME HERE TO MY PLACE AND MADE DINNER FOR TWO. SHE'S A SUPERB COOK, MIKE.
THEN, WE STOOD HAND-IN-HAND LOOKING OUT THIS WINDOW AT THE STARS.
WHERE'S NED?
WHAT?!!!
WHERE'S NED? HE'S NOT STUCK TO THE WINDOW WHERE HE SHOULD BE!
CARLEEN LIKED HIM, SO I GAVE HIM TO HER.
YOU GAVE NED AWAY? WEED!.... HOW COULD YOU?
I DUNNO. IT WAS AN IMPULSE. I WASN'T THINKING.
NEDLESS TO SAY.
LYNN

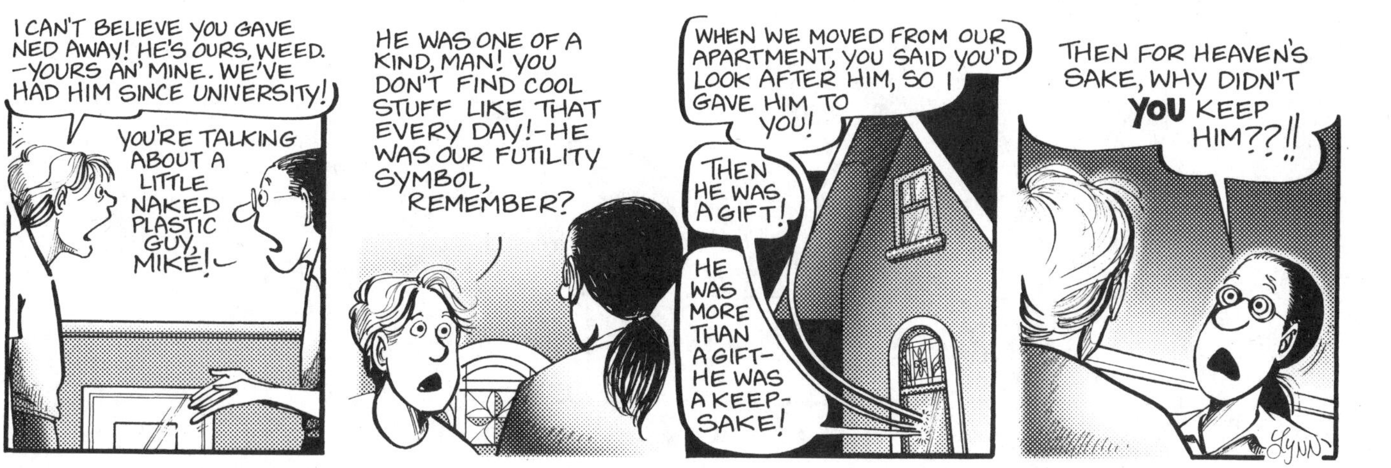
I CAN'T BELIEVE YOU GAVE NED AWAY! HE'S OURS, WEED. -YOURS AN' MINE. WE'VE HAD HIM SINCE UNIVERSITY!
YOU'RE TALKING ABOUT A LITTLE NAKED PLASTIC GUY, MIKE!
HE WAS ONE OF A KIND, MAN! YOU DON'T FIND COOL STUFF LIKE THAT EVERY DAY! -HE WAS OUR FUTILITY SYMBOL, REMEMBER?
WHEN WE MOVED FROM OUR APARTMENT, YOU SAID YOU'D LOOK AFTER HIM, SO I GAVE HIM TO YOU!
THEN HE WAS A GIFT!
HE WAS MORE THAN A GIFT- HE WAS A KEEP-SAKE!
THEN FOR HEAVEN'S SAKE, WHY DIDN'T YOU KEEP HIM??!!
LYNN

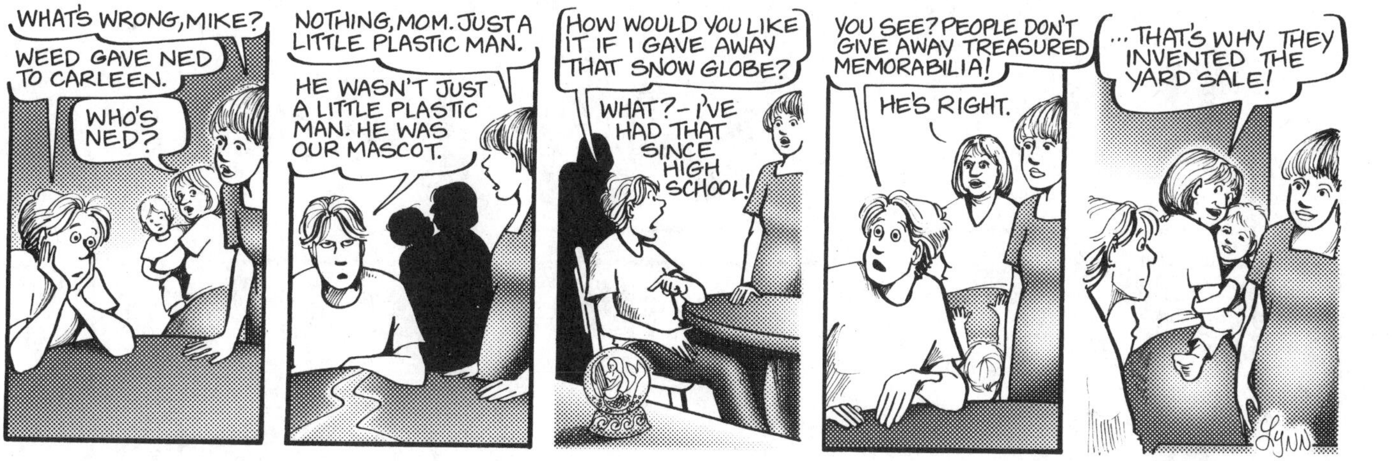
WHAT'S WRONG, MIKE?
WEED GAVE NED TO CARLEEN.
WHO'S NED?
NOTHING, MOM. JUST A LITTLE PLASTIC MAN.
HE WASN'T JUST A LITTLE PLASTIC MAN. HE WAS OUR MASCOT.
HOW WOULD YOU LIKE IT IF I GAVE AWAY THAT SNOW GLOBE?
WHAT?- I'VE HAD THAT SINCE HIGH SCHOOL!
YOU SEE? PEOPLE DON'T GIVE AWAY TREASURED MEMORABILIA!
HE'S RIGHT.
...THAT'S WHY THEY INVENTED THE YARD SALE!
LYNN

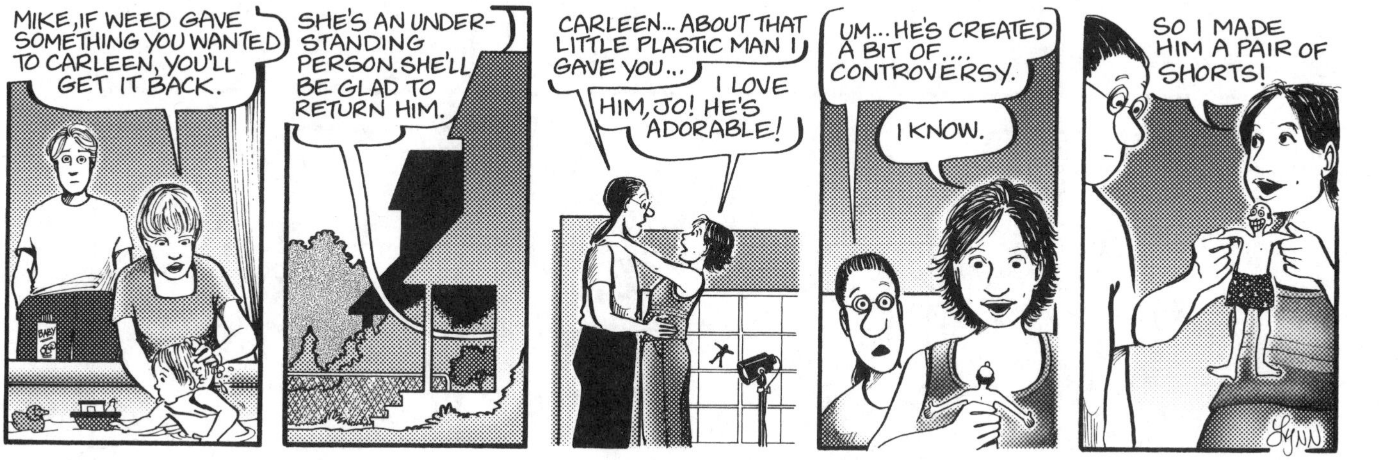
MIKE, IF WEED GAVE SOMETHING YOU WANTED TO CARLEEN, YOU'LL GET IT BACK.
SHE'S AN UNDER-STANDING PERSON. SHE'LL BE GLAD TO RETURN HIM.
CARLEEN... ABOUT THAT LITTLE PLASTIC MAN I GAVE YOU...
I LOVE HIM, JO! HE'S ADORABLE!
UM... HE'S CREATED A BIT OF.... CONTROVERSY.
I KNOW.
SO I MADE HIM A PAIR OF SHORTS!
LYNN

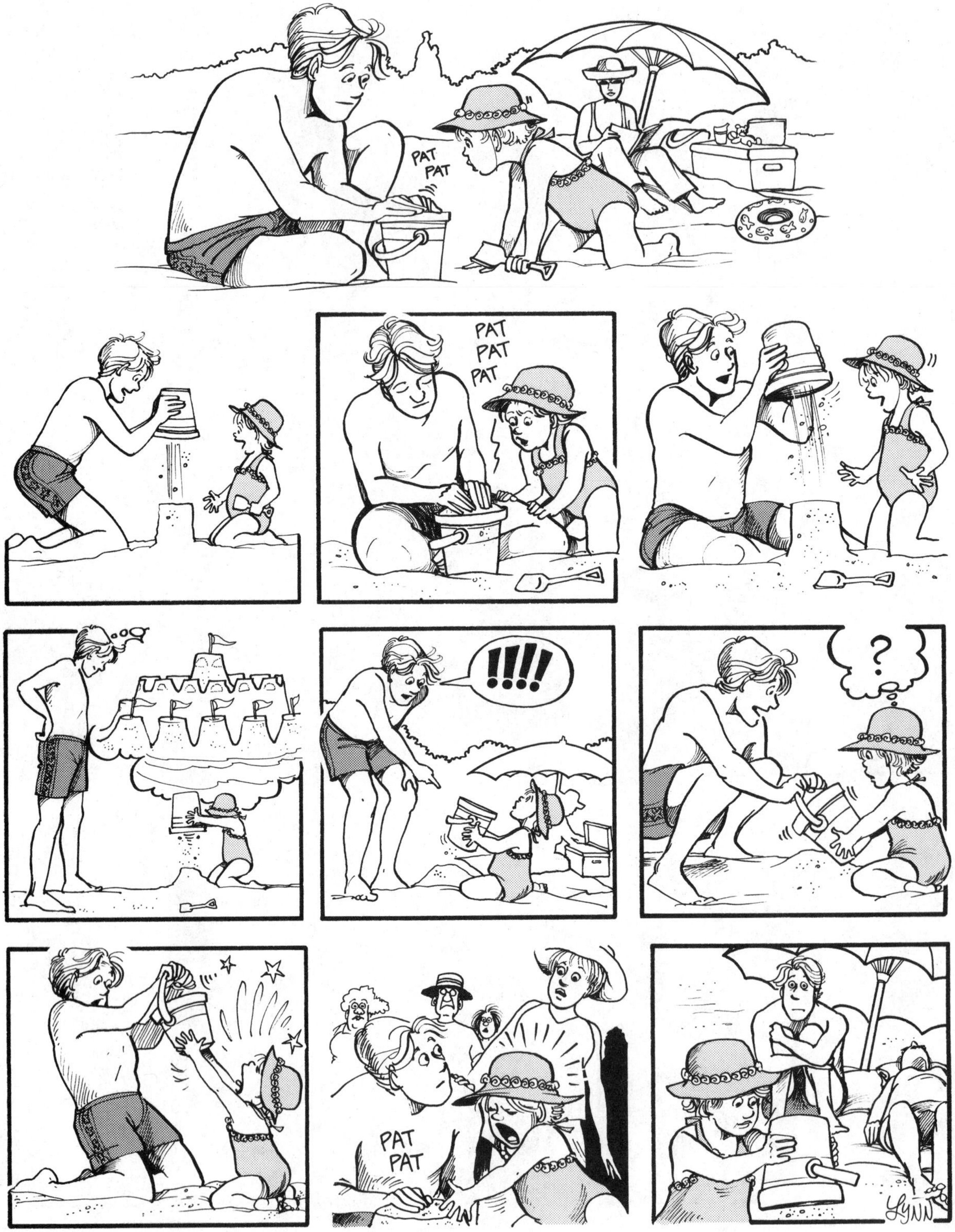
PAT
PAT
PAT
PAT
PAT
!!!!!
?
PAT
PAT
LYNN

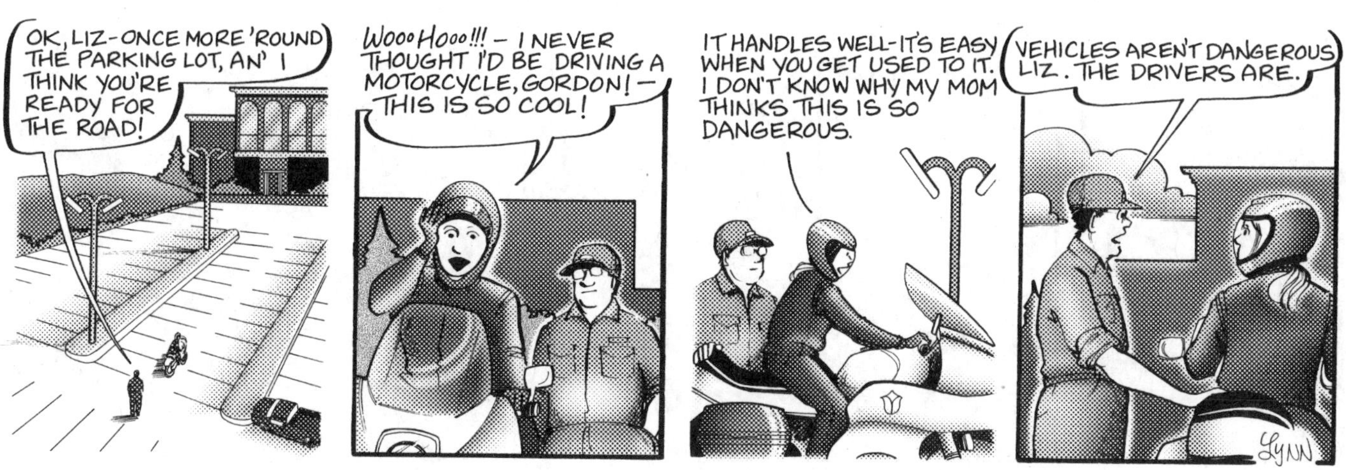
OK, LIZ-ONCE MORE 'ROUND THE PARKING LOT, AN' I THINK YOU'RE READY FOR THE ROAD!
WoooHooo!!! - I NEVER THOUGHT I'D BE DRIVING A MOTORCYCLE, GORDON! - THIS IS SO COOL!
IT HANDLES WELL-IT'S EASY WHEN YOU GET USED TO IT. I DON'T KNOW WHY MY MOM THINKS THIS IS SO DANGEROUS.
VEHICLES AREN'T DANGEROUS LIZ. THE DRIVERS ARE.
LYNN

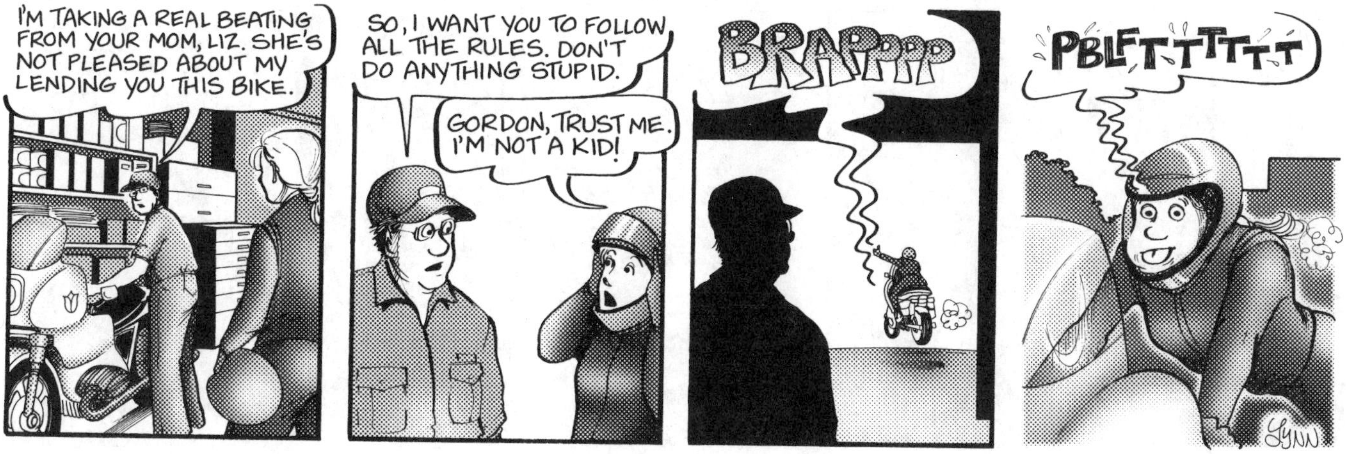
I'M TAKING A REAL BEATING FROM YOUR MOM, LIZ. SHE'S NOT PLEASED ABOUT MY LENDING YOU THIS BIKE.
SO, I WANT YOU TO FOLLOW ALL THE RULES. DON'T DO ANYTHING STUPID.
GORDON, TRUST ME. I'M NOT A KID!
BRAPPPP
PBLFTTTTTT
LYNN

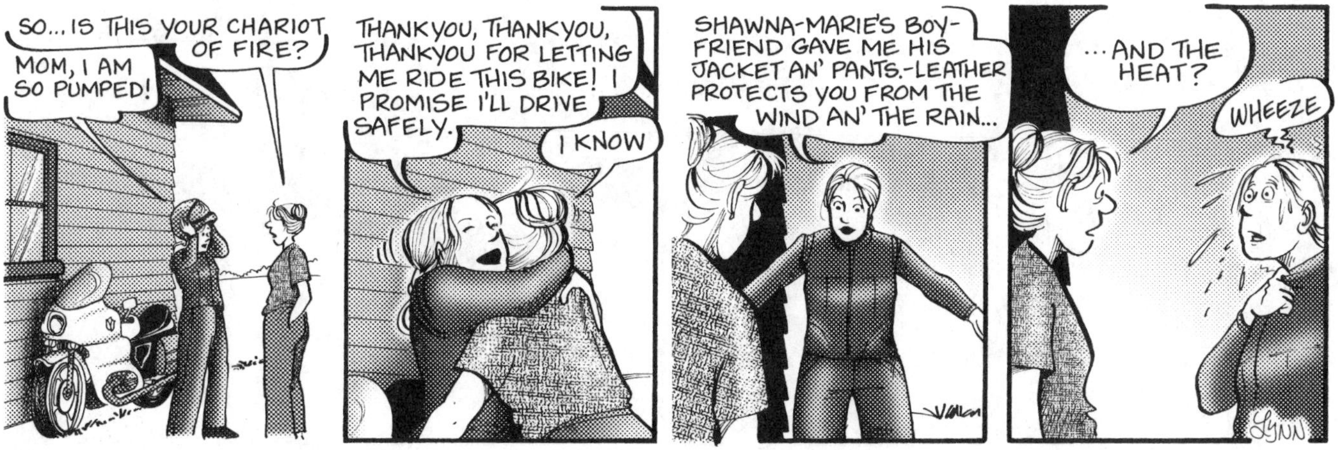
SO... IS THIS YOUR CHARIOT OF FIRE?
MOM, I AM SO PUMPED!
THANKYOU, THANKYOU, THANKYOU FOR LETTING ME RIDE THIS BIKE! I PROMISE I'LL DRIVE SAFELY.
I KNOW
SHAWNA-MARIE'S BOYFRIEND GAVE ME HIS JACKET AN' PANTS.-LEATHER PROTECTS YOU FROM THE WIND AN' THE RAIN...
...AND THE HEAT?
WHEEZE
LYNN

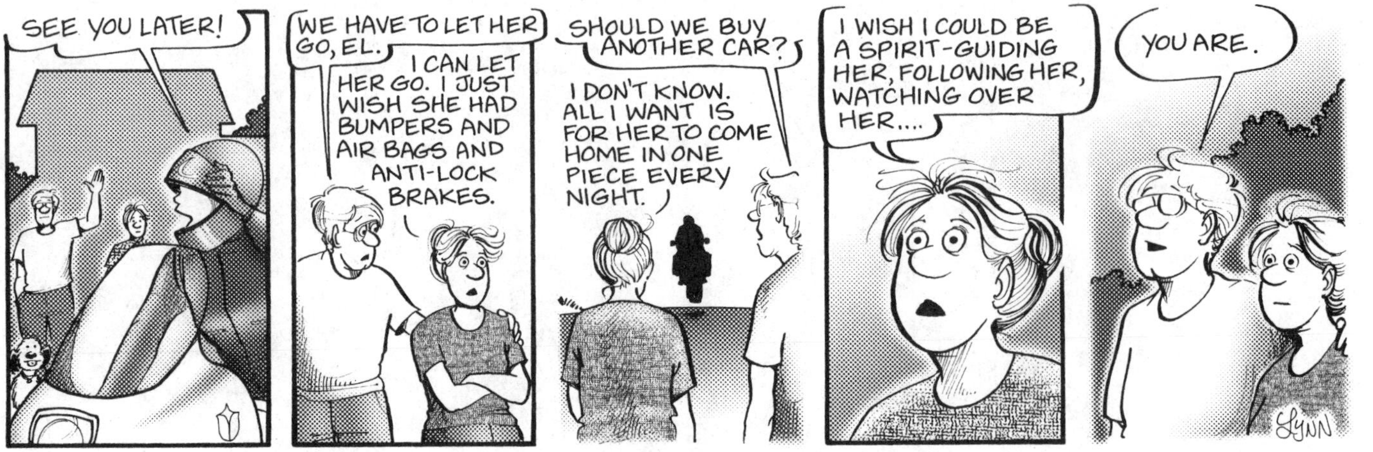
SEE YOU LATER!
WE HAVE TO LET HER GO, EL.
I CAN LET HER GO. I JUST WISH SHE HAD BUMPERS AND AIR BAGS AND ANTI-LOCK BRAKES.
SHOULD WE BUY ANOTHER CAR?
I DON'T KNOW. ALL I WANT IS FOR HER TO COME HOME IN ONE PIECE EVERY NIGHT.
I WISH I COULD BE A SPIRIT-GUIDING HER, FOLLOWING HER, WATCHING OVER HER....
YOU ARE.
LYNN

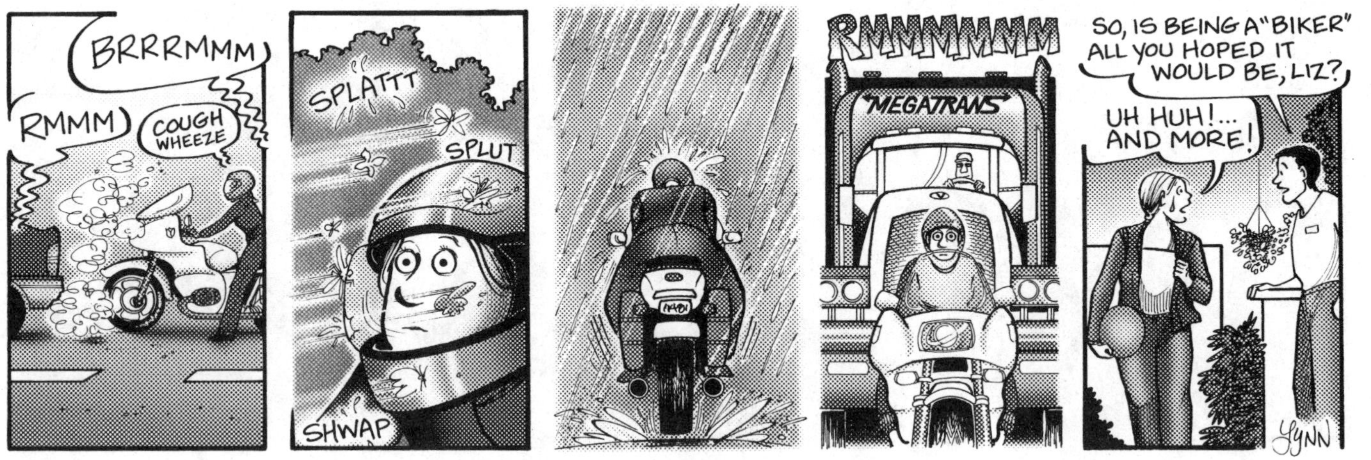
BRRRMMM
RMMM
COUGH WHEEZE
SPLATTT
SPLUT
SHWAP
RMMMMMMM
"MEGATRANS"
SO, IS BEING A "BIKER" ALL YOU HOPED IT WOULD BE, LIZ?
UH HUH!... AND MORE!
LYNN

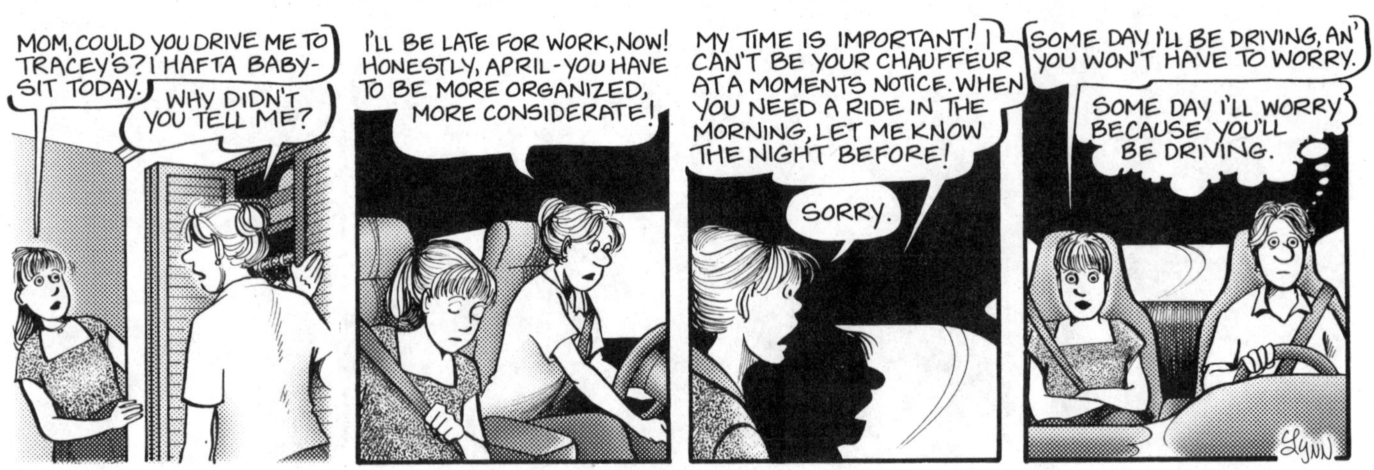
MOM, COULD YOU DRIVE ME TO TRACEY'S? I HAFTA BABY-SIT TODAY.
WHY DIDN'T YOU TELL ME?
I'LL BE LATE FOR WORK, NOW! HONESTLY, APRIL - YOU HAVE TO BE MORE ORGANIZED, MORE CONSIDERATE!
MY TIME IS IMPORTANT! I CAN'T BE YOUR CHAUFFEUR AT A MOMENTS NOTICE. WHEN YOU NEED A RIDE IN THE MORNING, LET ME KNOW THE NIGHT BEFORE!
SORRY.
SOME DAY I'LL BE DRIVING, AN' YOU WON'T HAVE TO WORRY.
SOME DAY I'LL WORRY BECAUSE YOU'LL BE DRIVING.
LYNN

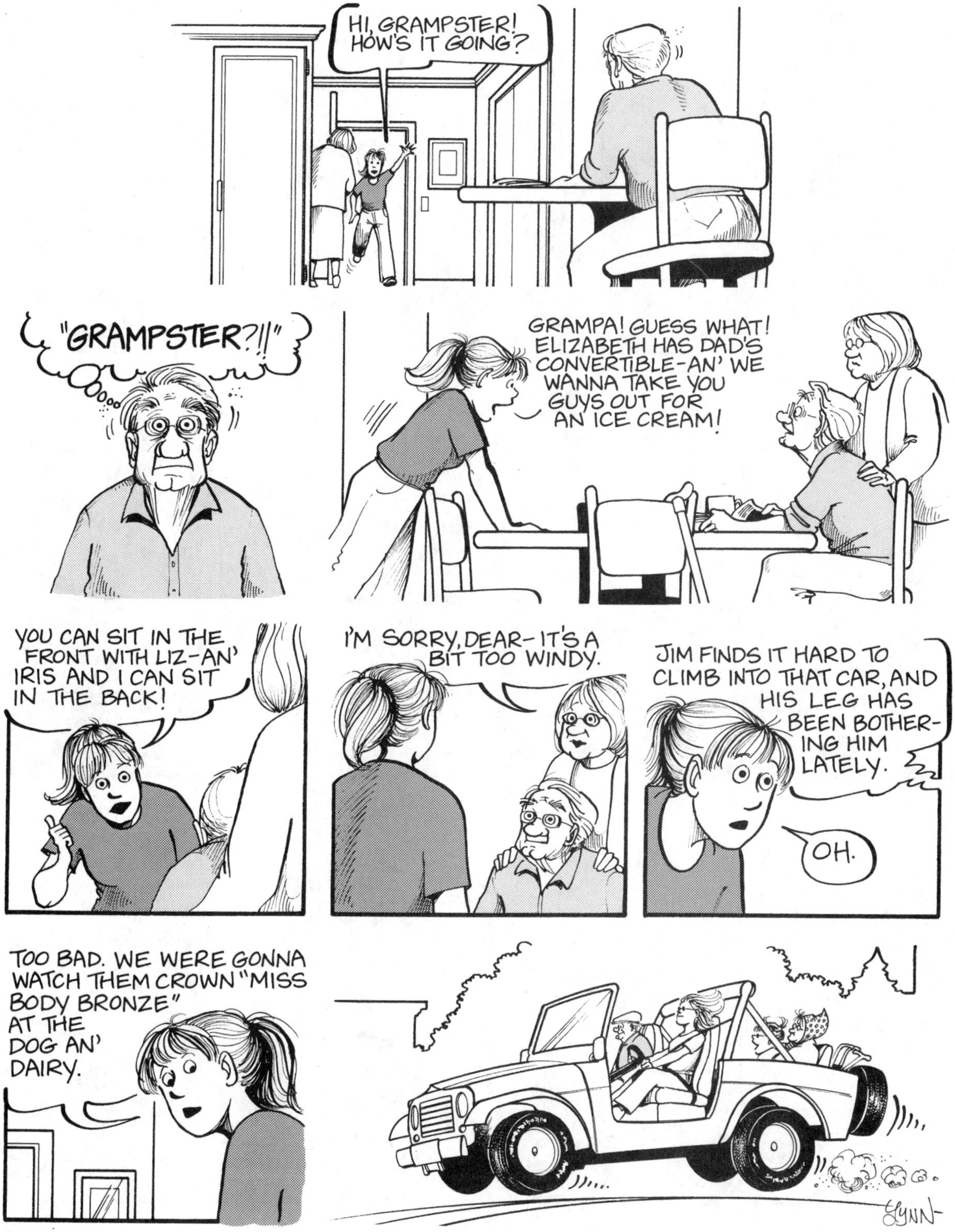
HI, GRAMPSTER! HOW'S IT GOING?
"GRAMPSTER?!!"
GRAMPA! GUESS WHAT! ELIZABETH HAS DAD'S CONVERTIBLE-AN' WE WANNA TAKE YOU GUYS OUT FOR AN ICE CREAM!
YOU CAN SIT IN THE FRONT WITH LIZ-AN' IRIS AND I CAN SIT IN THE BACK!
I'M SORRY, DEAR- IT'S A BIT TOO WINDY.
JIM FINDS IT HARD TO CLIMB INTO THAT CAR, AND HIS LEG HAS BEEN BOTHERING HIM LATELY.
OH.
TOO BAD. WE WERE GONNA WATCH THEM CROWN "MISS BODY BRONZE" AT THE DOG AN' DAIRY.
LYNN

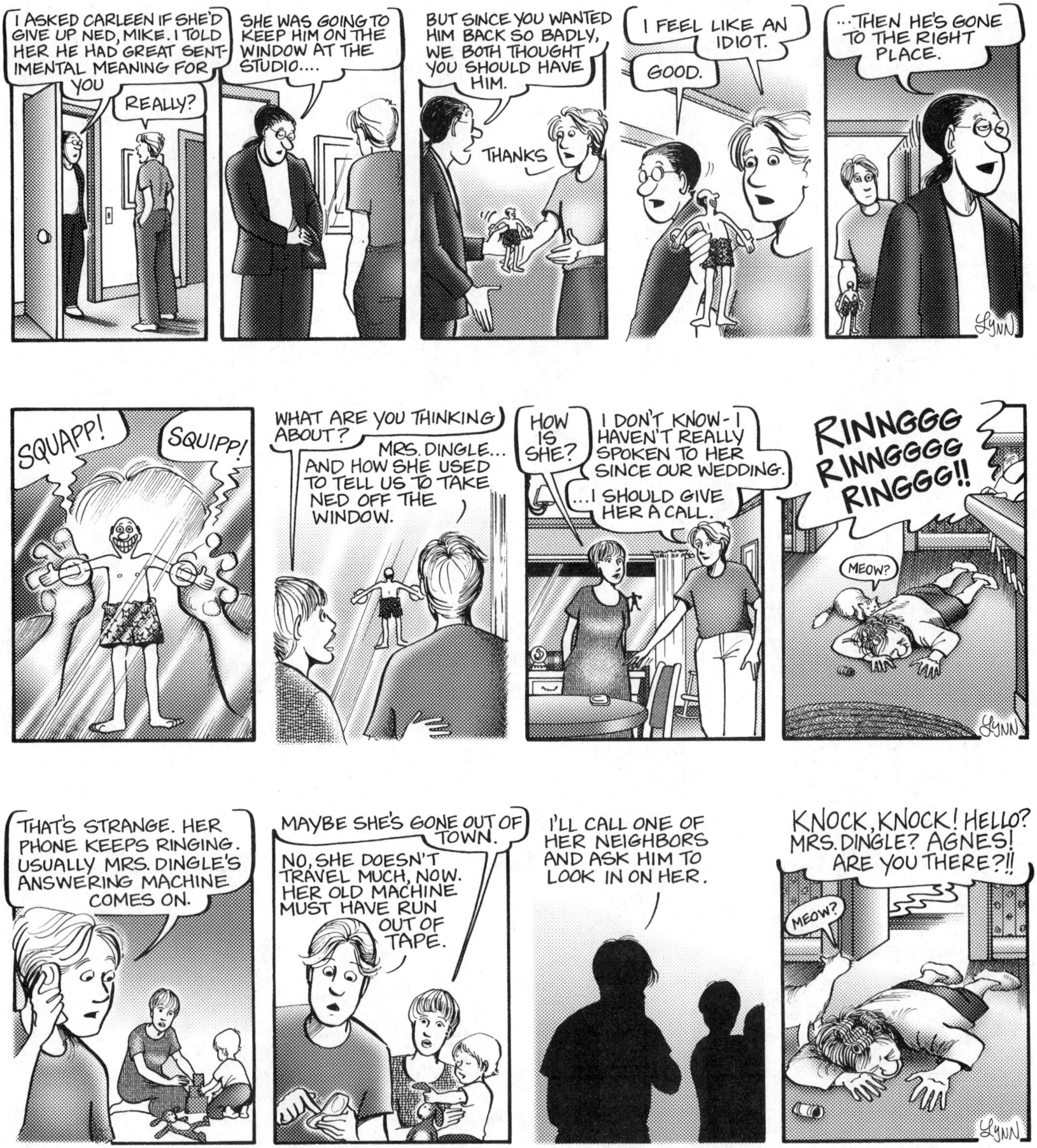
I ASKED CARLEEN IF SHE'D GIVE UP NED, MIKE. I TOLD HER HE HAD GREAT SENT-IMENTAL MEANING FOR YOU
REALLY?
SHE WAS GOING TO KEEP HIM ON THE WINDOW AT THE STUDIO....
BUT SINCE YOU WANTED HIM BACK SO BADLY, WE BOTH THOUGHT YOU SHOULD HAVE HIM.
THANKS
I FEEL LIKE AN IDIOT.
GOOD.
...THEN HE'S GONE TO THE RIGHT PLACE.
LYNN
SQUAPP!
SQUIPP!
WHAT ARE YOU THINKING ABOUT?
MRS. DINGLE... AND HOW SHE USED TO TELL US TO TAKE NED OFF THE WINDOW.
HOW IS SHE?
I DON'T KNOW- I HAVEN'T REALLY SPOKEN TO HER SINCE OUR WEDDING.
...I SHOULD GIVE HER A CALL.
RINNGGG RINNGGGG RINGGG!!
MEOW?
LYNN
THAT'S STRANGE. HER PHONE KEEPS RINGING. USUALLY MRS. DINGLE'S ANSWERING MACHINE COMES ON.
MAYBE SHE'S GONE OUT OF TOWN.
NO, SHE DOESN'T TRAVEL MUCH, NOW. HER OLD MACHINE MUST HAVE RUN OUT OF TAPE.
I'LL CALL ONE OF HER NEIGHBORS AND ASK HIM TO LOOK IN ON HER.
KNOCK, KNOCK! HELLO? MRS. DINGLE? AGNES! ARE YOU THERE?!!
MEOW?
LYNN

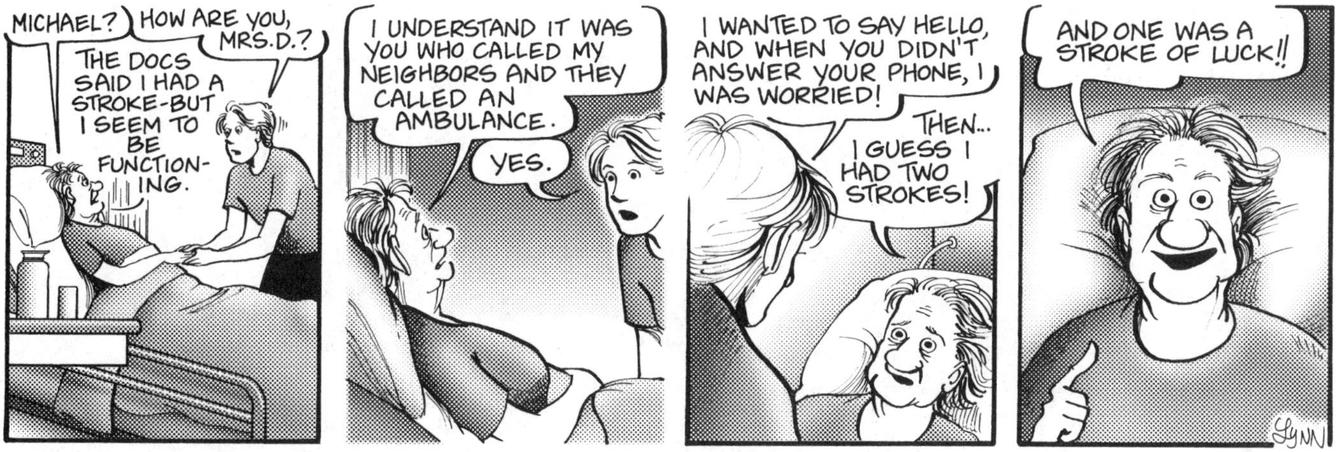
MICHAEL?
HOW ARE YOU, MRS. D.?
THE DOCS SAID I HAD A STROKE-BUT I SEEM TO BE FUNCTION-ING.
I UNDERSTAND IT WAS YOU WHO CALLED MY NEIGHBORS AND THEY CALLED AN AMBULANCE.
YES.
I WANTED TO SAY HELLO, AND WHEN YOU DIDN'T ANSWER YOUR PHONE, I WAS WORRIED!
THEN... I GUESS I HAD TWO STROKES!
AND ONE WAS A STROKE OF LUCK!!
LYNN

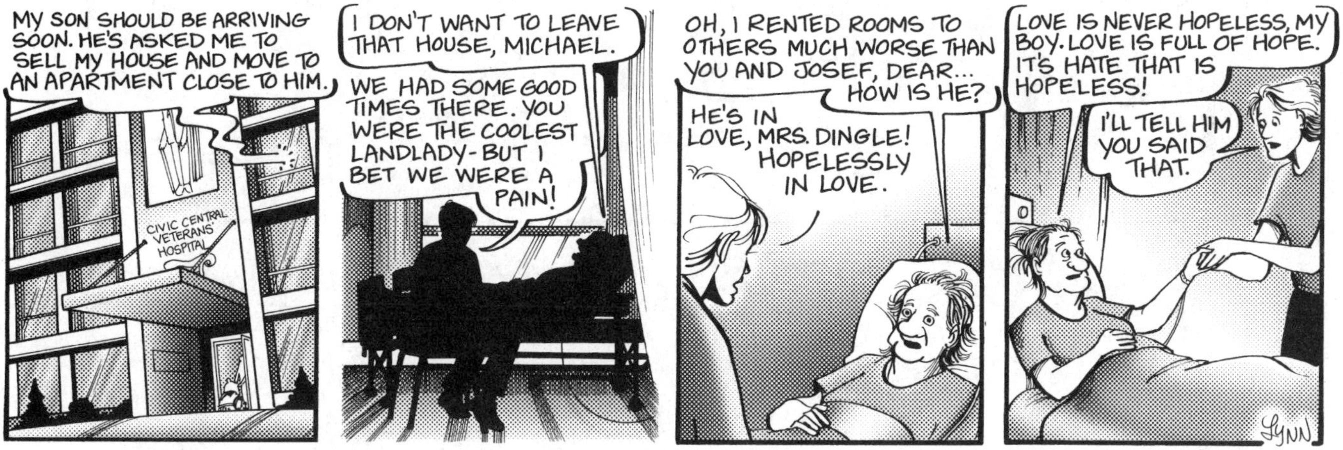
MY SON SHOULD BE ARRIVING SOON. HE'S ASKED ME TO SELL MY HOUSE AND MOVE TO AN APARTMENT CLOSE TO HIM.
CIVIC CENTRAL VETERANS' HOSPITAL
I DON'T WANT TO LEAVE THAT HOUSE, MICHAEL.
WE HAD SOME GOOD TIMES THERE. YOU WERE THE COOLEST LANDLADY- BUT I BET WE WERE A PAIN!
OH, I RENTED ROOMS TO OTHERS MUCH WORSE THAN YOU AND JOSEF, DEAR...
HOW IS HE?
HE'S IN LOVE, MRS. DINGLE! HOPELESSLY IN LOVE.
LOVE IS NEVER HOPELESS, MY BOY. LOVE IS FULL OF HOPE. IT'S HATE THAT IS HOPELESS!
I'LL TELL HIM YOU SAID THAT.
LYNN

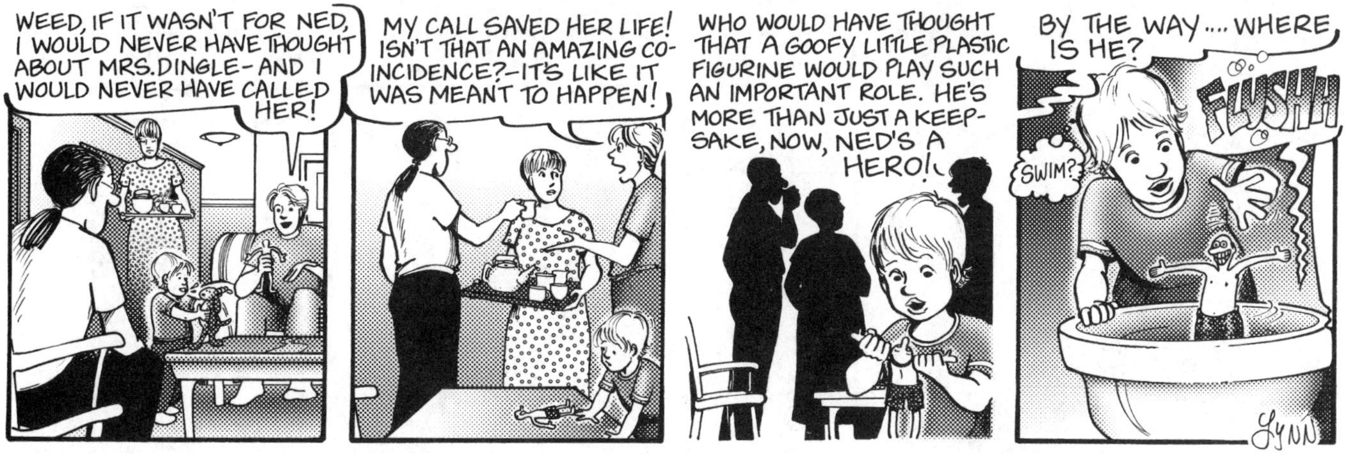
WEED, IF IT WASN'T FOR NED, I WOULD NEVER HAVE THOUGHT ABOUT MRS. DINGLE- AND I WOULD NEVER HAVE CALLED HER!
MY CALL SAVED HER LIFE! ISN'T THAT AN AMAZING CO-INCIDENCE?-IT'S LIKE IT WAS MEANT TO HAPPEN!
WHO WOULD HAVE THOUGHT THAT A GOOFY LITTLE PLASTIC FIGURINE WOULD PLAY SUCH AN IMPORTANT ROLE. HE'S MORE THAN JUST A KEEP-SAKE, NOW, NED'S A HERO!
BY THE WAY.... WHERE IS HE?
SWIM?
FLUSHH
LYNN

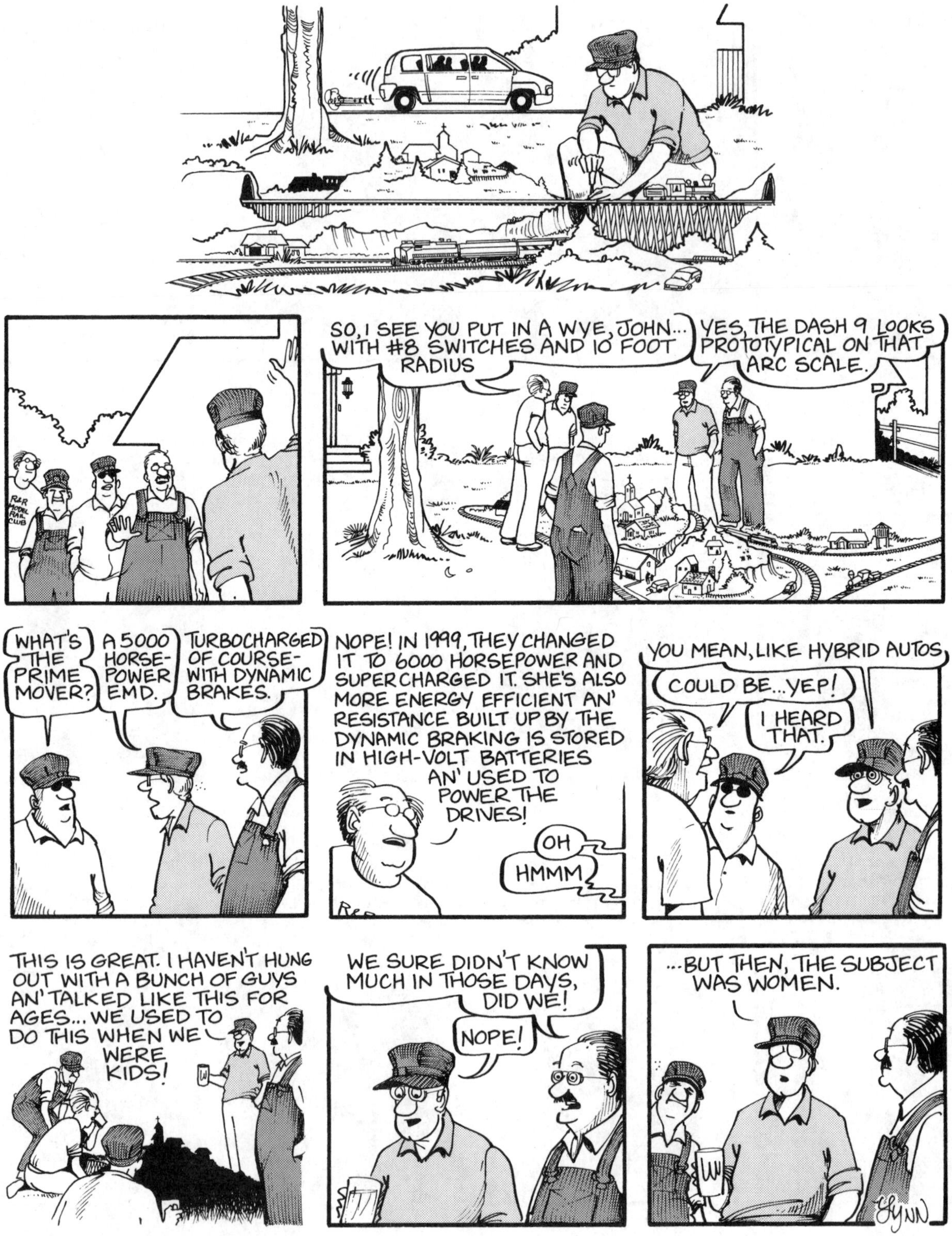
R&R MODEL RAIL CLUB
SO, I SEE YOU PUT IN A WYE, JOHN... WITH #8 SWITCHES AND 10 FOOT RADIUS
YES, THE DASH 9 LOOKS PROTOTYPICAL ON THAT ARC SCALE.
WHAT'S THE PRIME MOVER?
A 5000 HORSE-POWER EMD.
TURBOCHARGED OF COURSE-WITH DYNAMIC BRAKES.
NOPE! IN 1999, THEY CHANGED IT TO 6000 HORSEPOWER AND SUPERCHARGED IT. SHE'S ALSO MORE ENERGY EFFICIENT AN' RESISTANCE BUILT UP BY THE DYNAMIC BRAKING IS STORED IN HIGH-VOLT BATTERIES AN' USED TO POWER THE DRIVES!
OH
HMMM
YOU MEAN, LIKE HYBRID AUTOS
COULD BE...YEP!
I HEARD THAT.
THIS IS GREAT. I HAVEN'T HUNG OUT WITH A BUNCH OF GUYS AN' TALKED LIKE THIS FOR AGES... WE USED TO DO THIS WHEN WE WERE KIDS!
WE SURE DIDN'T KNOW MUCH IN THOSE DAYS, DID WE!
NOPE!
...BUT THEN, THE SUBJECT WAS WOMEN.
LYNN

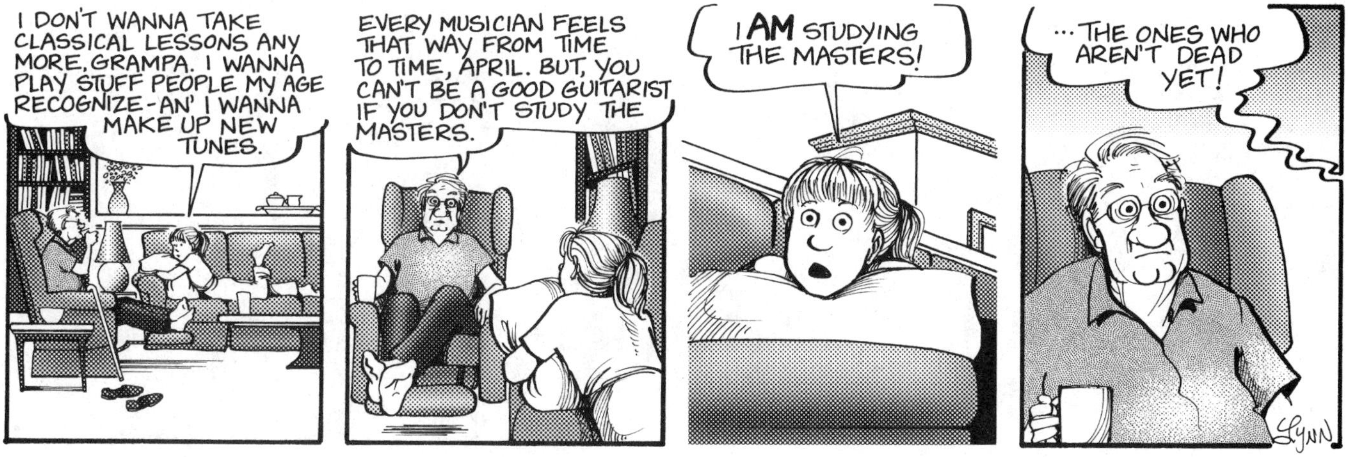
I DON'T WANNA TAKE CLASSICAL LESSONS ANY MORE, GRAMPA. I WANNA PLAY STUFF PEOPLE MY AGE RECOGNIZE - AN' I WANNA MAKE UP NEW TUNES.
EVERY MUSICIAN FEELS THAT WAY FROM TIME TO TIME, APRIL. BUT, YOU CAN'T BE A GOOD GUITARIST IF YOU DON'T STUDY THE MASTERS.
I **AM** STUDYING THE MASTERS!
... THE ONES WHO AREN'T DEAD YET!

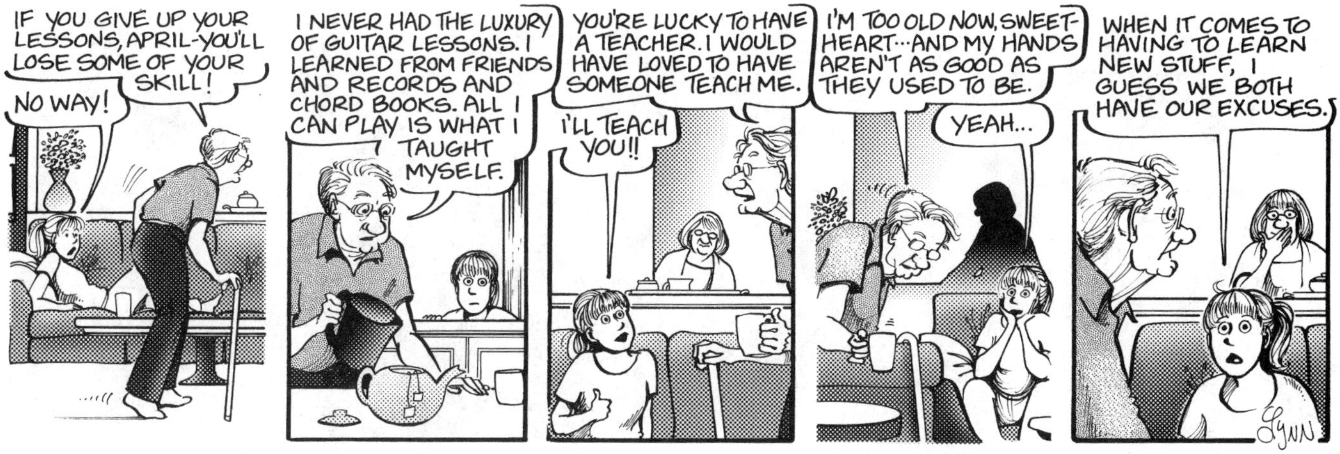
IF YOU GIVE UP YOUR LESSONS, APRIL - YOU'LL LOSE SOME OF YOUR SKILL!
NO WAY!
I NEVER HAD THE LUXURY OF GUITAR LESSONS. I LEARNED FROM FRIENDS AND RECORDS AND CHORD BOOKS. ALL I CAN PLAY IS WHAT I TAUGHT MYSELF.
YOU'RE LUCKY TO HAVE A TEACHER. I WOULD HAVE LOVED TO HAVE SOMEONE TEACH ME.
I'LL TEACH YOU!!
I'M TOO OLD NOW, SWEETHEART... AND MY HANDS AREN'T AS GOOD AS THEY USED TO BE.
YEAH...
WHEN IT COMES TO HAVING TO LEARN NEW STUFF, I GUESS WE BOTH HAVE OUR EXCUSES.

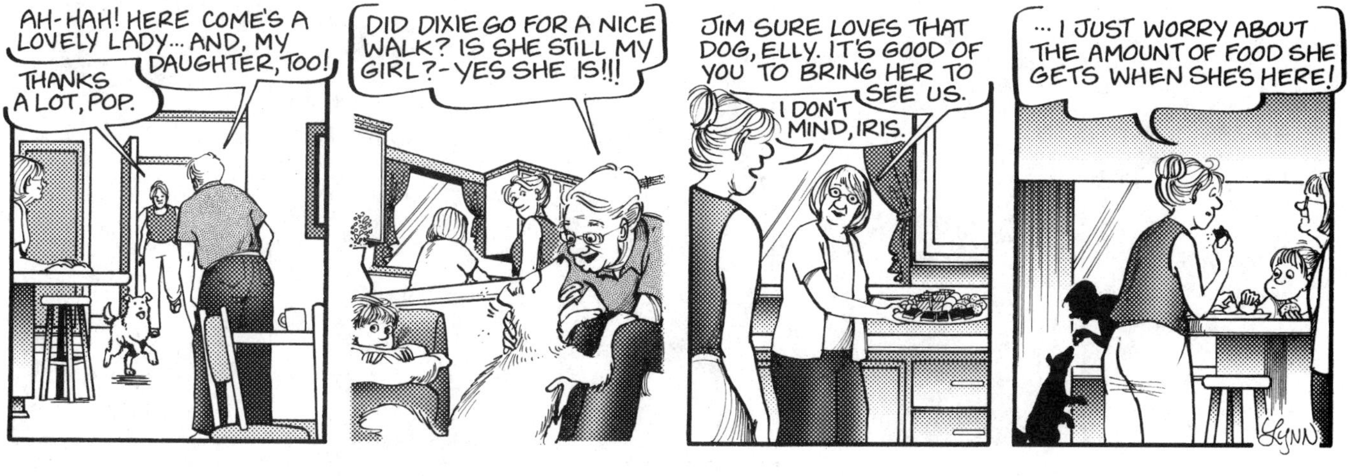
AH-HAH! HERE COME'S A LOVELY LADY... AND, MY DAUGHTER, TOO!
THANKS A LOT, POP.
DID DIXIE GO FOR A NICE WALK? IS SHE STILL MY GIRL? - YES SHE IS!!!
JIM SURE LOVES THAT DOG, ELLY. IT'S GOOD OF YOU TO BRING HER TO SEE US.
I DON'T MIND, IRIS.
... I JUST WORRY ABOUT THE AMOUNT OF FOOD SHE GETS WHEN SHE'S HERE!

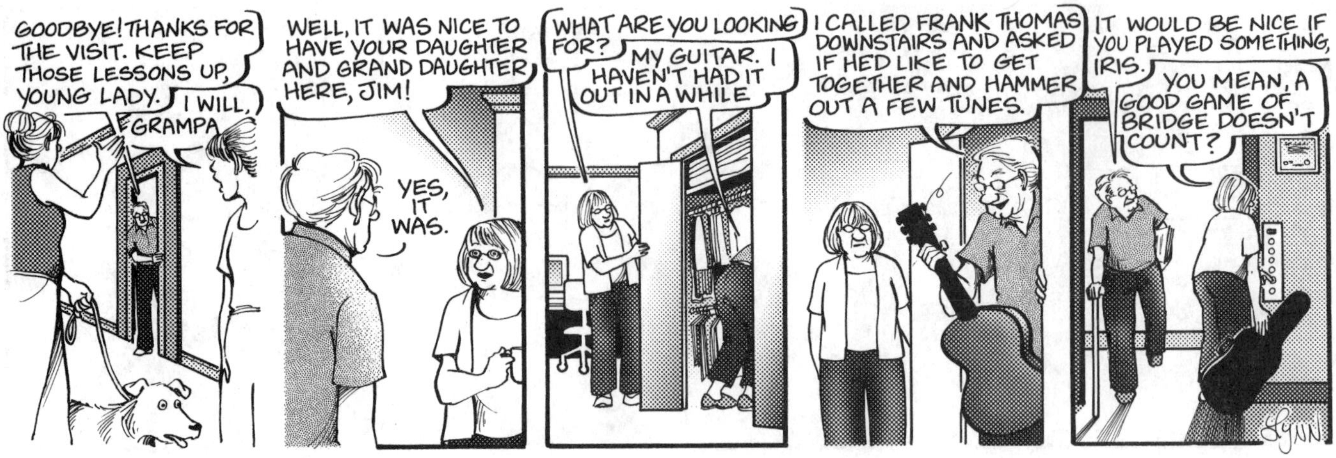
GOODBYE! THANKS FOR THE VISIT. KEEP THOSE LESSONS UP, YOUNG LADY.
I WILL, GRAMPA
WELL, IT WAS NICE TO HAVE YOUR DAUGHTER AND GRAND DAUGHTER HERE, JIM!
YES, IT WAS.
WHAT ARE YOU LOOKING FOR?
MY GUITAR. I HAVEN'T HAD IT OUT IN A WHILE
I CALLED FRANK THOMAS DOWNSTAIRS AND ASKED IF HED LIKE TO GET TOGETHER AND HAMMER OUT A FEW TUNES.
IT WOULD BE NICE IF YOU PLAYED SOMETHING, IRIS.
YOU MEAN, A GOOD GAME OF BRIDGE DOESN'T COUNT?
LYNN

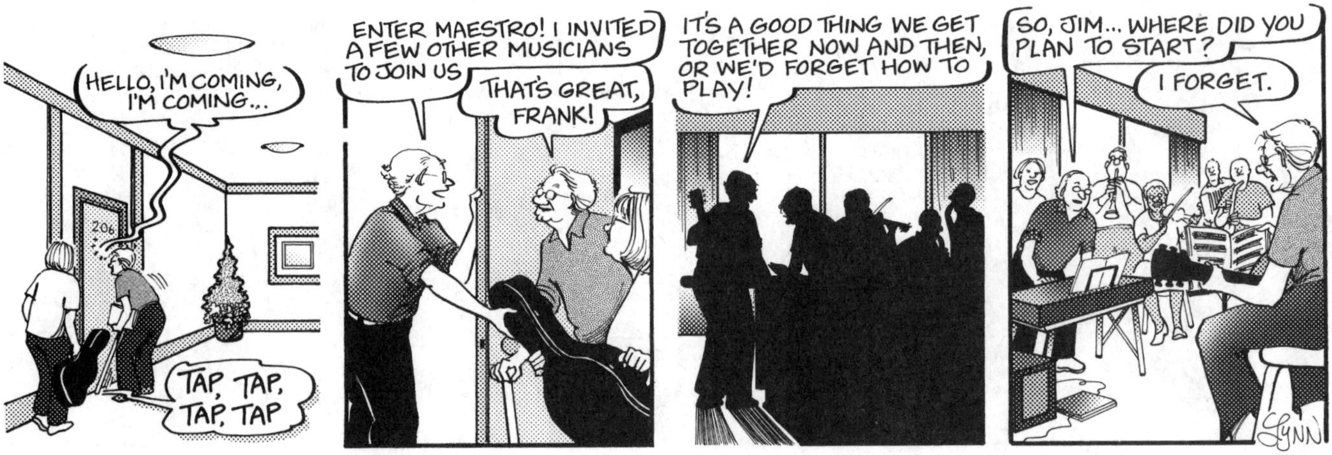
HELLO, I'M COMING, I'M COMING...
206
TAP, TAP, TAP, TAP
ENTER MAESTRO! I INVITED A FEW OTHER MUSICIANS TO JOIN US
THAT'S GREAT, FRANK!
IT'S A GOOD THING WE GET TOGETHER NOW AND THEN, OR WE'D FORGET HOW TO PLAY!
SO, JIM... WHERE DID YOU PLAN TO START?
I FORGET.
LYNN

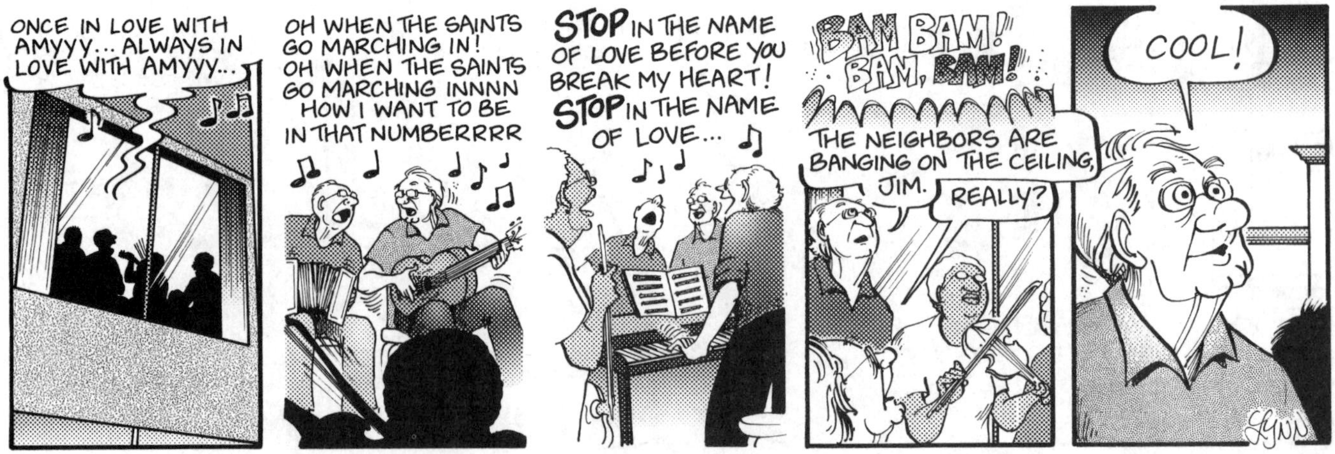
ONCE IN LOVE WITH AMYYY... ALWAYS IN LOVE WITH AMYYY...
OH WHEN THE SAINTS GO MARCHING IN! OH WHEN THE SAINTS GO MARCHING INNNN HOW I WANT TO BE IN THAT NUMBERRRR
STOP IN THE NAME OF LOVE BEFORE YOU BREAK MY HEART! STOP IN THE NAME OF LOVE...
BAM BAM! BAM, BAM!
THE NEIGHBORS ARE BANGING ON THE CEILING, JIM.
REALLY?
COOL!
LYNN

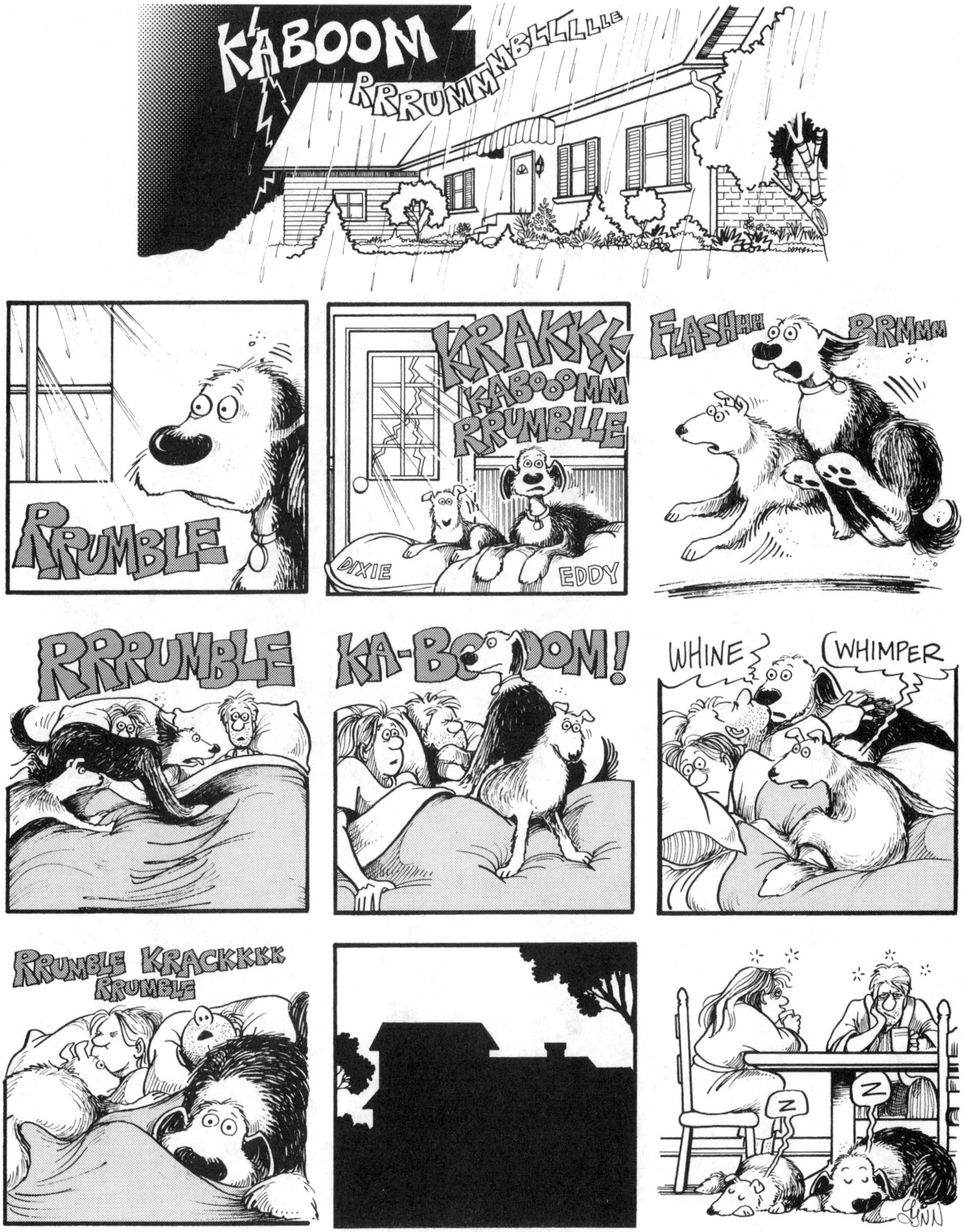
KABOOM
RRRUMMMBLLLLLLE
RRRUMBLE
KRAKKK
KABOOOMM
RRUMBLLE
DIXIE
EDDY
FLASHHH
BRMMM
RRRUMBLE
KA-BOOOM!
WHINE
WHIMPER
RRUMBLE KRACKKKK
RRUMBLE
Z
Z
LYNN

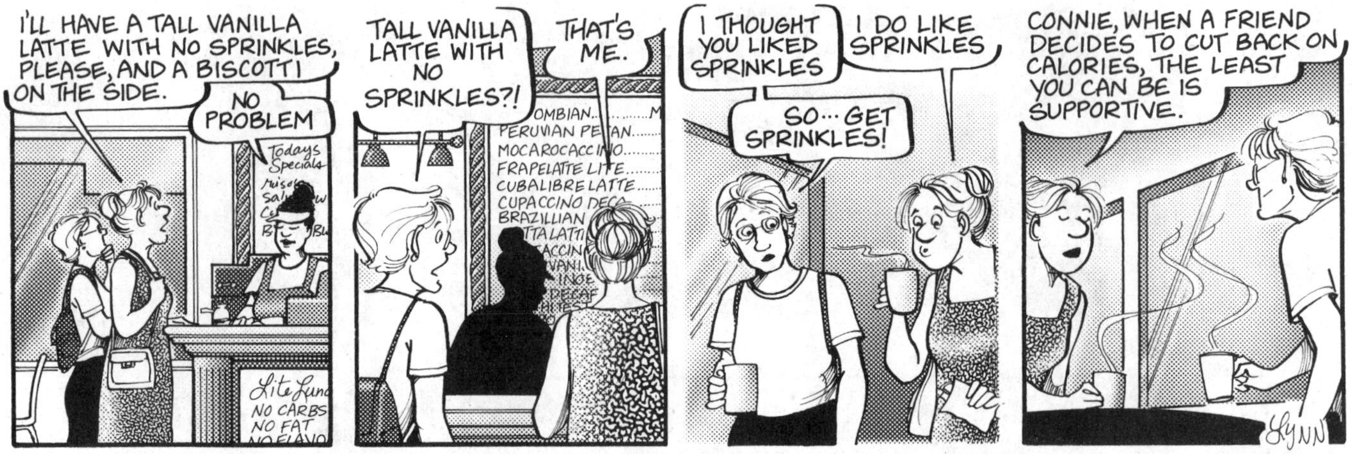
I'LL HAVE A TALL VANILLA LATTE WITH NO SPRINKLES, PLEASE, AND A BISCOTTI ON THE SIDE.
NO PROBLEM
TALL VANILLA LATTE WITH NO SPRINKLES?!
THAT'S ME.
I THOUGHT YOU LIKED SPRINKLES
SO... GET SPRINKLES!
I DO LIKE SPRINKLES
CONNIE, WHEN A FRIEND DECIDES TO CUT BACK ON CALORIES, THE LEAST YOU CAN BE IS SUPPORTIVE.

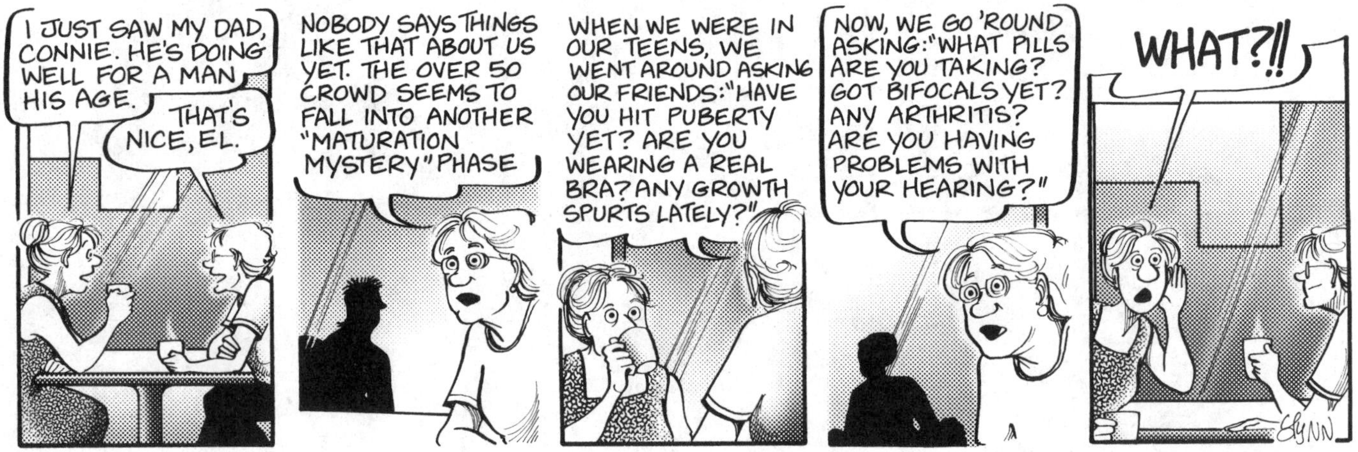
I JUST SAW MY DAD, CONNIE. HE'S DOING WELL FOR A MAN HIS AGE.
THAT'S NICE, EL.
NOBODY SAYS THINGS LIKE THAT ABOUT US YET. THE OVER 50 CROWD SEEMS TO FALL INTO ANOTHER "MATURATION MYSTERY" PHASE
WHEN WE WERE IN OUR TEENS, WE WENT AROUND ASKING OUR FRIENDS: "HAVE YOU HIT PUBERTY YET? ARE YOU WEARING A REAL BRA? ANY GROWTH SPURTS LATELY?"
NOW, WE GO 'ROUND ASKING: "WHAT PILLS ARE YOU TAKING? GOT BIFOCALS YET? ANY ARTHRITIS? ARE YOU HAVING PROBLEMS WITH YOUR HEARING?"
WHAT?!!

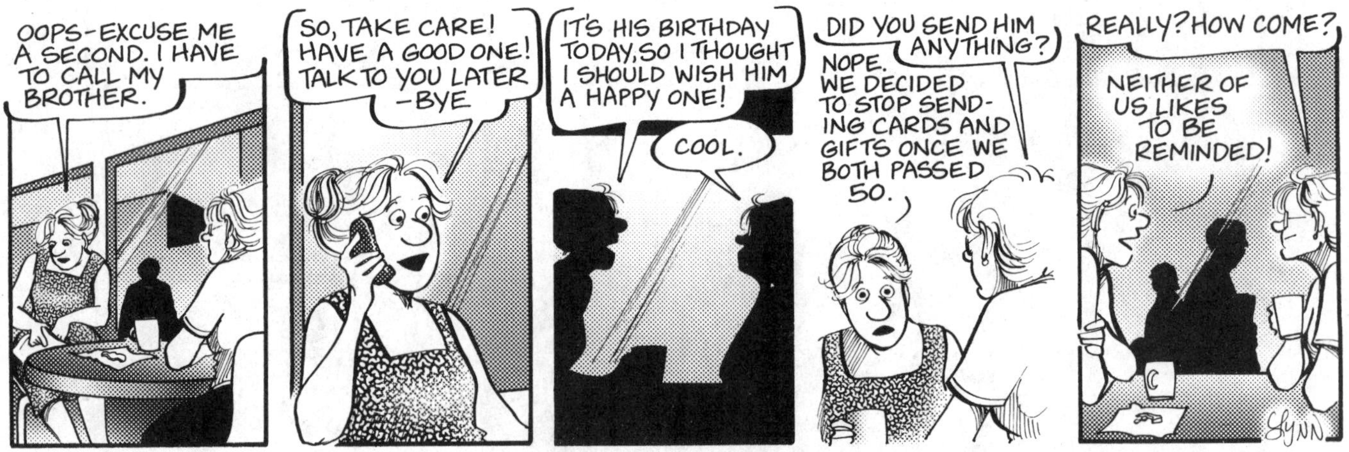
OOPS-EXCUSE ME A SECOND. I HAVE TO CALL MY BROTHER.
SO, TAKE CARE! HAVE A GOOD ONE! TALK TO YOU LATER -BYE
IT'S HIS BIRTHDAY TODAY, SO I THOUGHT I SHOULD WISH HIM A HAPPY ONE!
COOL.
DID YOU SEND HIM ANYTHING?
NOPE. WE DECIDED TO STOP SENDING CARDS AND GIFTS ONCE WE BOTH PASSED 50.
REALLY? HOW COME?
NEITHER OF US LIKES TO BE REMINDED!

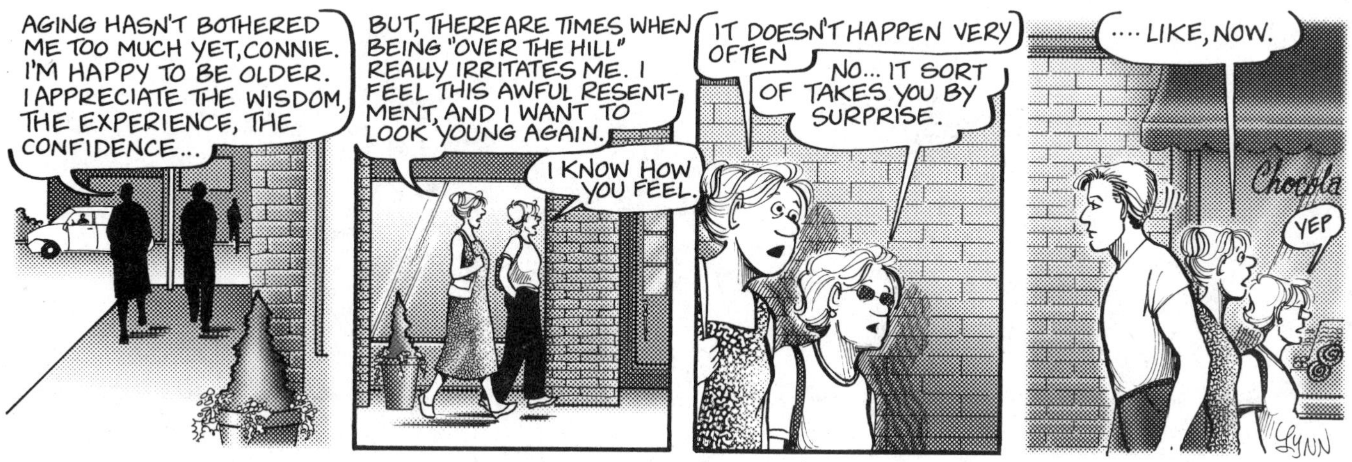
AGING HASN'T BOTHERED ME TOO MUCH YET, CONNIE. I'M HAPPY TO BE OLDER. I APPRECIATE THE WISDOM, THE EXPERIENCE, THE CONFIDENCE...
BUT, THERE ARE TIMES WHEN BEING "OVER THE HILL" REALLY IRRITATES ME. I FEEL THIS AWFUL RESENTMENT, AND I WANT TO LOOK YOUNG AGAIN.
I KNOW HOW YOU FEEL.
IT DOESN'T HAPPEN VERY OFTEN
NO... IT SORT OF TAKES YOU BY SURPRISE.
.... LIKE, NOW.
Chocola
YEP
LYNN

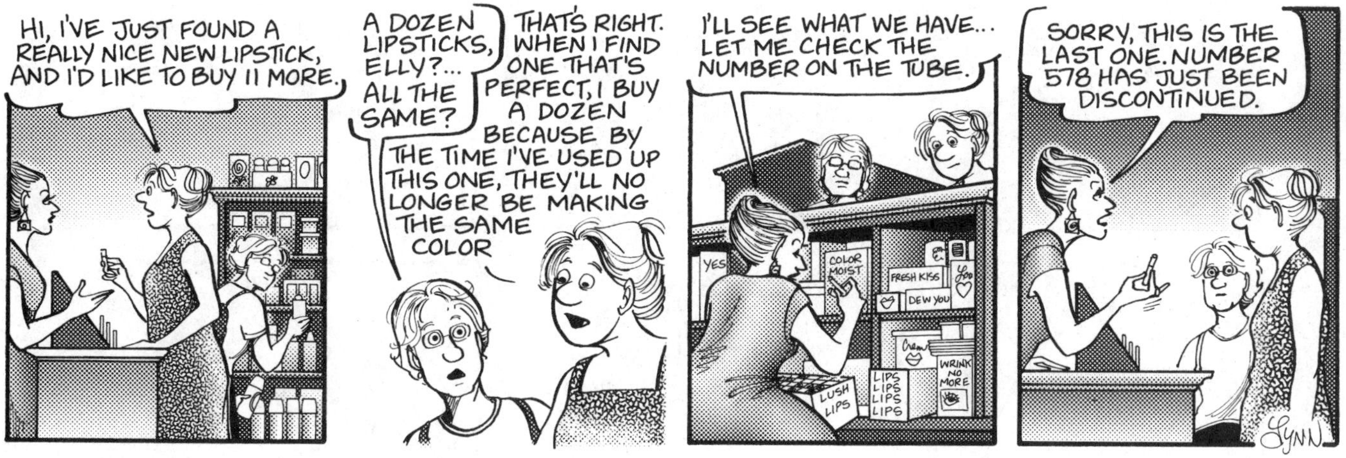
HI, I'VE JUST FOUND A REALLY NICE NEW LIPSTICK, AND I'D LIKE TO BUY 11 MORE.
A DOZEN LIPSTICKS, ELLY?... ALL THE SAME?
THAT'S RIGHT. WHEN I FIND ONE THAT'S PERFECT, I BUY A DOZEN BECAUSE BY THE TIME I'VE USED UP THIS ONE, THEY'LL NO LONGER BE MAKING THE SAME COLOR
I'LL SEE WHAT WE HAVE... LET ME CHECK THE NUMBER ON THE TUBE.
YES
COLOR MOIST
FRESH KISS
DEW YOU
LUSH LIPS
LIPS LIPS LIPS LIPS
WRINK NO MORE
SORRY, THIS IS THE LAST ONE. NUMBER 578 HAS JUST BEEN DISCONTINUED.
LYNN

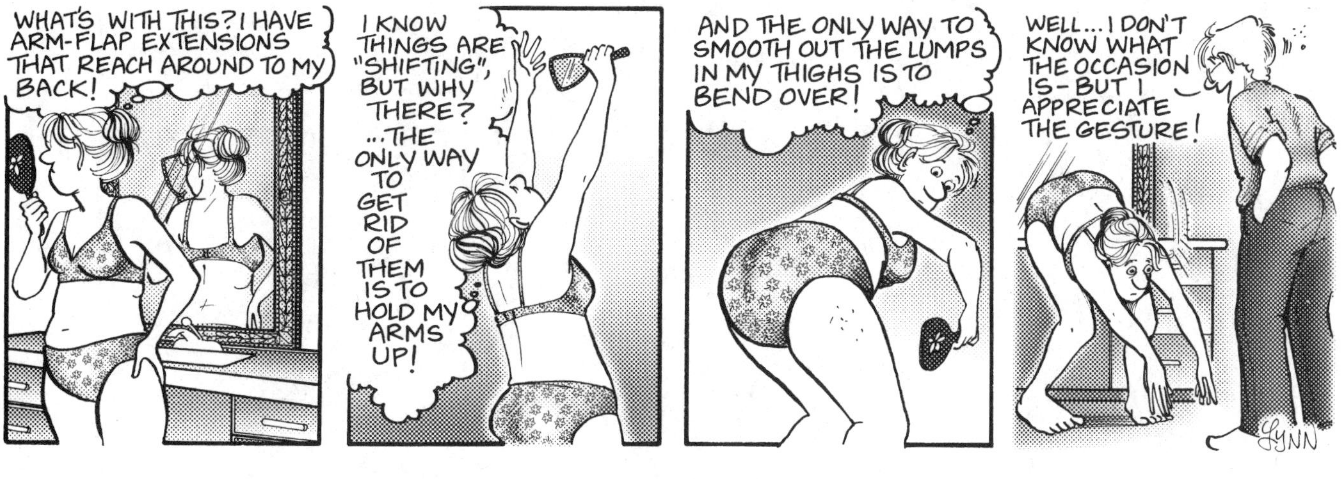
WHAT'S WITH THIS? I HAVE ARM-FLAP EXTENSIONS THAT REACH AROUND TO MY BACK!
I KNOW THINGS ARE "SHIFTING", BUT WHY THERE? ...THE ONLY WAY TO GET RID OF THEM IS TO HOLD MY ARMS UP!
AND THE ONLY WAY TO SMOOTH OUT THE LUMPS IN MY THIGHS IS TO BEND OVER!
WELL... I DON'T KNOW WHAT THE OCCASION IS - BUT I APPRECIATE THE GESTURE!
LYNN

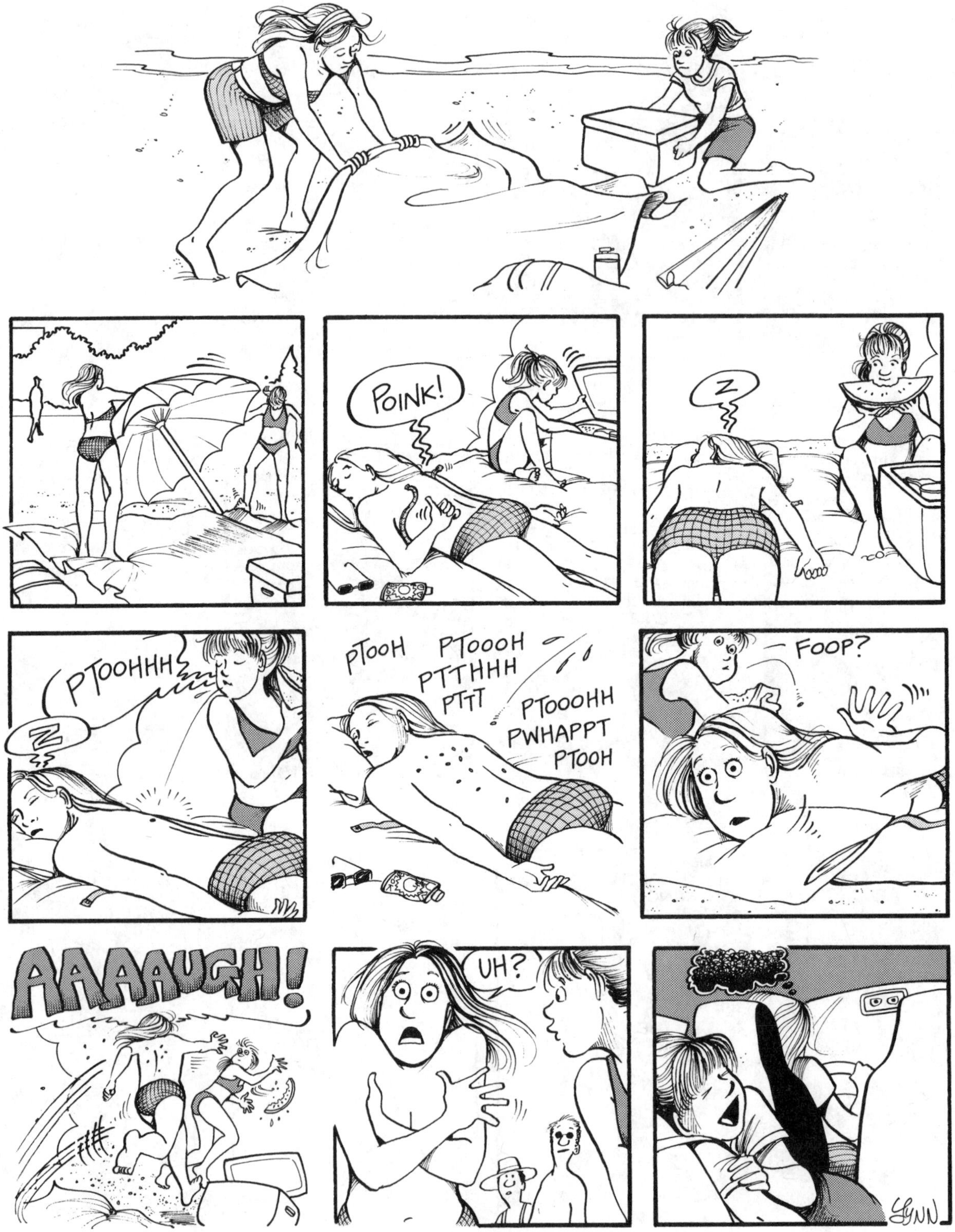
POINK!
Z
PTOOHHH
Z
PTOOH PTOOOH
PTTHHH
PTTT
PTOOOHH
PWHAPPT
PTOOH
FOOP?
AAAAUGH!
UH?
LYNN

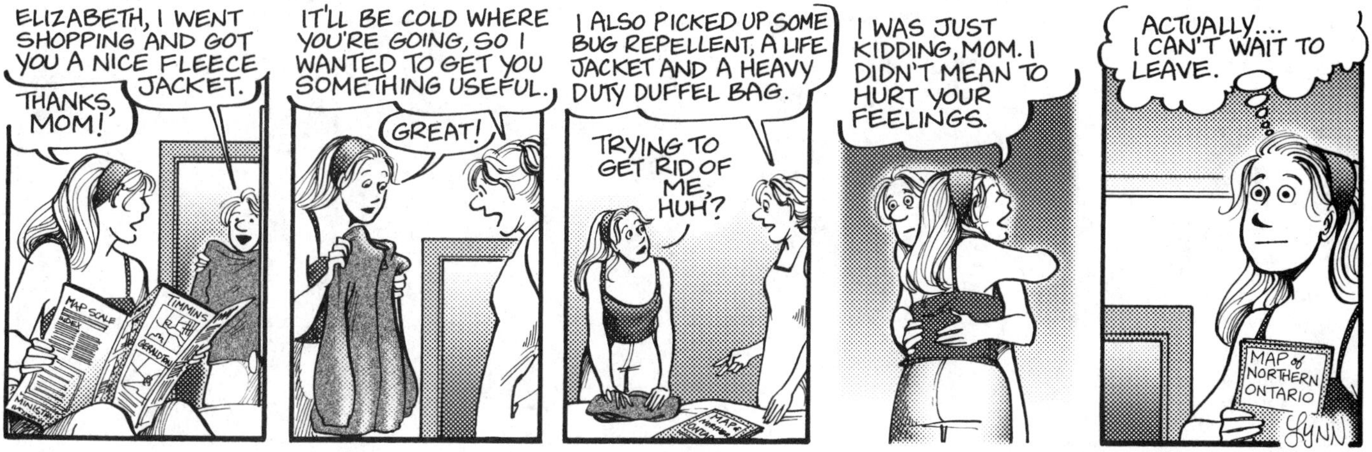
ELIZABETH, I WENT SHOPPING AND GOT YOU A NICE FLEECE JACKET.
THANKS, MOM!
MAP SCALE
TIMMINS
IT'LL BE COLD WHERE YOU'RE GOING, SO I WANTED TO GET YOU SOMETHING USEFUL.
GREAT!
I ALSO PICKED UP SOME BUG REPELLENT, A LIFE JACKET AND A HEAVY DUTY DUFFEL BAG.
TRYING TO GET RID OF ME, HUH?
I WAS JUST KIDDING, MOM. I DIDN'T MEAN TO HURT YOUR FEELINGS.
ACTUALLY.... I CAN'T WAIT TO LEAVE.
MAP of NORTHERN ONTARIO
LYNN

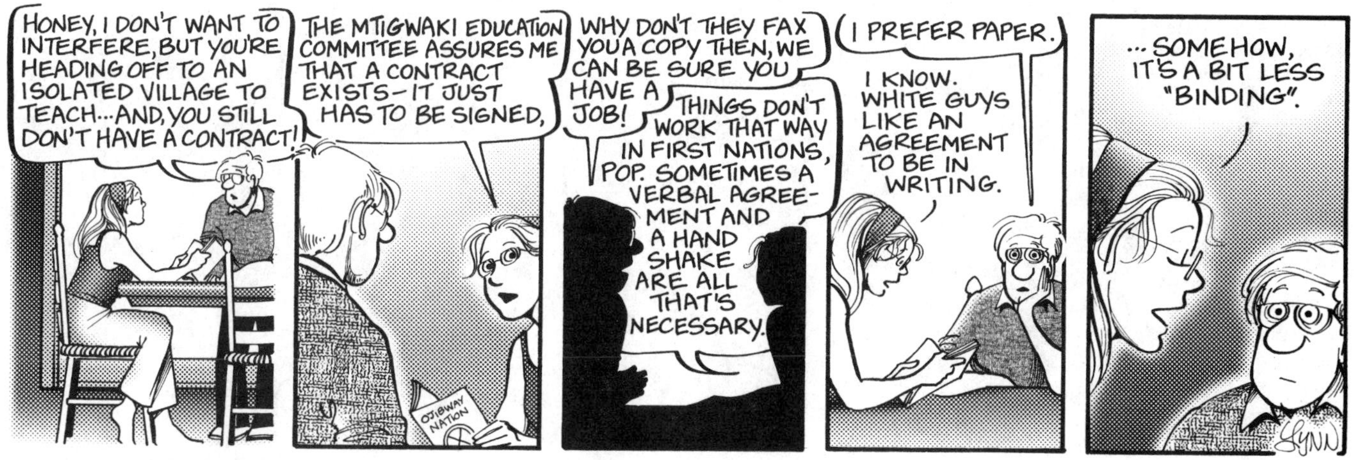
HONEY, I DON'T WANT TO INTERFERE, BUT YOU'RE HEADING OFF TO AN ISOLATED VILLAGE TO TEACH...AND, YOU STILL DON'T HAVE A CONTRACT!
THE MTIGWAKI EDUCATION COMMITTEE ASSURES ME THAT A CONTRACT EXISTS—IT JUST HAS TO BE SIGNED,
OJIBWAY NATION
WHY DON'T THEY FAX YOU A COPY THEN, WE CAN BE SURE YOU HAVE A JOB!
THINGS DON'T WORK THAT WAY IN FIRST NATIONS, POP. SOMETIMES A VERBAL AGREE-MENT AND A HAND SHAKE ARE ALL THAT'S NECESSARY.
I PREFER PAPER.
I KNOW. WHITE GUYS LIKE AN AGREEMENT TO BE IN WRITING.
...SOMEHOW, IT'S A BIT LESS "BINDING".
LYNN

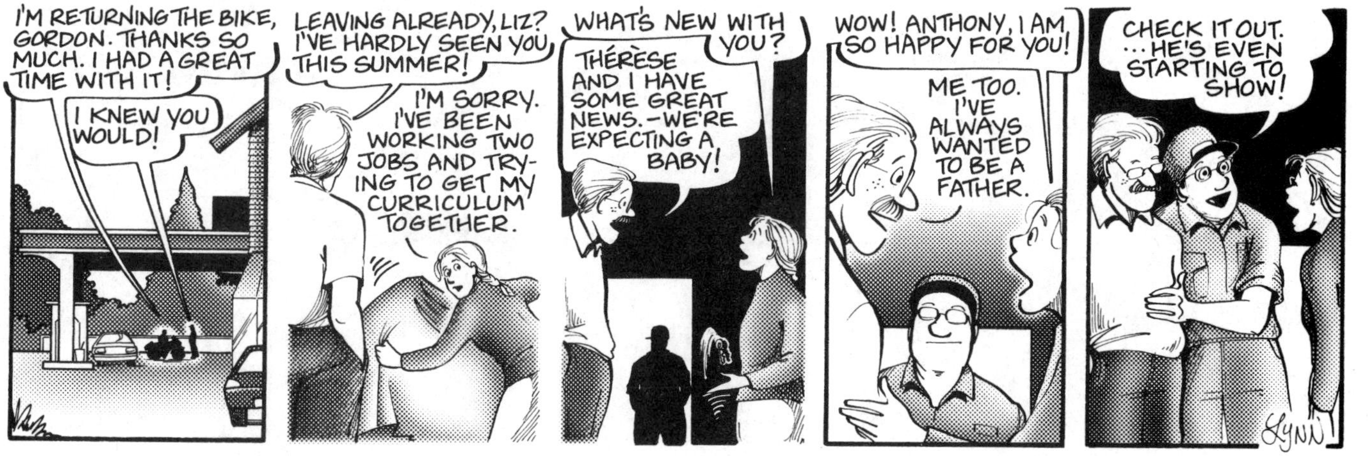
I'M RETURNING THE BIKE, GORDON. THANKS SO MUCH. I HAD A GREAT TIME WITH IT!
I KNEW YOU WOULD!
LEAVING ALREADY, LIZ? I'VE HARDLY SEEN YOU THIS SUMMER!
I'M SORRY. I'VE BEEN WORKING TWO JOBS AND TRY-ING TO GET MY CURRICULUM TOGETHER.
WHAT'S NEW WITH YOU?
THÉRÈSE AND I HAVE SOME GREAT NEWS.—WE'RE EXPECTING A BABY!
WOW! ANTHONY, I AM SO HAPPY FOR YOU!
ME TOO. I'VE ALWAYS WANTED TO BE A FATHER.
CHECK IT OUT. ...HE'S EVEN STARTING TO SHOW!
LYNN

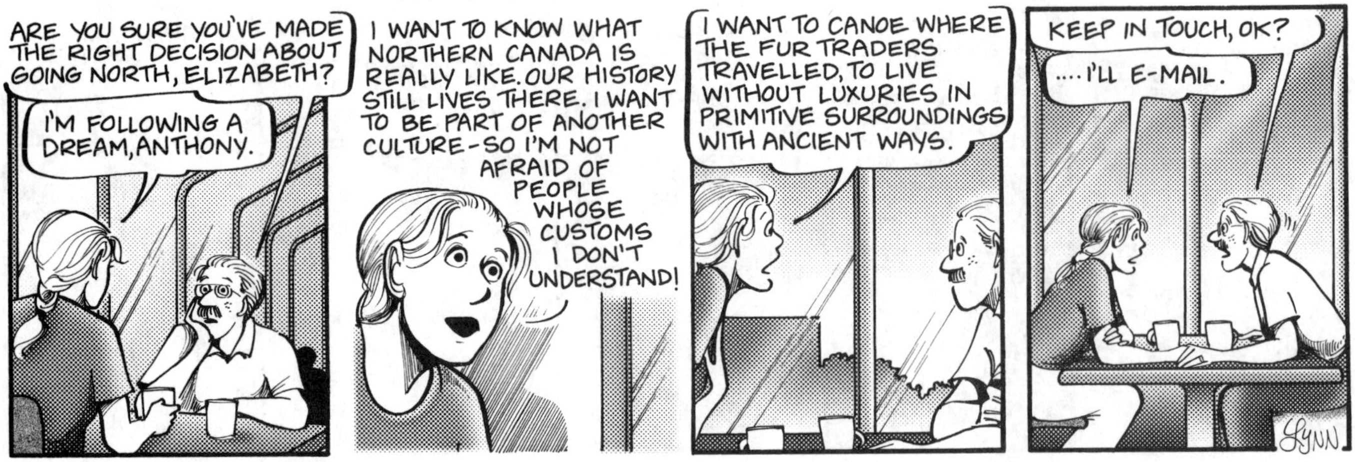
ARE YOU SURE YOU'VE MADE THE RIGHT DECISION ABOUT GOING NORTH, ELIZABETH?
I'M FOLLOWING A DREAM, ANTHONY.
I WANT TO KNOW WHAT NORTHERN CANADA IS REALLY LIKE. OUR HISTORY STILL LIVES THERE. I WANT TO BE PART OF ANOTHER CULTURE - SO I'M NOT AFRAID OF PEOPLE WHOSE CUSTOMS I DON'T UNDERSTAND!
I WANT TO CANOE WHERE THE FUR TRADERS TRAVELLED, TO LIVE WITHOUT LUXURIES IN PRIMITIVE SURROUNDINGS WITH ANCIENT WAYS.
KEEP IN TOUCH, OK?
.... I'LL E-MAIL.
LYNN

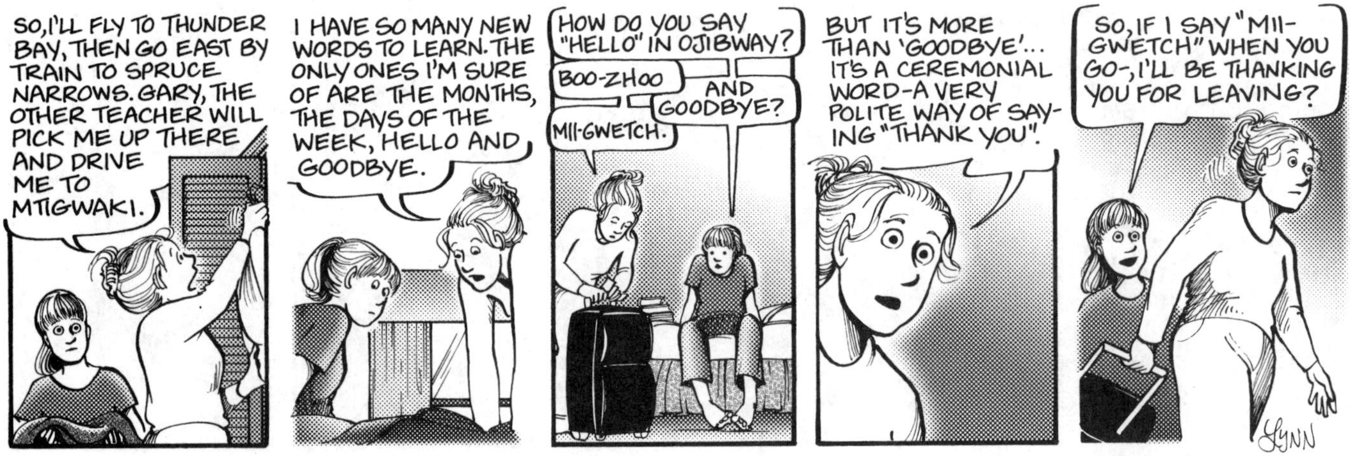
SO, I'LL FLY TO THUNDER BAY, THEN GO EAST BY TRAIN TO SPRUCE NARROWS. GARY, THE OTHER TEACHER WILL PICK ME UP THERE AND DRIVE ME TO MTIGWAKI.
I HAVE SO MANY NEW WORDS TO LEARN. THE ONLY ONES I'M SURE OF ARE THE MONTHS, THE DAYS OF THE WEEK, HELLO AND GOODBYE.
HOW DO YOU SAY "HELLO" IN OJIBWAY?
BOO-ZHOO
AND GOODBYE?
MII-GWETCH.
BUT IT'S MORE THAN 'GOODBYE'... IT'S A CEREMONIAL WORD-A VERY POLITE WAY OF SAYING "THANK YOU".
SO, IF I SAY "MII-GWETCH" WHEN YOU GO-, I'LL BE THANKING YOU FOR LEAVING?
LYNN

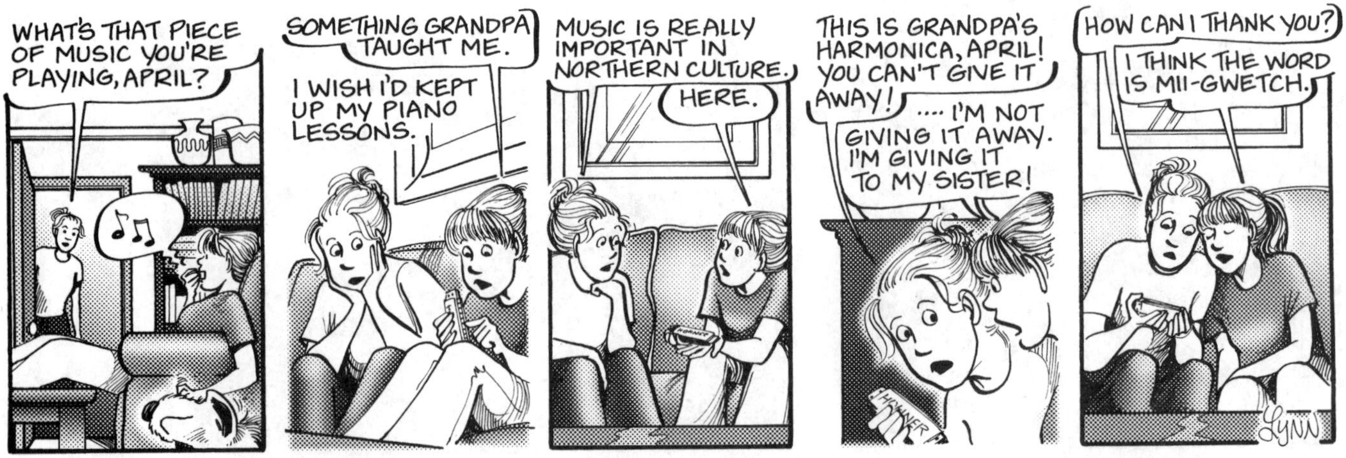
WHAT'S THAT PIECE OF MUSIC YOU'RE PLAYING, APRIL?
SOMETHING GRANDPA TAUGHT ME.
I WISH I'D KEPT UP MY PIANO LESSONS.
MUSIC IS REALLY IMPORTANT IN NORTHERN CULTURE.
HERE.
THIS IS GRANDPA'S HARMONICA, APRIL! YOU CAN'T GIVE IT AWAY!
.... I'M NOT GIVING IT AWAY. I'M GIVING IT TO MY SISTER!
HOW CAN I THANK YOU?
I THINK THE WORD IS MII-GWETCH.
LYNN

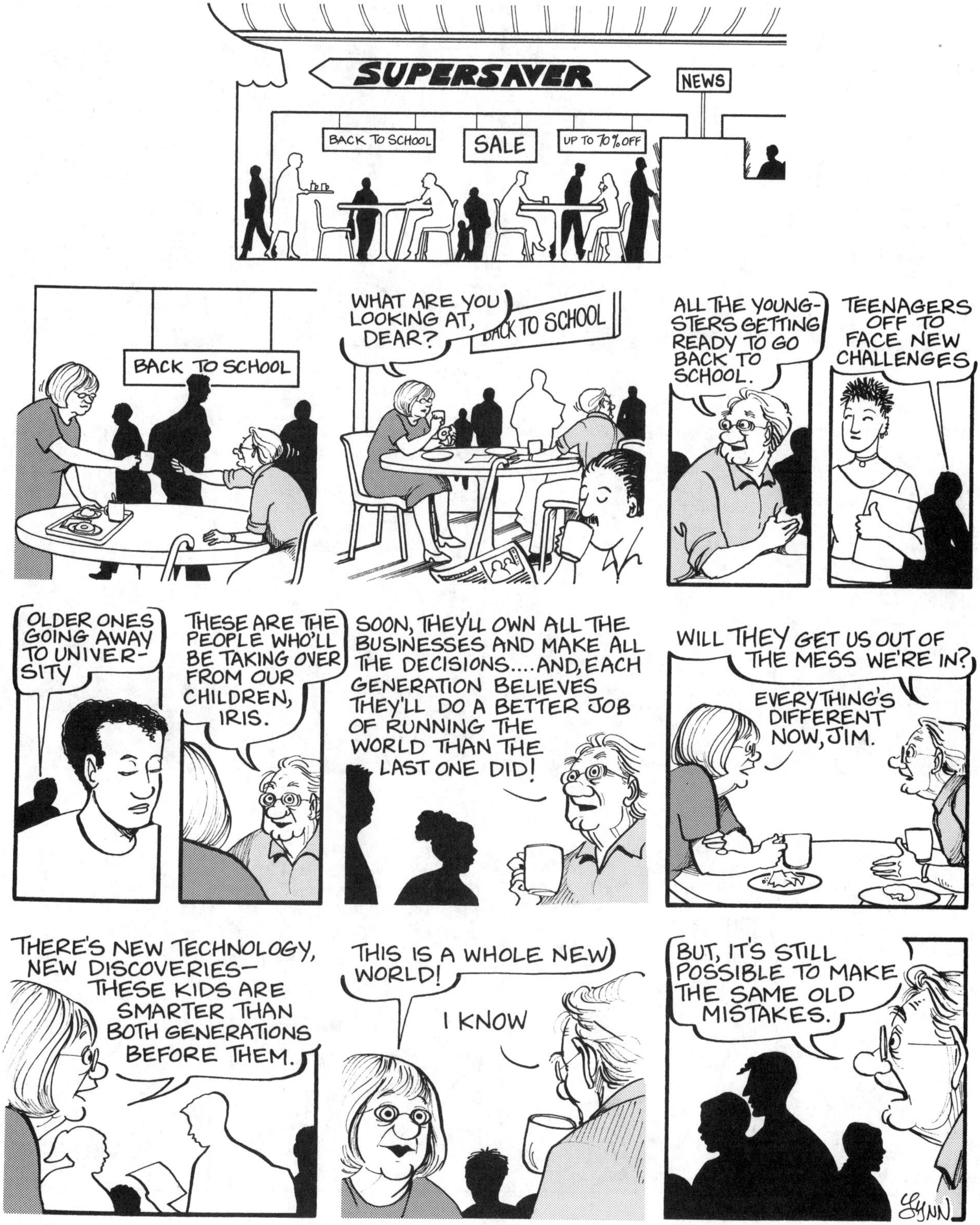
SUPERSAVER
NEWS
BACK TO SCHOOL
SALE
UP TO 70% OFF
BACK TO SCHOOL
WHAT ARE YOU LOOKING AT, DEAR?
BACK TO SCHOOL
ALL THE YOUNGSTERS GETTING READY TO GO BACK TO SCHOOL.
TEENAGERS OFF TO FACE NEW CHALLENGES
OLDER ONES GOING AWAY TO UNIVERSITY
THESE ARE THE PEOPLE WHO'LL BE TAKING OVER FROM OUR CHILDREN, IRIS.
SOON, THEY'LL OWN ALL THE BUSINESSES AND MAKE ALL THE DECISIONS....AND, EACH GENERATION BELIEVES THEY'LL DO A BETTER JOB OF RUNNING THE WORLD THAN THE LAST ONE DID!
WILL THEY GET US OUT OF THE MESS WE'RE IN?
EVERYTHING'S DIFFERENT NOW, JIM.
THERE'S NEW TECHNOLOGY, NEW DISCOVERIES— THESE KIDS ARE SMARTER THAN BOTH GENERATIONS BEFORE THEM.
THIS IS A WHOLE NEW WORLD!
I KNOW
BUT, IT'S STILL POSSIBLE TO MAKE THE SAME OLD MISTAKES.
LYNN

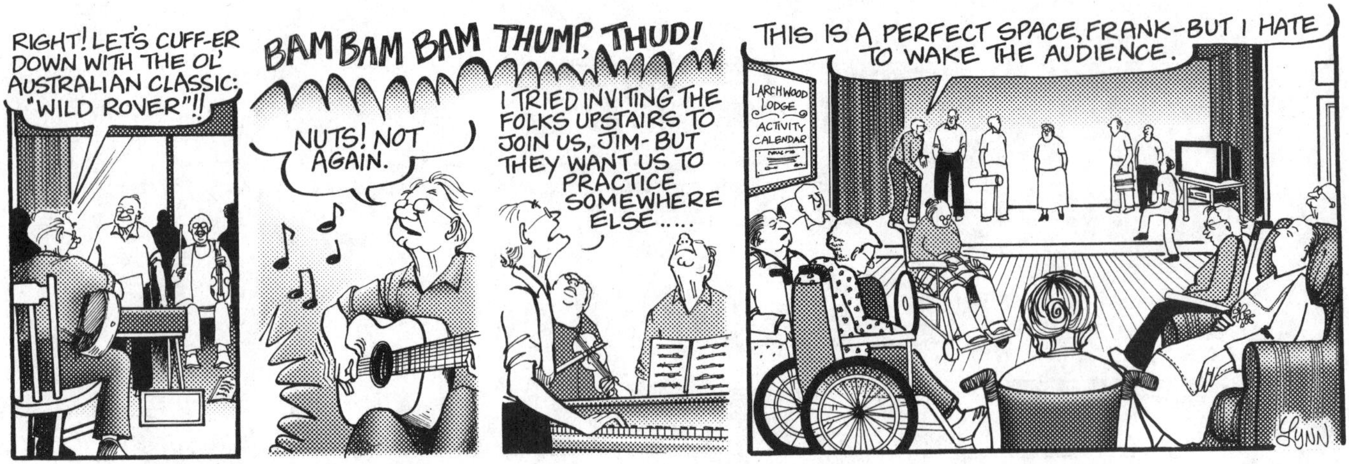
RIGHT! LET'S CUFF-ER DOWN WITH THE OL' AUSTRALIAN CLASSIC: "WILD ROVER"!!
BAM BAM BAM THUMP, THUD!
NUTS! NOT AGAIN.
I TRIED INVITING THE FOLKS UPSTAIRS TO JOIN US, JIM- BUT THEY WANT US TO PRACTICE SOMEWHERE ELSE.....
THIS IS A PERFECT SPACE, FRANK-BUT I HATE TO WAKE THE AUDIENCE.
LARCHWOOD LODGE ACTIVITY CALENDAR
LYNN

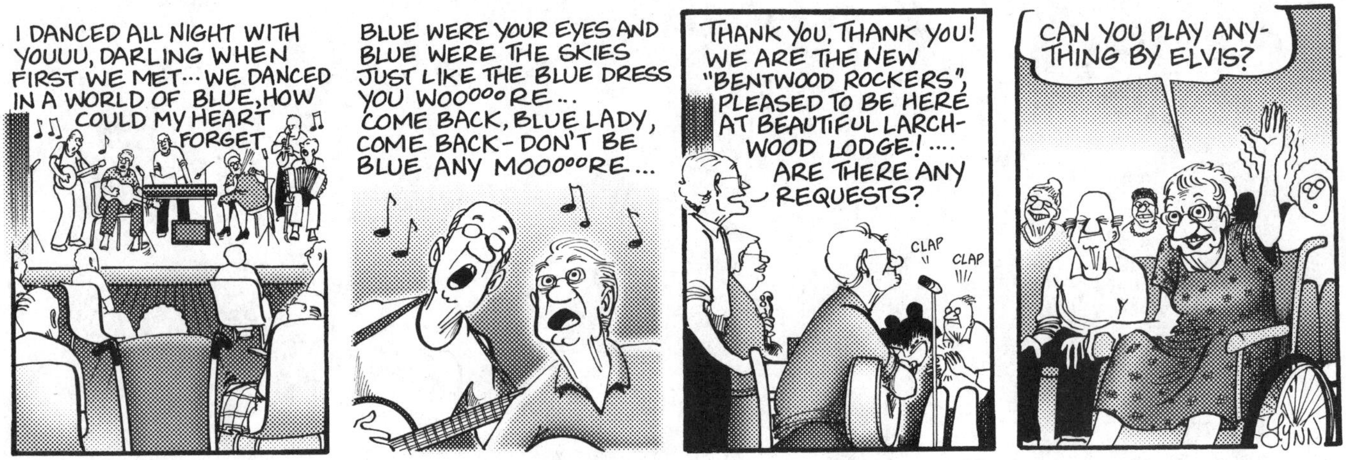
I DANCED ALL NIGHT WITH YOUUU, DARLING WHEN FIRST WE MET··· WE DANCED IN A WORLD OF BLUE, HOW COULD MY HEART FORGET
BLUE WERE YOUR EYES AND BLUE WERE THE SKIES JUST LIKE THE BLUE DRESS YOU WOOOOORE... COME BACK, BLUE LADY, COME BACK- DON'T BE BLUE ANY MOOOOORE...
THANK YOU, THANK YOU! WE ARE THE NEW "BENTWOOD ROCKERS", PLEASED TO BE HERE AT BEAUTIFUL LARCH-WOOD LODGE!.... ARE THERE ANY REQUESTS?
CLAP
CLAP
CAN YOU PLAY ANY-THING BY ELVIS?
LYNN

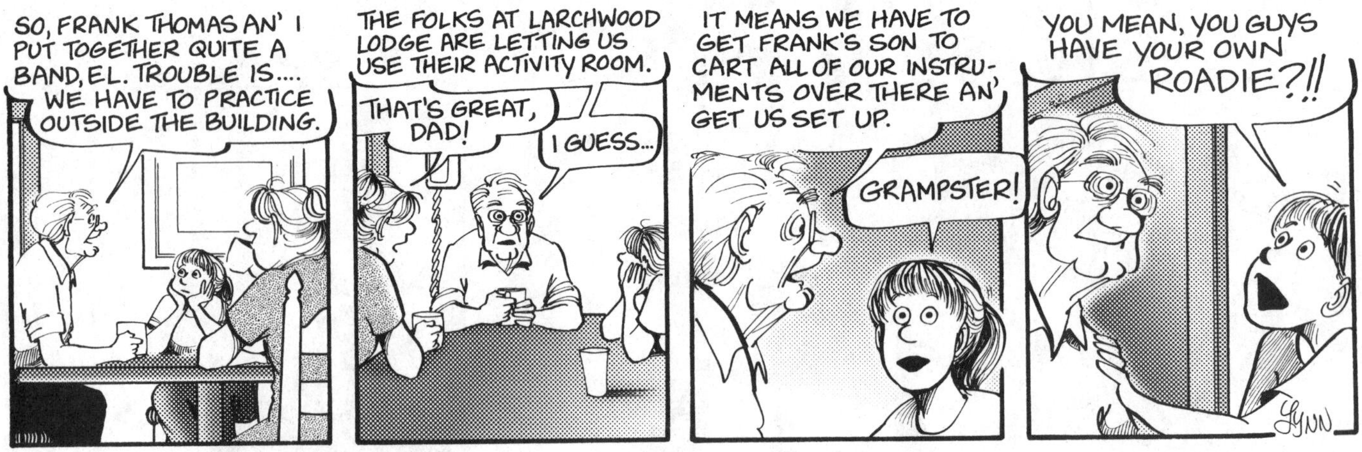
SO, FRANK THOMAS AN' I PUT TOGETHER QUITE A BAND, EL. TROUBLE IS....
WE HAVE TO PRACTICE OUTSIDE THE BUILDING.
THE FOLKS AT LARCHWOOD LODGE ARE LETTING US USE THEIR ACTIVITY ROOM.
THAT'S GREAT, DAD!
I GUESS...
IT MEANS WE HAVE TO GET FRANK'S SON TO CART ALL OF OUR INSTRU-MENTS OVER THERE AN' GET US SET UP.
GRAMPSTER!
YOU MEAN, YOU GUYS HAVE YOUR OWN ROADIE?!!
LYNN

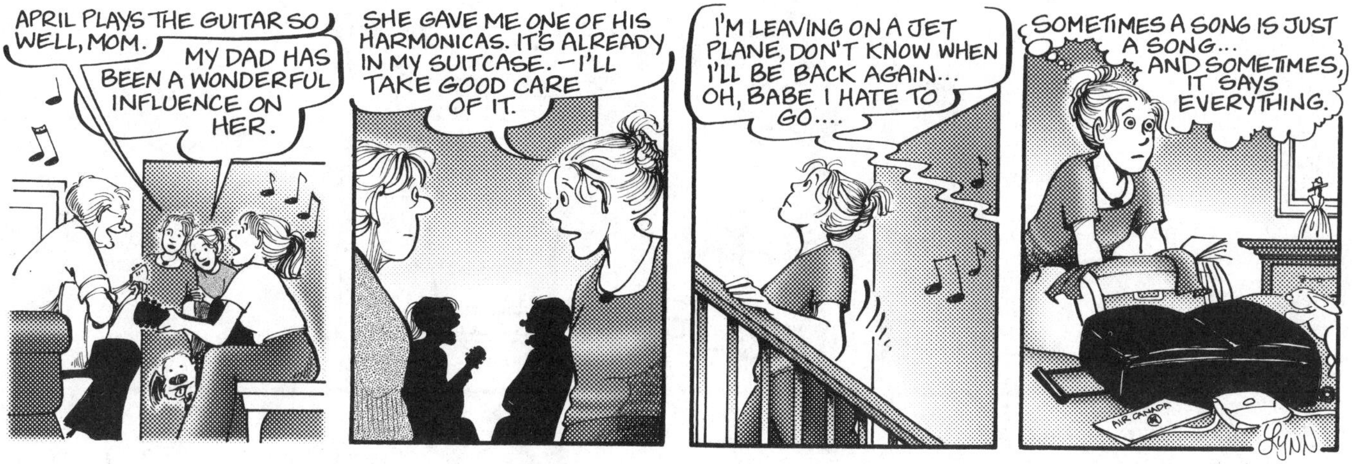
APRIL PLAYS THE GUITAR SO WELL, MOM.
MY DAD HAS BEEN A WONDERFUL INFLUENCE ON HER.
SHE GAVE ME ONE OF HIS HARMONICAS. IT'S ALREADY IN MY SUITCASE. —I'LL TAKE GOOD CARE OF IT.
I'M LEAVING ON A JET PLANE, DON'T KNOW WHEN I'LL BE BACK AGAIN... OH, BABE I HATE TO GO....
SOMETIMES A SONG IS JUST A SONG... AND SOMETIMES, IT SAYS EVERYTHING.
AIR CANADA
LYNN

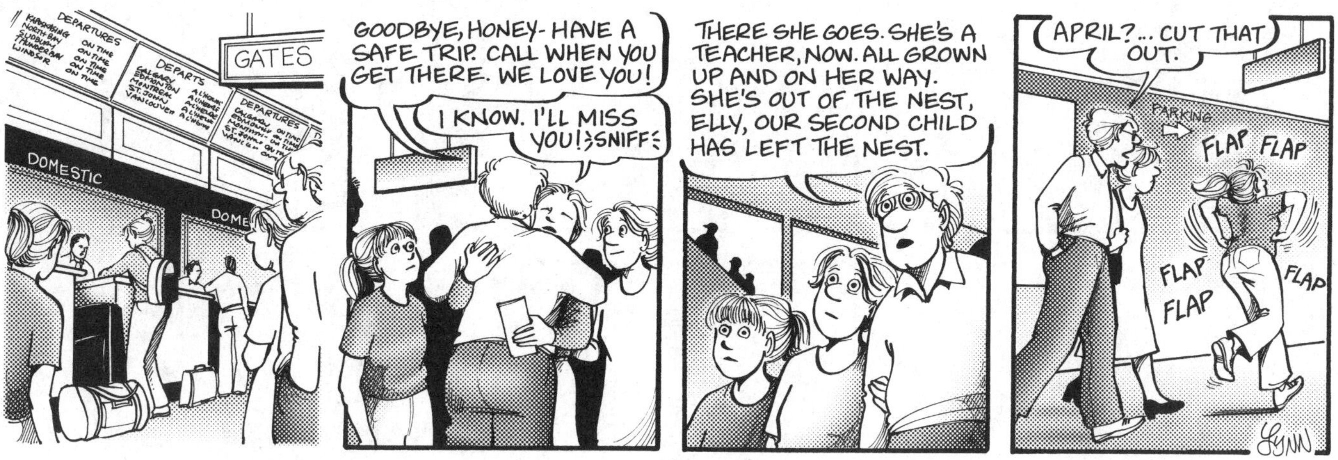
DEPARTURES
GATES
DEPARTS
DEPARTURES
DOMESTIC
DOME
GOODBYE, HONEY- HAVE A SAFE TRIP. CALL WHEN YOU GET THERE. WE LOVE YOU!
I KNOW. I'LL MISS YOU! SNIFF
THERE SHE GOES. SHE'S A TEACHER, NOW. ALL GROWN UP AND ON HER WAY. SHE'S OUT OF THE NEST, ELLY, OUR SECOND CHILD HAS LEFT THE NEST.
APRIL?... CUT THAT OUT.
PARKING
FLAP FLAP
FLAP
FLAP
FLAP
LYNN

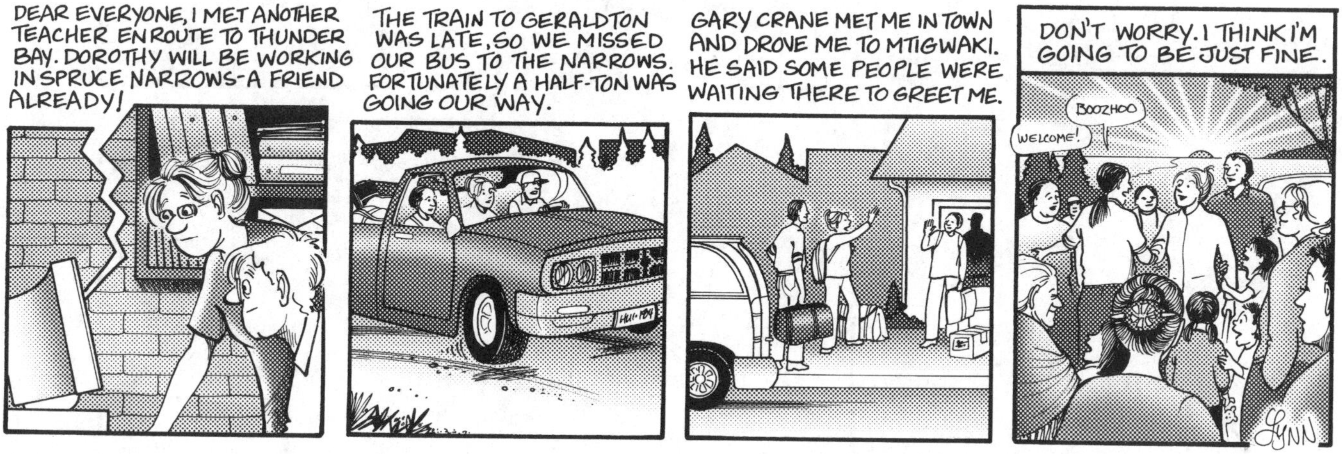
DEAR EVERYONE, I MET ANOTHER TEACHER EN ROUTE TO THUNDER BAY. DOROTHY WILL BE WORKING IN SPRUCE NARROWS-A FRIEND ALREADY!
THE TRAIN TO GERALDTON WAS LATE, SO WE MISSED OUR BUS TO THE NARROWS. FORTUNATELY A HALF-TON WAS GOING OUR WAY.
GARY CRANE MET ME IN TOWN AND DROVE ME TO MTIGWAKI. HE SAID SOME PEOPLE WERE WAITING THERE TO GREET ME.
DON'T WORRY. I THINK I'M GOING TO BE JUST FINE.
BOOZHOO
WELCOME!
LYNN

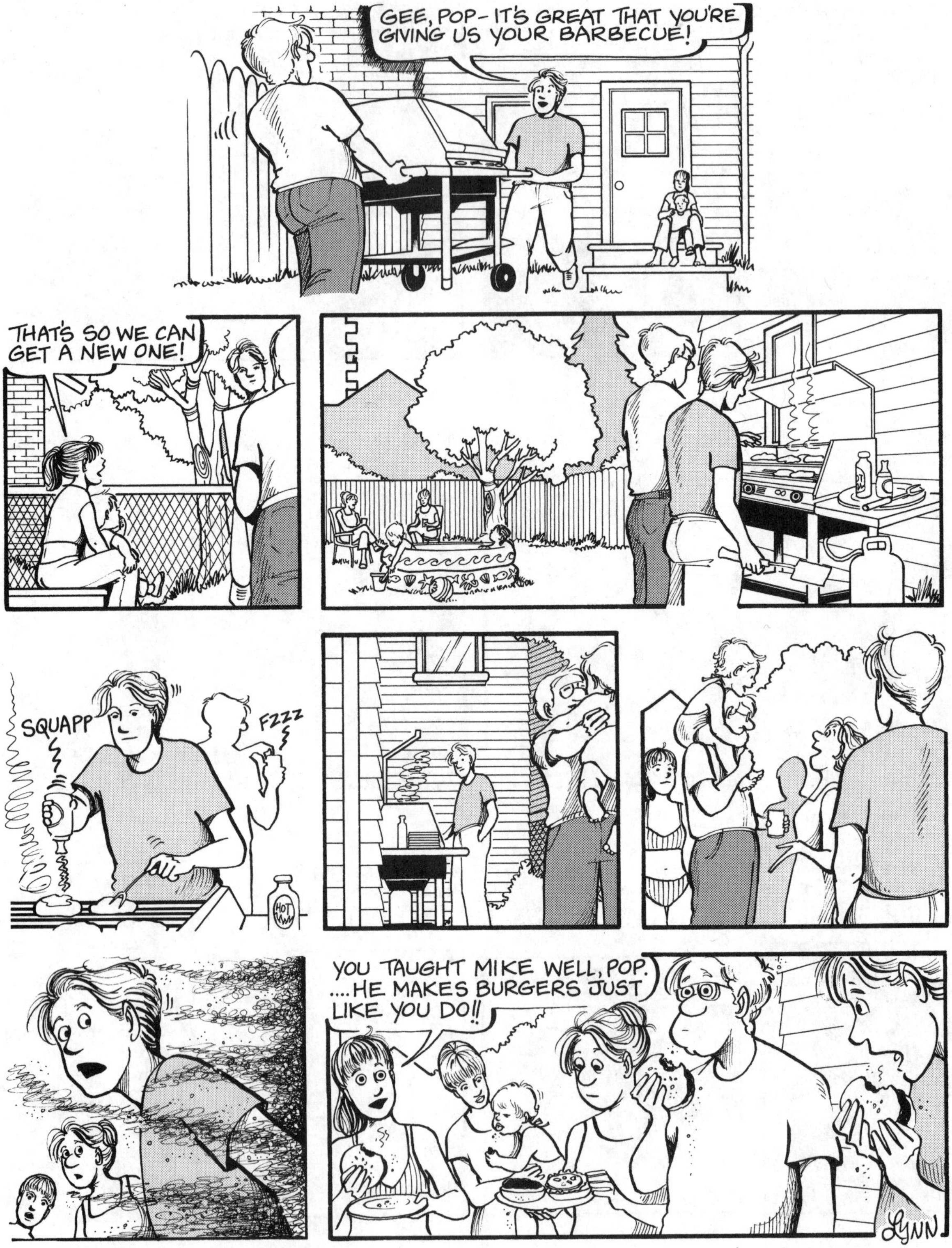
GEE, POP- IT'S GREAT THAT YOU'RE GIVING US YOUR BARBECUE!
THAT'S SO WE CAN GET A NEW ONE!
SQUAPP
FZZZ
HOT
YOU TAUGHT MIKE WELL, POP. ....HE MAKES BURGERS JUST LIKE YOU DO!!
LYNN

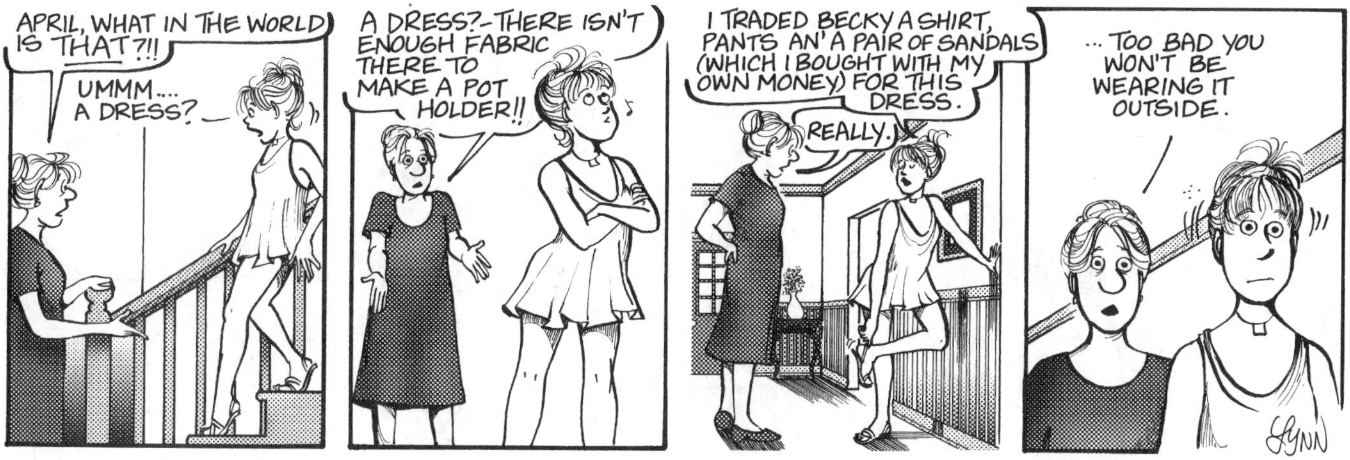
APRIL, WHAT IN THE WORLD IS THAT?!!
UMMM.... A DRESS?
A DRESS?- THERE ISN'T ENOUGH FABRIC THERE TO MAKE A POT HOLDER!!
I TRADED BECKY A SHIRT, PANTS AN' A PAIR OF SANDALS (WHICH I BOUGHT WITH MY OWN MONEY) FOR THIS DRESS.
REALLY.
... TOO BAD YOU WON'T BE WEARING IT OUTSIDE.
LYNN

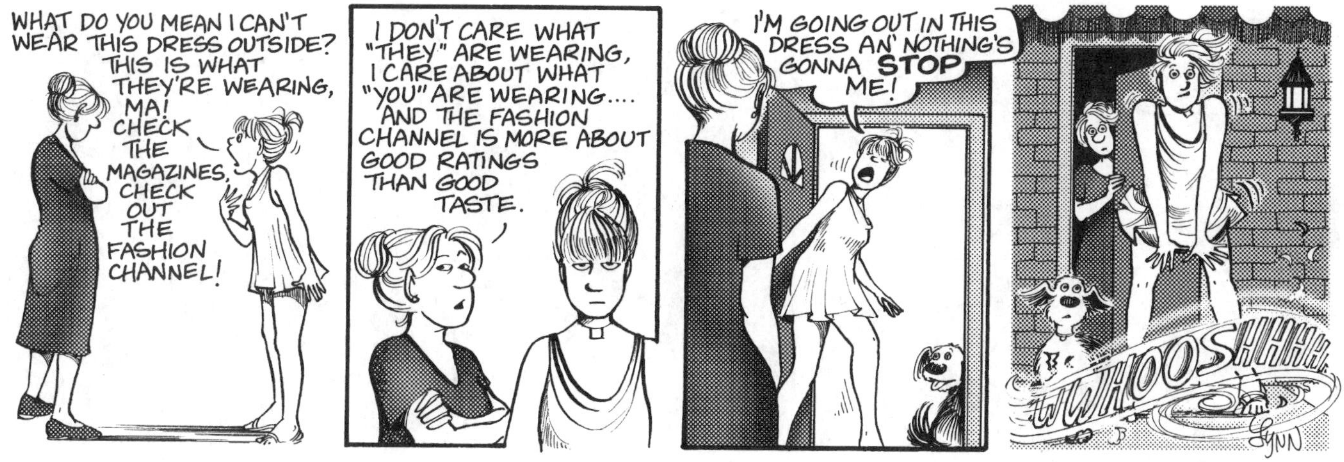
WHAT DO YOU MEAN I CAN'T WEAR THIS DRESS OUTSIDE? THIS IS WHAT THEY'RE WEARING, MA! CHECK THE MAGAZINES. CHECK OUT THE FASHION CHANNEL!
I DON'T CARE WHAT "THEY" ARE WEARING, I CARE ABOUT WHAT "YOU" ARE WEARING.... AND THE FASHION CHANNEL IS MORE ABOUT GOOD RATINGS THAN GOOD TASTE.
I'M GOING OUT IN THIS DRESS AN' NOTHING'S GONNA STOP ME!
WWHOOSHHHH
LYNN

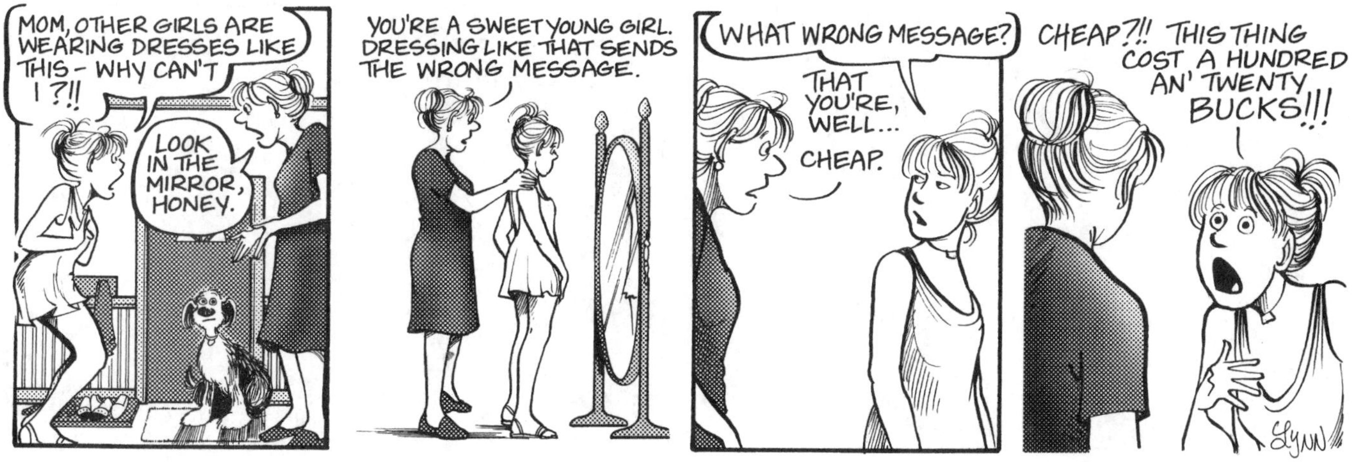
MOM, OTHER GIRLS ARE WEARING DRESSES LIKE THIS - WHY CAN'T I?!!
LOOK IN THE MIRROR, HONEY.
YOU'RE A SWEET YOUNG GIRL. DRESSING LIKE THAT SENDS THE WRONG MESSAGE.
WHAT WRONG MESSAGE?
THAT YOU'RE, WELL...
CHEAP.
CHEAP?!! THIS THING COST A HUNDRED AN' TWENTY BUCKS!!!
LYNN

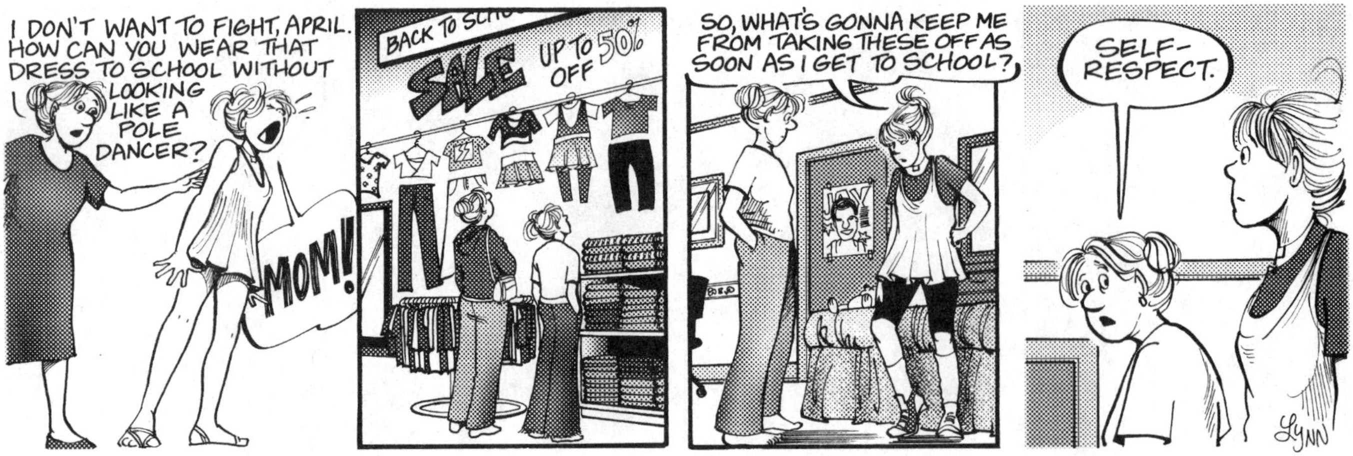
I DON'T WANT TO FIGHT, APRIL. HOW CAN YOU WEAR THAT DRESS TO SCHOOL WITHOUT LOOKING LIKE A POLE DANCER?
MOM!
BACK TO SCHO
SALE
UP TO 50% OFF
SO, WHAT'S GONNA KEEP ME FROM TAKING THESE OFF AS SOON AS I GET TO SCHOOL?
SELF-RESPECT.
LYNN

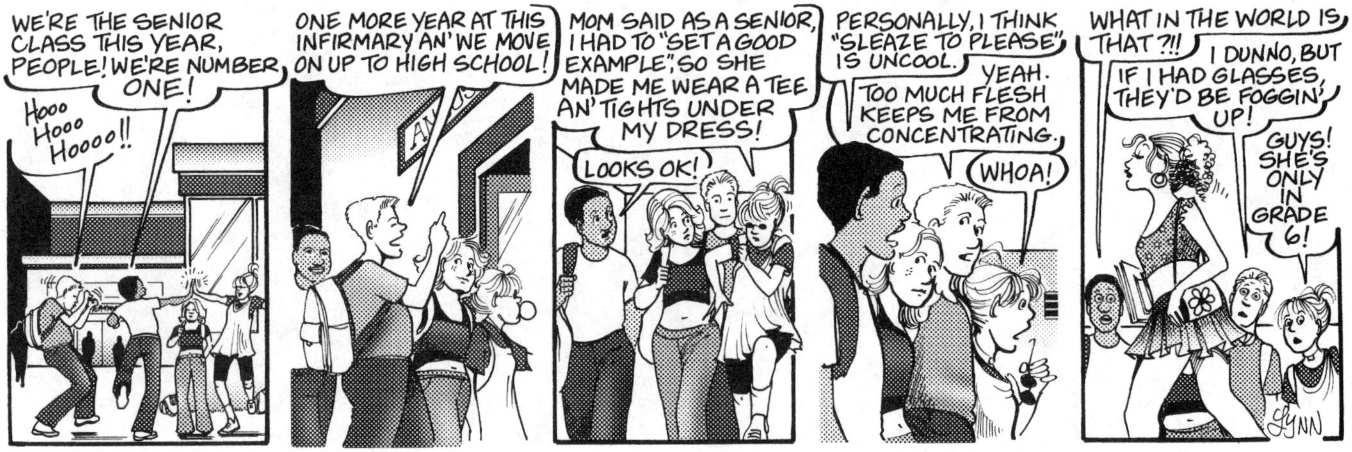
WE'RE THE SENIOR CLASS THIS YEAR, PEOPLE! WE'RE NUMBER ONE!
Hooo Hooo Hoooo!!
ONE MORE YEAR AT THIS INFIRMARY AN' WE MOVE ON UP TO HIGH SCHOOL!
MOM SAID AS A SENIOR, I HAD TO "SET A GOOD EXAMPLE", SO SHE MADE ME WEAR A TEE AN' TIGHTS UNDER MY DRESS!
LOOKS OK!
PERSONALLY, I THINK "SLEAZE TO PLEASE" IS UNCOOL.
YEAH. TOO MUCH FLESH KEEPS ME FROM CONCENTRATING.
WHOA!
WHAT IN THE WORLD IS THAT?!!
I DUNNO, BUT IF I HAD GLASSES, THEY'D BE FOGGIN' UP!
GUYS! SHE'S ONLY IN GRADE 6!
LYNN

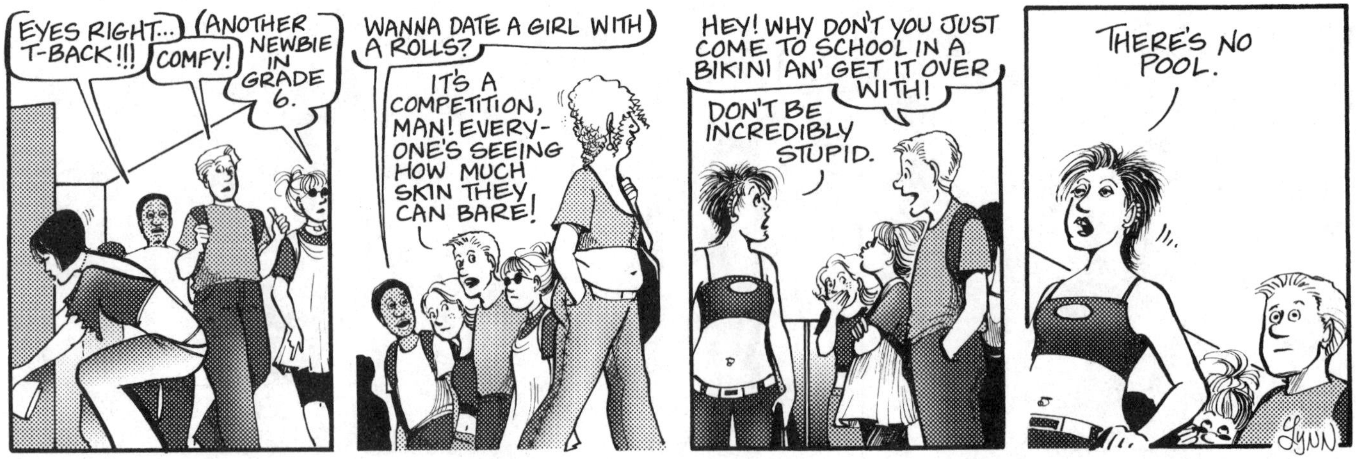
EYES RIGHT... T-BACK!!!
COMFY!
(ANOTHER NEWBIE IN GRADE 6.
WANNA DATE A GIRL WITH A ROLLS?
IT'S A COMPETITION, MAN! EVERYONE'S SEEING HOW MUCH SKIN THEY CAN BARE!
HEY! WHY DON'T YOU JUST COME TO SCHOOL IN A BIKINI AN' GET IT OVER WITH!
DON'T BE INCREDIBLY STUPID.
THERE'S NO POOL.
LYNN

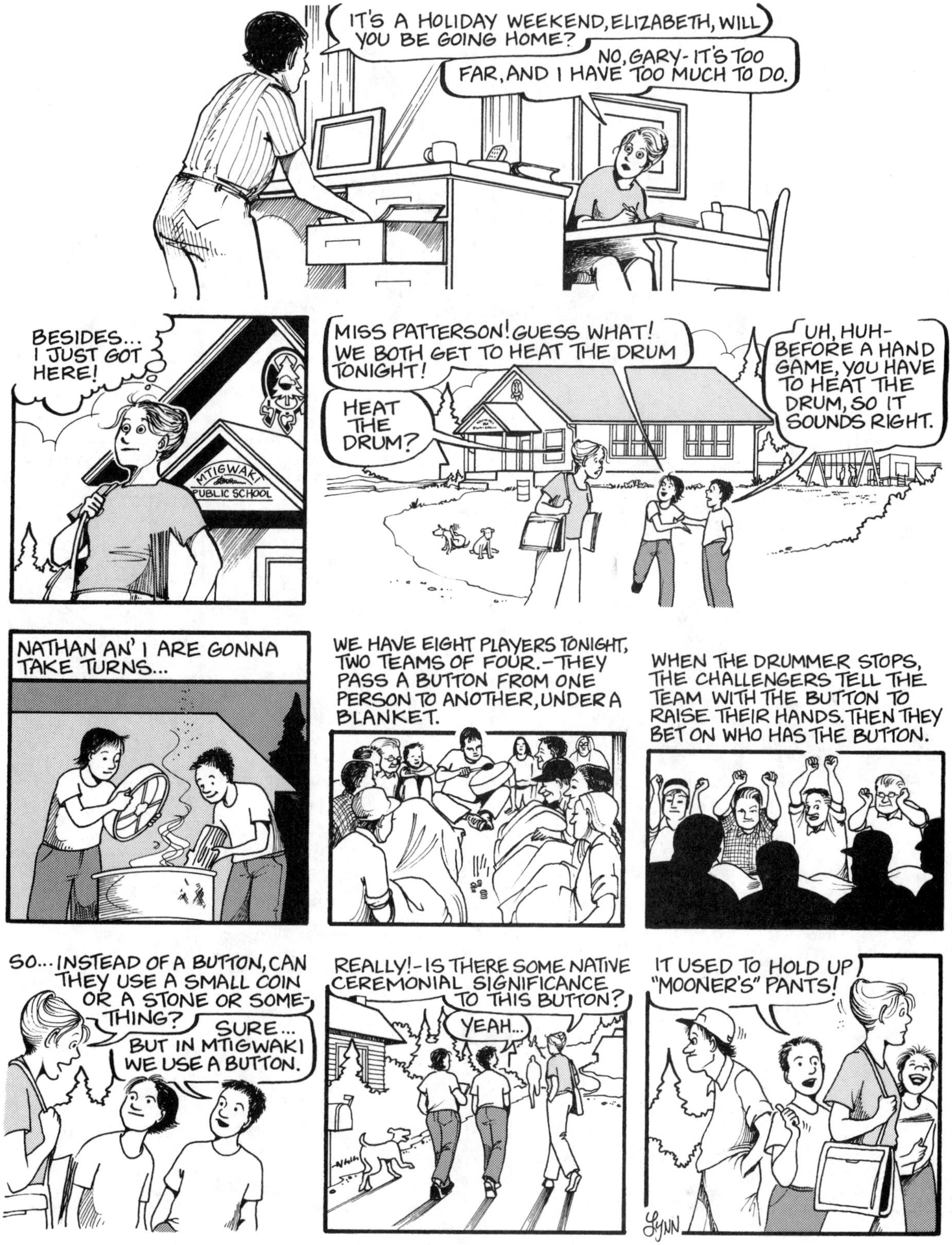
IT'S A HOLIDAY WEEKEND, ELIZABETH, WILL YOU BE GOING HOME?
NO, GARY- IT'S TOO FAR, AND I HAVE TOO MUCH TO DO.
BESIDES... I JUST GOT HERE!
MTIGWAKI PUBLIC SCHOOL
MISS PATTERSON! GUESS WHAT! WE BOTH GET TO HEAT THE DRUM TONIGHT!
HEAT THE DRUM?
UH, HUH- BEFORE A HAND GAME, YOU HAVE TO HEAT THE DRUM, SO IT SOUNDS RIGHT.
NATHAN AN' I ARE GONNA TAKE TURNS...
WE HAVE EIGHT PLAYERS TONIGHT, TWO TEAMS OF FOUR.-THEY PASS A BUTTON FROM ONE PERSON TO ANOTHER, UNDER A BLANKET.
WHEN THE DRUMMER STOPS, THE CHALLENGERS TELL THE TEAM WITH THE BUTTON TO RAISE THEIR HANDS. THEN THEY BET ON WHO HAS THE BUTTON.
SO... INSTEAD OF A BUTTON, CAN THEY USE A SMALL COIN OR A STONE OR SOME-THING?
SURE... BUT IN MTIGWAKI WE USE A BUTTON.
REALLY!-IS THERE SOME NATIVE CEREMONIAL SIGNIFICANCE TO THIS BUTTON?
YEAH...
IT USED TO HOLD UP "MOONER'S" PANTS!
LYNN

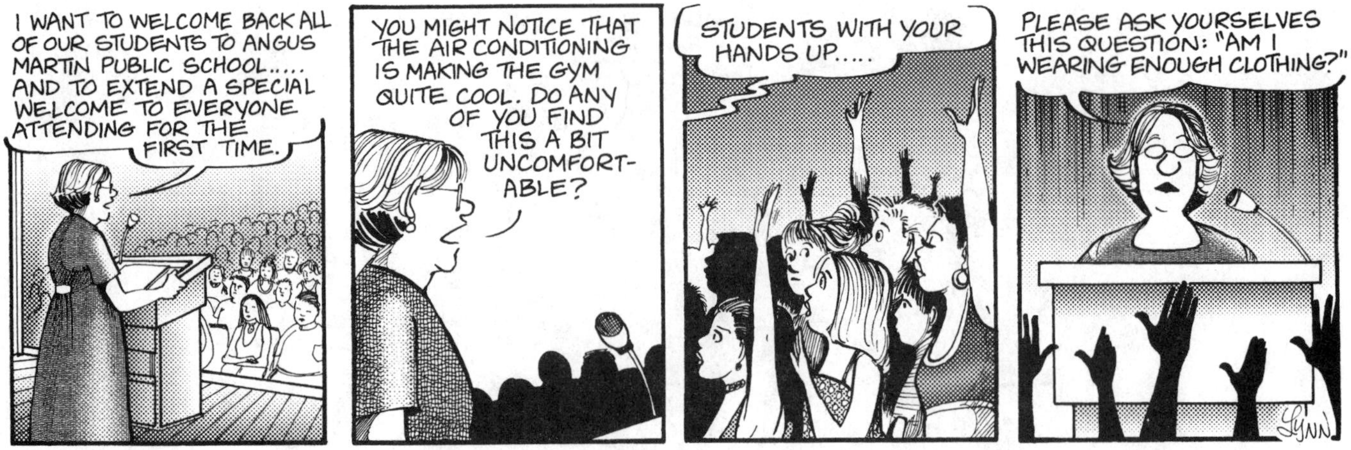
I WANT TO WELCOME BACK ALL OF OUR STUDENTS TO ANGUS MARTIN PUBLIC SCHOOL..... AND TO EXTEND A SPECIAL WELCOME TO EVERYONE ATTENDING FOR THE FIRST TIME.
YOU MIGHT NOTICE THAT THE AIR CONDITIONING IS MAKING THE GYM QUITE COOL. DO ANY OF YOU FIND THIS A BIT UNCOMFORTABLE?
STUDENTS WITH YOUR HANDS UP.....
PLEASE ASK YOURSELVES THIS QUESTION: "AM I WEARING ENOUGH CLOTHING?"
LYNN

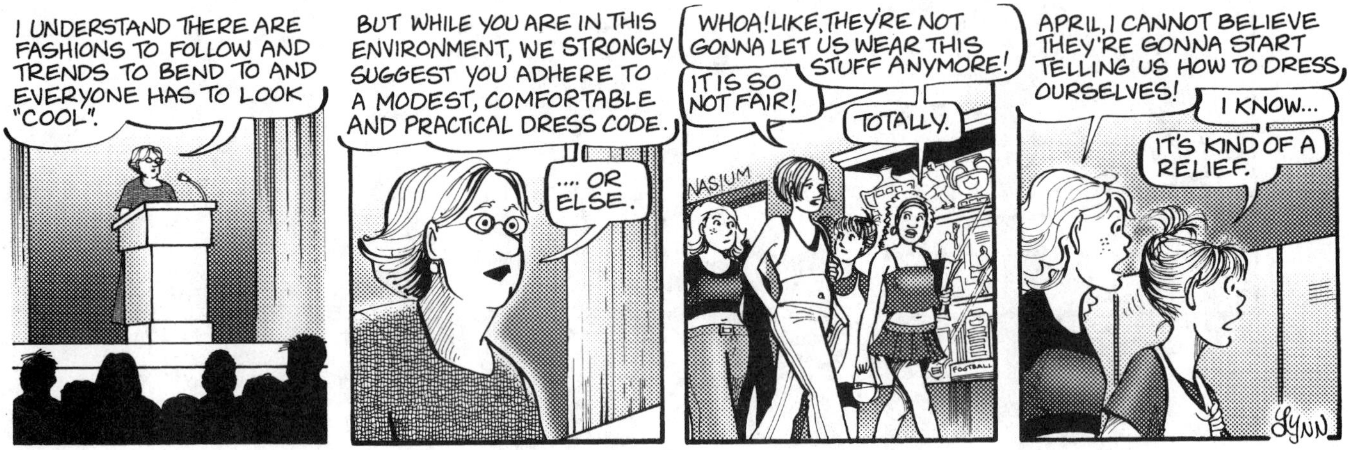
I UNDERSTAND THERE ARE FASHIONS TO FOLLOW AND TRENDS TO BEND TO AND EVERYONE HAS TO LOOK "COOL".
BUT WHILE YOU ARE IN THIS ENVIRONMENT, WE STRONGLY SUGGEST YOU ADHERE TO A MODEST, COMFORTABLE AND PRACTICAL DRESS CODE.
.... OR ELSE.
WHOA! LIKE, THEY'RE NOT GONNA LET US WEAR THIS STUFF ANYMORE!
IT IS SO NOT FAIR!
TOTALLY.
NASIUM
FOOTBALL
APRIL, I CANNOT BELIEVE THEY'RE GONNA START TELLING US HOW TO DRESS OURSELVES!
I KNOW...
IT'S KIND OF A RELIEF.
LYNN

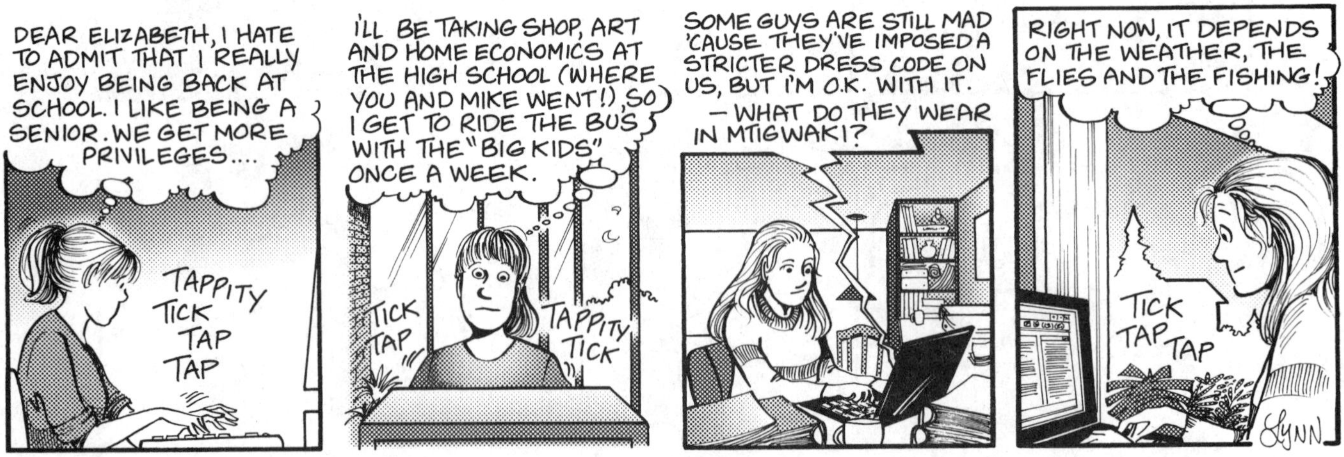
DEAR ELIZABETH, I HATE TO ADMIT THAT I REALLY ENJOY BEING BACK AT SCHOOL. I LIKE BEING A SENIOR. WE GET MORE PRIVILEGES....
TAPPITY TICK TAP TAP
I'LL BE TAKING SHOP, ART AND HOME ECONOMICS AT THE HIGH SCHOOL (WHERE YOU AND MIKE WENT!), SO I GET TO RIDE THE BUS WITH THE "BIG KIDS" ONCE A WEEK.
TICK TAP
TAPPITY TICK
SOME GUYS ARE STILL MAD 'CAUSE THEY'VE IMPOSED A STRICTER DRESS CODE ON US, BUT I'M O.K. WITH IT.
— WHAT DO THEY WEAR IN MTIGWAKI?
RIGHT NOW, IT DEPENDS ON THE WEATHER, THE FLIES AND THE FISHING!
TICK TAP TAP
LYNN

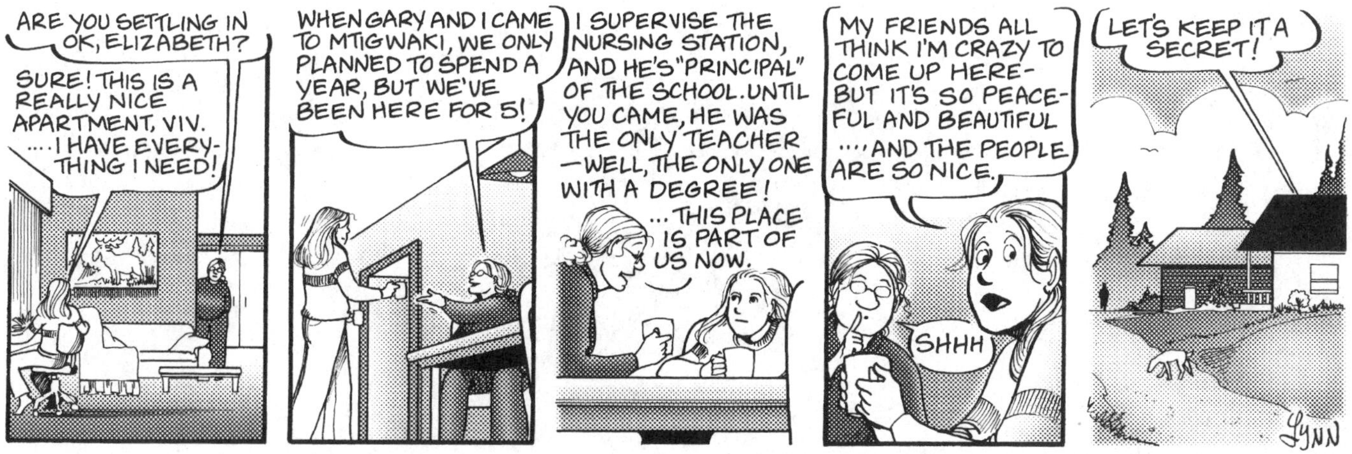
ARE YOU SETTLING IN OK, ELIZABETH?
SURE! THIS IS A REALLY NICE APARTMENT, VIV. ....I HAVE EVERYTHING I NEED!
WHEN GARY AND I CAME TO MTIGWAKI, WE ONLY PLANNED TO SPEND A YEAR, BUT WE'VE BEEN HERE FOR 5!
I SUPERVISE THE NURSING STATION, AND HE'S "PRINCIPAL" OF THE SCHOOL. UNTIL YOU CAME, HE WAS THE ONLY TEACHER —WELL, THE ONLY ONE WITH A DEGREE!
...THIS PLACE IS PART OF US NOW.
MY FRIENDS ALL THINK I'M CRAZY TO COME UP HERE- BUT IT'S SO PEACEFUL AND BEAUTIFUL ....AND THE PEOPLE ARE SO NICE.
SHHH
LET'S KEEP IT A SECRET!
LYNN

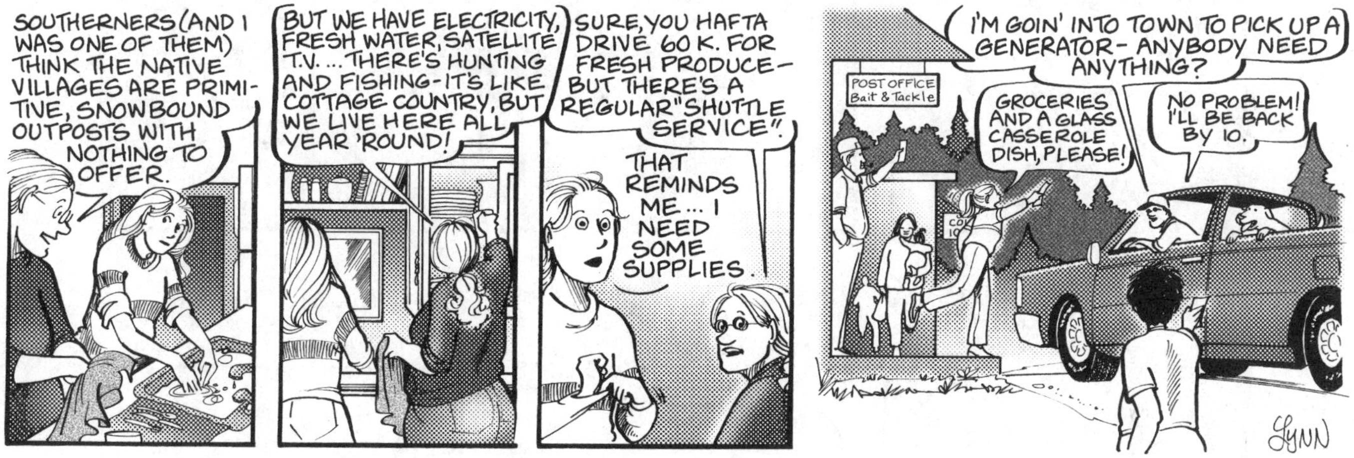
SOUTHERNERS (AND I WAS ONE OF THEM) THINK THE NATIVE VILLAGES ARE PRIMITIVE, SNOWBOUND OUTPOSTS WITH NOTHING TO OFFER.
BUT WE HAVE ELECTRICITY, FRESH WATER, SATELLITE T.V. ... THERE'S HUNTING AND FISHING- IT'S LIKE COTTAGE COUNTRY, BUT WE LIVE HERE ALL YEAR 'ROUND!
SURE, YOU HAFTA DRIVE 60 K. FOR FRESH PRODUCE- BUT THERE'S A REGULAR "SHUTTLE SERVICE".
THAT REMINDS ME... I NEED SOME SUPPLIES.
POST OFFICE
Bait & Tackle
I'M GOIN' INTO TOWN TO PICK UP A GENERATOR- ANYBODY NEED ANYTHING?
GROCERIES AND A GLASS CASSEROLE DISH, PLEASE!
NO PROBLEM! I'LL BE BACK BY 10.
LYNN

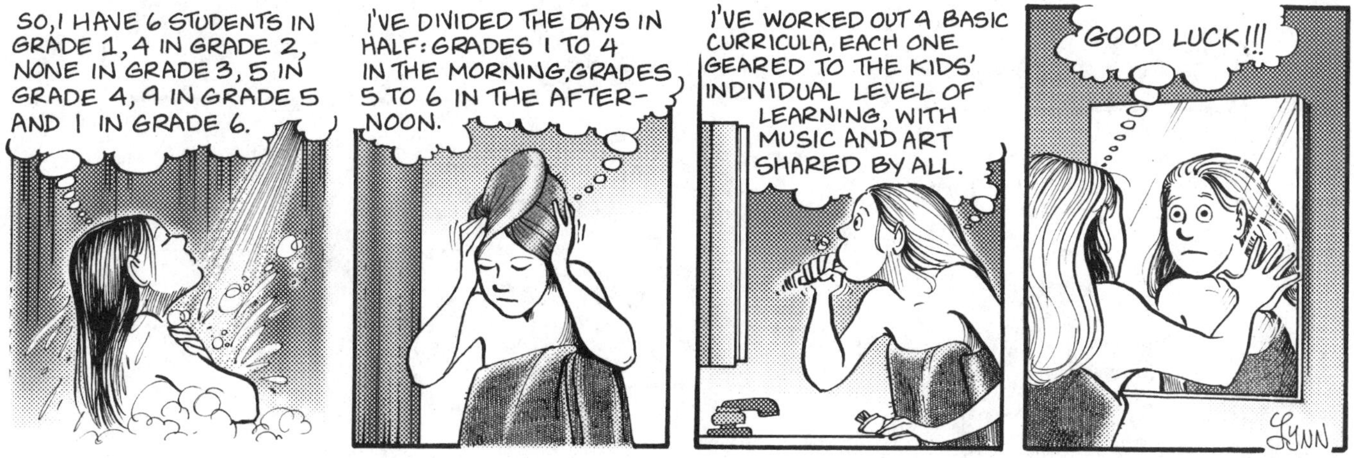
SO, I HAVE 6 STUDENTS IN GRADE 1, 4 IN GRADE 2, NONE IN GRADE 3, 5 IN GRADE 4, 9 IN GRADE 5 AND 1 IN GRADE 6.
I'VE DIVIDED THE DAYS IN HALF: GRADES 1 TO 4 IN THE MORNING, GRADES 5 TO 6 IN THE AFTERNOON.
I'VE WORKED OUT 4 BASIC CURRICULA, EACH ONE GEARED TO THE KIDS' INDIVIDUAL LEVEL OF LEARNING, WITH MUSIC AND ART SHARED BY ALL.
GOOD LUCK!!!
LYNN

WELL, IT'S ONE FOR THE MONEY, TWO FOR THE SHOW....
THREE TO GET READY, NOW GO CAT GO, AN'.....
DON'T YEEW STEP ON MAH BLUE SUEDE SHOES.... YOU CAN DO ANYTHING, BUT STAY OFFA THEM BLUE SUEDE SHOES!
MOMMA DON'T ALLOW NO GUITAR PICKIN' 'ROUND HERE-OH, NO... MOMMA DON'T ALLOW NO GUITAR PICKIN' HEEEERE!!!
KISS ME ONCE AND KISS ME TWICE AND KISS ME ONCE AGAIN, IT'S BEEN A LONG, LONG TIIIME.
AND, WE'LL END THE SHOW WITH OUR VERSION OF "THE CHATTANOOGA CHOO-CHOO"!!
WE ARE THE NEW "BENTWOOD ROCKERS"! THANK YOU AND GOOD NIGHT!
YOU'RE NOT 20 YEARS OLD, JIM...
YOU'RE GOING TO ACHE FOR A WEEK!
I KNOW, BUT IT WAS WORTH IT.
LYNN

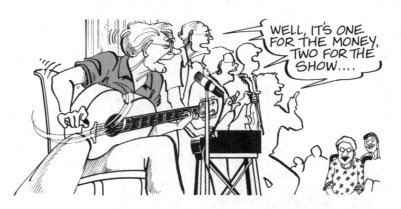

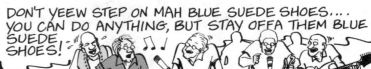

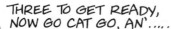

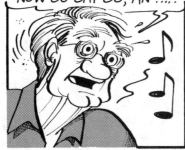

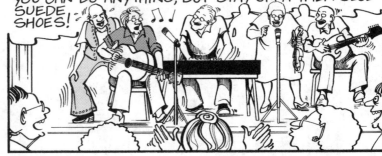

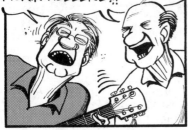

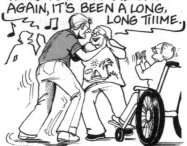

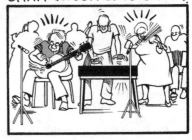

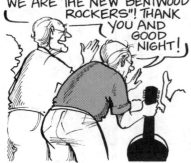

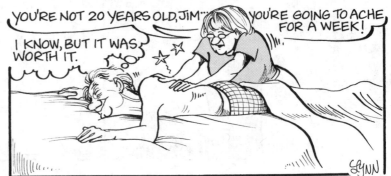

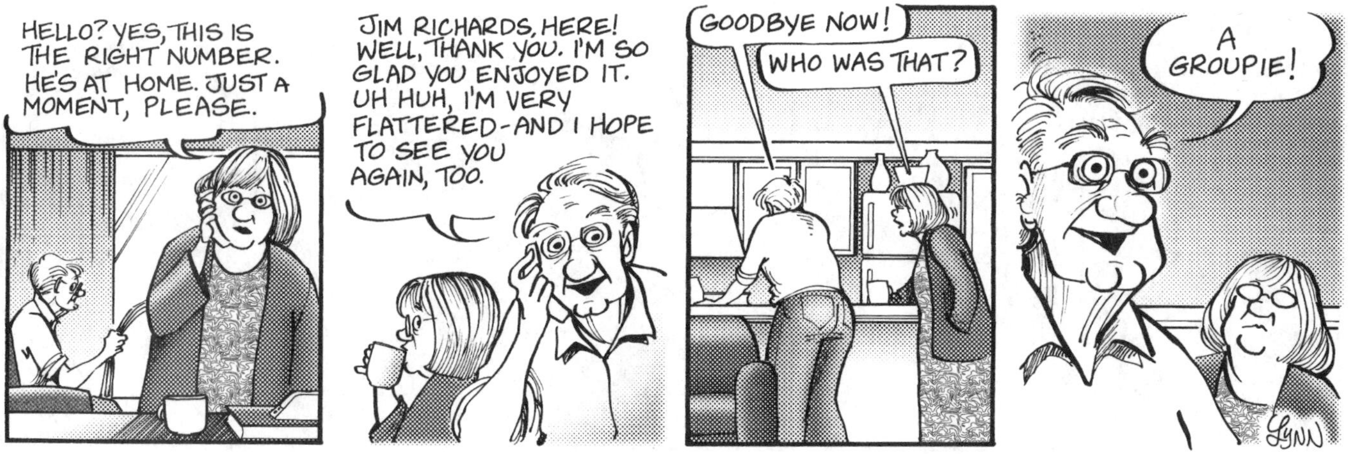
HELLO? YES, THIS IS THE RIGHT NUMBER. HE'S AT HOME. JUST A MOMENT, PLEASE.
JIM RICHARDS, HERE! WELL, THANK YOU. I'M SO GLAD YOU ENJOYED IT. UH HUH, I'M VERY FLATTERED-AND I HOPE TO SEE YOU AGAIN, TOO.
GOODBYE NOW!
WHO WAS THAT?
A GROUPIE!
LYNN

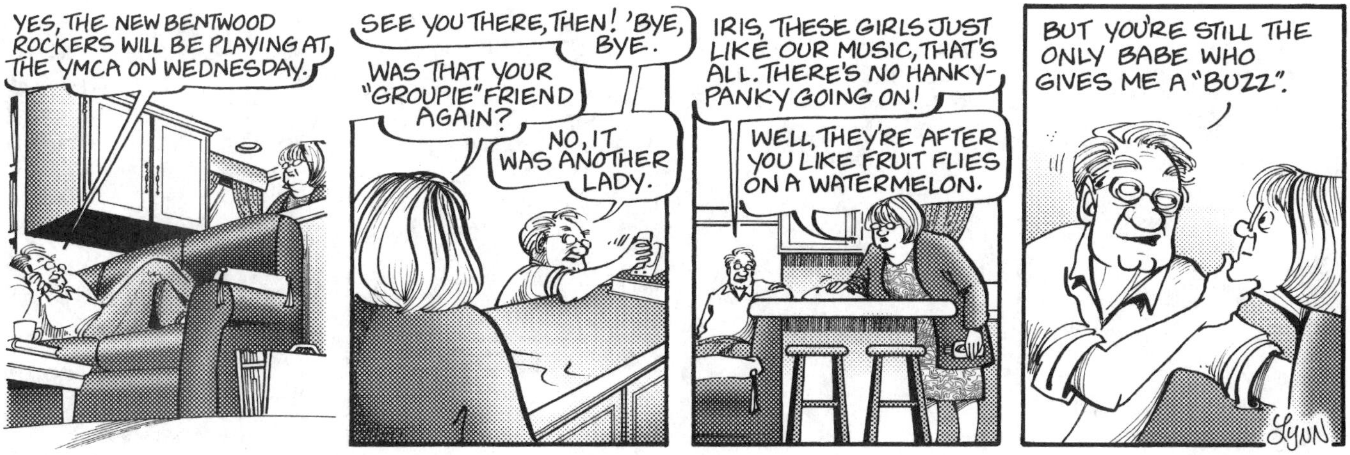
YES, THE NEW BENTWOOD ROCKERS WILL BE PLAYING AT THE YMCA ON WEDNESDAY.
SEE YOU THERE, THEN! 'BYE, BYE.
WAS THAT YOUR "GROUPIE" FRIEND AGAIN?
NO, IT WAS ANOTHER LADY.
IRIS, THESE GIRLS JUST LIKE OUR MUSIC, THAT'S ALL. THERE'S NO HANKY-PANKY GOING ON!
WELL, THEY'RE AFTER YOU LIKE FRUIT FLIES ON A WATERMELON.
BUT YOU'RE STILL THE ONLY BABE WHO GIVES ME A "BUZZ".
LYNN

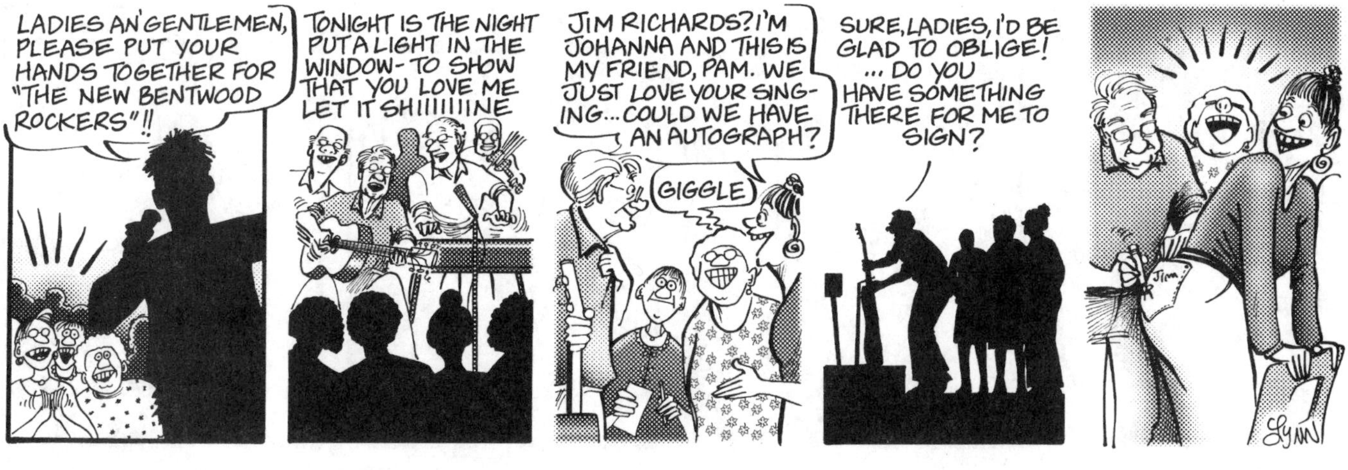
LADIES AN' GENTLEMEN, PLEASE PUT YOUR HANDS TOGETHER FOR "THE NEW BENTWOOD ROCKERS"!!
TONIGHT IS THE NIGHT PUT A LIGHT IN THE WINDOW- TO SHOW THAT YOU LOVE ME LET IT SHIIIIIIINE
JIM RICHARDS? I'M JOHANNA AND THIS IS MY FRIEND, PAM. WE JUST LOVE YOUR SINGING... COULD WE HAVE AN AUTOGRAPH?
GIGGLE
SURE, LADIES, I'D BE GLAD TO OBLIGE! ... DO YOU HAVE SOMETHING THERE FOR ME TO SIGN?
Jim
LYNN

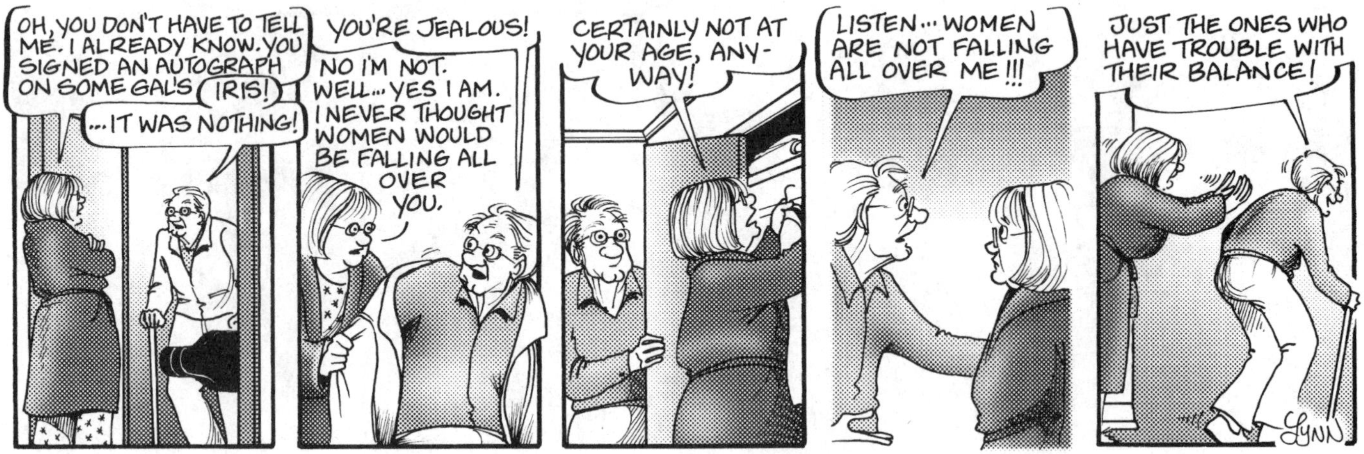
OH, YOU DON'T HAVE TO TELL ME. I ALREADY KNOW. YOU SIGNED AN AUTOGRAPH ON SOME GAL'S
IRIS!
...IT WAS NOTHING!
YOU'RE JEALOUS!
NO I'M NOT. WELL... YES I AM. I NEVER THOUGHT WOMEN WOULD BE FALLING ALL OVER YOU.
CERTAINLY NOT AT YOUR AGE, ANY-WAY!
LISTEN... WOMEN ARE NOT FALLING ALL OVER ME!!!
JUST THE ONES WHO HAVE TROUBLE WITH THEIR BALANCE!
LYNN

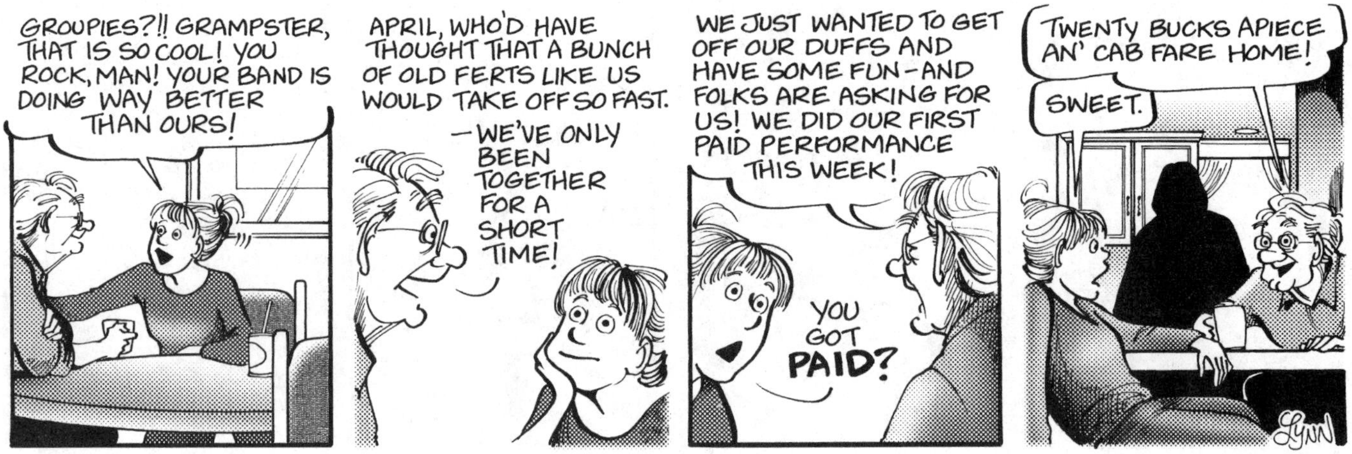
GROUPIES?!! GRAMPSTER, THAT IS SO COOL! YOU ROCK, MAN! YOUR BAND IS DOING WAY BETTER THAN OURS!
APRIL, WHO'D HAVE THOUGHT THAT A BUNCH OF OLD FERTS LIKE US WOULD TAKE OFF SO FAST.
-WE'VE ONLY BEEN TOGETHER FOR A SHORT TIME!
WE JUST WANTED TO GET OFF OUR DUFFS AND HAVE SOME FUN-AND FOLKS ARE ASKING FOR US! WE DID OUR FIRST PAID PERFORMANCE THIS WEEK!
YOU GOT PAID?
TWENTY BUCKS APIECE AN' CAB FARE HOME!
SWEET.
LYNN

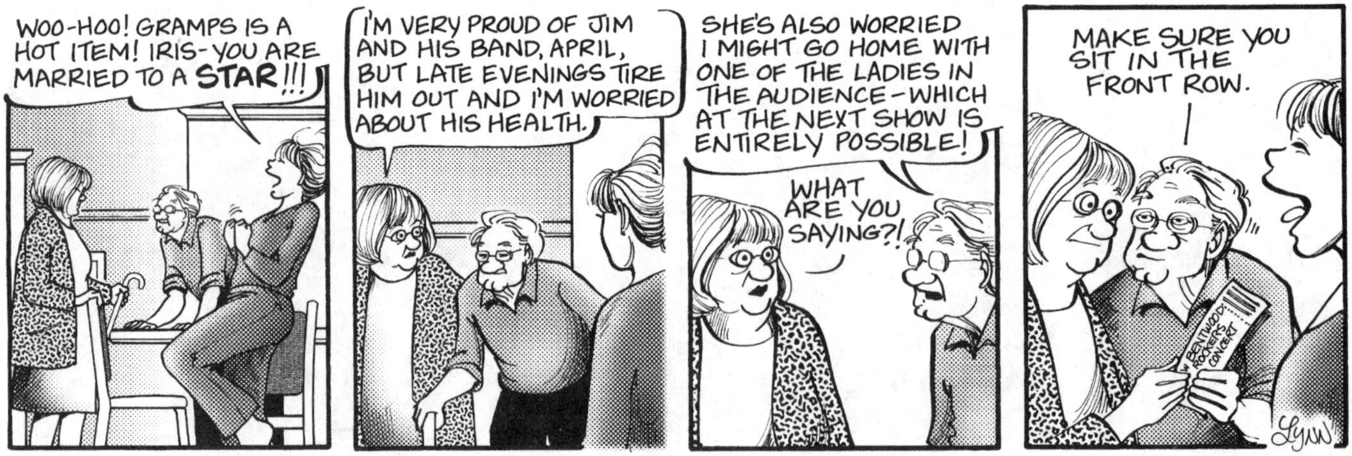
WOO-HOO! GRAMPS IS A HOT ITEM! IRIS-YOU ARE MARRIED TO A STAR!!!
I'M VERY PROUD OF JIM AND HIS BAND, APRIL, BUT LATE EVENINGS TIRE HIM OUT AND I'M WORRIED ABOUT HIS HEALTH.
SHE'S ALSO WORRIED I MIGHT GO HOME WITH ONE OF THE LADIES IN THE AUDIENCE-WHICH AT THE NEXT SHOW IS ENTIRELY POSSIBLE!
WHAT ARE YOU SAYING?!
MAKE SURE YOU SIT IN THE FRONT ROW.
LYNN

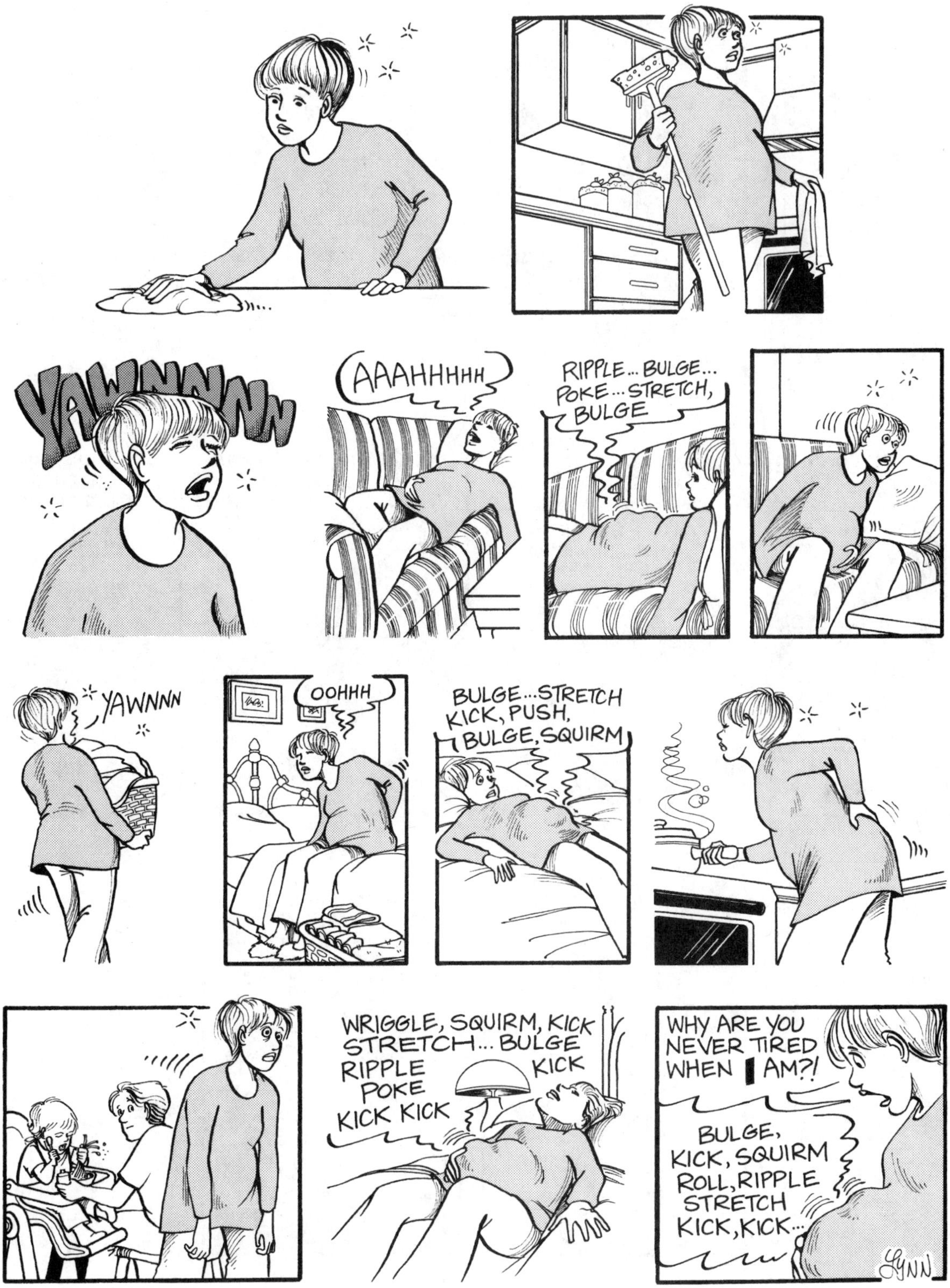
YAWNNNN
AAAHHHHH
RIPPLE... BULGE... POKE... STRETCH, BULGE
YAWNNN
OOHHH
BULGE...STRETCH KICK, PUSH, BULGE, SQUIRM
WRIGGLE, SQUIRM, KICK STRETCH... BULGE RIPPLE POKE KICK KICK KICK
WHY ARE YOU NEVER TIRED WHEN I AM?!
BULGE, KICK, SQUIRM ROLL, RIPPLE STRETCH KICK, KICK...
LYNN

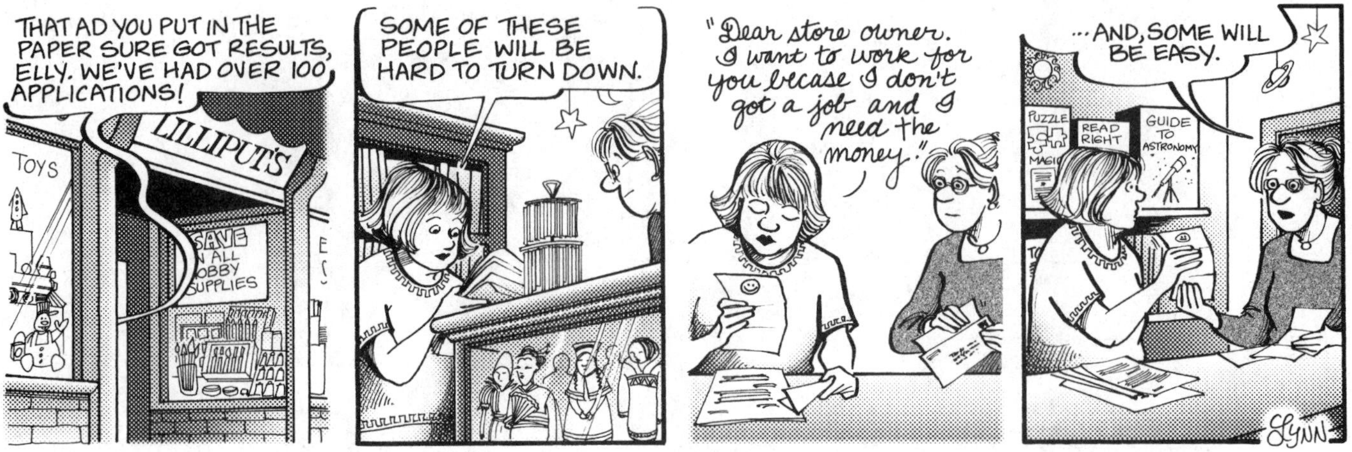

THAT AD YOU PUT IN THE PAPER SURE GOT RESULTS, ELLY. WE'VE HAD OVER 100 APPLICATIONS!
LILLIPUT'S
TOYS
SAVE ON ALL HOBBY SUPPLIES
SOME OF THESE PEOPLE WILL BE HARD TO TURN DOWN.
"Dear store owner. I want to work for you becase I don't got a job and I need the money."
...AND, SOME WILL BE EASY.
PUZZLE
READ RIGHT
GUIDE TO ASTRONOMY
LYNN

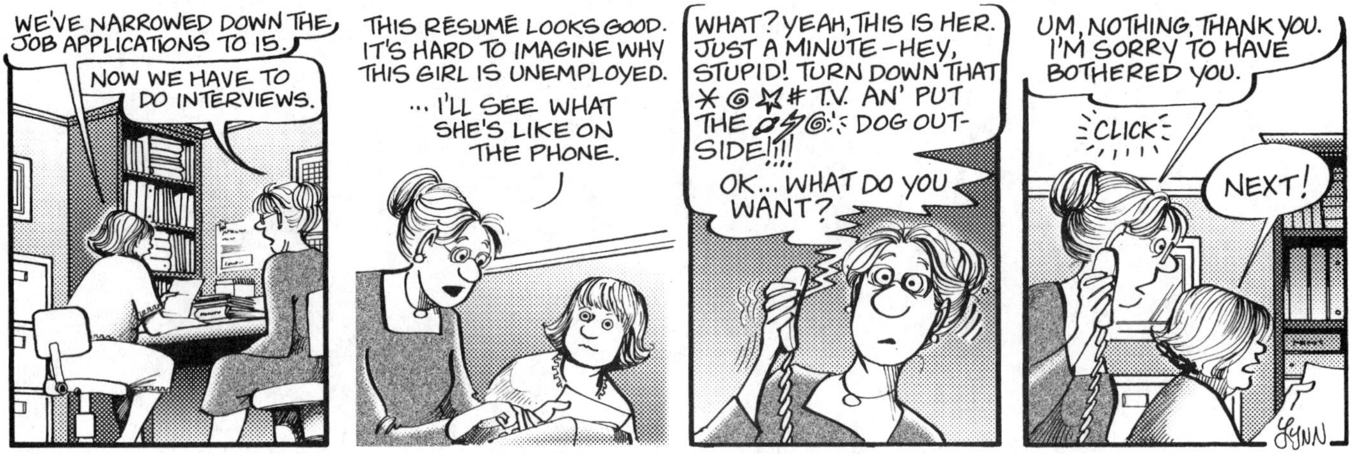

WE'VE NARROWED DOWN THE JOB APPLICATIONS TO 15.
NOW WE HAVE TO DO INTERVIEWS.
THIS RESUMÉ LOOKS GOOD. IT'S HARD TO IMAGINE WHY THIS GIRL IS UNEMPLOYED.
... I'LL SEE WHAT SHE'S LIKE ON THE PHONE.
WHAT? YEAH, THIS IS HER. JUST A MINUTE – HEY, STUPID! TURN DOWN THAT *@*# T.V. AN' PUT THE @*@ DOG OUT-SIDE!!!!
OK... WHAT DO YOU WANT?
UM, NOTHING, THANK YOU. I'M SORRY TO HAVE BOTHERED YOU.
CLICK
NEXT!
LYNN

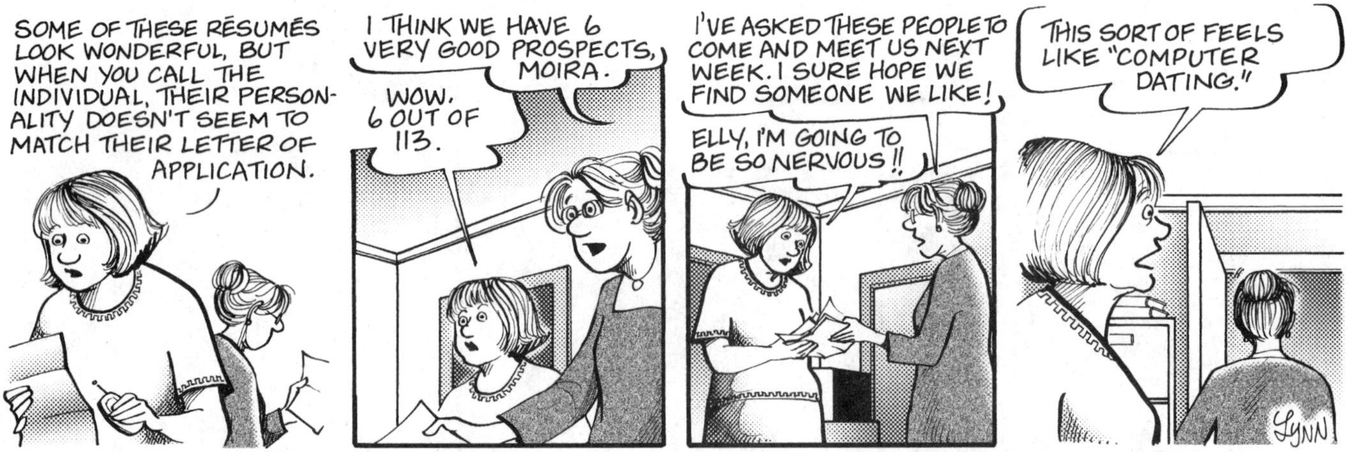

SOME OF THESE RÉSUMÉS LOOK WONDERFUL, BUT WHEN YOU CALL THE INDIVIDUAL, THEIR PERSON-ALITY DOESN'T SEEM TO MATCH THEIR LETTER OF APPLICATION.
I THINK WE HAVE 6 VERY GOOD PROSPECTS, MOIRA.
WOW. 6 OUT OF 113.
I'VE ASKED THESE PEOPLE TO COME AND MEET US NEXT WEEK. I SURE HOPE WE FIND SOMEONE WE LIKE!
ELLY, I'M GOING TO BE SO NERVOUS!!
THIS SORT OF FEELS LIKE "COMPUTER DATING."
LYNN

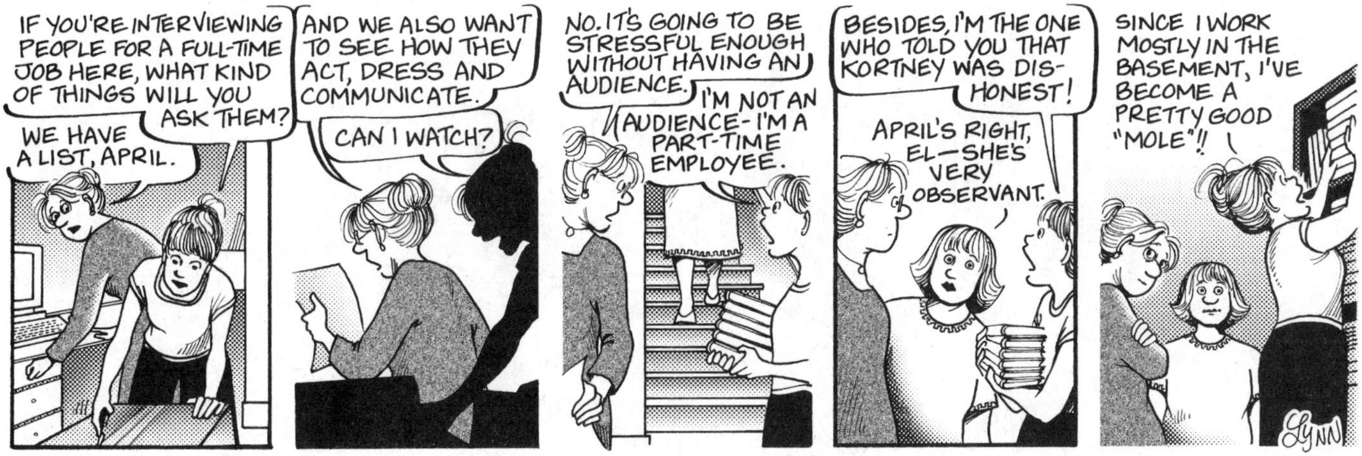
IF YOU'RE INTERVIEWING PEOPLE FOR A FULL-TIME JOB HERE, WHAT KIND OF THINGS WILL YOU ASK THEM?
WE HAVE A LIST, APRIL.
AND WE ALSO WANT TO SEE HOW THEY ACT, DRESS AND COMMUNICATE.
CAN I WATCH?
NO. IT'S GOING TO BE STRESSFUL ENOUGH WITHOUT HAVING AN AUDIENCE.
I'M NOT AN AUDIENCE - I'M A PART-TIME EMPLOYEE.
BESIDES, I'M THE ONE WHO TOLD YOU THAT KORTNEY WAS DIS-HONEST!
APRIL'S RIGHT, EL—SHE'S VERY OBSERVANT.
SINCE I WORK MOSTLY IN THE BASEMENT, I'VE BECOME A PRETTY GOOD "MOLE"!!
LYNN

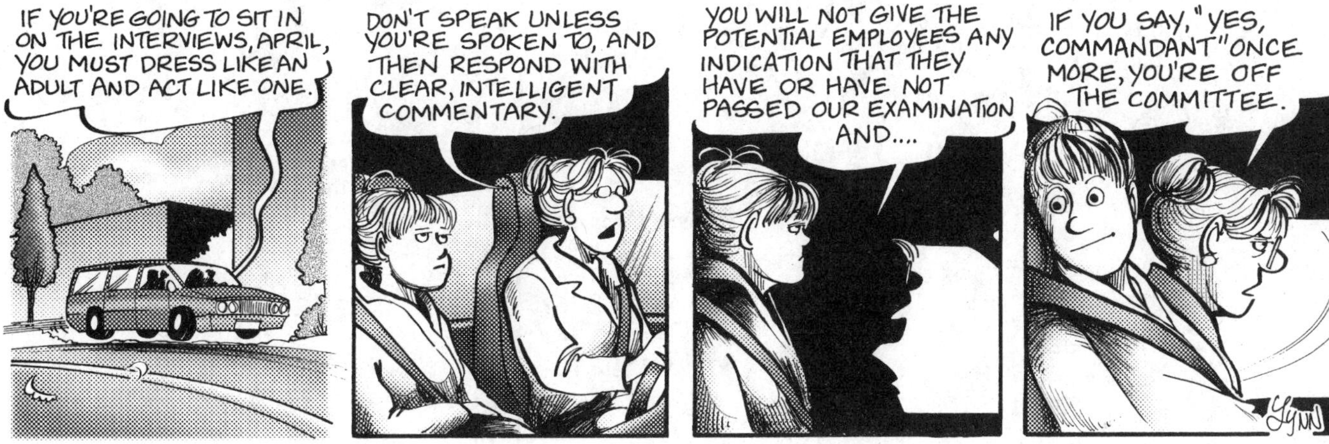
IF YOU'RE GOING TO SIT IN ON THE INTERVIEWS, APRIL, YOU MUST DRESS LIKE AN ADULT AND ACT LIKE ONE.
DON'T SPEAK UNLESS YOU'RE SPOKEN TO, AND THEN RESPOND WITH CLEAR, INTELLIGENT COMMENTARY.
YOU WILL NOT GIVE THE POTENTIAL EMPLOYEES ANY INDICATION THAT THEY HAVE OR HAVE NOT PASSED OUR EXAMINATION AND....
IF YOU SAY, "YES, COMMANDANT" ONCE MORE, YOU'RE OFF THE COMMITTEE.
LYNN

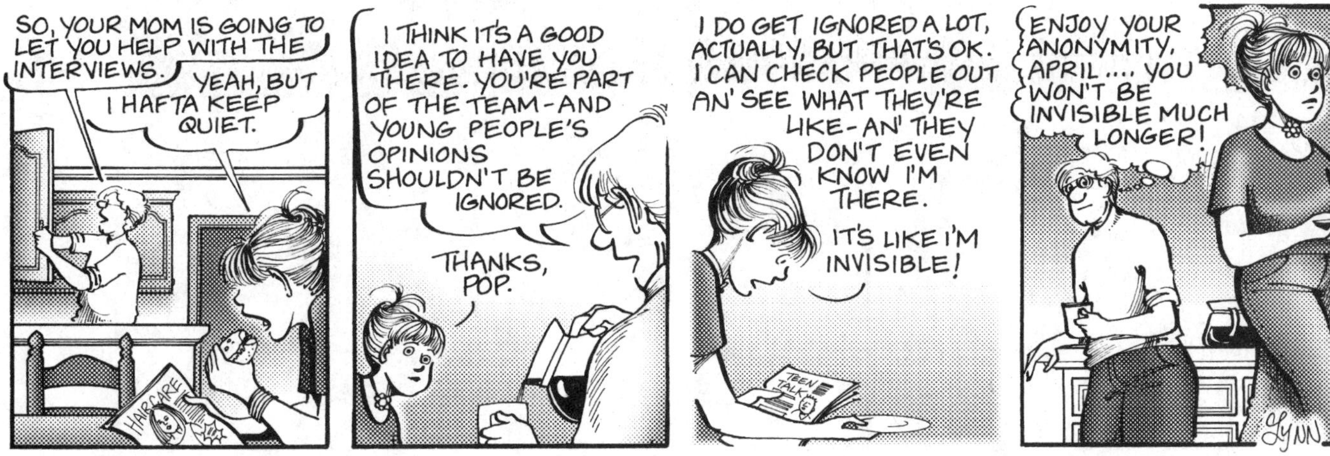
SO, YOUR MOM IS GOING TO LET YOU HELP WITH THE INTERVIEWS.
YEAH, BUT I HAFTA KEEP QUIET.
HAIRCARE!
I THINK IT'S A GOOD IDEA TO HAVE YOU THERE. YOU'RE PART OF THE TEAM - AND YOUNG PEOPLE'S OPINIONS SHOULDN'T BE IGNORED.
THANKS, POP.
I DO GET IGNORED A LOT, ACTUALLY, BUT THAT'S OK. I CAN CHECK PEOPLE OUT AN' SEE WHAT THEY'RE LIKE - AN' THEY DON'T EVEN KNOW I'M THERE.
IT'S LIKE I'M INVISIBLE!
TEEN TALK
ENJOY YOUR ANONYMITY, APRIL.... YOU WON'T BE INVISIBLE MUCH LONGER!
LYNN

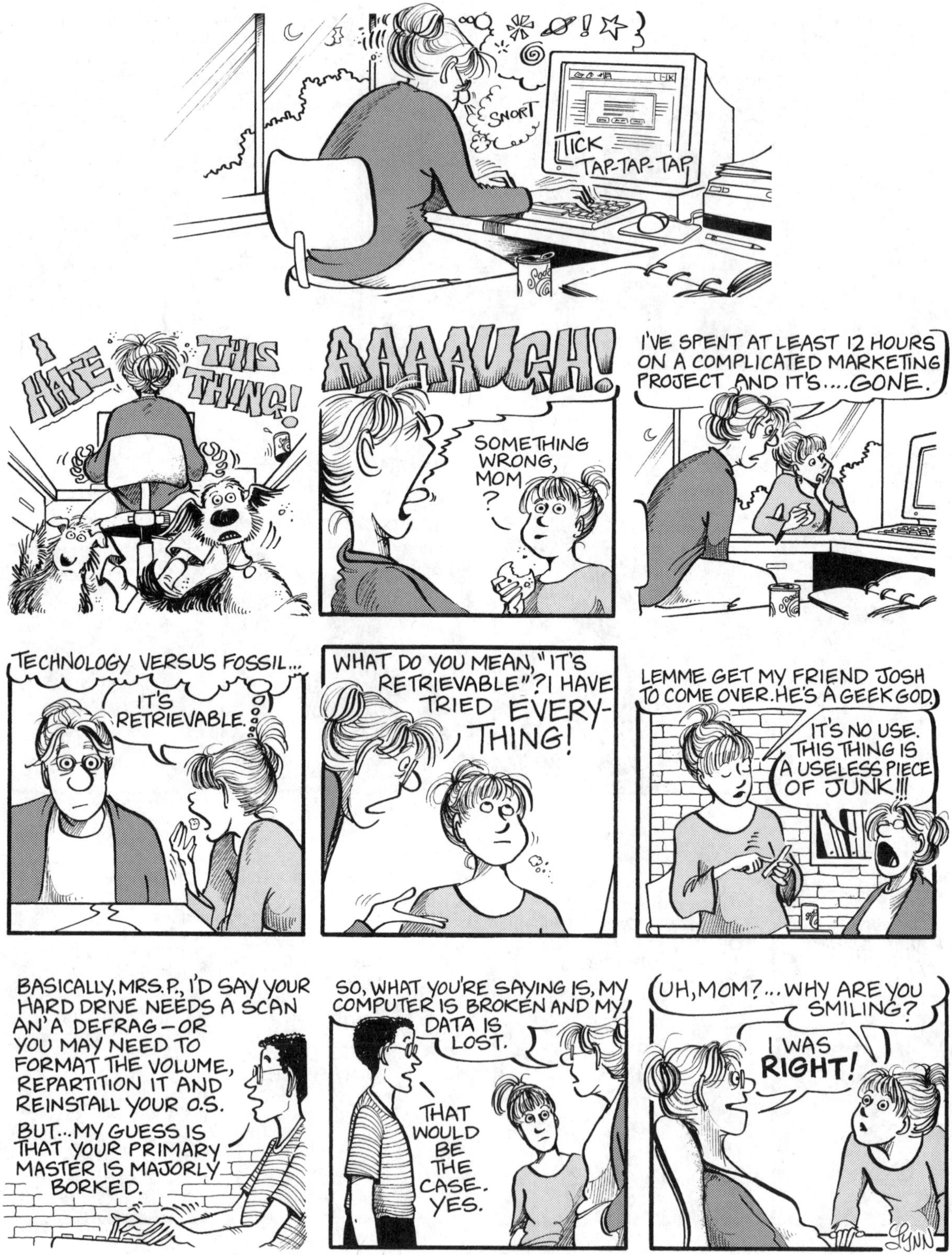
SNORT
TICK
TAP-TAP-TAP
I HATE THIS THING!
AAAAUGH!
SOMETHING WRONG, MOM ?
I'VE SPENT AT LEAST 12 HOURS ON A COMPLICATED MARKETING PROJECT AND IT'S.... GONE.
TECHNOLOGY VERSUS FOSSIL...
IT'S RETRIEVABLE.
WHAT DO YOU MEAN, "IT'S RETRIEVABLE"? I HAVE TRIED EVERY-THING!
LEMME GET MY FRIEND JOSH TO COME OVER. HE'S A GEEK GOD.
IT'S NO USE. THIS THING IS A USELESS PIECE OF JUNK!!!
BASICALLY, MRS. P., I'D SAY YOUR HARD DRIVE NEEDS A SCAN AN' A DEFRAG—OR YOU MAY NEED TO FORMAT THE VOLUME, REPARTITION IT AND REINSTALL YOUR O.S.
BUT... MY GUESS IS THAT YOUR PRIMARY MASTER IS MAJORLY BORKED.
SO, WHAT YOU'RE SAYING IS, MY COMPUTER IS BROKEN AND MY DATA IS LOST.
THAT WOULD BE THE CASE. YES.
UH, MOM?... WHY ARE YOU SMILING?
I WAS RIGHT!
LYNN

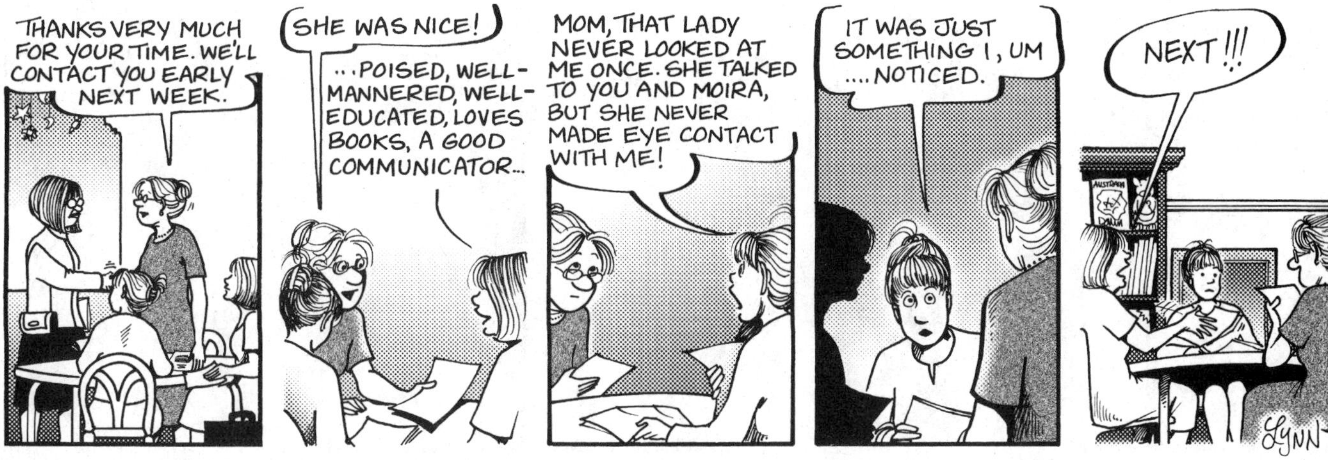
THANKS VERY MUCH FOR YOUR TIME. WE'LL CONTACT YOU EARLY NEXT WEEK.
SHE WAS NICE!
...POISED, WELL-MANNERED, WELL-EDUCATED, LOVES BOOKS, A GOOD COMMUNICATOR...
MOM, THAT LADY NEVER LOOKED AT ME ONCE. SHE TALKED TO YOU AND MOIRA, BUT SHE NEVER MADE EYE CONTACT WITH ME!
IT WAS JUST SOMETHING I, UM ....NOTICED.
NEXT!!!
LYNN

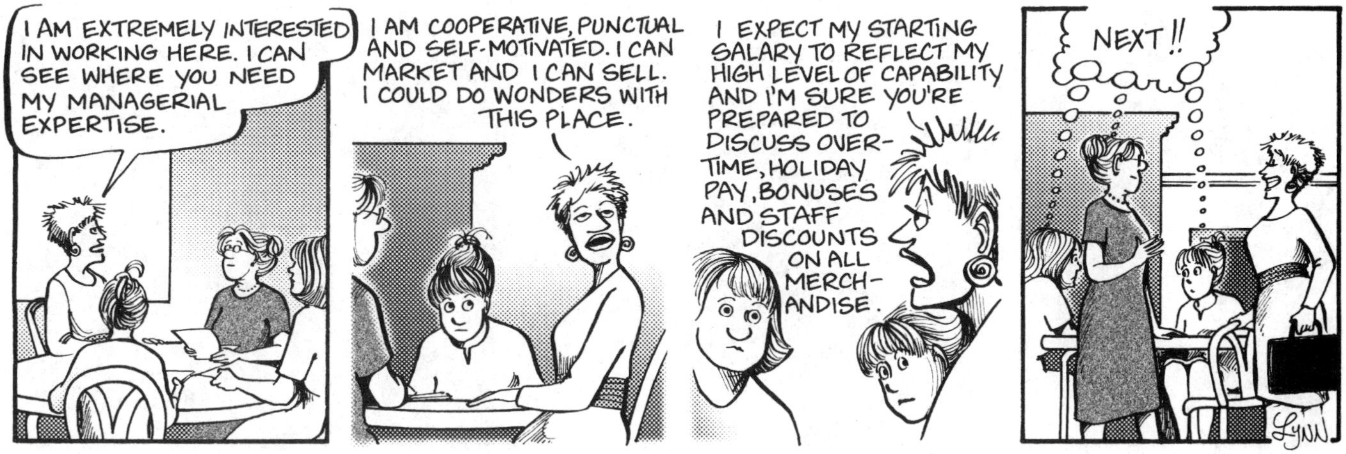
I AM EXTREMELY INTERESTED IN WORKING HERE. I CAN SEE WHERE YOU NEED MY MANAGERIAL EXPERTISE.
I AM COOPERATIVE, PUNCTUAL AND SELF-MOTIVATED. I CAN MARKET AND I CAN SELL. I COULD DO WONDERS WITH THIS PLACE.
I EXPECT MY STARTING SALARY TO REFLECT MY HIGH LEVEL OF CAPABILITY AND I'M SURE YOU'RE PREPARED TO DISCUSS OVER-TIME, HOLIDAY PAY, BONUSES AND STAFF DISCOUNTS ON ALL MERCH-ANDISE.
NEXT!!
LYNN

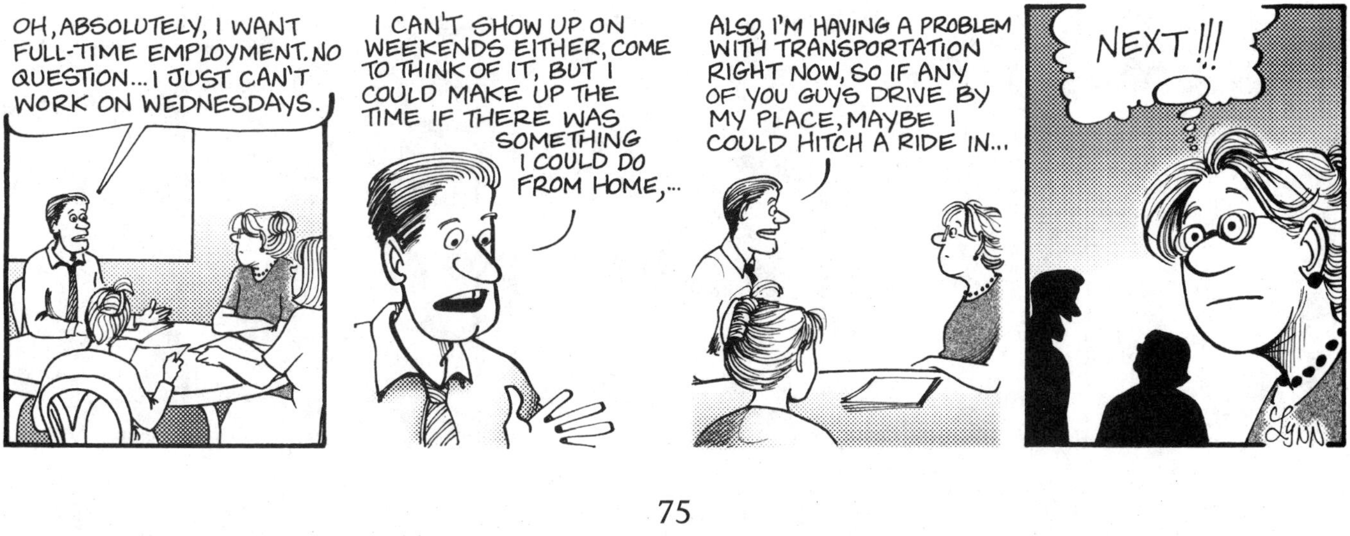
OH, ABSOLUTELY, I WANT FULL-TIME EMPLOYMENT. NO QUESTION... I JUST CAN'T WORK ON WEDNESDAYS.
I CAN'T SHOW UP ON WEEKENDS EITHER, COME TO THINK OF IT, BUT I COULD MAKE UP THE TIME IF THERE WAS SOMETHING I COULD DO FROM HOME,...
ALSO, I'M HAVING A PROBLEM WITH TRANSPORTATION RIGHT NOW, SO IF ANY OF YOU GUYS DRIVE BY MY PLACE, MAYBE I COULD HITCH A RIDE IN...
NEXT!!!
LYNN

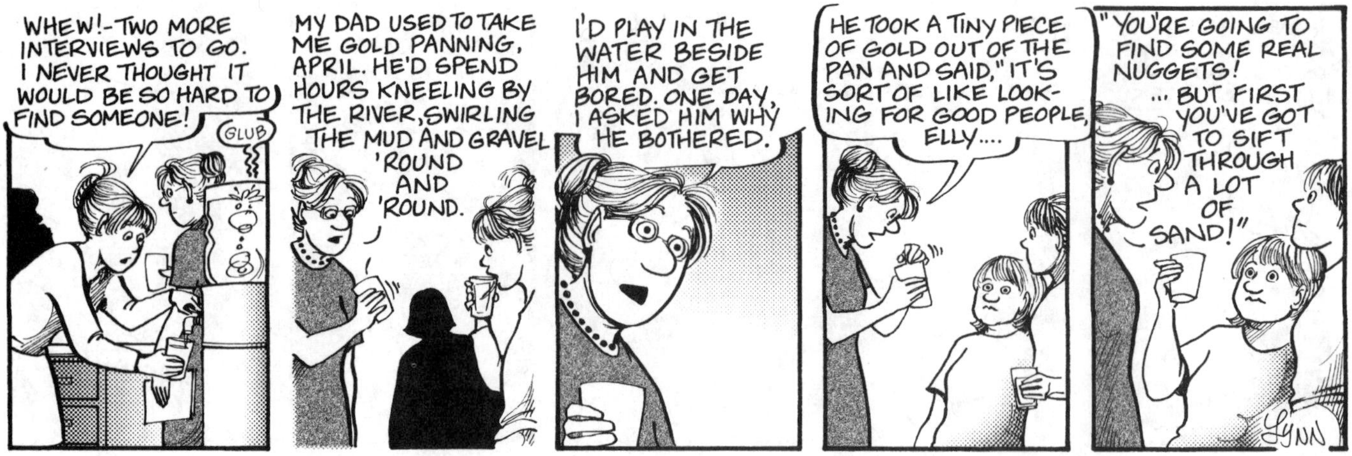
WHEW! - TWO MORE INTERVIEWS TO GO. I NEVER THOUGHT IT WOULD BE SO HARD TO FIND SOMEONE!
GLUB
MY DAD USED TO TAKE ME GOLD PANNING, APRIL. HE'D SPEND HOURS KNEELING BY THE RIVER, SWIRLING THE MUD AND GRAVEL 'ROUND AND 'ROUND.
I'D PLAY IN THE WATER BESIDE HIM AND GET BORED. ONE DAY, I ASKED HIM WHY HE BOTHERED.
HE TOOK A TINY PIECE OF GOLD OUT OF THE PAN AND SAID, "IT'S SORT OF LIKE LOOKING FOR GOOD PEOPLE, ELLY....
"YOU'RE GOING TO FIND SOME REAL NUGGETS! ... BUT FIRST YOU'VE GOT TO SIFT THROUGH A LOT OF SAND!"
LYNN

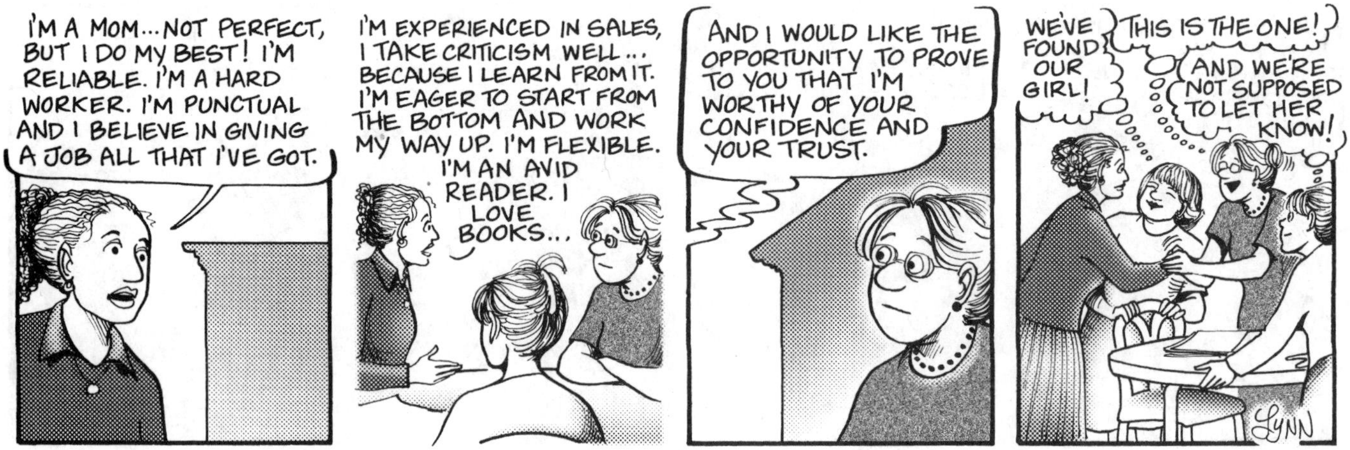
I'M A MOM... NOT PERFECT, BUT I DO MY BEST! I'M RELIABLE. I'M A HARD WORKER. I'M PUNCTUAL AND I BELIEVE IN GIVING A JOB ALL THAT I'VE GOT.
I'M EXPERIENCED IN SALES, I TAKE CRITICISM WELL... BECAUSE I LEARN FROM IT. I'M EAGER TO START FROM THE BOTTOM AND WORK MY WAY UP. I'M FLEXIBLE.
I'M AN AVID READER. I LOVE BOOKS...
AND I WOULD LIKE THE OPPORTUNITY TO PROVE TO YOU THAT I'M WORTHY OF YOUR CONFIDENCE AND YOUR TRUST.
WE'VE FOUND OUR GIRL!
THIS IS THE ONE!
AND WE'RE NOT SUPPOSED TO LET HER KNOW!
LYNN

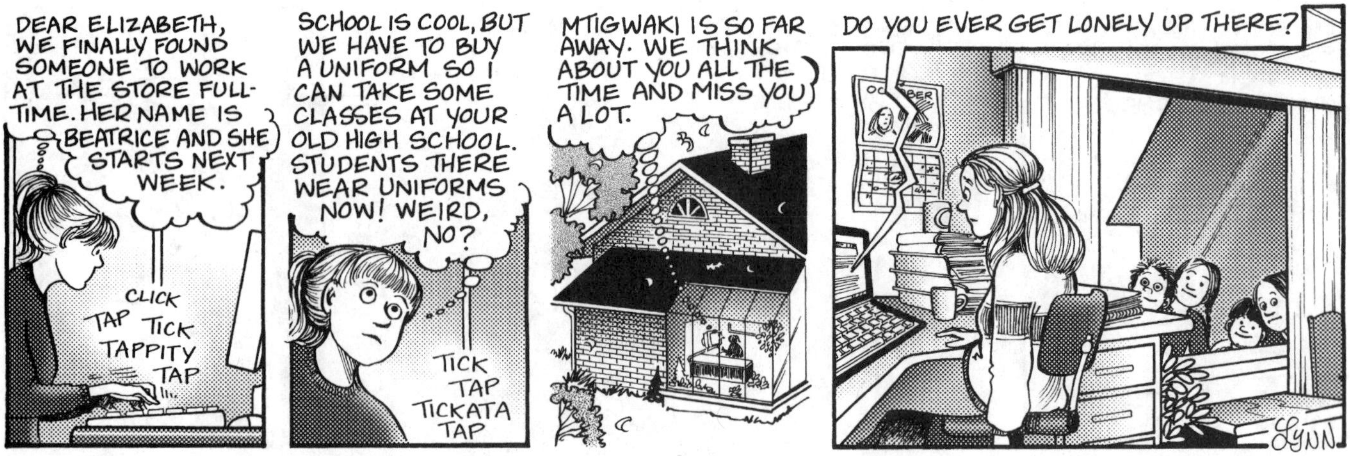
DEAR ELIZABETH, WE FINALLY FOUND SOMEONE TO WORK AT THE STORE FULL-TIME. HER NAME IS BEATRICE AND SHE STARTS NEXT WEEK.
CLICK TAP TICK TAPPITY TAP
SCHOOL IS COOL, BUT WE HAVE TO BUY A UNIFORM SO I CAN TAKE SOME CLASSES AT YOUR OLD HIGH SCHOOL. STUDENTS THERE WEAR UNIFORMS NOW! WEIRD, NO?
TICK TAP TICKATA TAP
MTIGWAKI IS SO FAR AWAY. WE THINK ABOUT YOU ALL THE TIME AND MISS YOU A LOT.
DO YOU EVER GET LONELY UP THERE?
LYNN

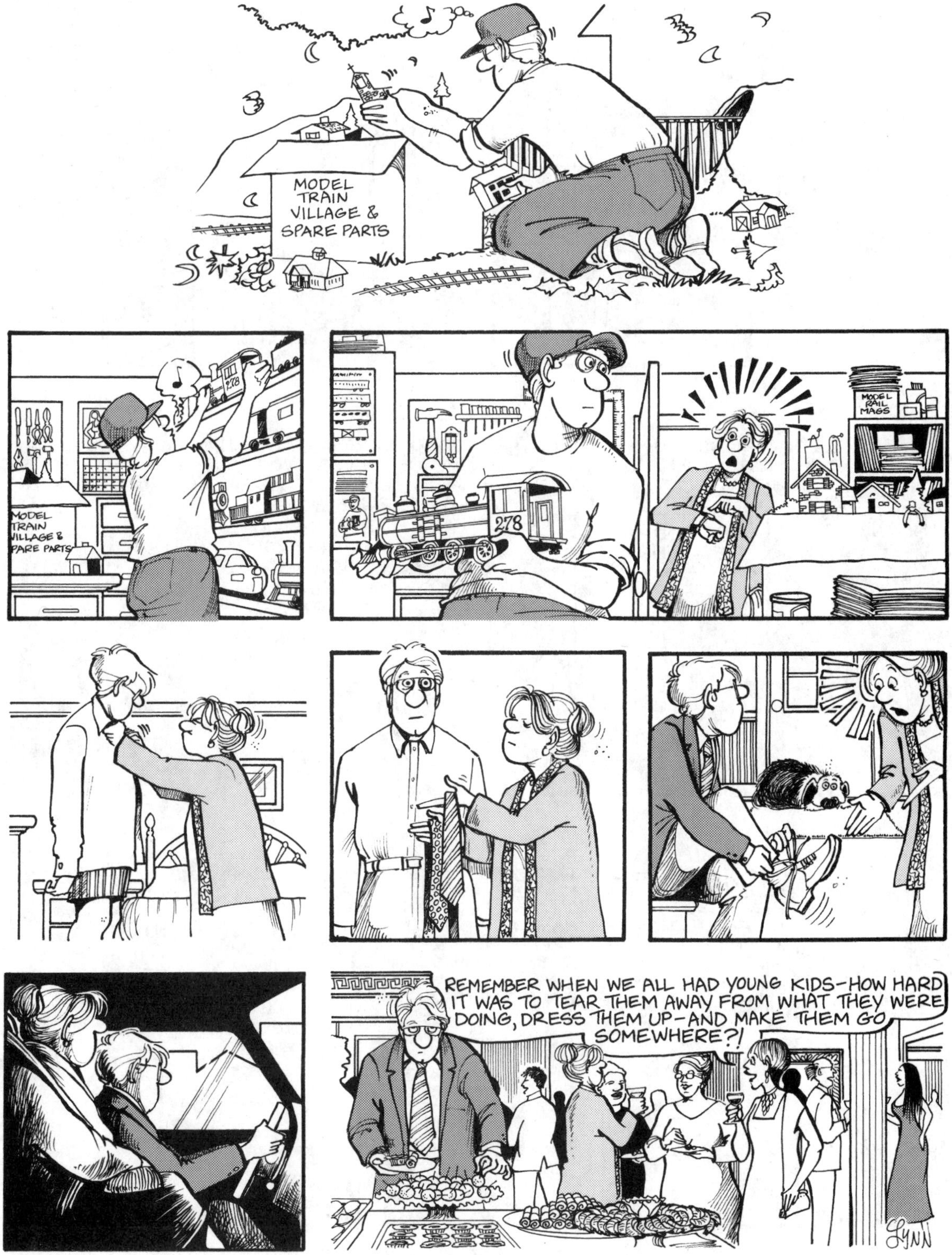
MODEL TRAIN VILLAGE & SPARE PARTS
278
MODEL RAIL MAGS
REMEMBER WHEN WE ALL HAD YOUNG KIDS–HOW HARD IT WAS TO TEAR THEM AWAY FROM WHAT THEY WERE DOING, DRESS THEM UP–AND MAKE THEM GO SOMEWHERE?!
LYNN

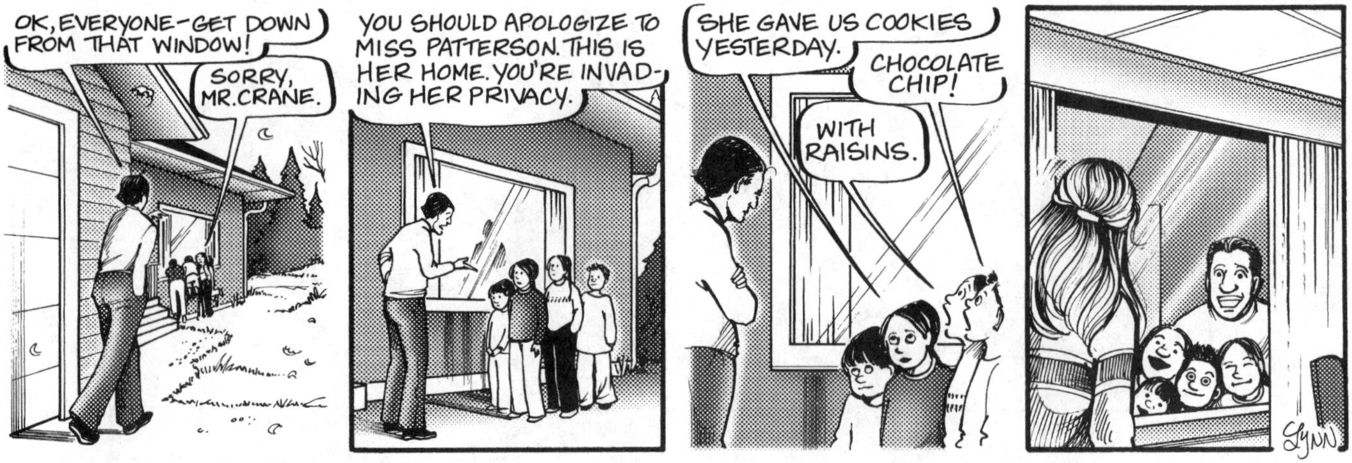
OK, EVERYONE-GET DOWN FROM THAT WINDOW!
SORRY, MR.CRANE.
YOU SHOULD APOLOGIZE TO MISS PATTERSON. THIS IS HER HOME. YOU'RE INVAD-ING HER PRIVACY.
SHE GAVE US COOKIES YESTERDAY.
CHOCOLATE CHIP!
WITH RAISINS.
LYNN

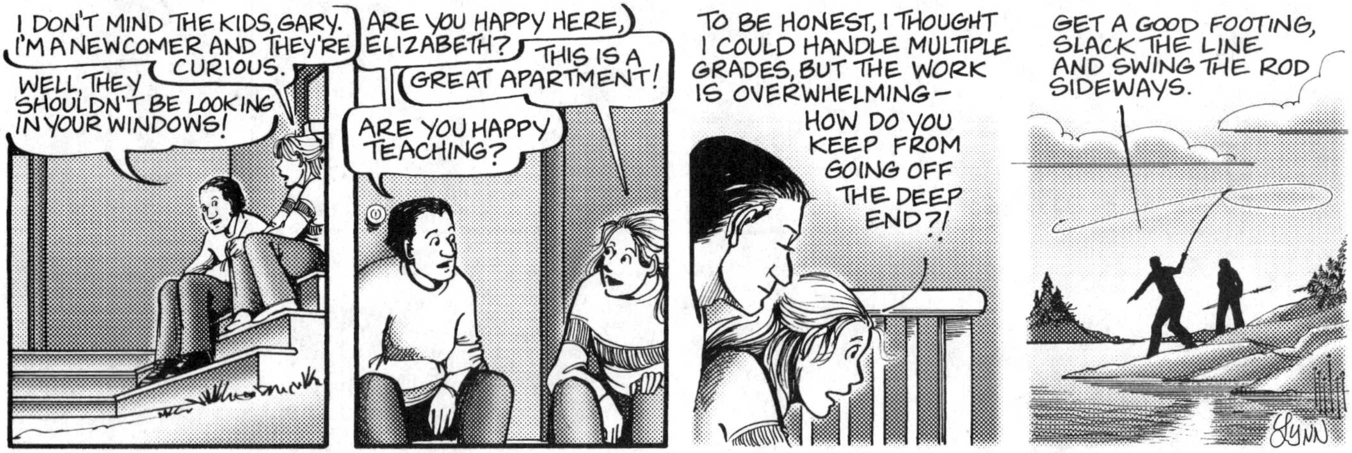
I DON'T MIND THE KIDS, GARY. I'M A NEWCOMER AND THEY'RE CURIOUS.
WELL, THEY SHOULDN'T BE LOOKING IN YOUR WINDOWS!
ARE YOU HAPPY HERE, ELIZABETH?
THIS IS A GREAT APARTMENT!
ARE YOU HAPPY TEACHING?
TO BE HONEST, I THOUGHT I COULD HANDLE MULTIPLE GRADES, BUT THE WORK IS OVERWHELMING—
HOW DO YOU KEEP FROM GOING OFF THE DEEP END?!
GET A GOOD FOOTING, SLACK THE LINE AND SWING THE ROD SIDEWAYS.
LYNN

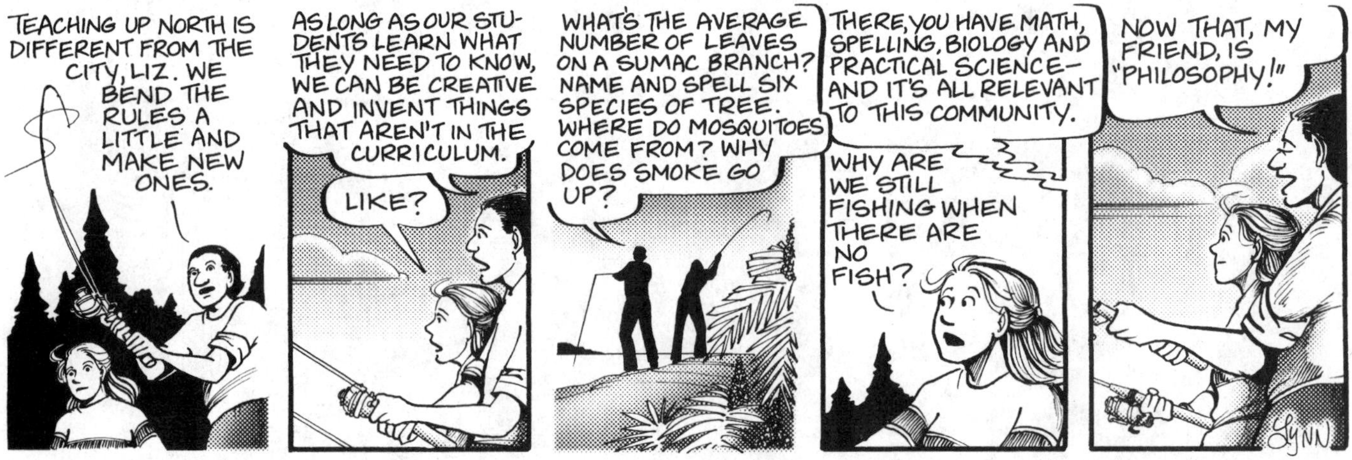
TEACHING UP NORTH IS DIFFERENT FROM THE CITY, LIZ. WE BEND THE RULES A LITTLE AND MAKE NEW ONES.
AS LONG AS OUR STU-DENTS LEARN WHAT THEY NEED TO KNOW, WE CAN BE CREATIVE AND INVENT THINGS THAT AREN'T IN THE CURRICULUM.
LIKE?
WHAT'S THE AVERAGE NUMBER OF LEAVES ON A SUMAC BRANCH? NAME AND SPELL SIX SPECIES OF TREE. WHERE DO MOSQUITOES COME FROM? WHY DOES SMOKE GO UP?
THERE, YOU HAVE MATH, SPELLING, BIOLOGY AND PRACTICAL SCIENCE—AND IT'S ALL RELEVANT TO THIS COMMUNITY.
WHY ARE WE STILL FISHING WHEN THERE ARE NO FISH?
NOW THAT, MY FRIEND, IS "PHILOSOPHY!"
LYNN

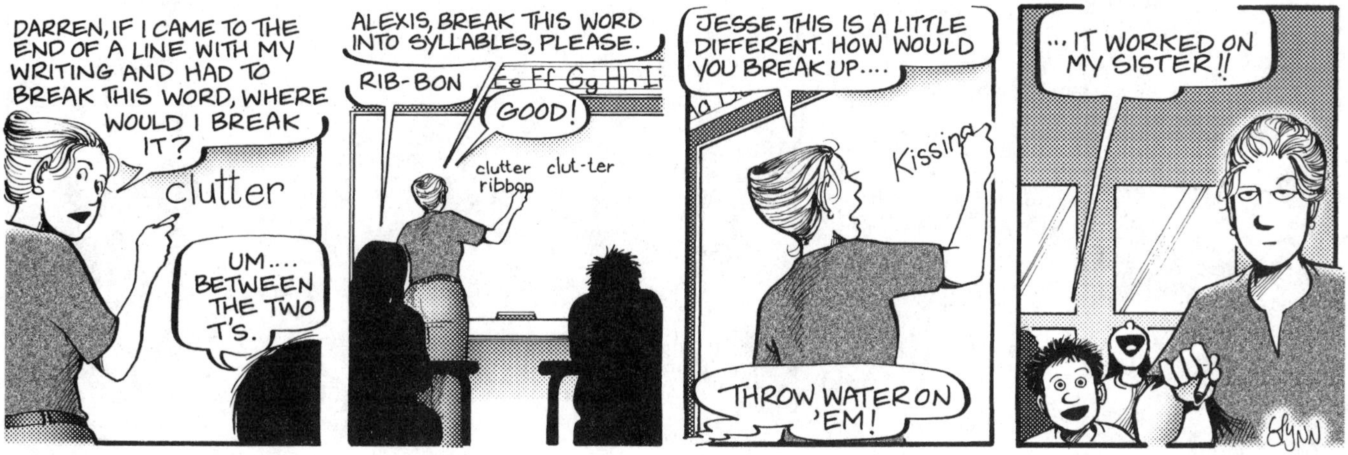
DARREN, IF I CAME TO THE END OF A LINE WITH MY WRITING AND HAD TO BREAK THIS WORD, WHERE WOULD I BREAK IT?
clutter
UM.... BETWEEN THE TWO T'S.
ALEXIS, BREAK THIS WORD INTO SYLLABLES, PLEASE.
RIB-BON
GOOD!
clutter clut-ter
ribbon
JESSE, THIS IS A LITTLE DIFFERENT. HOW WOULD YOU BREAK UP....
Kissing
THROW WATER ON 'EM!
...IT WORKED ON MY SISTER!!

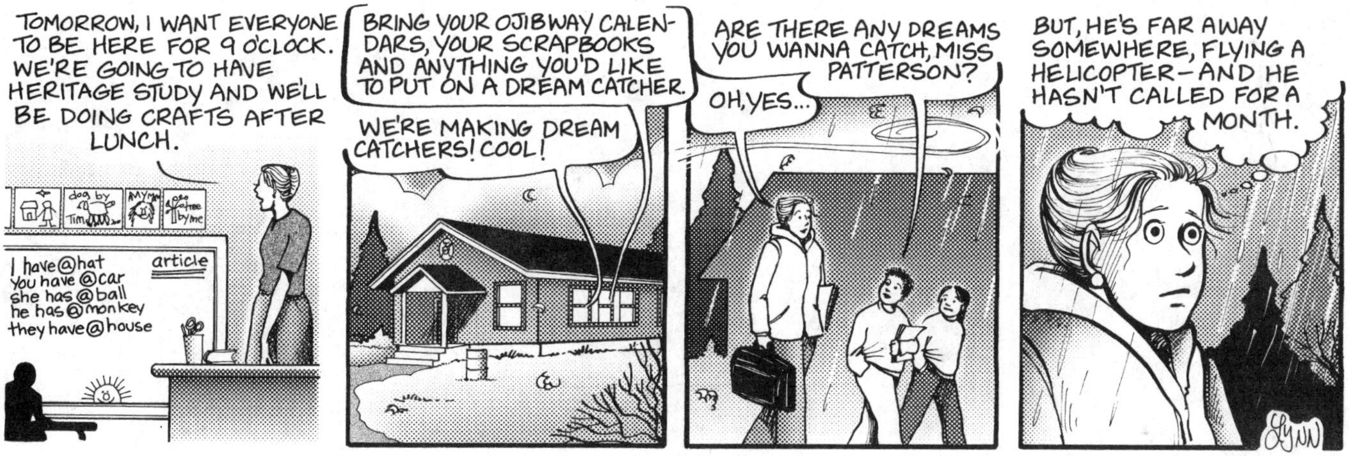
TOMORROW, I WANT EVERYONE TO BE HERE FOR 9 O'CLOCK. WE'RE GOING TO HAVE HERITAGE STUDY AND WE'LL BE DOING CRAFTS AFTER LUNCH.
article
I have @hat
You have @car
she has @ball
he has @monkey
they have @house
BRING YOUR OJIBWAY CALENDARS, YOUR SCRAPBOOKS AND ANYTHING YOU'D LIKE TO PUT ON A DREAM CATCHER.
WE'RE MAKING DREAM CATCHERS! COOL!
ARE THERE ANY DREAMS YOU WANNA CATCH, MISS PATTERSON?
OH, YES...
BUT, HE'S FAR AWAY SOMEWHERE, FLYING A HELICOPTER—AND HE HASN'T CALLED FOR A MONTH.

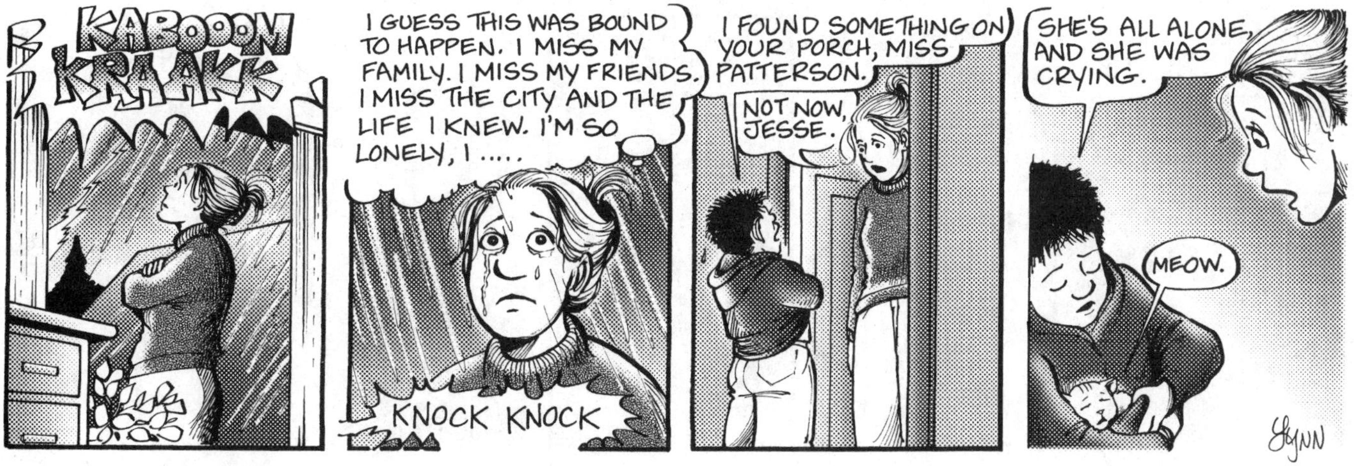
KABOOOM
KRAAKK
I GUESS THIS WAS BOUND TO HAPPEN. I MISS MY FAMILY. I MISS MY FRIENDS. I MISS THE CITY AND THE LIFE I KNEW. I'M SO LONELY, I .....
KNOCK KNOCK
I FOUND SOMETHING ON YOUR PORCH, MISS PATTERSON.
NOT NOW, JESSE.
SHE'S ALL ALONE, AND SHE WAS CRYING.
MEOW.

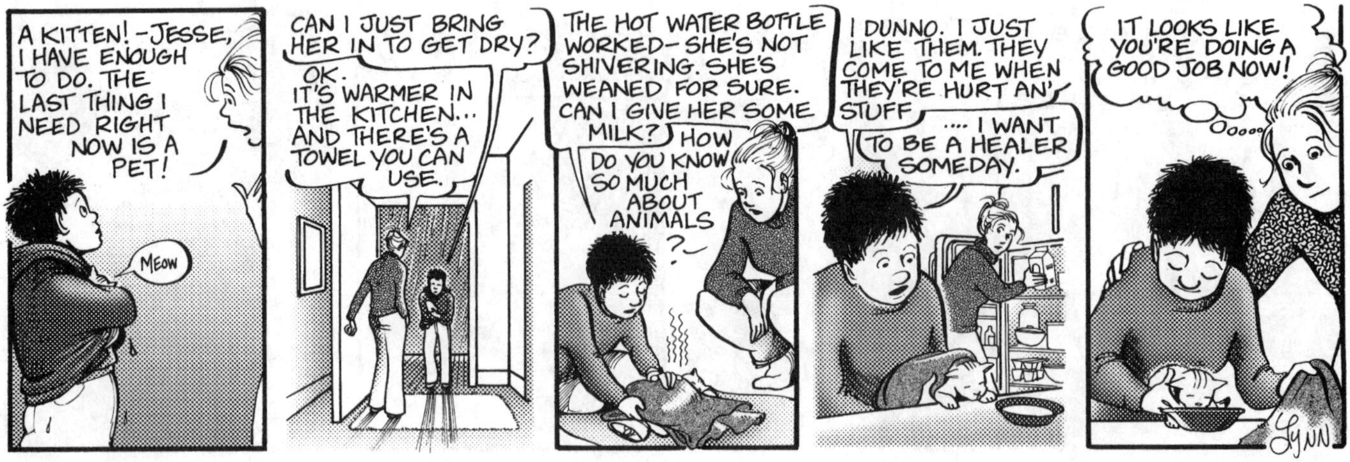
A KITTEN! -JESSE, I HAVE ENOUGH TO DO. THE LAST THING I NEED RIGHT NOW IS A PET!
MEOW
CAN I JUST BRING HER IN TO GET DRY?
OK. IT'S WARMER IN THE KITCHEN... AND THERE'S A TOWEL YOU CAN USE.
THE HOT WATER BOTTLE WORKED- SHE'S NOT SHIVERING. SHE'S WEANED FOR SURE. CAN I GIVE HER SOME MILK?
HOW DO YOU KNOW SO MUCH ABOUT ANIMALS ?
I DUNNO. I JUST LIKE THEM. THEY COME TO ME WHEN THEY'RE HURT AN' STUFF
.... I WANT TO BE A HEALER SOMEDAY.
IT LOOKS LIKE YOU'RE DOING A GOOD JOB NOW!
LYNN

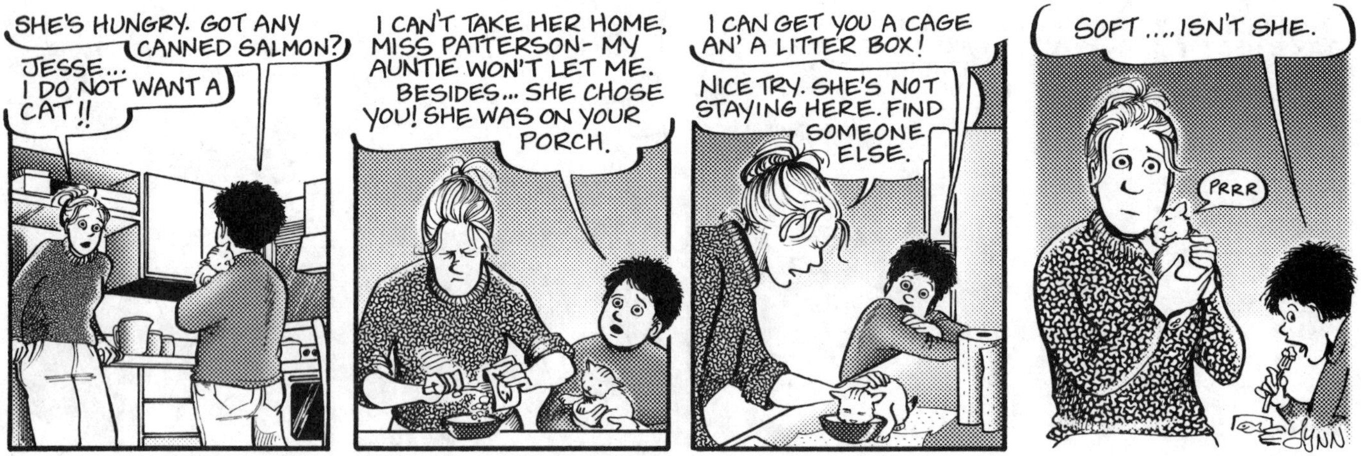
SHE'S HUNGRY. GOT ANY CANNED SALMON?
JESSE... I DO NOT WANT A CAT!!
I CAN'T TAKE HER HOME, MISS PATTERSON- MY AUNTIE WON'T LET ME. BESIDES... SHE CHOSE YOU! SHE WAS ON YOUR PORCH.
I CAN GET YOU A CAGE AN' A LITTER BOX!
NICE TRY. SHE'S NOT STAYING HERE. FIND SOMEONE ELSE.
SOFT .... ISN'T SHE.
PRRR
LYNN

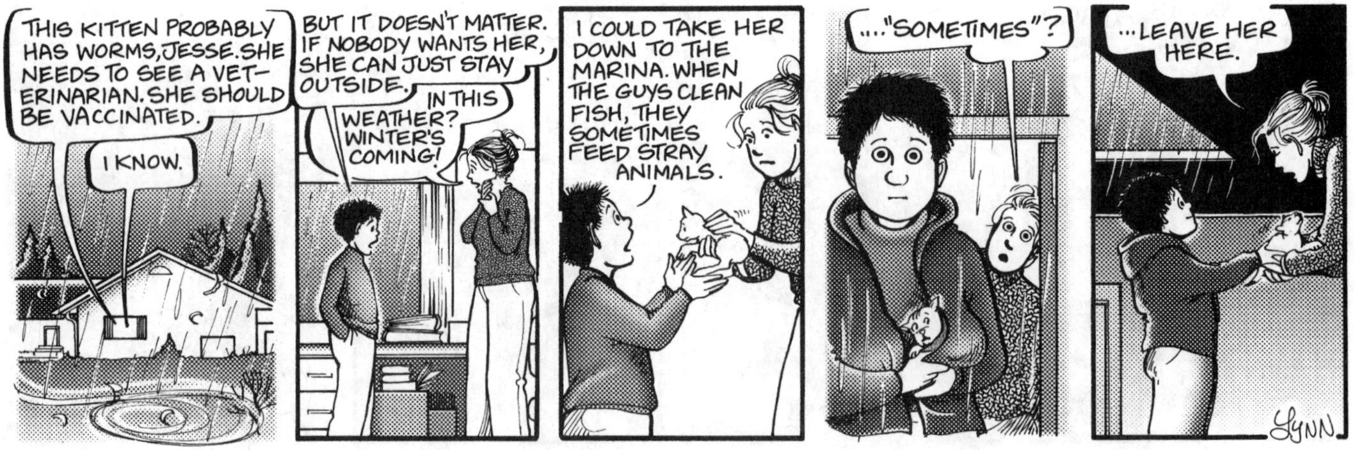
THIS KITTEN PROBABLY HAS WORMS, JESSE. SHE NEEDS TO SEE A VET-ERINARIAN. SHE SHOULD BE VACCINATED.
I KNOW.
BUT IT DOESN'T MATTER. IF NOBODY WANTS HER, SHE CAN JUST STAY OUTSIDE.
IN THIS WEATHER? WINTER'S COMING!
I COULD TAKE HER DOWN TO THE MARINA. WHEN THE GUYS CLEAN FISH, THEY SOMETIMES FEED STRAY ANIMALS.
...."SOMETIMES"?
...LEAVE HER HERE.
LYNN

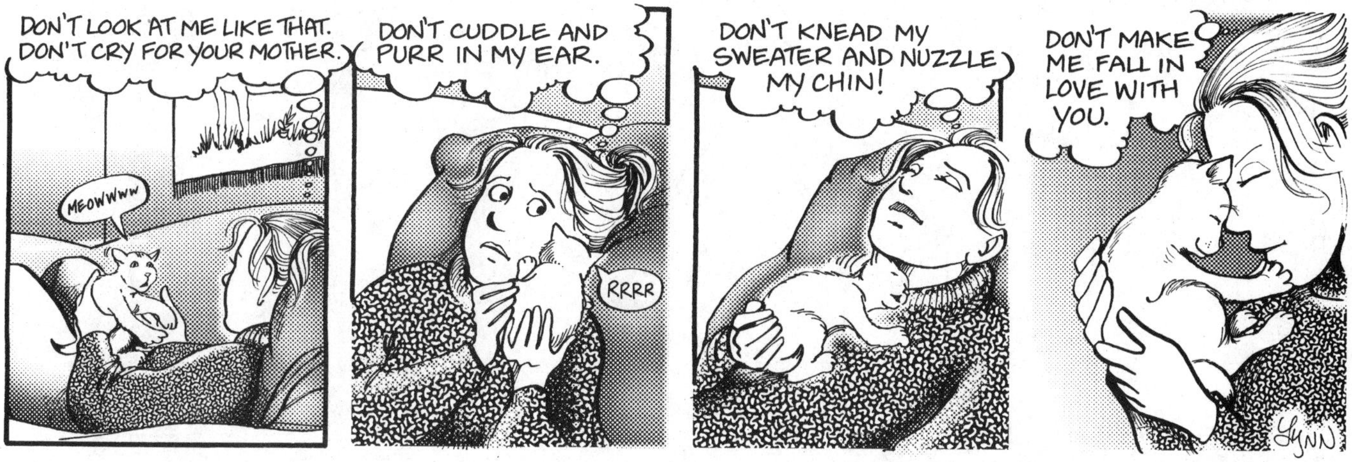
DON'T LOOK AT ME LIKE THAT. DON'T CRY FOR YOUR MOTHER.
MEOWWWW
DON'T CUDDLE AND PURR IN MY EAR.
RRRR
DON'T KNEAD MY SWEATER AND NUZZLE MY CHIN!
DON'T MAKE ME FALL IN LOVE WITH YOU.

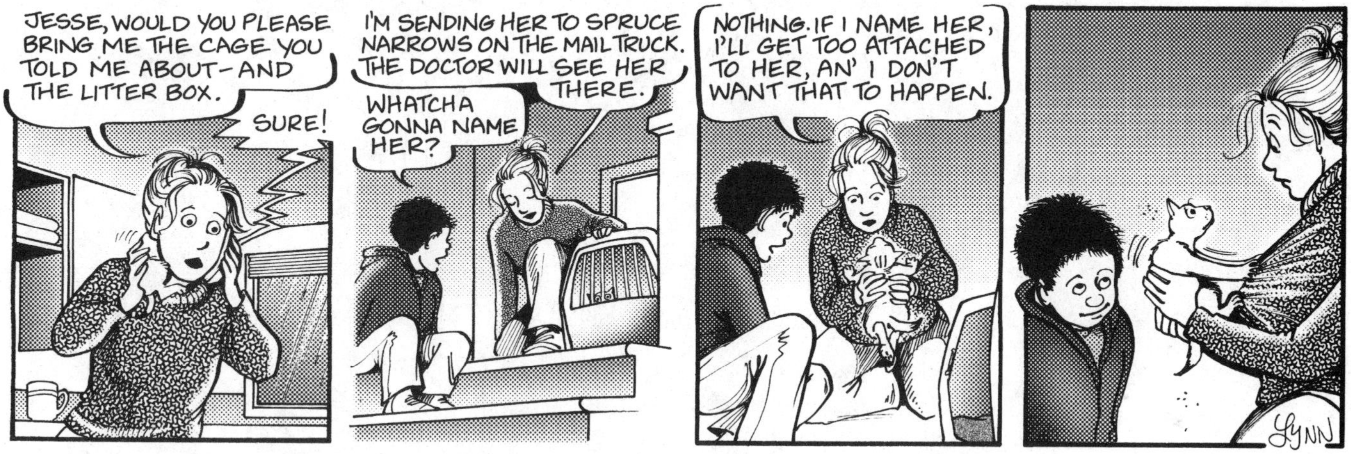
JESSE, WOULD YOU PLEASE BRING ME THE CAGE YOU TOLD ME ABOUT– AND THE LITTER BOX.
SURE!
I'M SENDING HER TO SPRUCE NARROWS ON THE MAIL TRUCK. THE DOCTOR WILL SEE HER THERE.
WHATCHA GONNA NAME HER?
NOTHING. IF I NAME HER, I'LL GET TOO ATTACHED TO HER, AN' I DON'T WANT THAT TO HAPPEN.

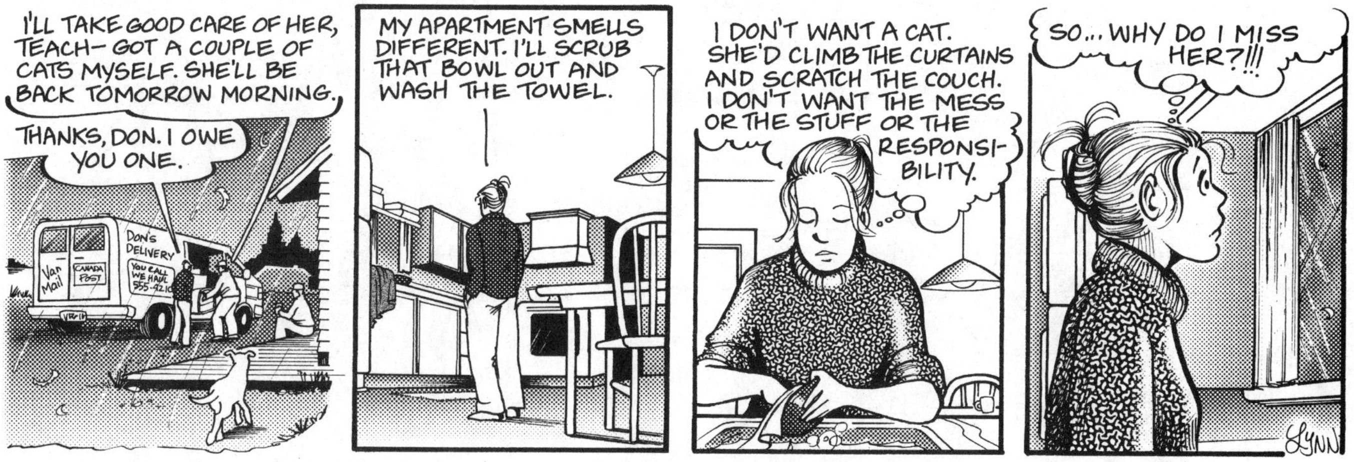
I'LL TAKE GOOD CARE OF HER, TEACH– GOT A COUPLE OF CATS MYSELF. SHE'LL BE BACK TOMORROW MORNING.
THANKS, DON. I OWE YOU ONE.
DON'S DELIVERY
MY APARTMENT SMELLS DIFFERENT. I'LL SCRUB THAT BOWL OUT AND WASH THE TOWEL.
I DON'T WANT A CAT. SHE'D CLIMB THE CURTAINS AND SCRATCH THE COUCH. I DON'T WANT THE MESS OR THE STUFF OR THE RESPONSI-BILITY.
SO... WHY DO I MISS HER?!!!

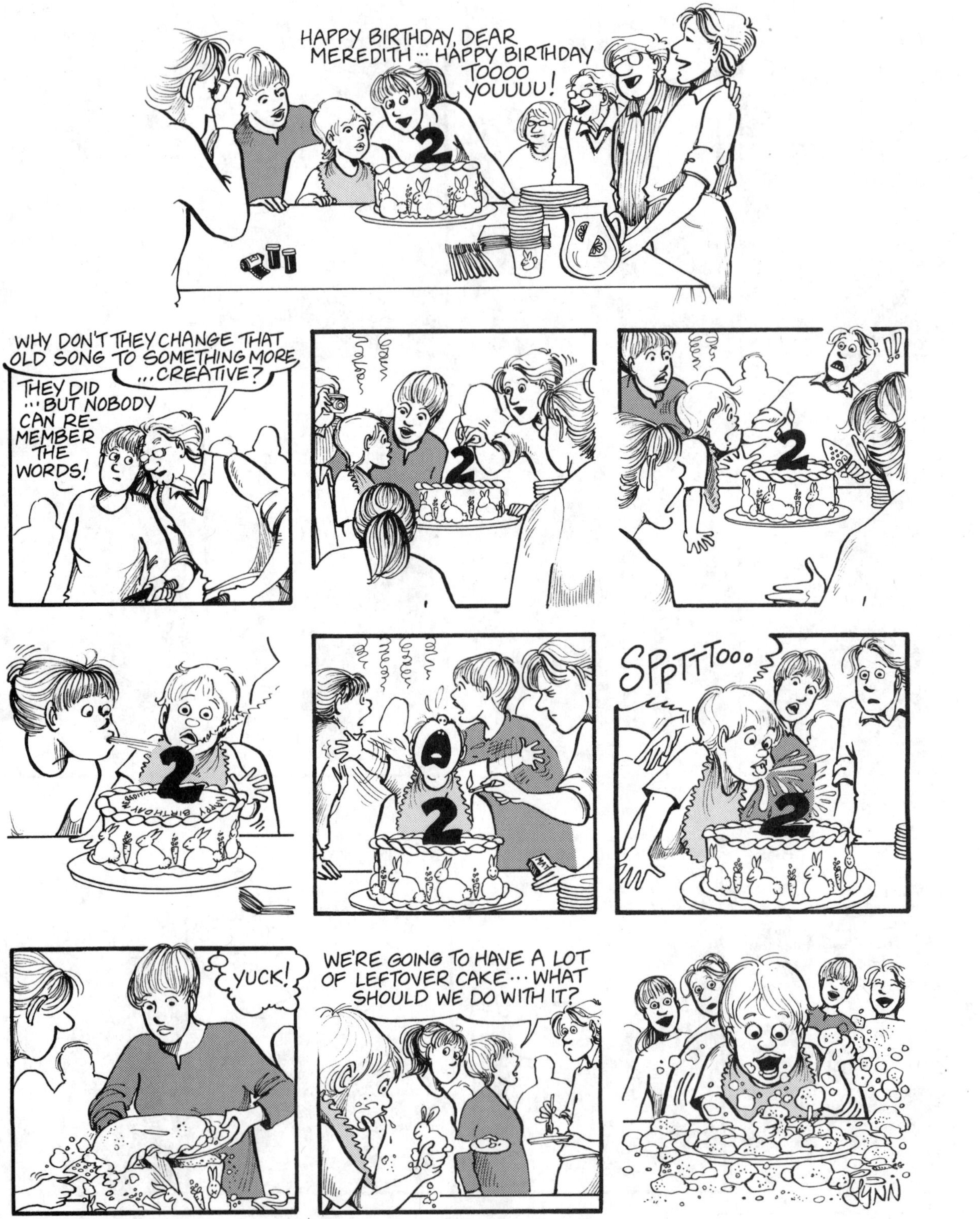

HAPPY BIRTHDAY, DEAR MEREDITH ... HAPPY BIRTHDAY TOOOO YOUUUU!
WHY DON'T THEY CHANGE THAT OLD SONG TO SOMETHING MORE ... CREATIVE?
THEY DID ... BUT NOBODY CAN REMEMBER THE WORDS!
!!
SPPTTTOoo
YUCK!
WE'RE GOING TO HAVE A LOT OF LEFTOVER CAKE ... WHAT SHOULD WE DO WITH IT?
LYNN

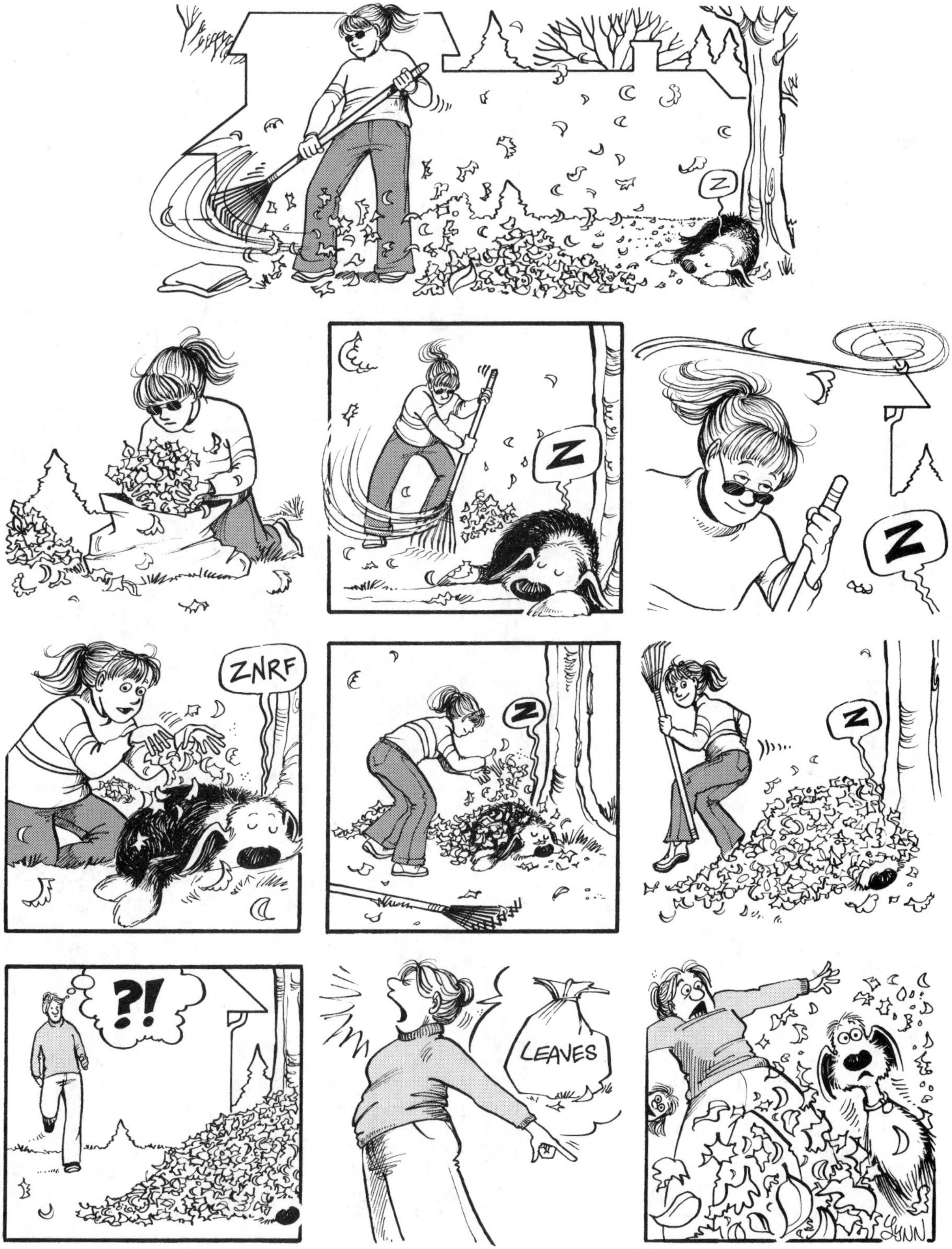

Z
Z
Z
ZNRF
Z
Z
?!
LEAVES
LYNN

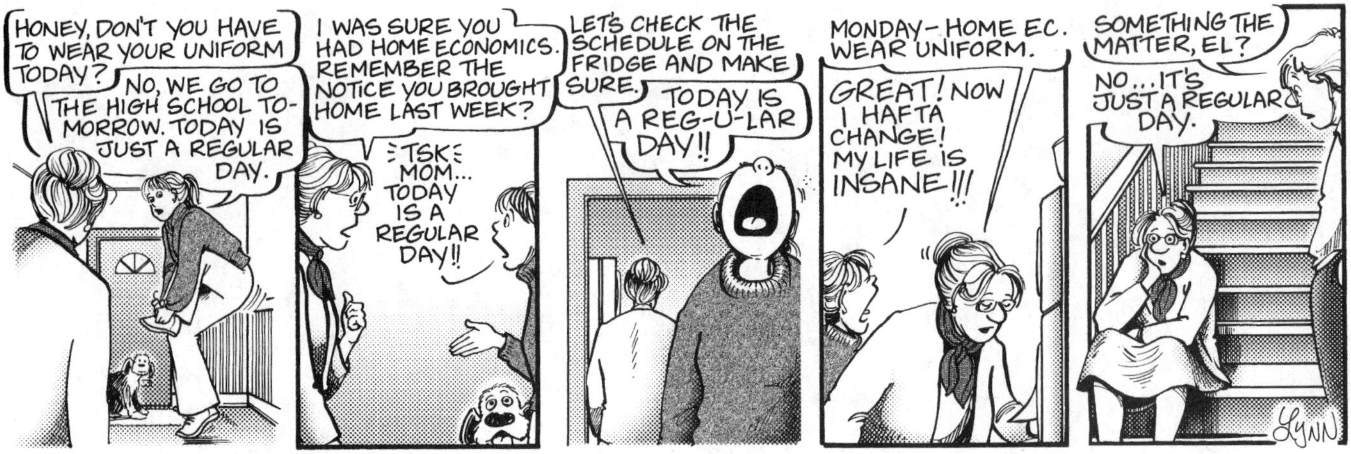
HONEY, DON'T YOU HAVE TO WEAR YOUR UNIFORM TODAY?
NO, WE GO TO THE HIGH SCHOOL TO-MORROW. TODAY IS JUST A REGULAR DAY.
I WAS SURE YOU HAD HOME ECONOMICS. REMEMBER THE NOTICE YOU BROUGHT HOME LAST WEEK?
TSK MOM... TODAY IS A REGULAR DAY!!
LET'S CHECK THE SCHEDULE ON THE FRIDGE AND MAKE SURE.
TODAY IS A REG-U-LAR DAY!!
MONDAY- HOME EC. WEAR UNIFORM.
GREAT! NOW I HAFTA CHANGE! MY LIFE IS INSANE!!!
SOMETHING THE MATTER, EL?
NO... IT'S JUST A REGULAR DAY.
LYNN

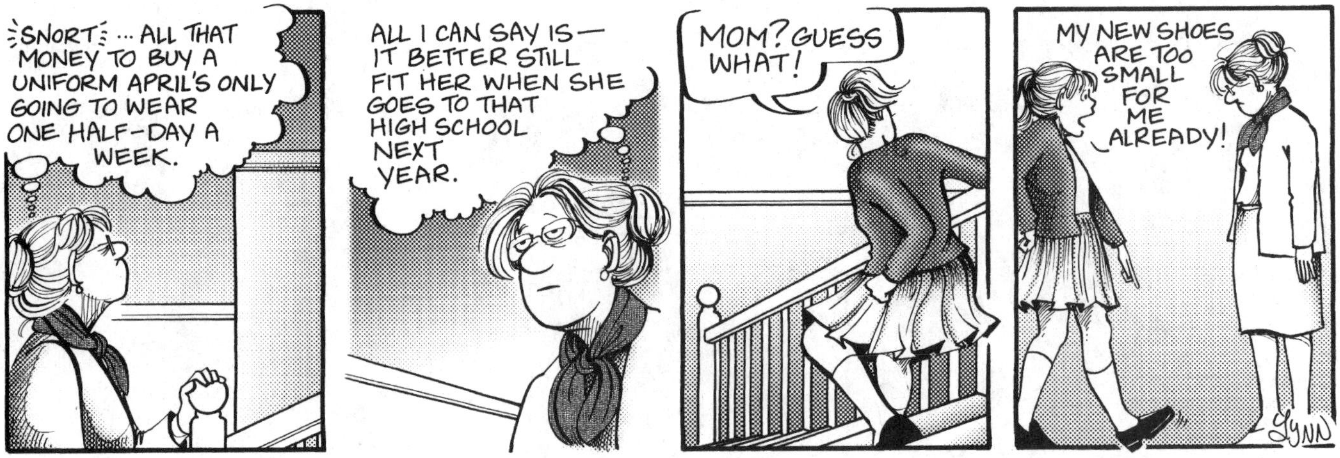
SNORT ... ALL THAT MONEY TO BUY A UNIFORM APRIL'S ONLY GOING TO WEAR ONE HALF-DAY A WEEK.
ALL I CAN SAY IS— IT BETTER STILL FIT HER WHEN SHE GOES TO THAT HIGH SCHOOL NEXT YEAR.
MOM? GUESS WHAT!
MY NEW SHOES ARE TOO SMALL FOR ME ALREADY!
LYNN

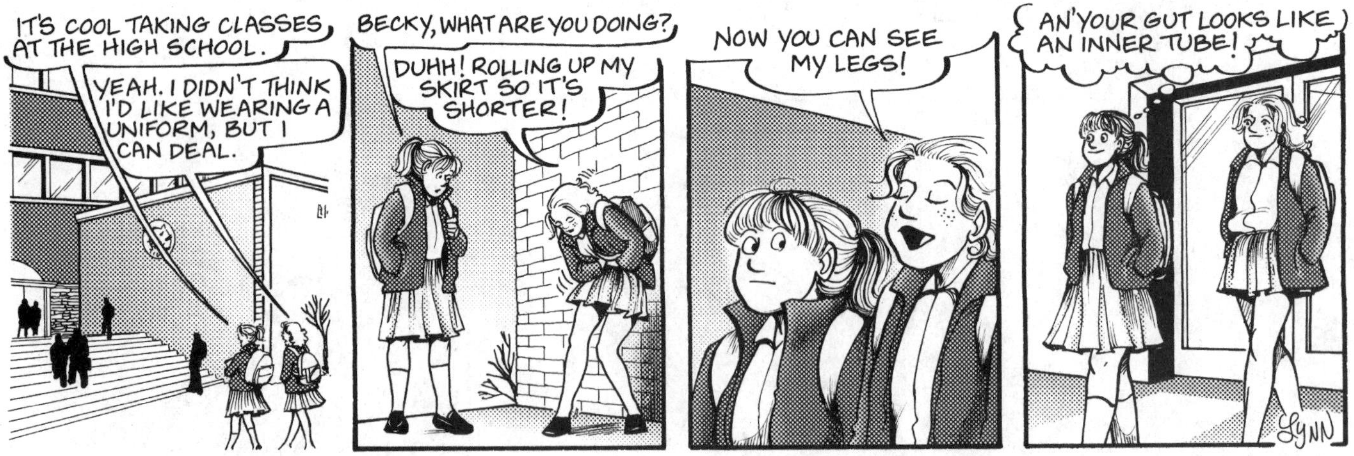
IT'S COOL TAKING CLASSES AT THE HIGH SCHOOL.
YEAH. I DIDN'T THINK I'D LIKE WEARING A UNIFORM, BUT I CAN DEAL.
BECKY, WHAT ARE YOU DOING?
DUHH! ROLLING UP MY SKIRT SO IT'S SHORTER!
NOW YOU CAN SEE MY LEGS!
AN' YOUR GUT LOOKS LIKE AN INNER TUBE!
LYNN

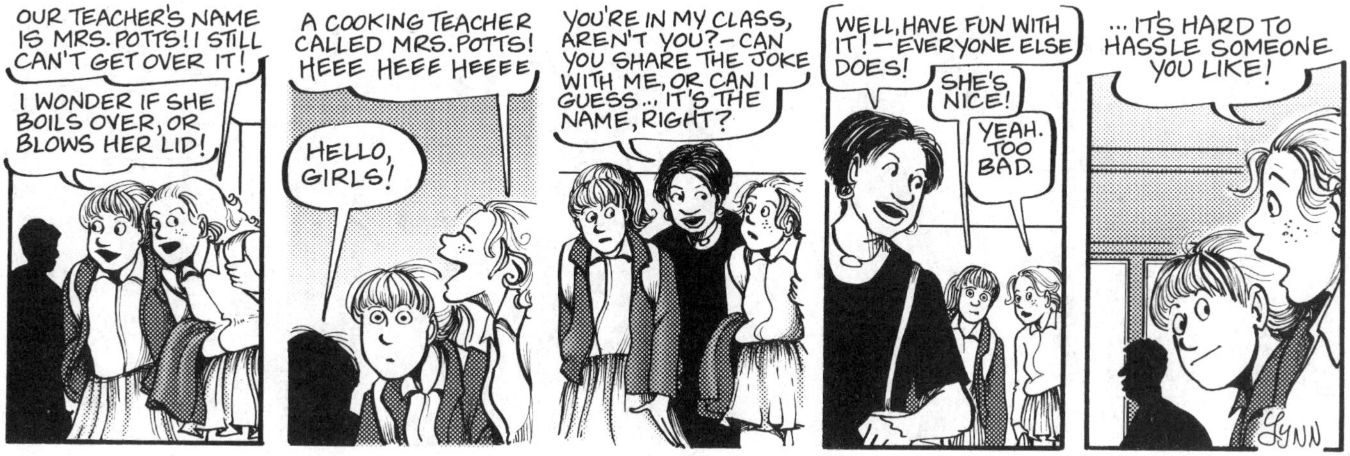
OUR TEACHER'S NAME IS MRS. POTTS! I STILL CAN'T GET OVER IT!
I WONDER IF SHE BOILS OVER, OR BLOWS HER LID!
A COOKING TEACHER CALLED MRS. POTTS! HEEE HEEE HEEEE
HELLO, GIRLS!
YOU'RE IN MY CLASS, AREN'T YOU?—CAN YOU SHARE THE JOKE WITH ME, OR CAN I GUESS... IT'S THE NAME, RIGHT?
WELL, HAVE FUN WITH IT!—EVERYONE ELSE DOES!
SHE'S NICE!
YEAH. TOO BAD.
...IT'S HARD TO HASSLE SOMEONE YOU LIKE!

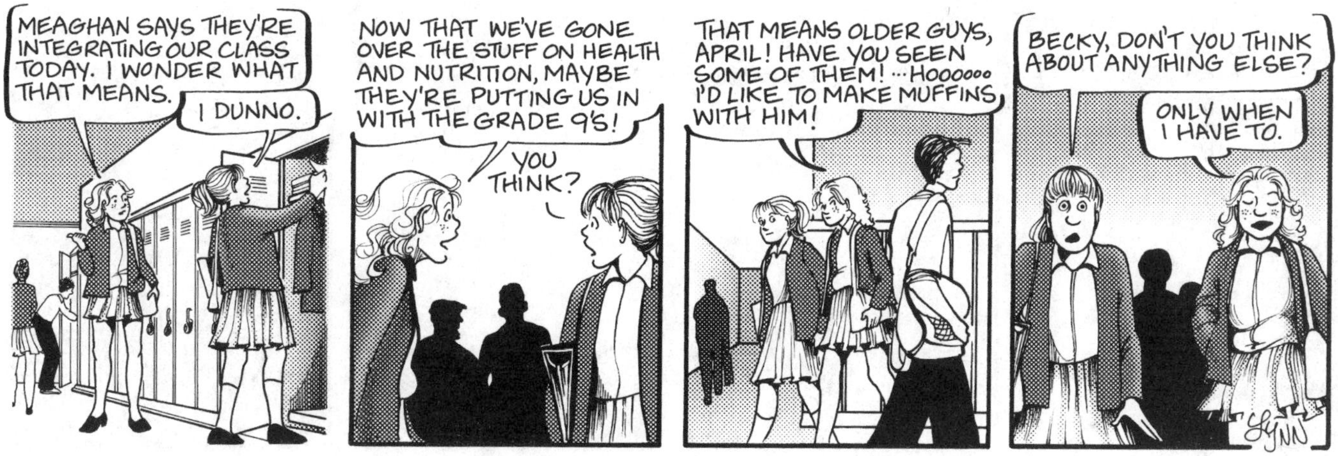
MEAGHAN SAYS THEY'RE INTEGRATING OUR CLASS TODAY. I WONDER WHAT THAT MEANS.
I DUNNO.
NOW THAT WE'VE GONE OVER THE STUFF ON HEALTH AND NUTRITION, MAYBE THEY'RE PUTTING US IN WITH THE GRADE 9'S!
YOU THINK?
THAT MEANS OLDER GUYS, APRIL! HAVE YOU SEEN SOME OF THEM! ...Hoooooo I'D LIKE TO MAKE MUFFINS WITH HIM!
BECKY, DON'T YOU THINK ABOUT ANYTHING ELSE?
ONLY WHEN I HAVE TO.

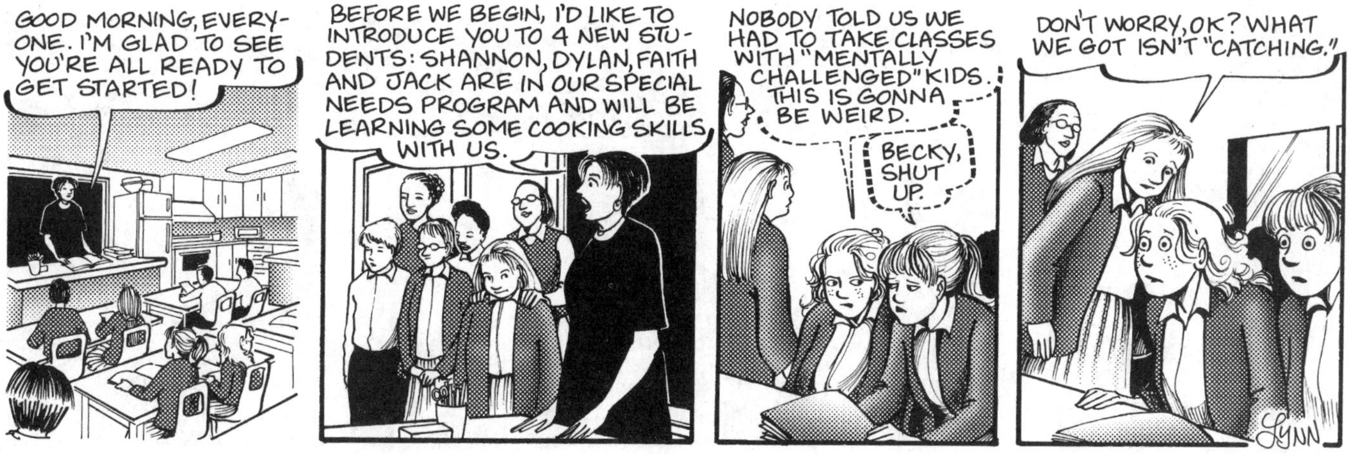
GOOD MORNING, EVERY-ONE. I'M GLAD TO SEE YOU'RE ALL READY TO GET STARTED!
BEFORE WE BEGIN, I'D LIKE TO INTRODUCE YOU TO 4 NEW STU-DENTS: SHANNON, DYLAN, FAITH AND JACK ARE IN OUR SPECIAL NEEDS PROGRAM AND WILL BE LEARNING SOME COOKING SKILLS WITH US.
NOBODY TOLD US WE HAD TO TAKE CLASSES WITH "MENTALLY CHALLENGED" KIDS. THIS IS GONNA BE WEIRD.
BECKY, SHUT UP.
DON'T WORRY, OK? WHAT WE GOT ISN'T "CATCHING."

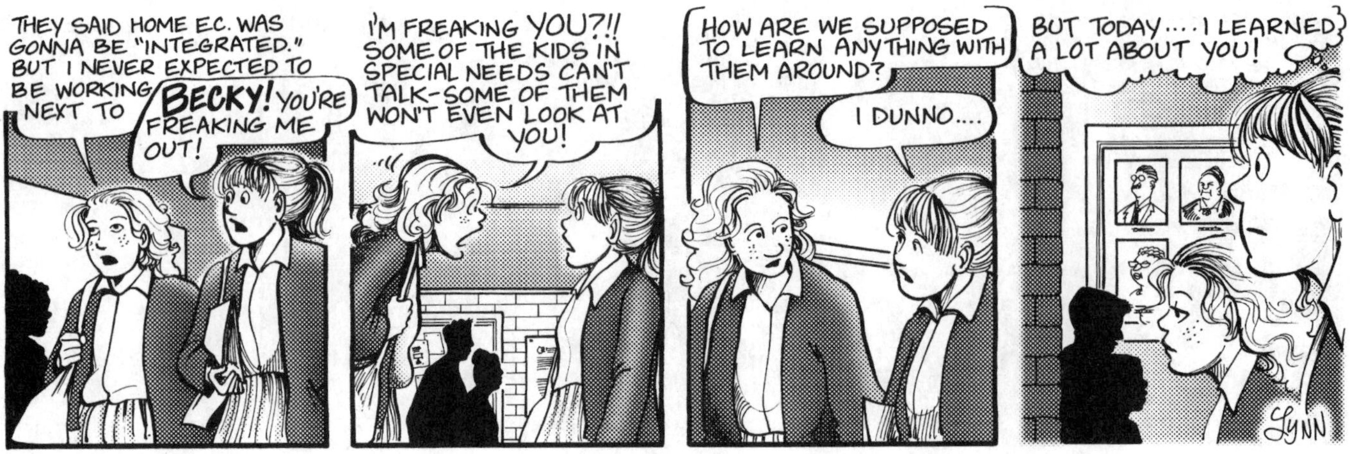
THEY SAID HOME EC. WAS GONNA BE "INTEGRATED." BUT I NEVER EXPECTED TO BE WORKING NEXT TO
BECKY! YOU'RE FREAKING ME OUT!
I'M FREAKING YOU?!! SOME OF THE KIDS IN SPECIAL NEEDS CAN'T TALK-SOME OF THEM WON'T EVEN LOOK AT YOU!
HOW ARE WE SUPPOSED TO LEARN ANYTHING WITH THEM AROUND?
I DUNNO....
BUT TODAY.... I LEARNED A LOT ABOUT YOU!
LYNN

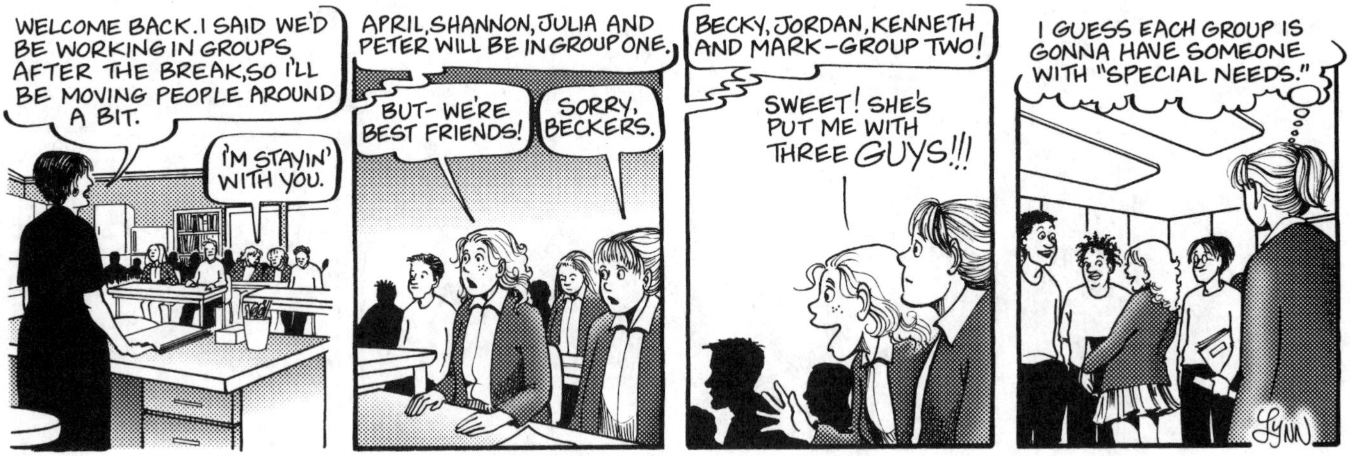
WELCOME BACK. I SAID WE'D BE WORKING IN GROUPS AFTER THE BREAK, SO I'LL BE MOVING PEOPLE AROUND A BIT.
I'M STAYIN' WITH YOU.
APRIL, SHANNON, JULIA AND PETER WILL BE IN GROUP ONE.
BUT- WE'RE BEST FRIENDS!
SORRY, BECKERS.
BECKY, JORDAN, KENNETH AND MARK-GROUP TWO!
SWEET! SHE'S PUT ME WITH THREE GUYS!!!
I GUESS EACH GROUP IS GONNA HAVE SOMEONE WITH "SPECIAL NEEDS."
LYNN

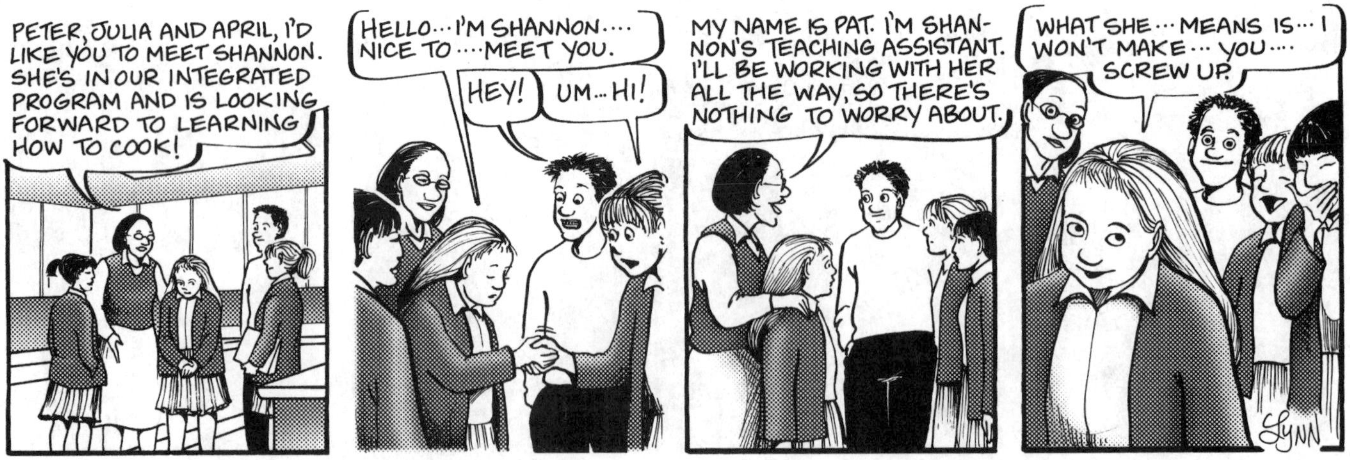
PETER, JULIA AND APRIL, I'D LIKE YOU TO MEET SHANNON. SHE'S IN OUR INTEGRATED PROGRAM AND IS LOOKING FORWARD TO LEARNING HOW TO COOK!
HELLO... I'M SHANNON.... NICE TO .... MEET YOU.
HEY!
UM... HI!
MY NAME IS PAT. I'M SHANNON'S TEACHING ASSISTANT. I'LL BE WORKING WITH HER ALL THE WAY, SO THERE'S NOTHING TO WORRY ABOUT.
WHAT SHE ... MEANS IS ... I WON'T MAKE ... YOU .... SCREW UP.
LYNN

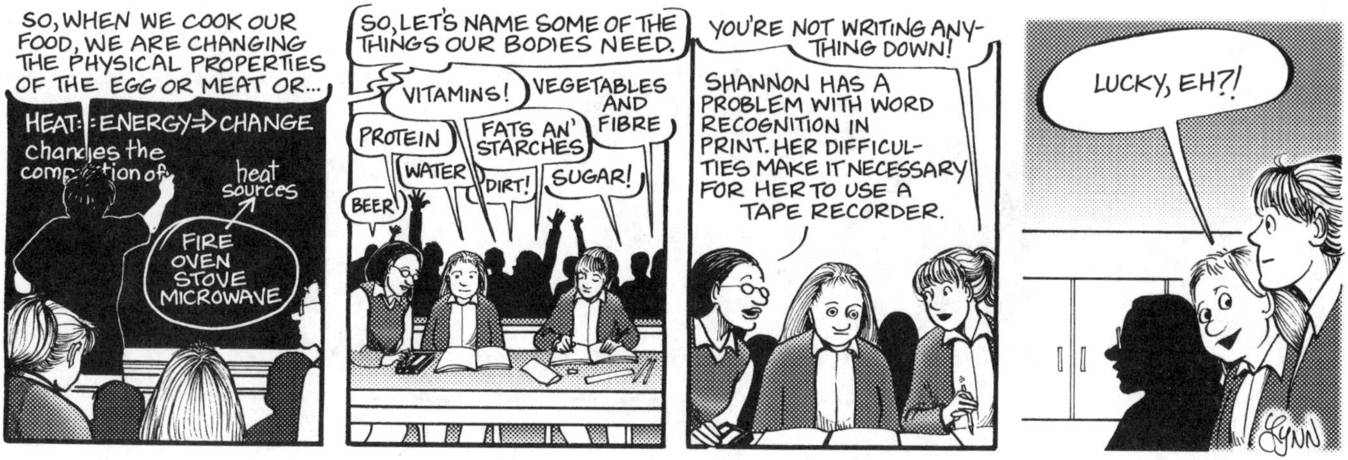

SO, WHEN WE COOK OUR FOOD, WE ARE CHANGING THE PHYSICAL PROPERTIES OF THE EGG OR MEAT OR...
HEAT = ENERGY ⇒ CHANGE
changes the
heat sources
FIRE OVEN STOVE MICROWAVE
SO, LET'S NAME SOME OF THE THINGS OUR BODIES NEED.
VITAMINS!
VEGETABLES AND FIBRE
PROTEIN
FATS AN' STARCHES
WATER
BEER
DIRT!
SUGAR!
YOU'RE NOT WRITING ANYTHING DOWN!
SHANNON HAS A PROBLEM WITH WORD RECOGNITION IN PRINT. HER DIFFICULTIES MAKE IT NECESSARY FOR HER TO USE A TAPE RECORDER.
LUCKY, EH?!
LYNN

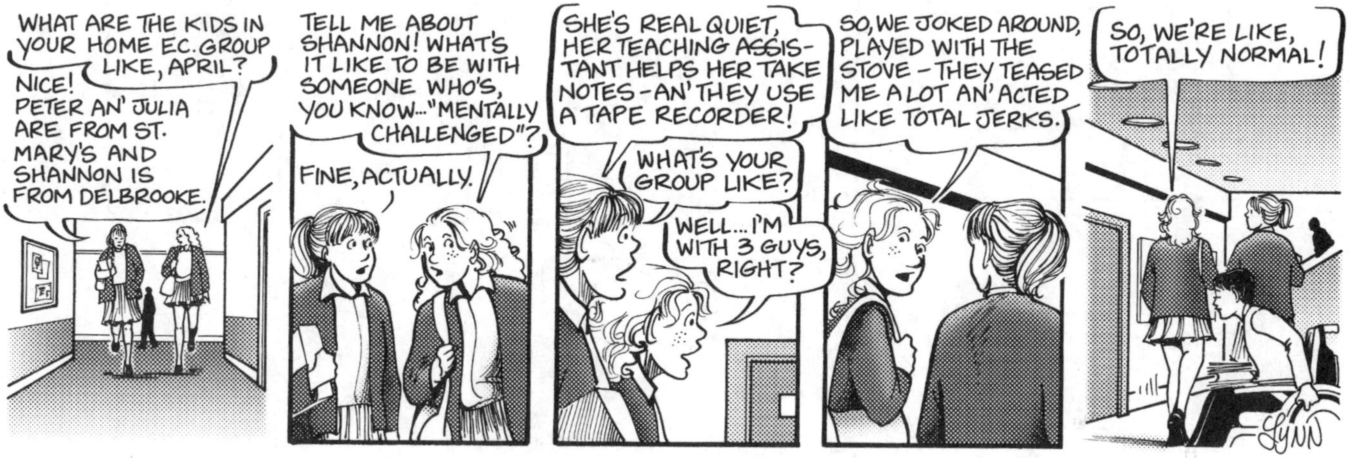

WHAT ARE THE KIDS IN YOUR HOME EC. GROUP LIKE, APRIL?
NICE! PETER AN' JULIA ARE FROM ST. MARY'S AND SHANNON IS FROM DELBROOKE.
TELL ME ABOUT SHANNON! WHAT'S IT LIKE TO BE WITH SOMEONE WHO'S, YOU KNOW..."MENTALLY CHALLENGED"?
FINE, ACTUALLY.
SHE'S REAL QUIET, HER TEACHING ASSISTANT HELPS HER TAKE NOTES - AN' THEY USE A TAPE RECORDER!
WHAT'S YOUR GROUP LIKE?
WELL... I'M WITH 3 GUYS, RIGHT?
SO, WE JOKED AROUND, PLAYED WITH THE STOVE - THEY TEASED ME A LOT AN' ACTED LIKE TOTAL JERKS.
SO, WE'RE LIKE, TOTALLY NORMAL!
LYNN

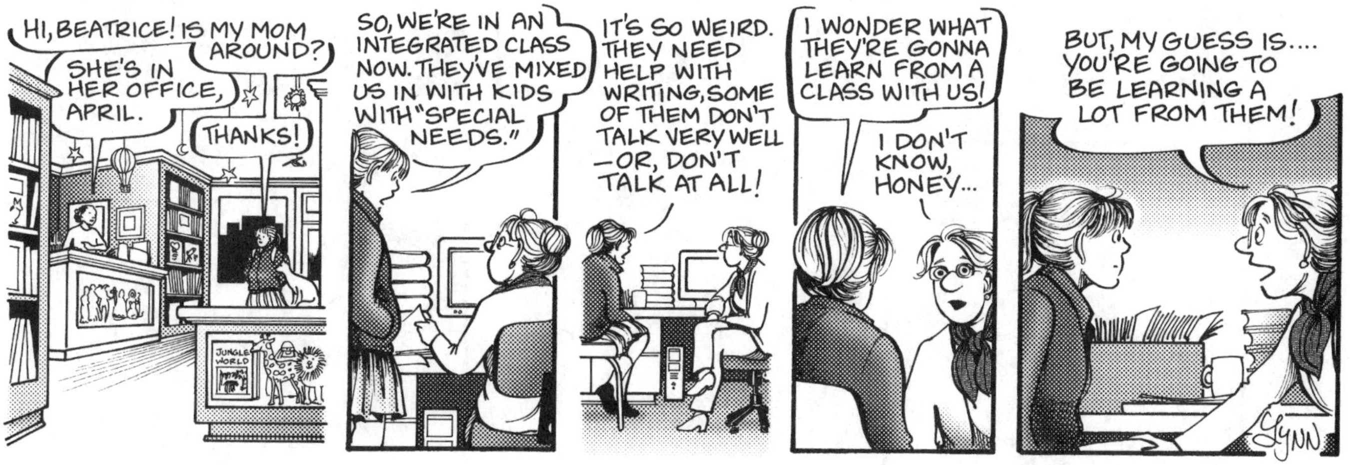

HI, BEATRICE! IS MY MOM AROUND?
SHE'S IN HER OFFICE, APRIL.
THANKS!
JUNGLE WORLD
SO, WE'RE IN AN INTEGRATED CLASS NOW. THEY'VE MIXED US IN WITH KIDS WITH "SPECIAL NEEDS."
IT'S SO WEIRD. THEY NEED HELP WITH WRITING, SOME OF THEM DON'T TALK VERY WELL - OR, DON'T TALK AT ALL!
I WONDER WHAT THEY'RE GONNA LEARN FROM A CLASS WITH US!
I DON'T KNOW, HONEY...
BUT, MY GUESS IS.... YOU'RE GOING TO BE LEARNING A LOT FROM THEM!
LYNN

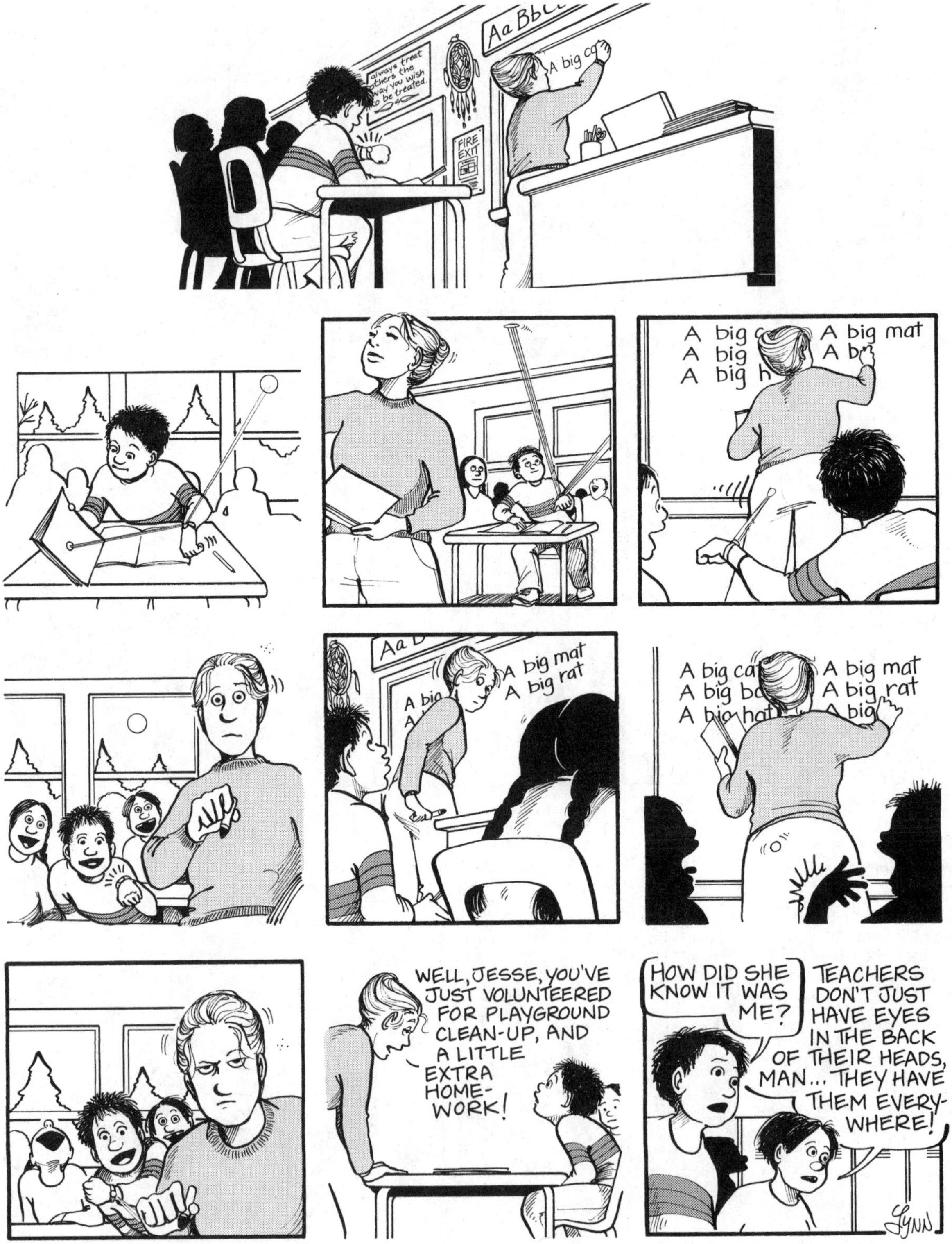
Aa Bb
always treat others the way you wish to be treated.
FIRE EXIT
A big mat
A big rat
WELL, JESSE, YOU'VE JUST VOLUNTEERED FOR PLAYGROUND CLEAN-UP, AND A LITTLE EXTRA HOME-WORK!
HOW DID SHE KNOW IT WAS ME?
TEACHERS DON'T JUST HAVE EYES IN THE BACK OF THEIR HEADS, MAN... THEY HAVE THEM EVERY-WHERE!
LYNN

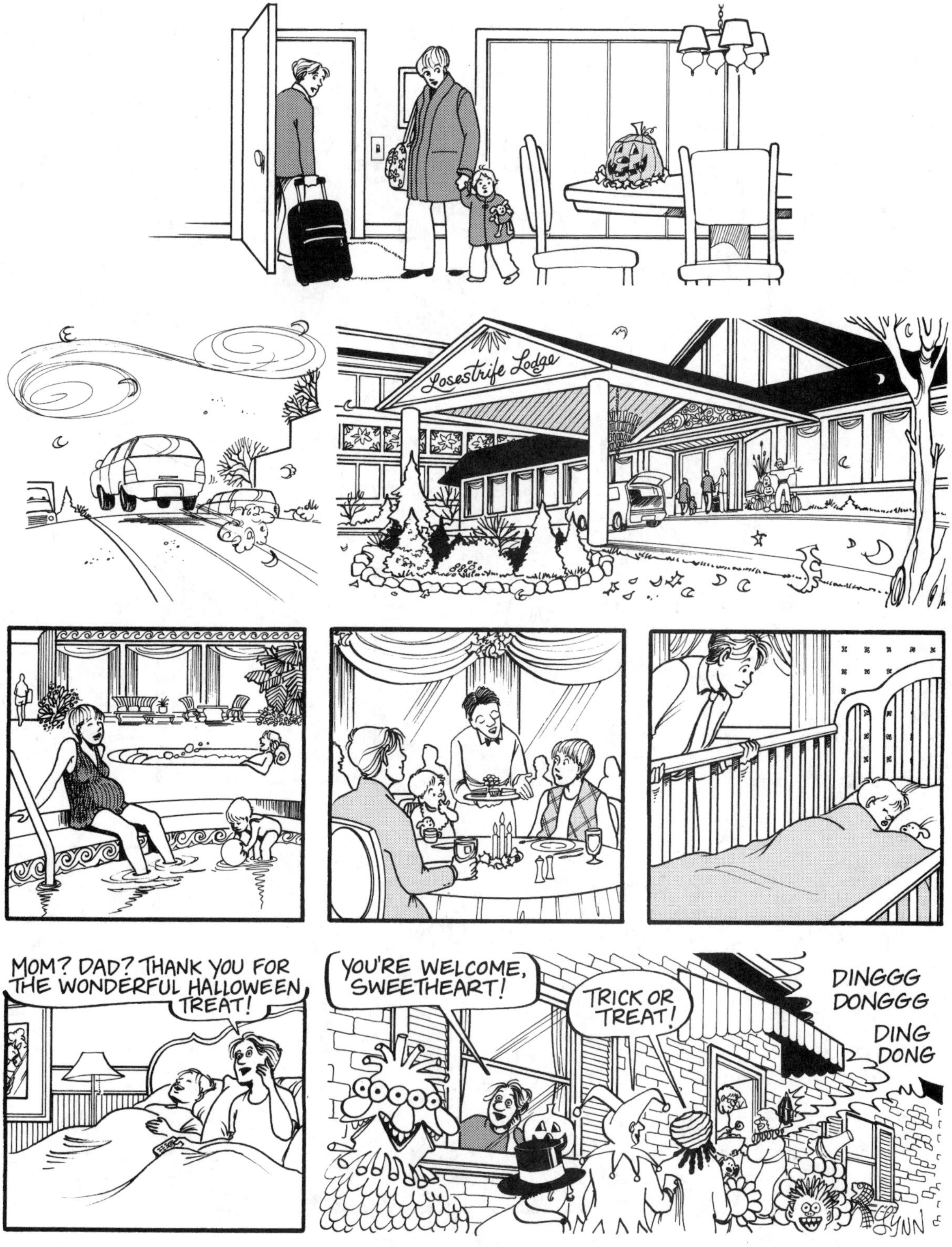
Losestrife Lodge
MOM? DAD? THANK YOU FOR THE WONDERFUL HALLOWEEN TREAT!
YOU'RE WELCOME, SWEETHEART!
TRICK OR TREAT!
DINGGG DONGGG
DING DONG
LYNN

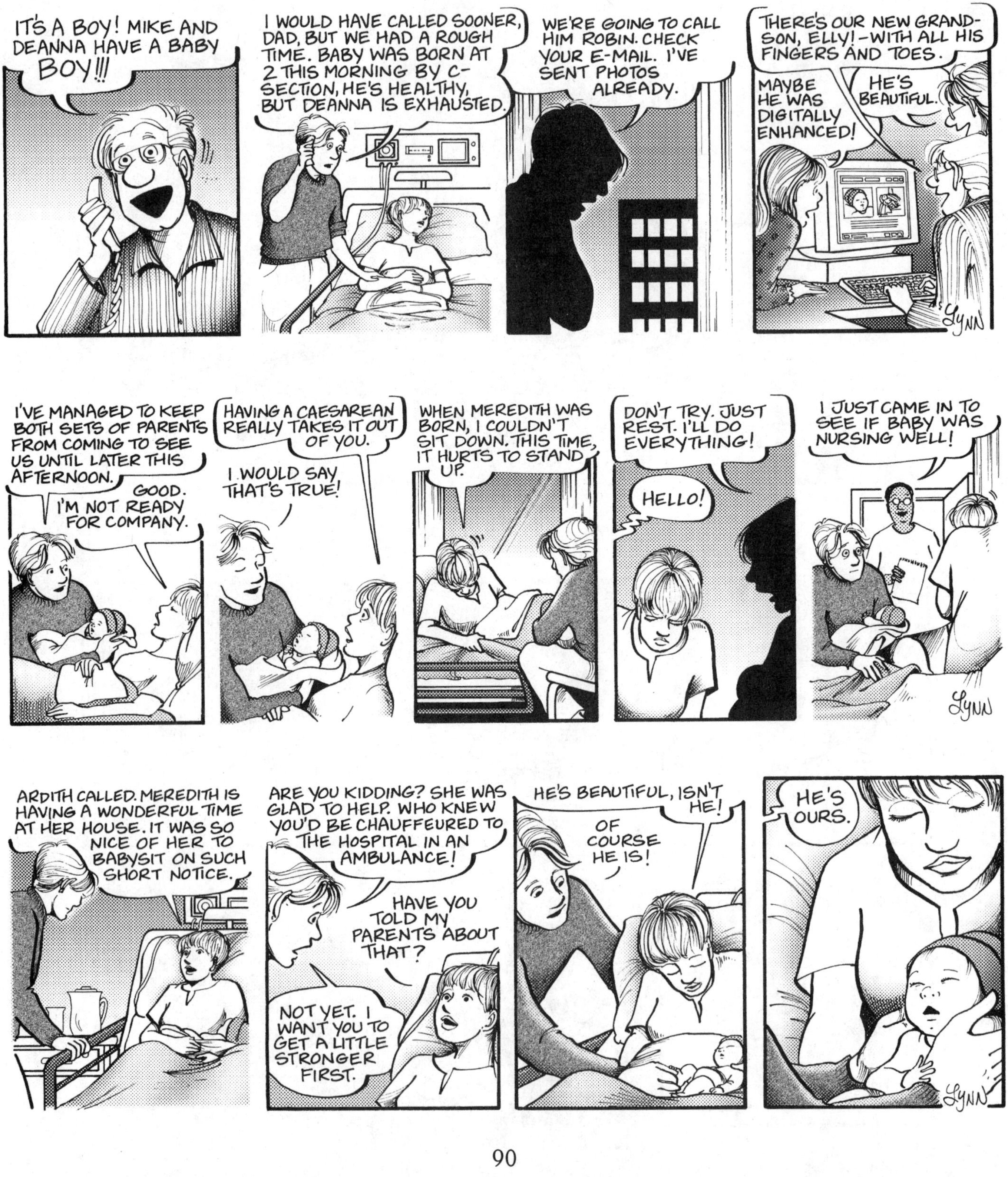
IT'S A BOY! MIKE AND DEANNA HAVE A BABY BOY!!!
I WOULD HAVE CALLED SOONER, DAD, BUT WE HAD A ROUGH TIME. BABY WAS BORN AT 2 THIS MORNING BY C-SECTION, HE'S HEALTHY, BUT DEANNA IS EXHAUSTED.
WE'RE GOING TO CALL HIM ROBIN. CHECK YOUR E-MAIL. I'VE SENT PHOTOS ALREADY.
THERE'S OUR NEW GRANDSON, ELLY! -WITH ALL HIS FINGERS AND TOES.
MAYBE HE WAS DIGITALLY ENHANCED!
HE'S BEAUTIFUL.
LYNN
I'VE MANAGED TO KEEP BOTH SETS OF PARENTS FROM COMING TO SEE US UNTIL LATER THIS AFTERNOON.
GOOD. I'M NOT READY FOR COMPANY.
HAVING A CAESAREAN REALLY TAKES IT OUT OF YOU.
I WOULD SAY THAT'S TRUE!
WHEN MEREDITH WAS BORN, I COULDN'T SIT DOWN. THIS TIME, IT HURTS TO STAND UP.
DON'T TRY. JUST REST. I'LL DO EVERYTHING!
HELLO!
I JUST CAME IN TO SEE IF BABY WAS NURSING WELL!
LYNN
ARDITH CALLED. MEREDITH IS HAVING A WONDERFUL TIME AT HER HOUSE. IT WAS SO NICE OF HER TO BABYSIT ON SUCH SHORT NOTICE.
ARE YOU KIDDING? SHE WAS GLAD TO HELP. WHO KNEW YOU'D BE CHAUFFEURED TO THE HOSPITAL IN AN AMBULANCE!
HAVE YOU TOLD MY PARENTS ABOUT THAT?
NOT YET. I WANT YOU TO GET A LITTLE STRONGER FIRST.
HE'S BEAUTIFUL, ISN'T HE!
OF COURSE HE IS!
HE'S OURS.
LYNN

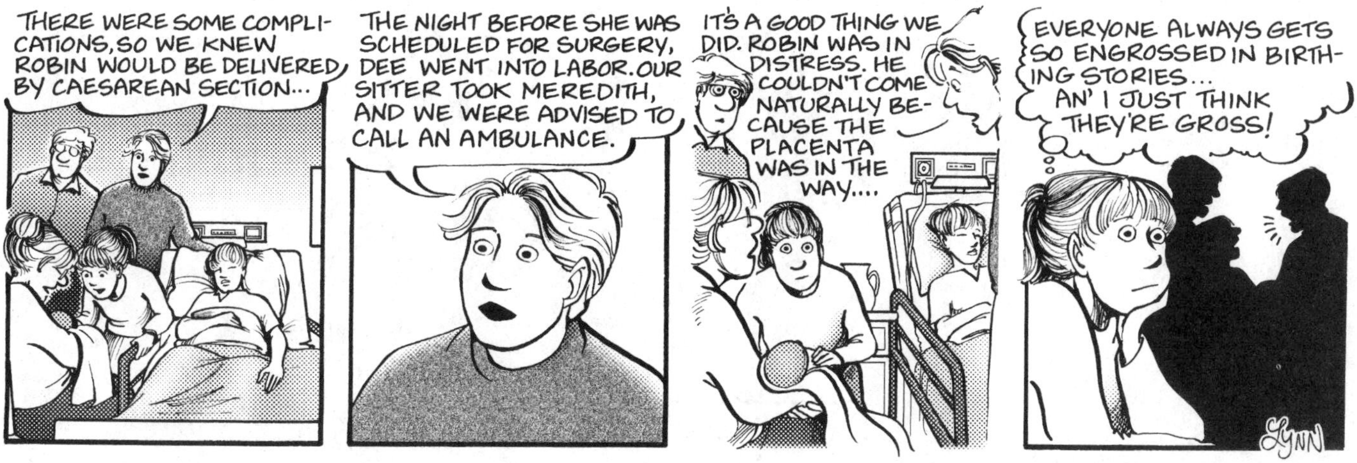
THERE WERE SOME COMPLICATIONS, SO WE KNEW ROBIN WOULD BE DELIVERED BY CAESAREAN SECTION...
THE NIGHT BEFORE SHE WAS SCHEDULED FOR SURGERY, DEE WENT INTO LABOR. OUR SITTER TOOK MEREDITH, AND WE WERE ADVISED TO CALL AN AMBULANCE.
IT'S A GOOD THING WE DID. ROBIN WAS IN DISTRESS. HE COULDN'T COME NATURALLY BECAUSE THE PLACENTA WAS IN THE WAY....
EVERYONE ALWAYS GETS SO ENGROSSED IN BIRTHING STORIES... AN' I JUST THINK THEY'RE GROSS!

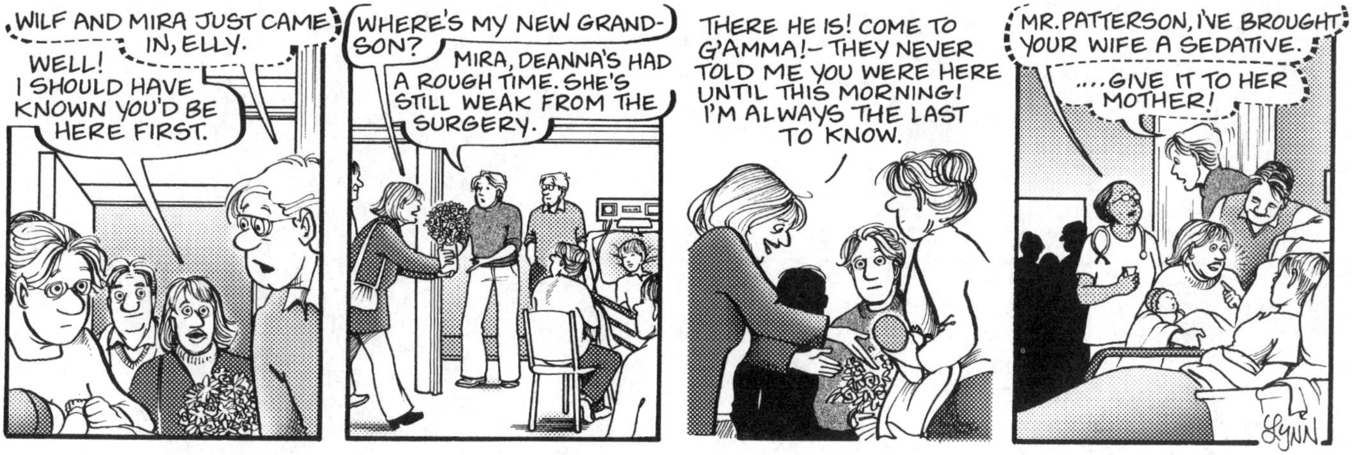
WILF AND MIRA JUST CAME IN, ELLY.
WELL! I SHOULD HAVE KNOWN YOU'D BE HERE FIRST.
WHERE'S MY NEW GRANDSON?
MIRA, DEANNA'S HAD A ROUGH TIME. SHE'S STILL WEAK FROM THE SURGERY.
THERE HE IS! COME TO G'AMMA! – THEY NEVER TOLD ME YOU WERE HERE UNTIL THIS MORNING! I'M ALWAYS THE LAST TO KNOW.
MR. PATTERSON, I'VE BROUGHT YOUR WIFE A SEDATIVE.
....GIVE IT TO HER MOTHER!

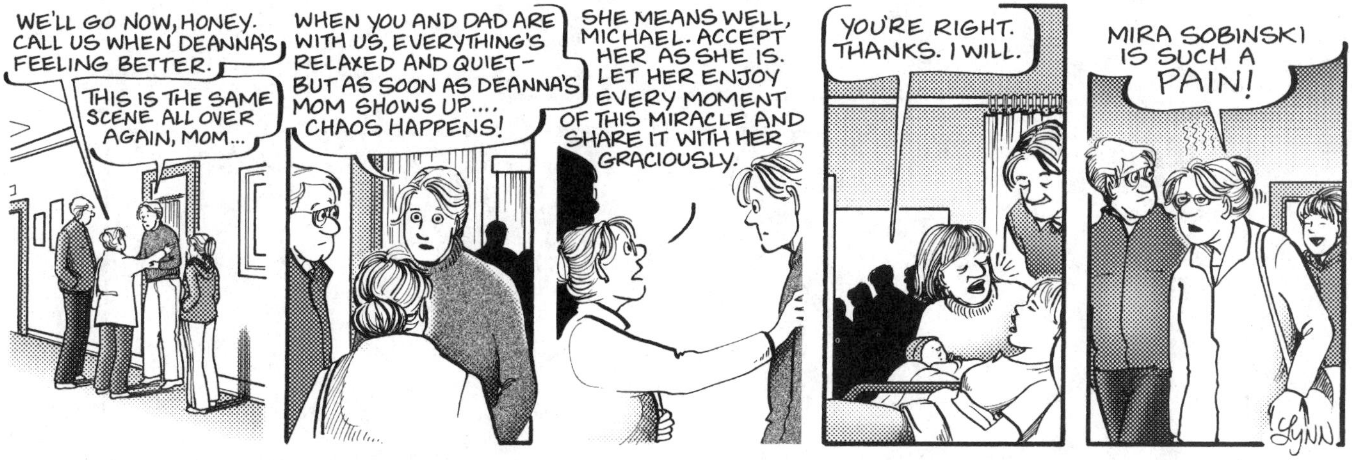
WE'LL GO NOW, HONEY. CALL US WHEN DEANNA'S FEELING BETTER.
THIS IS THE SAME SCENE ALL OVER AGAIN, MOM...
WHEN YOU AND DAD ARE WITH US, EVERYTHING'S RELAXED AND QUIET – BUT AS SOON AS DEANNA'S MOM SHOWS UP...., CHAOS HAPPENS!
SHE MEANS WELL, MICHAEL. ACCEPT HER AS SHE IS. LET HER ENJOY EVERY MOMENT OF THIS MIRACLE AND SHARE IT WITH HER GRACIOUSLY.
YOU'RE RIGHT. THANKS. I WILL.
MIRA SOBINSKI IS SUCH A PAIN!

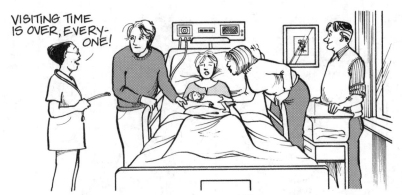

VISITING TIME IS OVER, EVERYONE!

GOOD NIGHT, MOM AND DAD.

GOOD NIGHT, DEAR.

EVERYONE'S GONE HOME, DEANNA. WE'RE ALONE WITH OUR NEW BABY BOY.

ROBIN. ARE YOU HAPPY WITH THAT NAME?

ROBIN MICHAEL. YES. I THINK SO.

PEOPLE TALK ABOUT PERFECTION. THEY SAY, "THIS IS PERFECT" OR "THAT IS PERFECT"— WHEN NOTHING ON EARTH IS REALLY PERFECT.

BUT LOOK AT HIM. A BABY IS PERFECT. THEIR MINDS ARE CLEAR OF ALL UNKIND THOUGHTS. THEY KNOW NOTHING ABOUT GOOD OR EVIL....

IN A BABY'S EYES, ONE SEES NO GREED OR GUILT OR MALICE. THEIR TINY BODIES ARE UNTOUCHED AND— BEAUTIFUL.

YOU'RE RIGHT. A BRAND-NEW BABY IS THE ONE THING THAT'S ABSOLUTELY PERFECT.

HIC!

WAAAHH

ALMOST.

Lynn

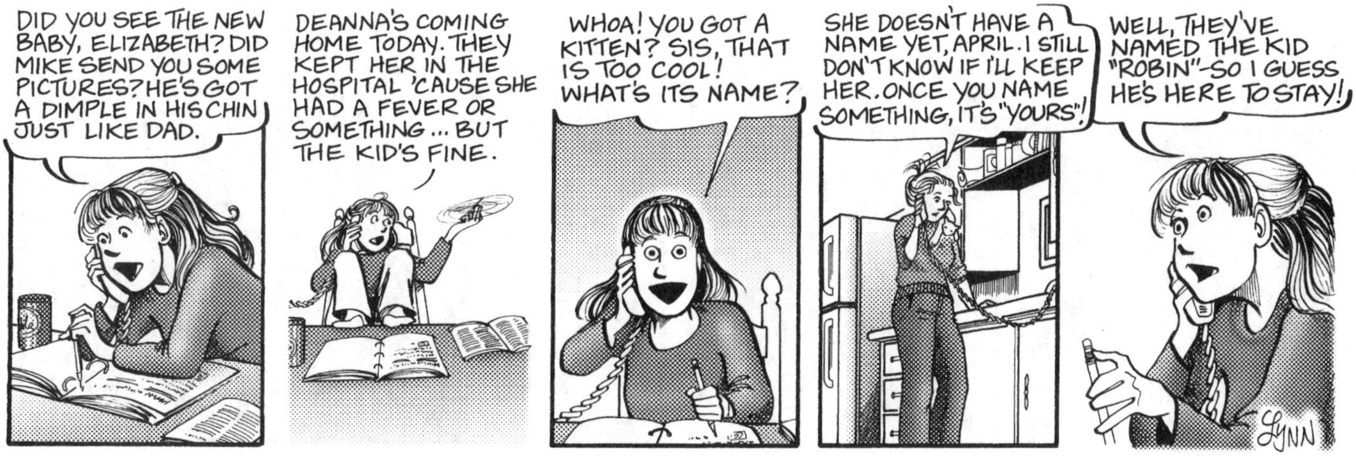
DID YOU SEE THE NEW BABY, ELIZABETH? DID MIKE SEND YOU SOME PICTURES? HE'S GOT A DIMPLE IN HIS CHIN JUST LIKE DAD.
DEANNA'S COMING HOME TODAY. THEY KEPT HER IN THE HOSPITAL 'CAUSE SHE HAD A FEVER OR SOMETHING ... BUT THE KID'S FINE.
WHOA! YOU GOT A KITTEN? SIS, THAT IS TOO COOL! WHAT'S ITS NAME?
SHE DOESN'T HAVE A NAME YET, APRIL. I STILL DON'T KNOW IF I'LL KEEP HER. ONCE YOU NAME SOMETHING, IT'S "YOURS"!
WELL, THEY'VE NAMED THE KID "ROBIN"—SO I GUESS HE'S HERE TO STAY!
LYNN

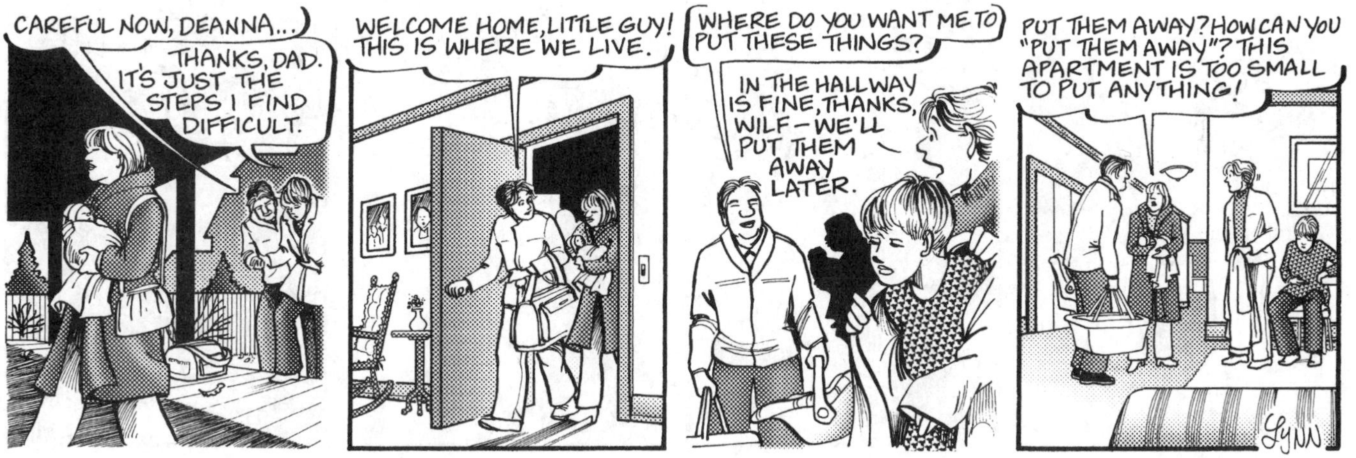
CAREFUL NOW, DEANNA...
THANKS, DAD. IT'S JUST THE STEPS I FIND DIFFICULT.
WELCOME HOME, LITTLE GUY! THIS IS WHERE WE LIVE.
WHERE DO YOU WANT ME TO PUT THESE THINGS?
IN THE HALLWAY IS FINE, THANKS, WILF—WE'LL PUT THEM AWAY LATER.
PUT THEM AWAY? HOW CAN YOU "PUT THEM AWAY"? THIS APARTMENT IS TOO SMALL TO PUT ANYTHING!
LYNN

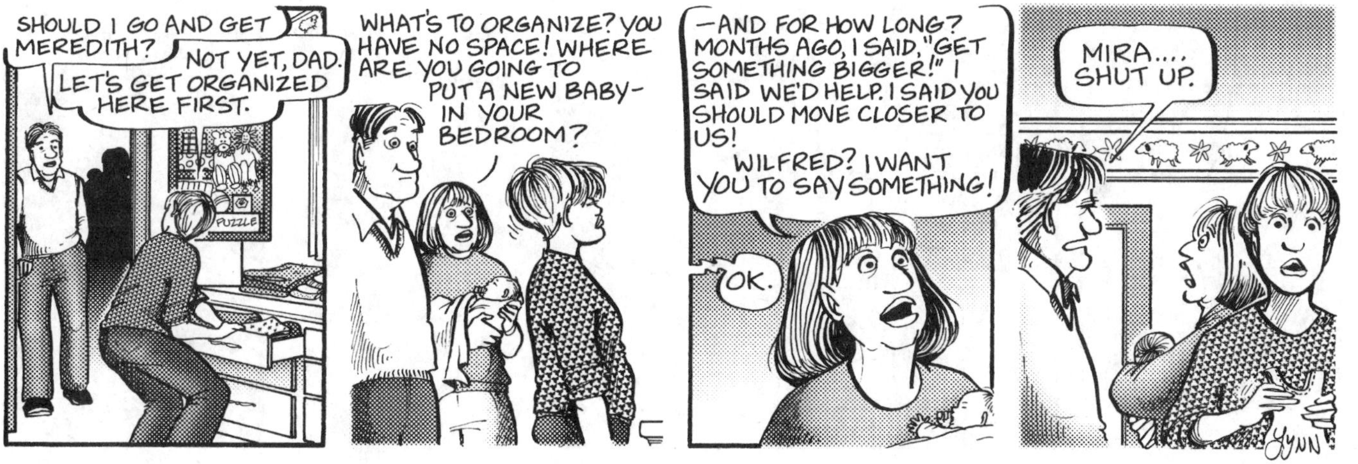
SHOULD I GO AND GET MEREDITH?
NOT YET, DAD. LET'S GET ORGANIZED HERE FIRST.
PUZZLE
WHAT'S TO ORGANIZE? YOU HAVE NO SPACE! WHERE ARE YOU GOING TO PUT A NEW BABY—IN YOUR BEDROOM?
—AND FOR HOW LONG? MONTHS AGO, I SAID, "GET SOMETHING BIGGER!" I SAID WE'D HELP. I SAID YOU SHOULD MOVE CLOSER TO US!
WILFRED? I WANT YOU TO SAY SOMETHING!
OK.
MIRA.... SHUT UP.
LYNN

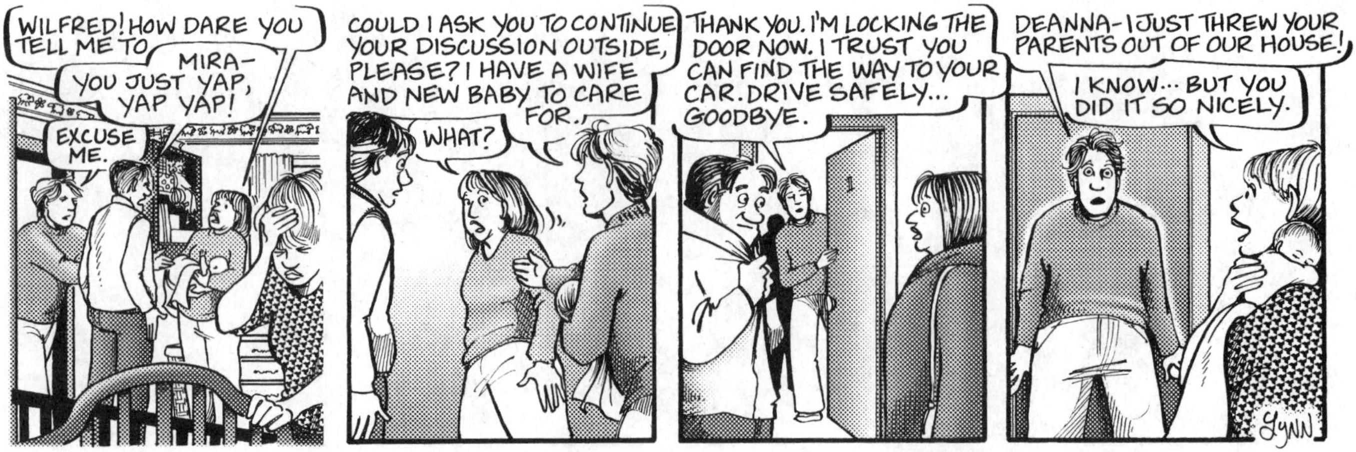
WILFRED! HOW DARE YOU TELL ME TO
MIRA- YOU JUST YAP, YAP YAP!
EXCUSE ME.
COULD I ASK YOU TO CONTINUE YOUR DISCUSSION OUTSIDE, PLEASE? I HAVE A WIFE AND NEW BABY TO CARE FOR.
WHAT?
THANK YOU. I'M LOCKING THE DOOR NOW. I TRUST YOU CAN FIND THE WAY TO YOUR CAR. DRIVE SAFELY... GOODBYE.
DEANNA- I JUST THREW YOUR PARENTS OUT OF OUR HOUSE!
I KNOW... BUT YOU DID IT SO NICELY.
LYNN

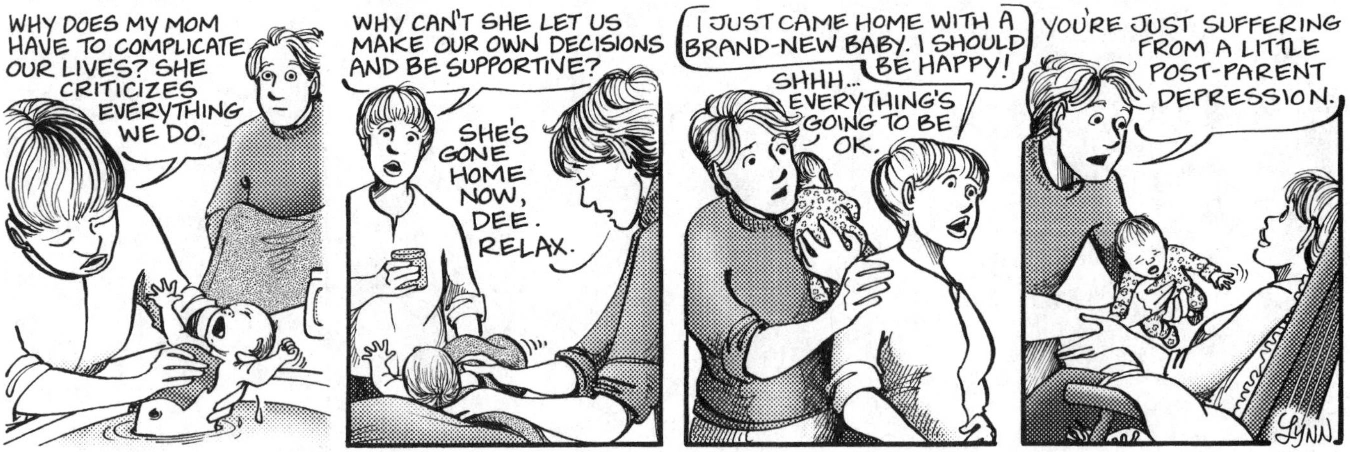
WHY DOES MY MOM HAVE TO COMPLICATE OUR LIVES? SHE CRITICIZES EVERYTHING WE DO.
WHY CAN'T SHE LET US MAKE OUR OWN DECISIONS AND BE SUPPORTIVE?
SHE'S GONE HOME NOW, DEE. RELAX.
I JUST CAME HOME WITH A BRAND-NEW BABY. I SHOULD BE HAPPY!
SHHH... EVERYTHING'S GOING TO BE OK.
YOU'RE JUST SUFFERING FROM A LITTLE POST-PARENT DEPRESSION.
LYNN

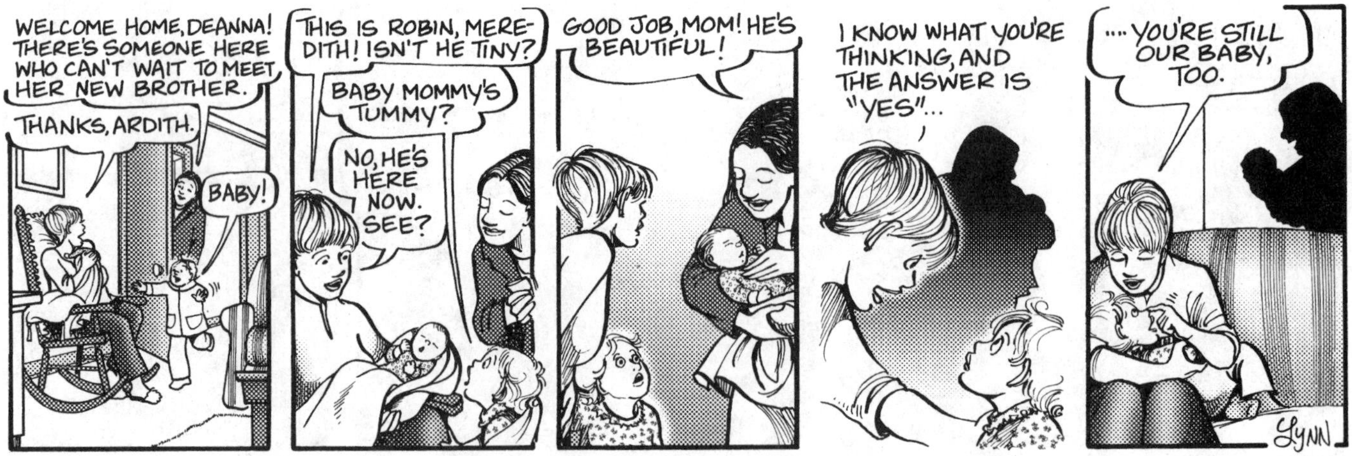
WELCOME HOME, DEANNA! THERE'S SOMEONE HERE WHO CAN'T WAIT TO MEET HER NEW BROTHER.
THANKS, ARDITH.
BABY!
THIS IS ROBIN, MEREDITH! ISN'T HE TINY?
BABY MOMMY'S TUMMY?
NO, HE'S HERE NOW. SEE?
GOOD JOB, MOM! HE'S BEAUTIFUL!
I KNOW WHAT YOU'RE THINKING, AND THE ANSWER IS "YES"...
....YOU'RE STILL OUR BABY, TOO.
LYNN

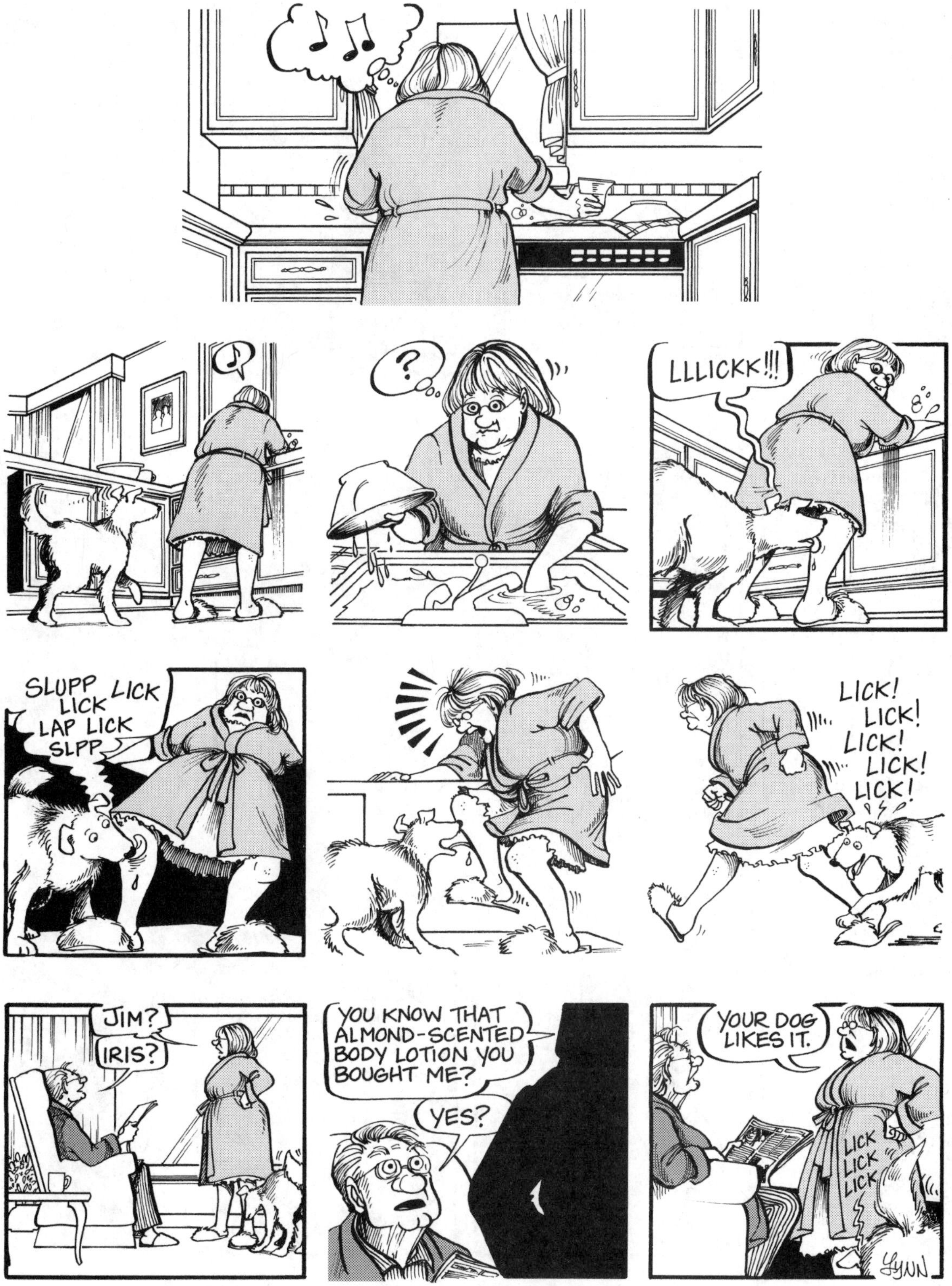
LLLICKK!!!
SLUPP LICK
LICK
LAP LICK
SLPP
LICK!
LICK!
LICK!
LICK!
LICK!
JIM?
IRIS?
YOU KNOW THAT ALMOND-SCENTED BODY LOTION YOU BOUGHT ME?
YES?
YOUR DOG LIKES IT.
LICK
LICK
LICK
LYNN

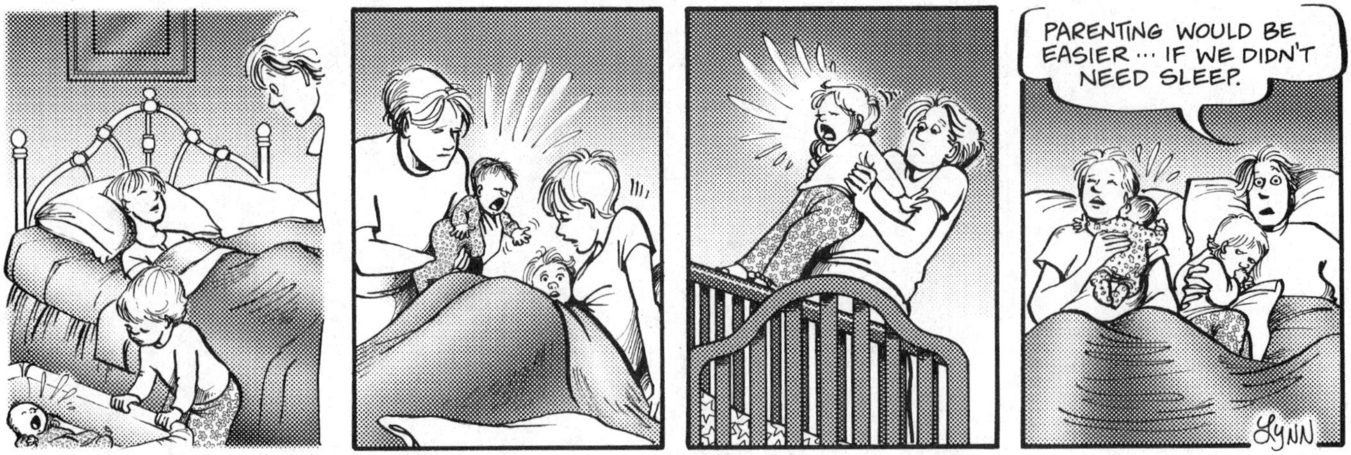
PARENTING WOULD BE EASIER ... IF WE DIDN'T NEED SLEEP.
LYNN

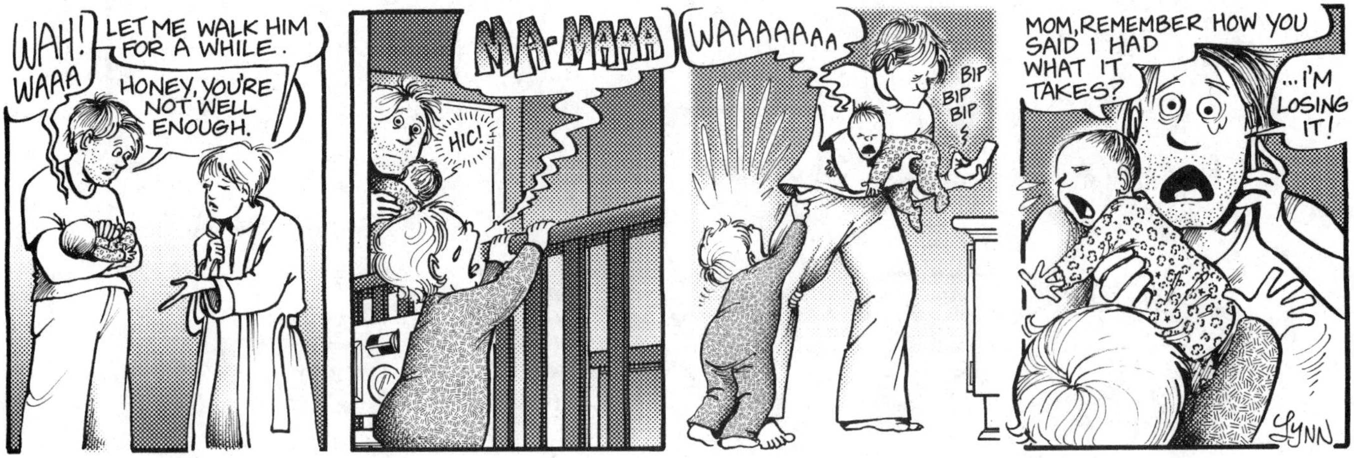
WAH! WAAA
LET ME WALK HIM FOR A WHILE.
HONEY, YOU'RE NOT WELL ENOUGH.
MA-MAAA
HIC!
WAAAAAAA
BIP BIP BIP
MOM, REMEMBER HOW YOU SAID I HAD WHAT IT TAKES?
...I'M LOSING IT!
LYNN

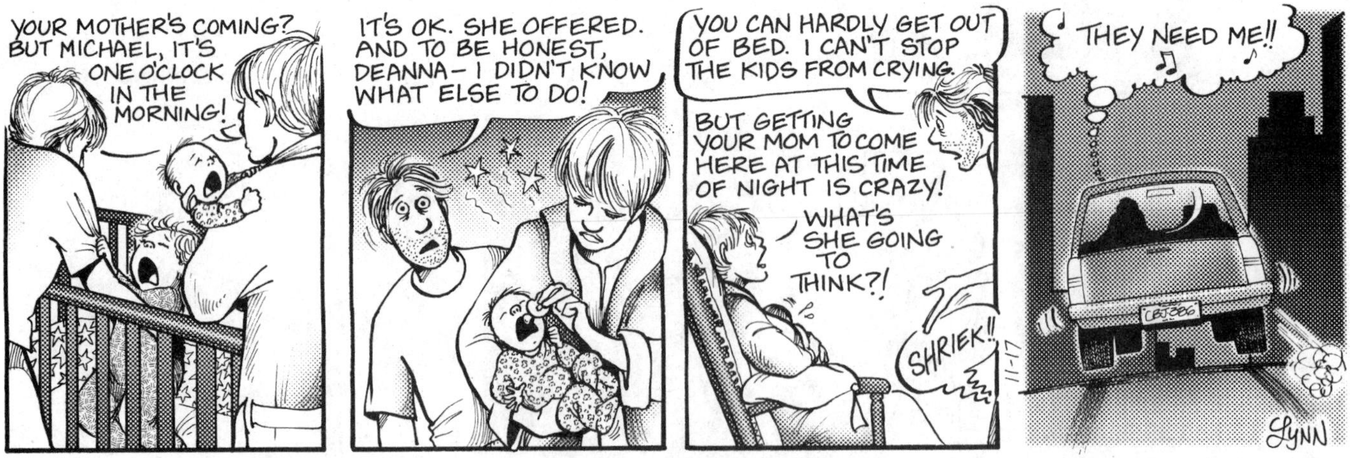
YOUR MOTHER'S COMING? BUT MICHAEL, IT'S ONE O'CLOCK IN THE MORNING!
IT'S OK. SHE OFFERED. AND TO BE HONEST, DEANNA– I DIDN'T KNOW WHAT ELSE TO DO!
YOU CAN HARDLY GET OUT OF BED. I CAN'T STOP THE KIDS FROM CRYING.
BUT GETTING YOUR MOM TO COME HERE AT THIS TIME OF NIGHT IS CRAZY!
WHAT'S SHE GOING TO THINK?!
SHRIEK!!
11-17
THEY NEED ME!!
LYNN

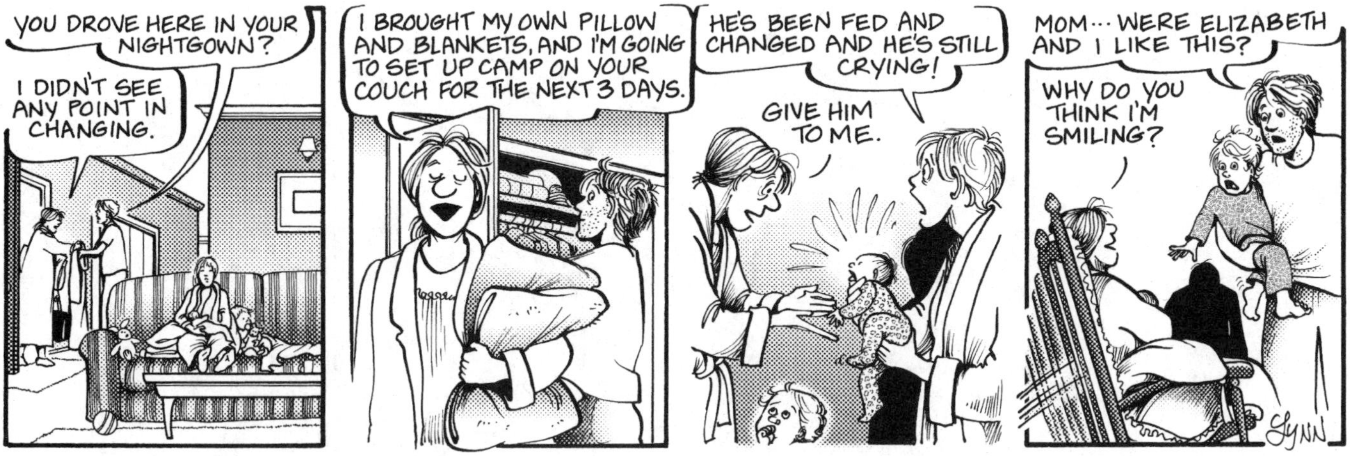
YOU DROVE HERE IN YOUR NIGHTGOWN?
I DIDN'T SEE ANY POINT IN CHANGING.
I BROUGHT MY OWN PILLOW AND BLANKETS, AND I'M GOING TO SET UP CAMP ON YOUR COUCH FOR THE NEXT 3 DAYS.
HE'S BEEN FED AND CHANGED AND HE'S STILL CRYING!
GIVE HIM TO ME.
MOM... WERE ELIZABETH AND I LIKE THIS?
WHY DO YOU THINK I'M SMILING?
LYNN

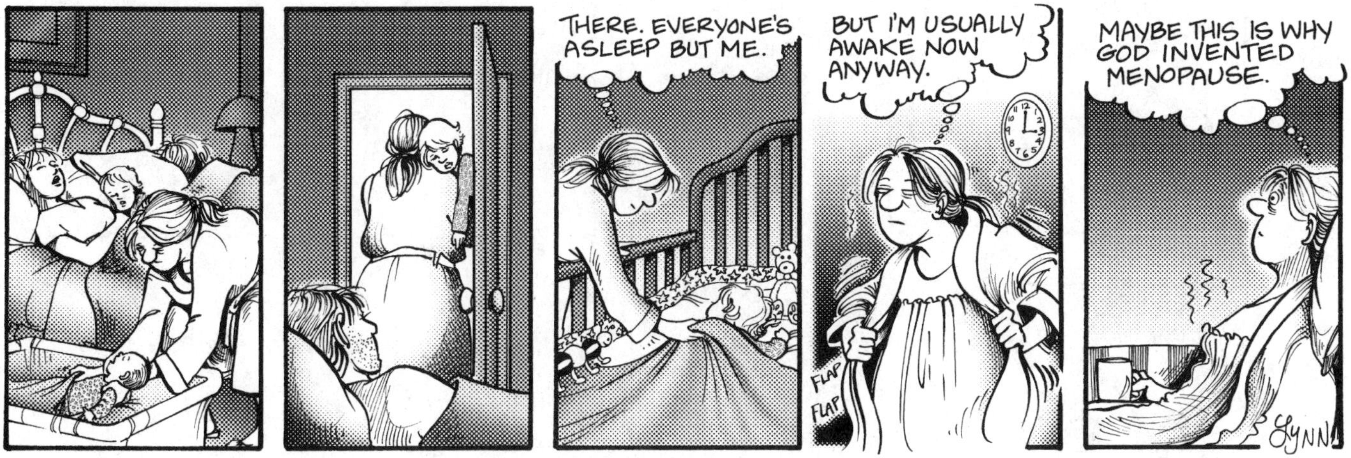
THERE. EVERYONE'S ASLEEP BUT ME.
BUT I'M USUALLY AWAKE NOW ANYWAY.
FLAP
FLAP
MAYBE THIS IS WHY GOD INVENTED MENOPAUSE.
LYNN

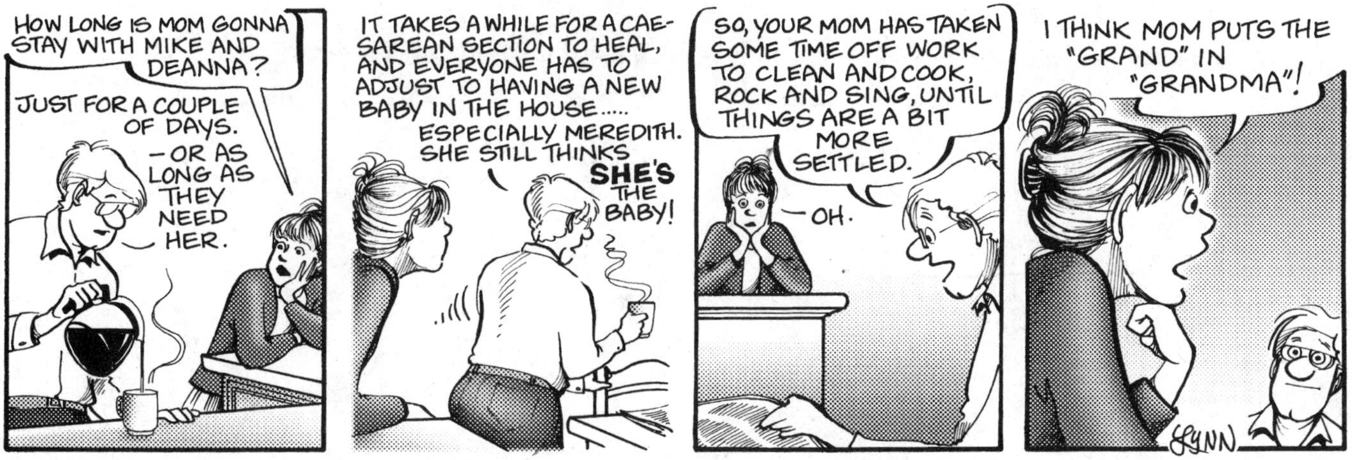
HOW LONG IS MOM GONNA STAY WITH MIKE AND DEANNA?
JUST FOR A COUPLE OF DAYS.
—OR AS LONG AS THEY NEED HER.
IT TAKES A WHILE FOR A CAESAREAN SECTION TO HEAL, AND EVERYONE HAS TO ADJUST TO HAVING A NEW BABY IN THE HOUSE.....
ESPECIALLY MEREDITH. SHE STILL THINKS SHE'S THE BABY!
SO, YOUR MOM HAS TAKEN SOME TIME OFF WORK TO CLEAN AND COOK, ROCK AND SING, UNTIL THINGS ARE A BIT MORE SETTLED.
—OH.
I THINK MOM PUTS THE "GRAND" IN "GRANDMA"!
LYNN

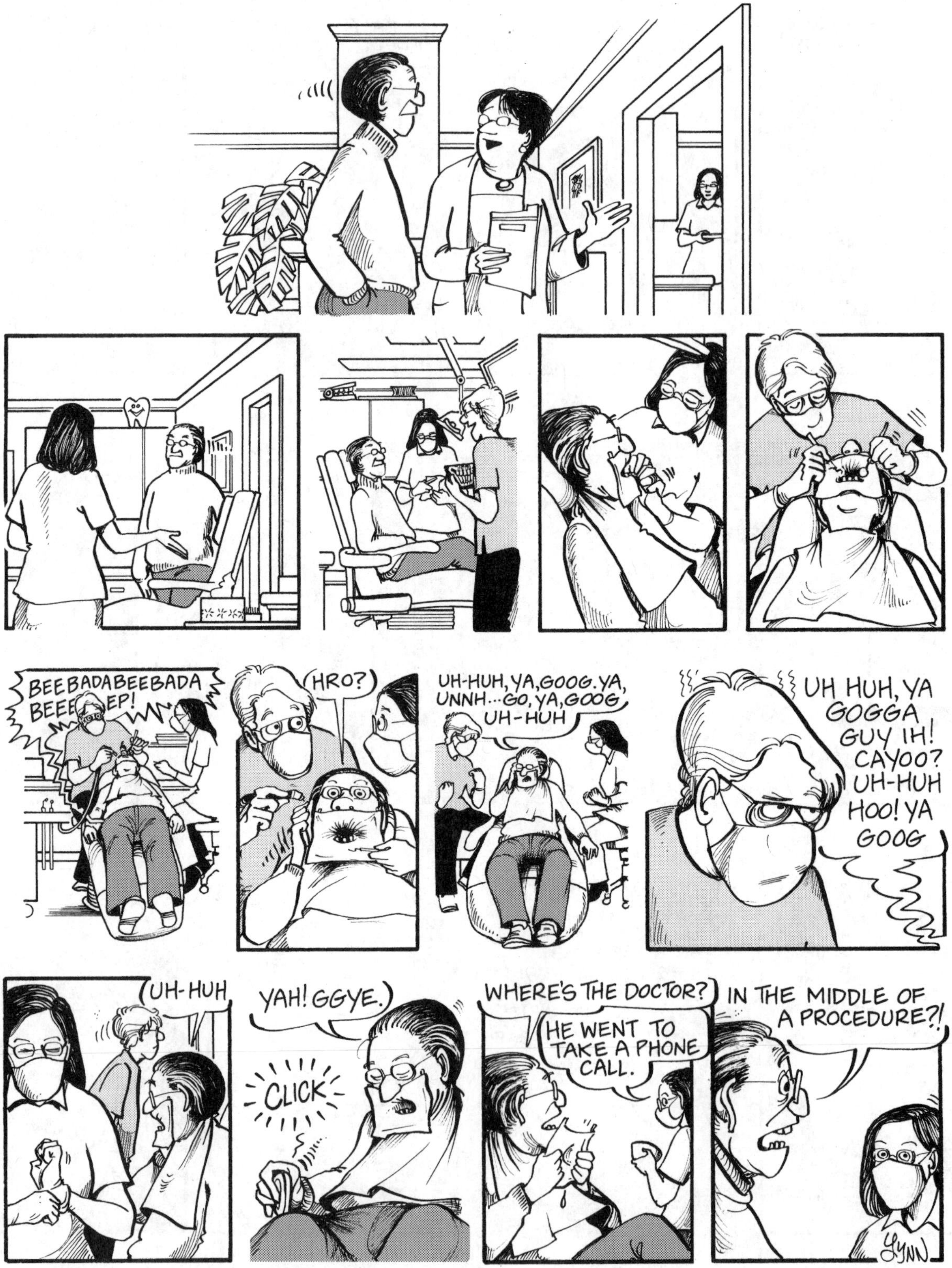
BEEBADABEEBADA
HRO?
UH-HUH, YA, GOOG. YA, UNNH...GO, YA, GOOG UH-HUH
UH HUH, YA GOGGA GUY IH! CAYOO? UH-HUH HOO! YA GOOG
UH-HUH
YAH! GGYE.
CLICK
WHERE'S THE DOCTOR?
HE WENT TO TAKE A PHONE CALL.
IN THE MIDDLE OF A PROCEDURE?!
LYNN

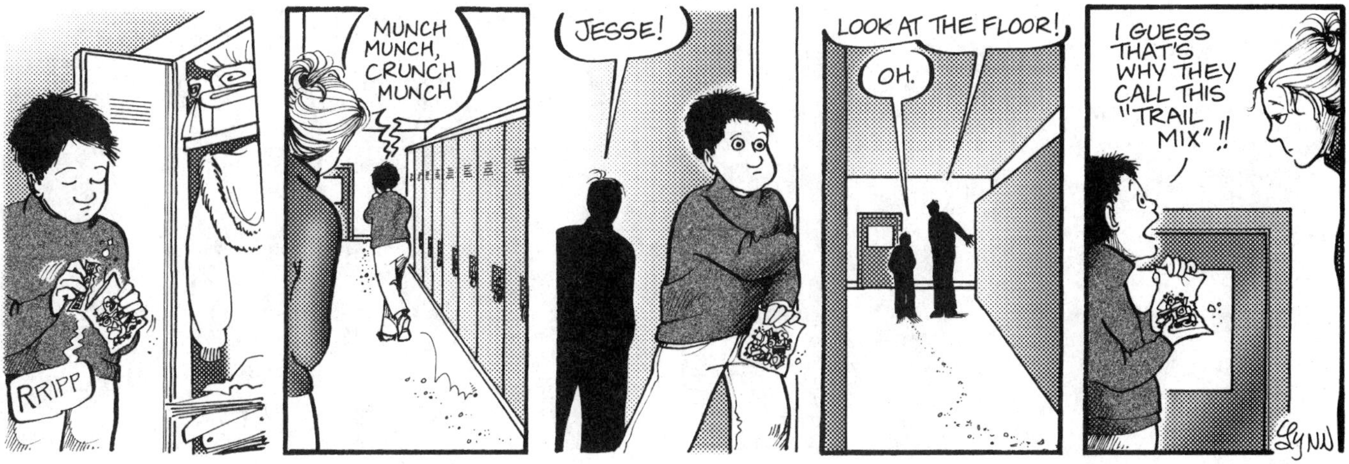
RRIPP
MUNCH MUNCH, CRUNCH MUNCH
JESSE!
LOOK AT THE FLOOR!
OH.
I GUESS THAT'S WHY THEY CALL THIS "TRAIL MIX"!!
LYNN

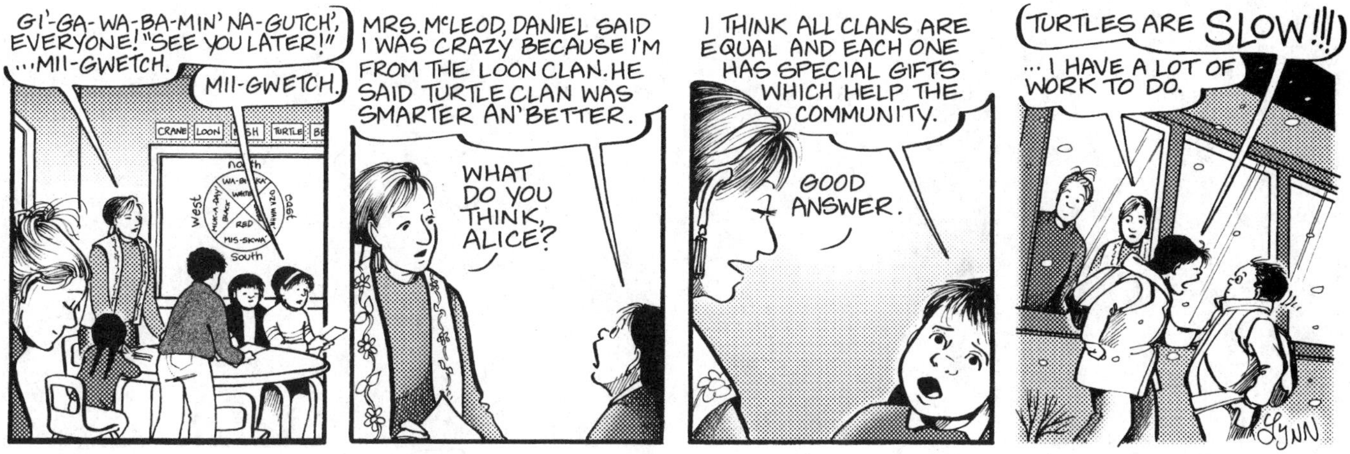
GI'-GA-WA-BA-MIN' NA-GUTCH', EVERYONE! "SEE YOU LATER!" ...MII-GWETCH.
MII-GWETCH.
CRANE
LOON
TURTLE
north
west
east
south
MRS. McLEOD, DANIEL SAID I WAS CRAZY BECAUSE I'M FROM THE LOON CLAN. HE SAID TURTLE CLAN WAS SMARTER AN' BETTER.
WHAT DO YOU THINK, ALICE?
I THINK ALL CLANS ARE EQUAL AND EACH ONE HAS SPECIAL GIFTS WHICH HELP THE COMMUNITY.
GOOD ANSWER.
TURTLES ARE SLOW!!!
...I HAVE A LOT OF WORK TO DO.
LYNN

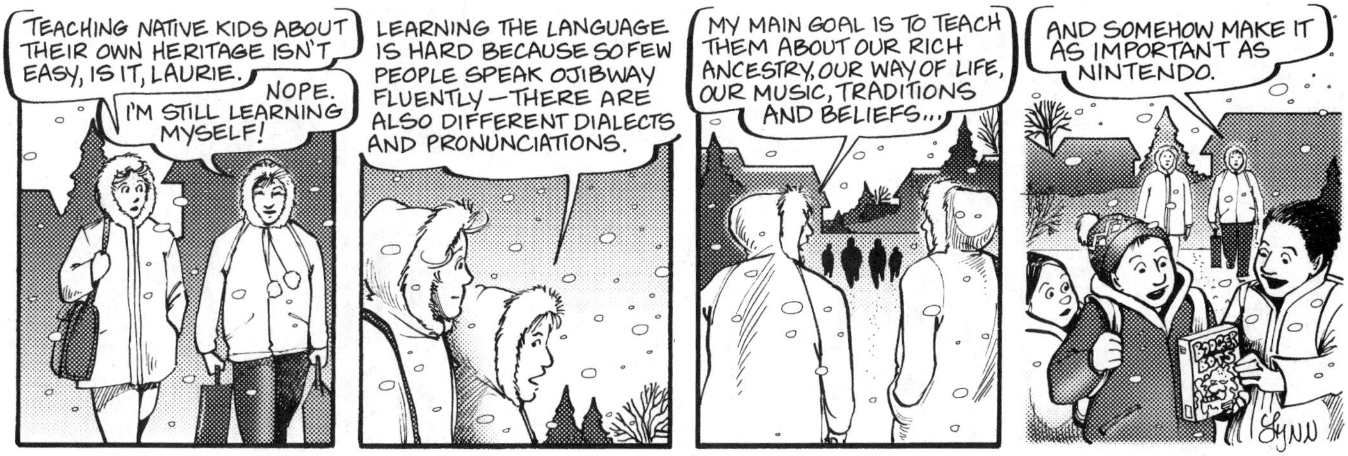
TEACHING NATIVE KIDS ABOUT THEIR OWN HERITAGE ISN'T EASY, IS IT, LAURIE.
NOPE. I'M STILL LEARNING MYSELF!
LEARNING THE LANGUAGE IS HARD BECAUSE SO FEW PEOPLE SPEAK OJIBWAY FLUENTLY—THERE ARE ALSO DIFFERENT DIALECTS AND PRONUNCIATIONS.
MY MAIN GOAL IS TO TEACH THEM ABOUT OUR RICH ANCESTRY, OUR WAY OF LIFE, OUR MUSIC, TRADITIONS AND BELIEFS...
AND SOMEHOW MAKE IT AS IMPORTANT AS NINTENDO.
LYNN

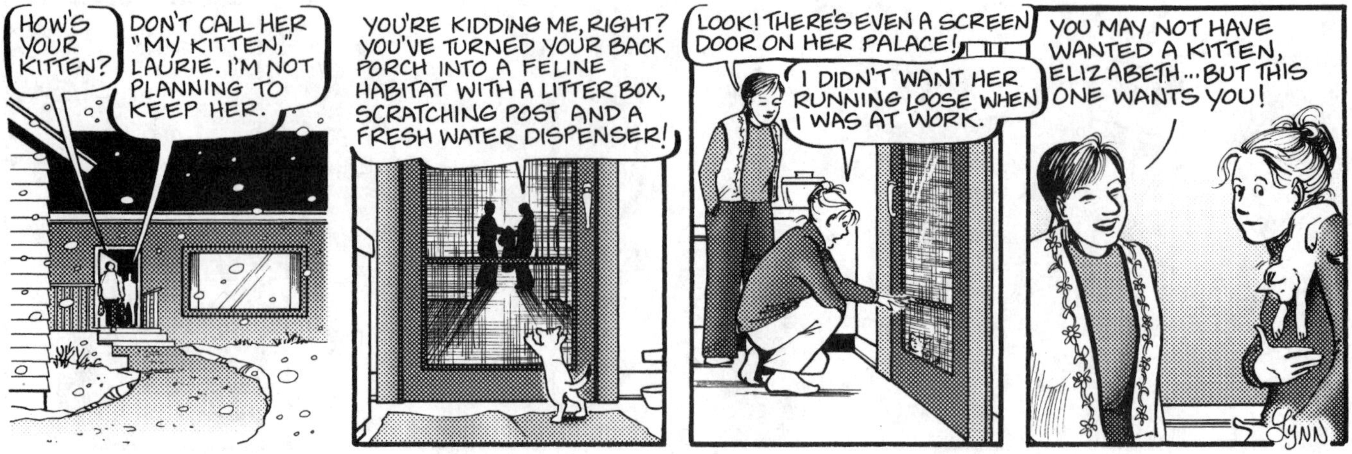
HOW'S YOUR KITTEN?
DON'T CALL HER "MY KITTEN," LAURIE. I'M NOT PLANNING TO KEEP HER.
YOU'RE KIDDING ME, RIGHT? YOU'VE TURNED YOUR BACK PORCH INTO A FELINE HABITAT WITH A LITTER BOX, SCRATCHING POST AND A FRESH WATER DISPENSER!
LOOK! THERE'S EVEN A SCREEN DOOR ON HER PALACE!
I DIDN'T WANT HER RUNNING LOOSE WHEN I WAS AT WORK.
YOU MAY NOT HAVE WANTED A KITTEN, ELIZABETH... BUT THIS ONE WANTS YOU!
LYNN

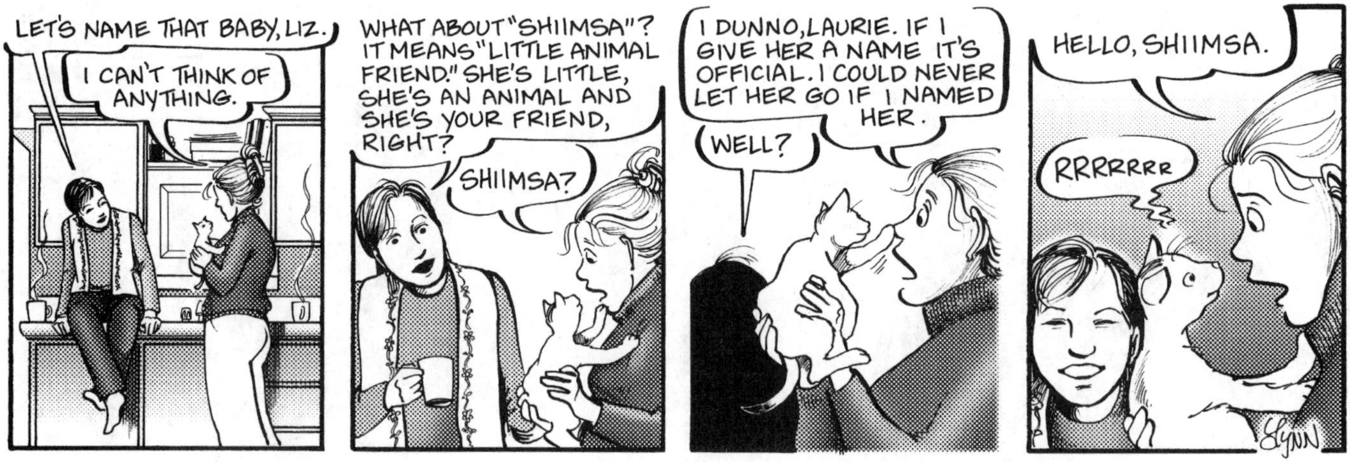
LET'S NAME THAT BABY, LIZ.
I CAN'T THINK OF ANYTHING.
WHAT ABOUT "SHIIMSA"? IT MEANS "LITTLE ANIMAL FRIEND." SHE'S LITTLE, SHE'S AN ANIMAL AND SHE'S YOUR FRIEND, RIGHT?
SHIIMSA?
I DUNNO, LAURIE. IF I GIVE HER A NAME IT'S OFFICIAL. I COULD NEVER LET HER GO IF I NAMED HER.
WELL?
HELLO, SHIIMSA.
RRRRRRR
LYNN

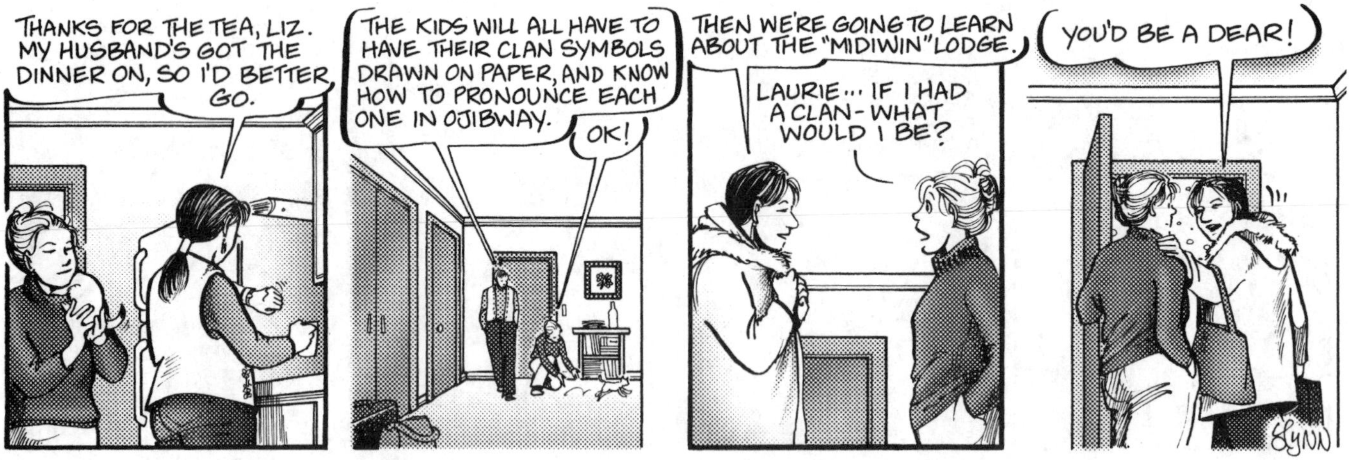
THANKS FOR THE TEA, LIZ. MY HUSBAND'S GOT THE DINNER ON, SO I'D BETTER GO.
THE KIDS WILL ALL HAVE TO HAVE THEIR CLAN SYMBOLS DRAWN ON PAPER, AND KNOW HOW TO PRONOUNCE EACH ONE IN OJIBWAY.
OK!
THEN WE'RE GOING TO LEARN ABOUT THE "MIDIWIN" LODGE.
LAURIE... IF I HAD A CLAN - WHAT WOULD I BE?
YOU'D BE A DEAR!
LYNN

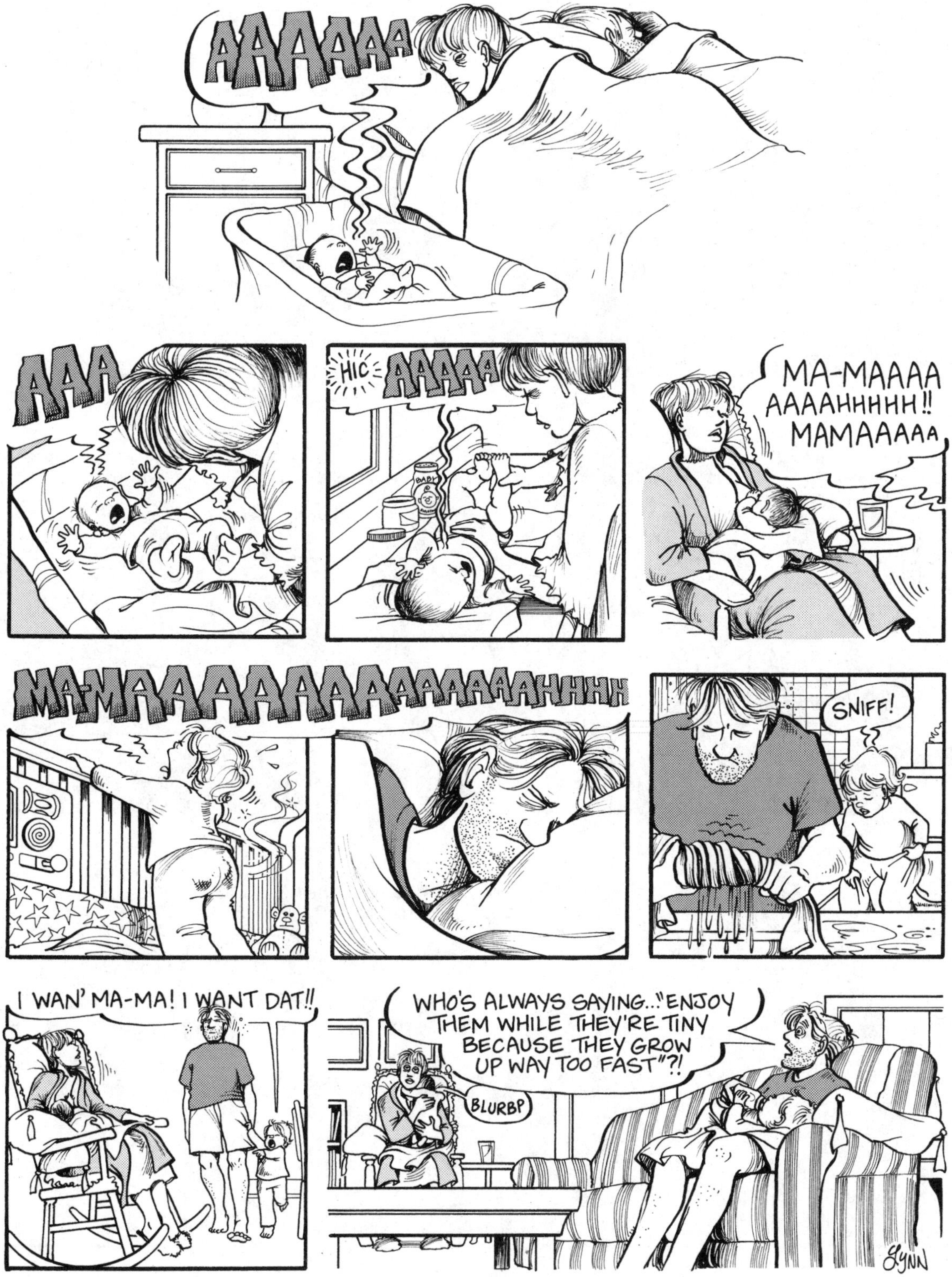
AAAAAA
AAA
HIC AAAAA
MA-MAAAA AAAAHHHHH!! MAMAAAAA
MA-MAAAAAAAAAAAAAHHHH
SNIFF!
I WAN' MA-MA! I WANT DAT!!
WHO'S ALWAYS SAYING..."ENJOY THEM WHILE THEY'RE TINY BECAUSE THEY GROW UP WAY TOO FAST"?!
BLURBP
LYNN

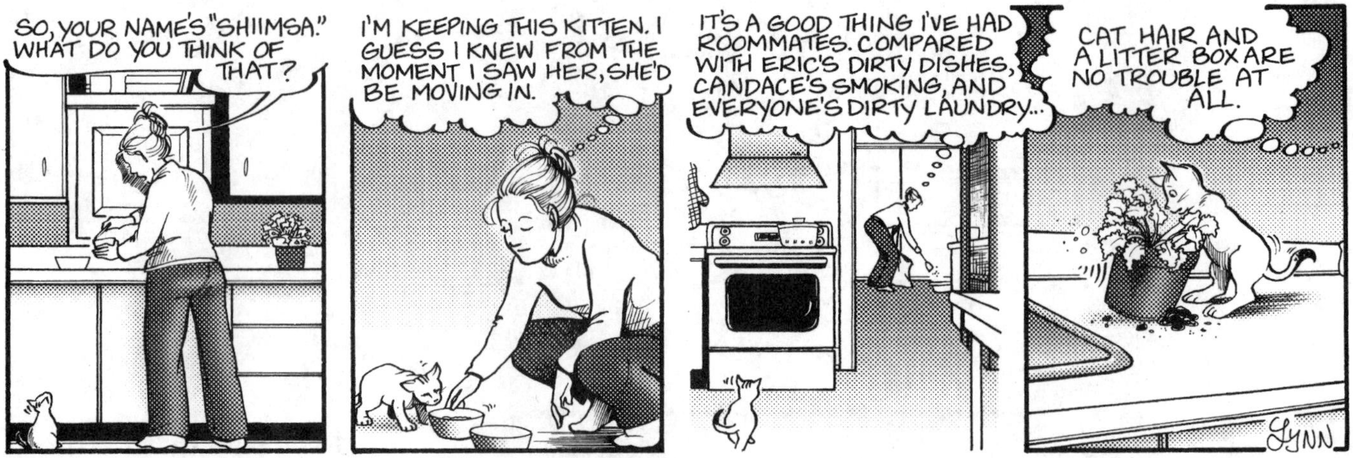
SO, YOUR NAME'S "SHIIMSA." WHAT DO YOU THINK OF THAT?
I'M KEEPING THIS KITTEN. I GUESS I KNEW FROM THE MOMENT I SAW HER, SHE'D BE MOVING IN.
IT'S A GOOD THING I'VE HAD ROOMMATES. COMPARED WITH ERIC'S DIRTY DISHES, CANDACE'S SMOKING, AND EVERYONE'S DIRTY LAUNDRY...
CAT HAIR AND A LITTER BOX ARE NO TROUBLE AT ALL.
LYNN

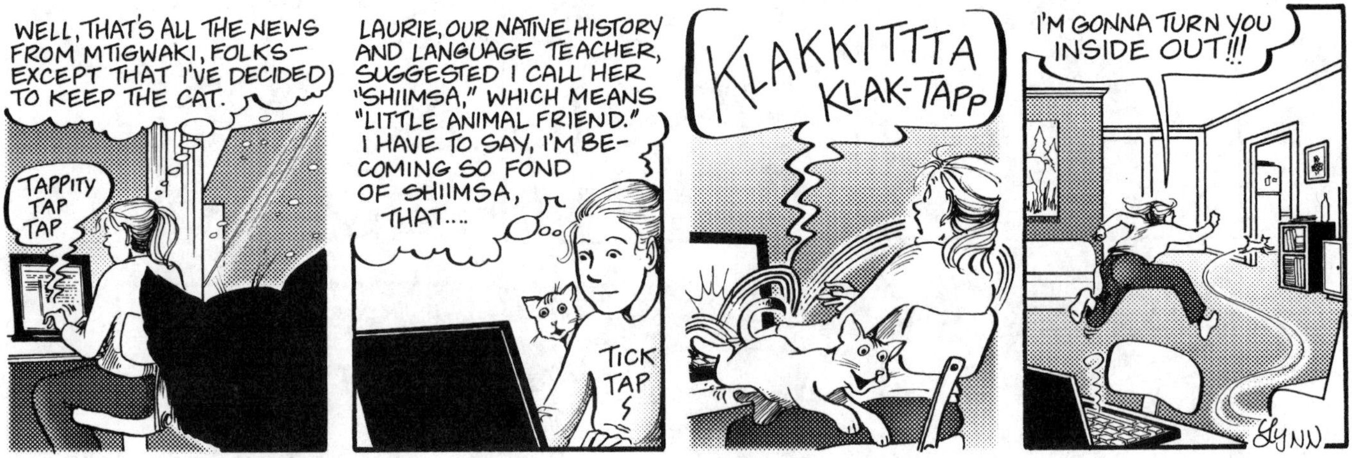
WELL, THAT'S ALL THE NEWS FROM MTIGWAKI, FOLKS— EXCEPT THAT I'VE DECIDED TO KEEP THE CAT.
TAPPITY TAP TAP
LAURIE, OUR NATIVE HISTORY AND LANGUAGE TEACHER, SUGGESTED I CALL HER "SHIIMSA," WHICH MEANS "LITTLE ANIMAL FRIEND." I HAVE TO SAY, I'M BECOMING SO FOND OF SHIIMSA, THAT....
TICK TAP
KLAKKITTTA KLAK-TAPP
I'M GONNA TURN YOU INSIDE OUT!!!
LYNN

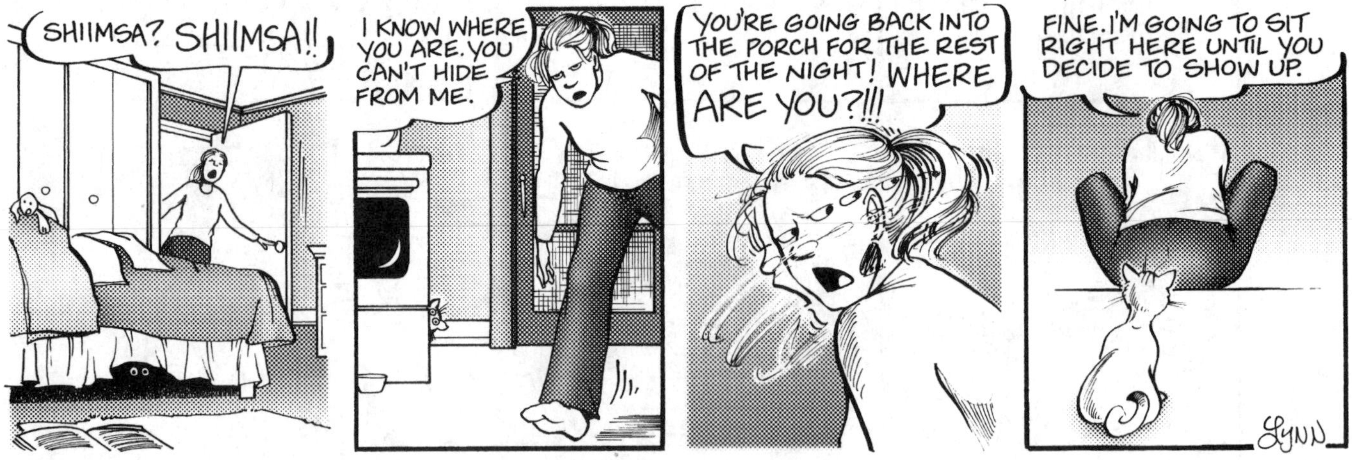
SHIIMSA? SHIIMSA!!
I KNOW WHERE YOU ARE. YOU CAN'T HIDE FROM ME.
YOU'RE GOING BACK INTO THE PORCH FOR THE REST OF THE NIGHT! WHERE ARE YOU?!!!
FINE. I'M GOING TO SIT RIGHT HERE UNTIL YOU DECIDE TO SHOW UP.
LYNN

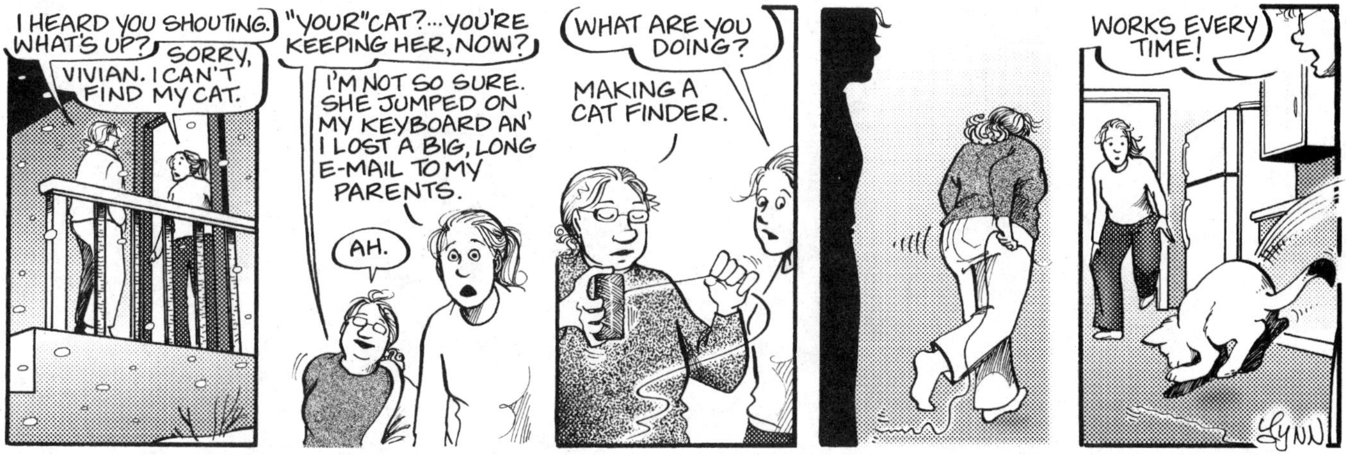
I HEARD YOU SHOUTING. WHAT'S UP?
SORRY, VIVIAN. I CAN'T FIND MY CAT.
"YOUR" CAT?... YOU'RE KEEPING HER, NOW?
I'M NOT SO SURE. SHE JUMPED ON MY KEYBOARD AN' I LOST A BIG, LONG E-MAIL TO MY PARENTS.
AH.
WHAT ARE YOU DOING?
MAKING A CAT FINDER.
WORKS EVERY TIME!
LYNN

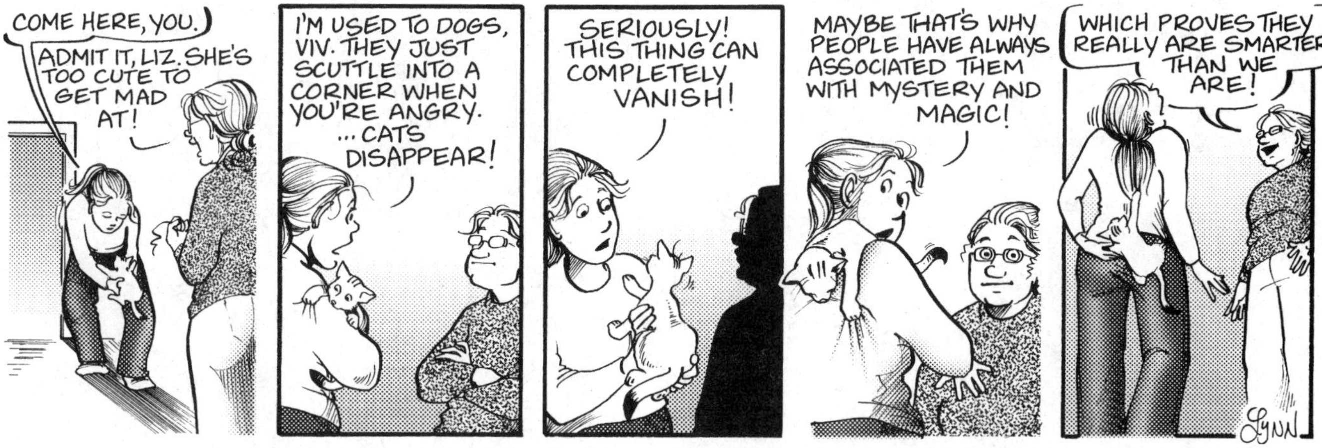
COME HERE, YOU.
ADMIT IT, LIZ. SHE'S TOO CUTE TO GET MAD AT!
I'M USED TO DOGS, VIV. THEY JUST SCUTTLE INTO A CORNER WHEN YOU'RE ANGRY. ...CATS DISAPPEAR!
SERIOUSLY! THIS THING CAN COMPLETELY VANISH!
MAYBE THAT'S WHY PEOPLE HAVE ALWAYS ASSOCIATED THEM WITH MYSTERY AND MAGIC!
WHICH PROVES THEY REALLY ARE SMARTER THAN WE ARE!
LYNN

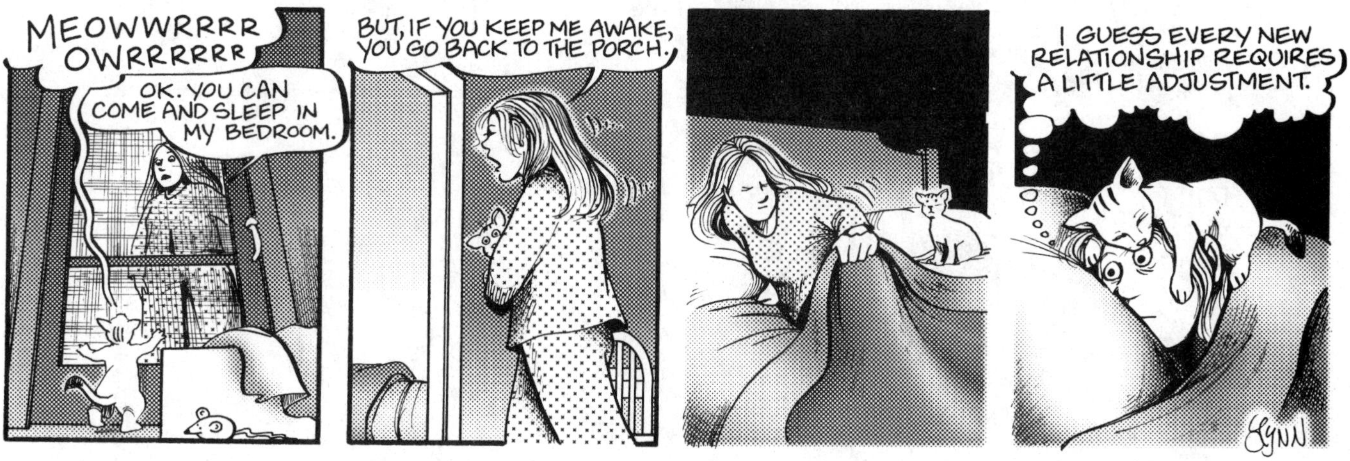
MEOWWRRRR OWRRRRRR
OK. YOU CAN COME AND SLEEP IN MY BEDROOM.
BUT, IF YOU KEEP ME AWAKE, YOU GO BACK TO THE PORCH.
I GUESS EVERY NEW RELATIONSHIP REQUIRES A LITTLE ADJUSTMENT.
LYNN

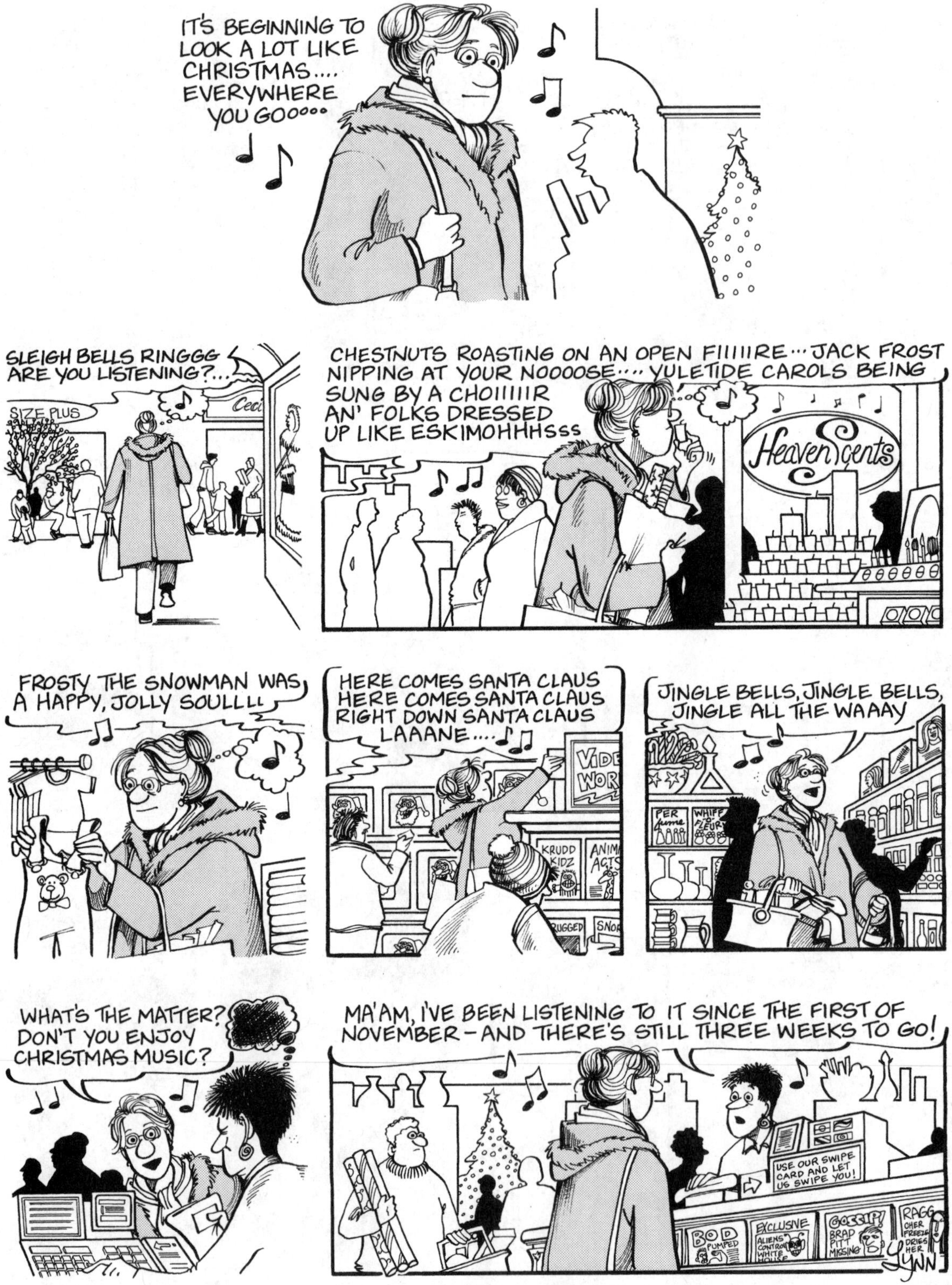

IT'S BEGINNING TO LOOK A LOT LIKE CHRISTMAS.... EVERYWHERE YOU GOoooo
SLEIGH BELLS RINGGG ARE YOU LISTENING?...
SIZE PLUS
CHESTNUTS ROASTING ON AN OPEN FIIIIIRE... JACK FROST NIPPING AT YOUR NOOOOSE.... YULETIDE CAROLS BEING SUNG BY A CHOIIIIIR AN' FOLKS DRESSED UP LIKE ESKIMOHHHSSS
Heaven Scents
FROSTY THE SNOWMAN WAS A HAPPY, JOLLY SOULLLLL
HERE COMES SANTA CLAUS HERE COMES SANTA CLAUS RIGHT DOWN SANTA CLAUS LAAANE....
KRUDD KIDZ
JINGLE BELLS, JINGLE BELLS, JINGLE ALL THE WAAAY
WHAT'S THE MATTER? DON'T YOU ENJOY CHRISTMAS MUSIC?
MA'AM, I'VE BEEN LISTENING TO IT SINCE THE FIRST OF NOVEMBER – AND THERE'S STILL THREE WEEKS TO GO!
USE OUR SWIPE CARD AND LET US SWIPE YOU!
GOSSIP! BRAD PITT MISSING
Lynn

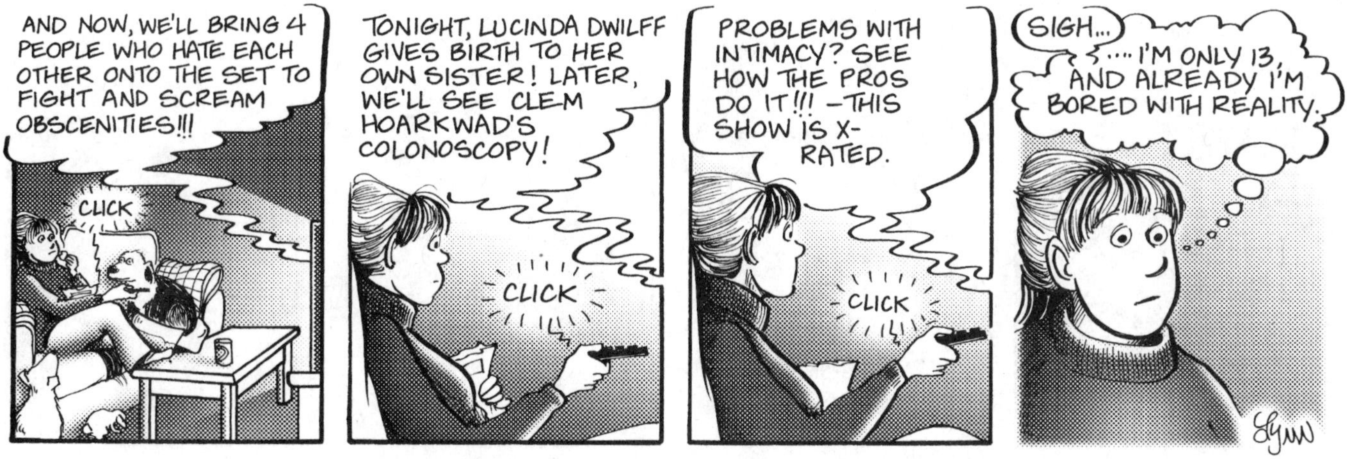
AND NOW, WE'LL BRING 4 PEOPLE WHO HATE EACH OTHER ONTO THE SET TO FIGHT AND SCREAM OBSCENITIES!!!
CLICK
TONIGHT, LUCINDA DWILFF GIVES BIRTH TO HER OWN SISTER! LATER, WE'LL SEE CLEM HOARKWAD'S COLONOSCOPY!
CLICK
PROBLEMS WITH INTIMACY? SEE HOW THE PROS DO IT!!! –THIS SHOW IS X-RATED.
CLICK
SIGH...
.... I'M ONLY 13, AND ALREADY I'M BORED WITH REALITY.

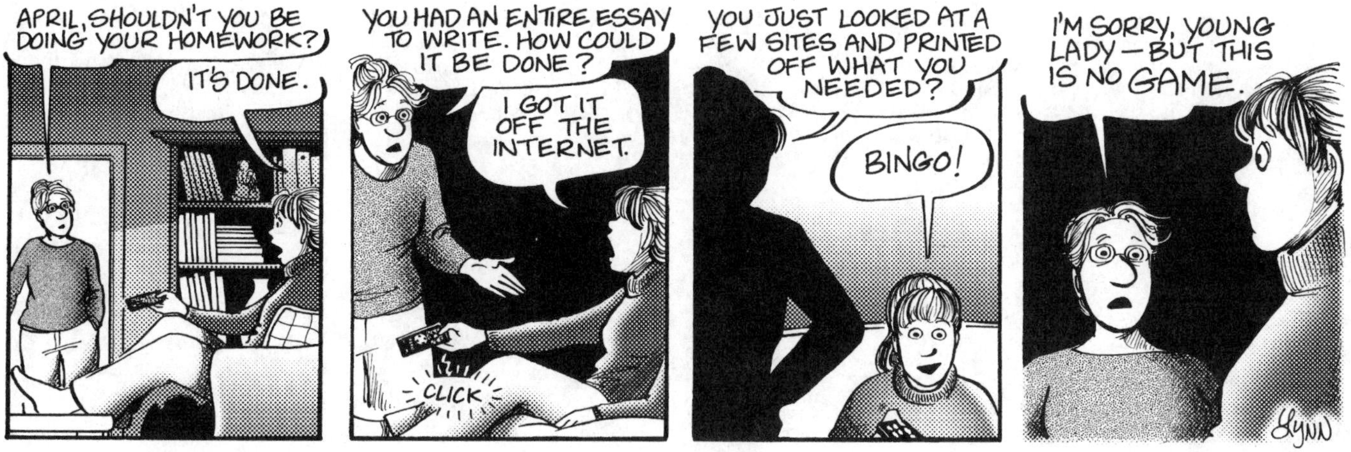
APRIL, SHOULDN'T YOU BE DOING YOUR HOMEWORK?
IT'S DONE.
YOU HAD AN ENTIRE ESSAY TO WRITE. HOW COULD IT BE DONE?
I GOT IT OFF THE INTERNET.
CLICK
YOU JUST LOOKED AT A FEW SITES AND PRINTED OFF WHAT YOU NEEDED?
BINGO!
I'M SORRY, YOUNG LADY – BUT THIS IS NO GAME.

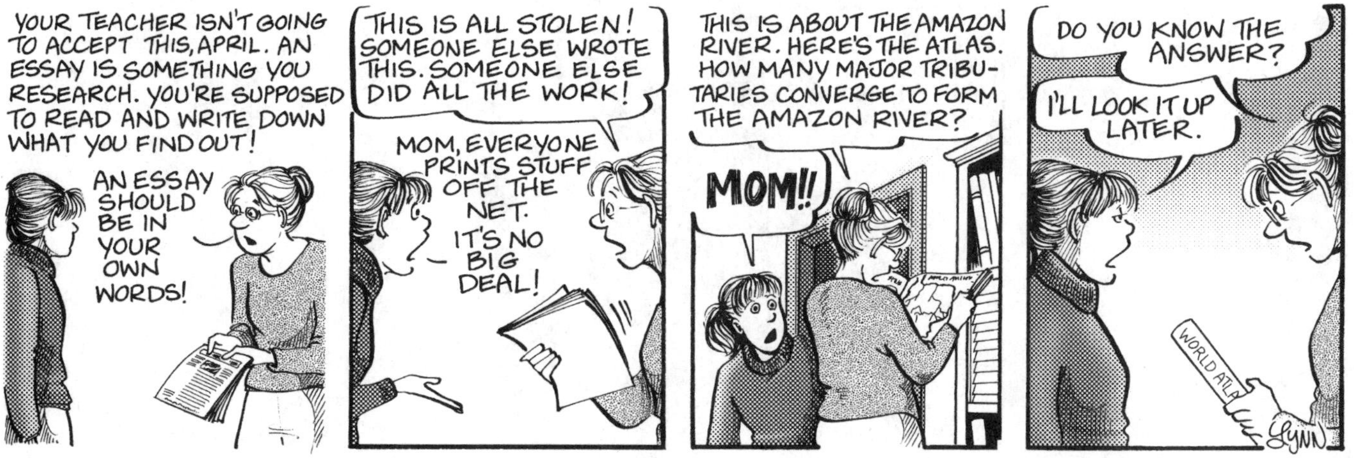
YOUR TEACHER ISN'T GOING TO ACCEPT THIS, APRIL. AN ESSAY IS SOMETHING YOU RESEARCH. YOU'RE SUPPOSED TO READ AND WRITE DOWN WHAT YOU FIND OUT!
AN ESSAY SHOULD BE IN YOUR OWN WORDS!
THIS IS ALL STOLEN! SOMEONE ELSE WROTE THIS. SOMEONE ELSE DID ALL THE WORK!
MOM, EVERYONE PRINTS STUFF OFF THE NET.
IT'S NO BIG DEAL!
THIS IS ABOUT THE AMAZON RIVER. HERE'S THE ATLAS. HOW MANY MAJOR TRIBUTARIES CONVERGE TO FORM THE AMAZON RIVER?
MOM!!
DO YOU KNOW THE ANSWER?
I'LL LOOK IT UP LATER.
WORLD ATLAS

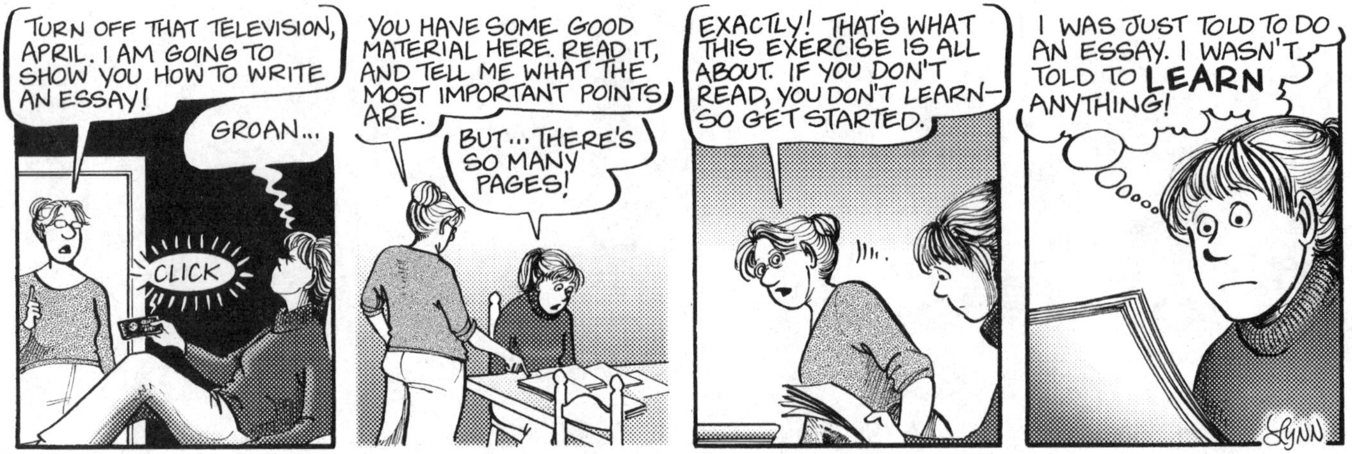
TURN OFF THAT TELEVISION, APRIL. I AM GOING TO SHOW YOU HOW TO WRITE AN ESSAY!
GROAN...
CLICK
YOU HAVE SOME GOOD MATERIAL HERE. READ IT, AND TELL ME WHAT THE MOST IMPORTANT POINTS ARE.
BUT... THERE'S SO MANY PAGES!
EXACTLY! THAT'S WHAT THIS EXERCISE IS ALL ABOUT. IF YOU DON'T READ, YOU DON'T LEARN— SO GET STARTED.
I WAS JUST TOLD TO DO AN ESSAY. I WASN'T TOLD TO LEARN ANYTHING!
LYNN

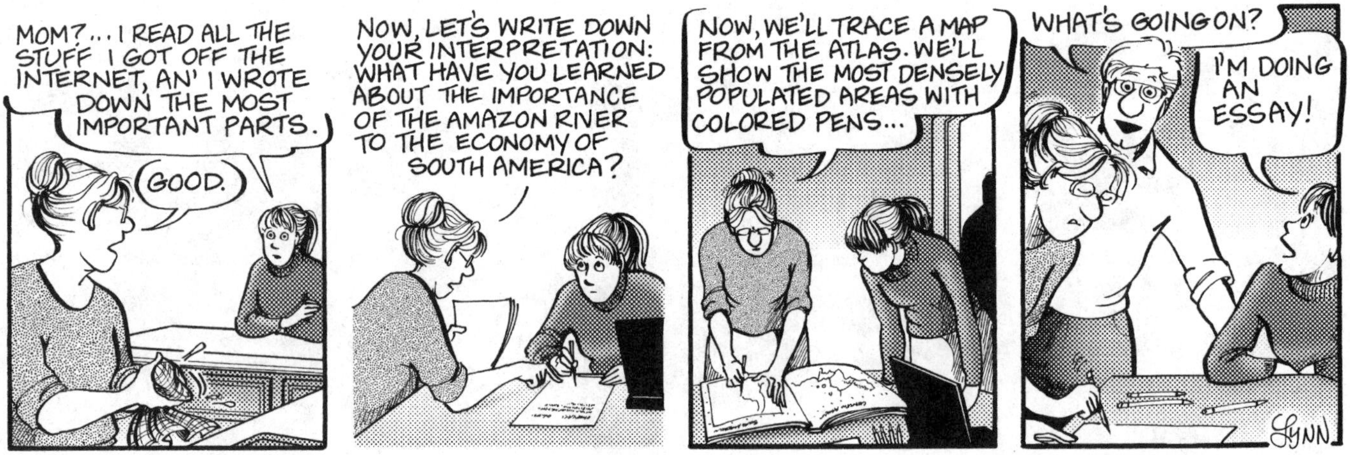
MOM?... I READ ALL THE STUFF I GOT OFF THE INTERNET, AN' I WROTE DOWN THE MOST IMPORTANT PARTS.
GOOD.
NOW, LET'S WRITE DOWN YOUR INTERPRETATION: WHAT HAVE YOU LEARNED ABOUT THE IMPORTANCE OF THE AMAZON RIVER TO THE ECONOMY OF SOUTH AMERICA?
NOW, WE'LL TRACE A MAP FROM THE ATLAS. WE'LL SHOW THE MOST DENSELY POPULATED AREAS WITH COLORED PENS...
WHAT'S GOING ON?
I'M DOING AN ESSAY!
LYNN

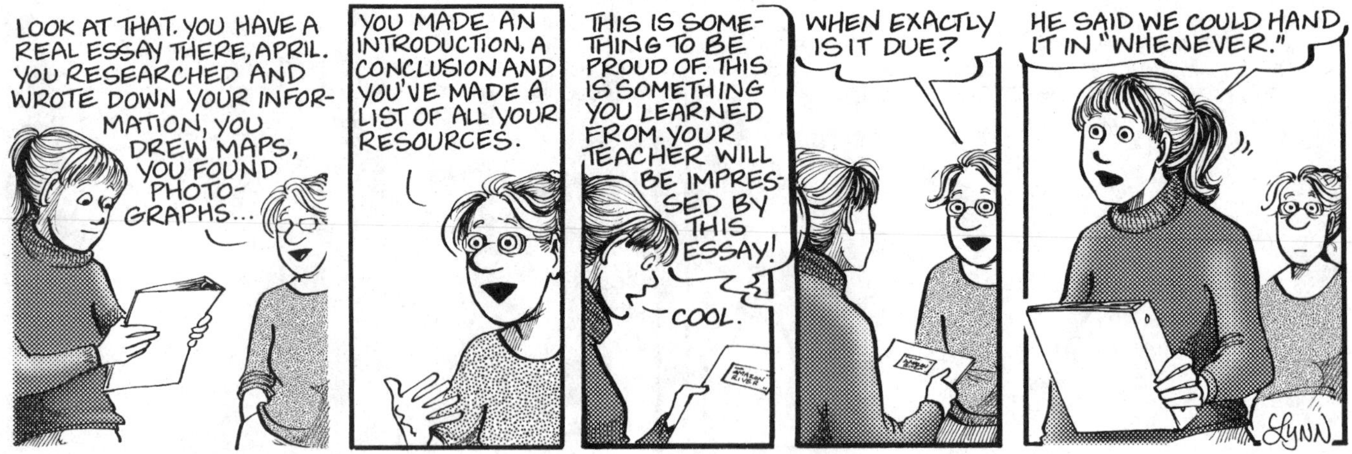
LOOK AT THAT. YOU HAVE A REAL ESSAY THERE, APRIL. YOU RESEARCHED AND WROTE DOWN YOUR INFORMATION, YOU DREW MAPS, YOU FOUND PHOTOGRAPHS...
YOU MADE AN INTRODUCTION, A CONCLUSION AND YOU'VE MADE A LIST OF ALL YOUR RESOURCES.
THIS IS SOMETHING TO BE PROUD OF. THIS IS SOMETHING YOU LEARNED FROM. YOUR TEACHER WILL BE IMPRESSED BY THIS ESSAY!
—COOL.
WHEN EXACTLY IS IT DUE?
HE SAID WE COULD HAND IT IN "WHENEVER."
LYNN

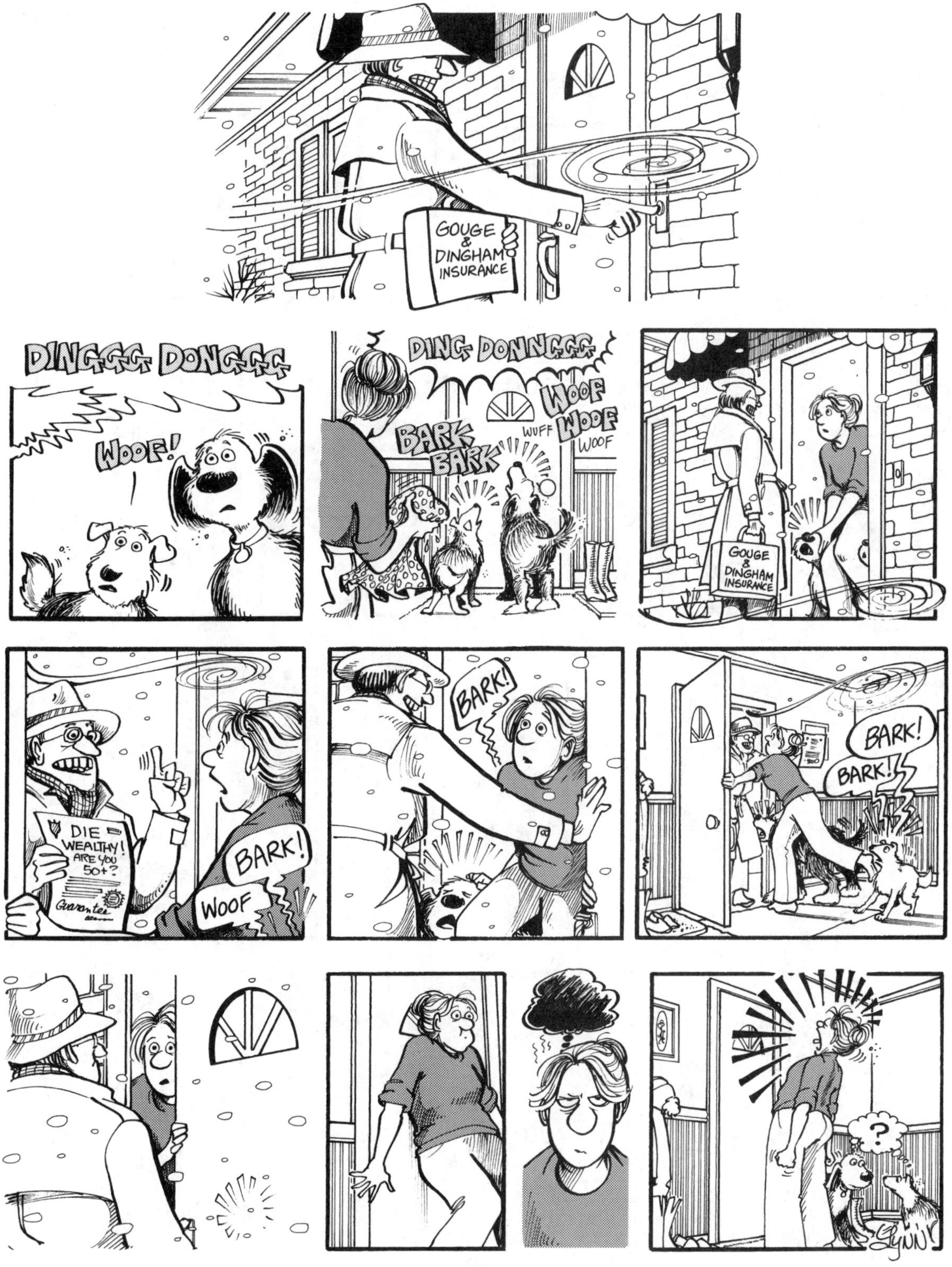
GOUGE & DINGHAM INSURANCE
DINGGG DONGGG
WOOF!
DING DONNGGG
BARK BARK
WOOF WOOF
WUFF
WOOF
GOUGE & DINGHAM INSURANCE
DIE WEALTHY! ARE YOU 50+?
Guarantee
BARK!
WOOF
BARK!
BARK!
BARK!
?
LYNN

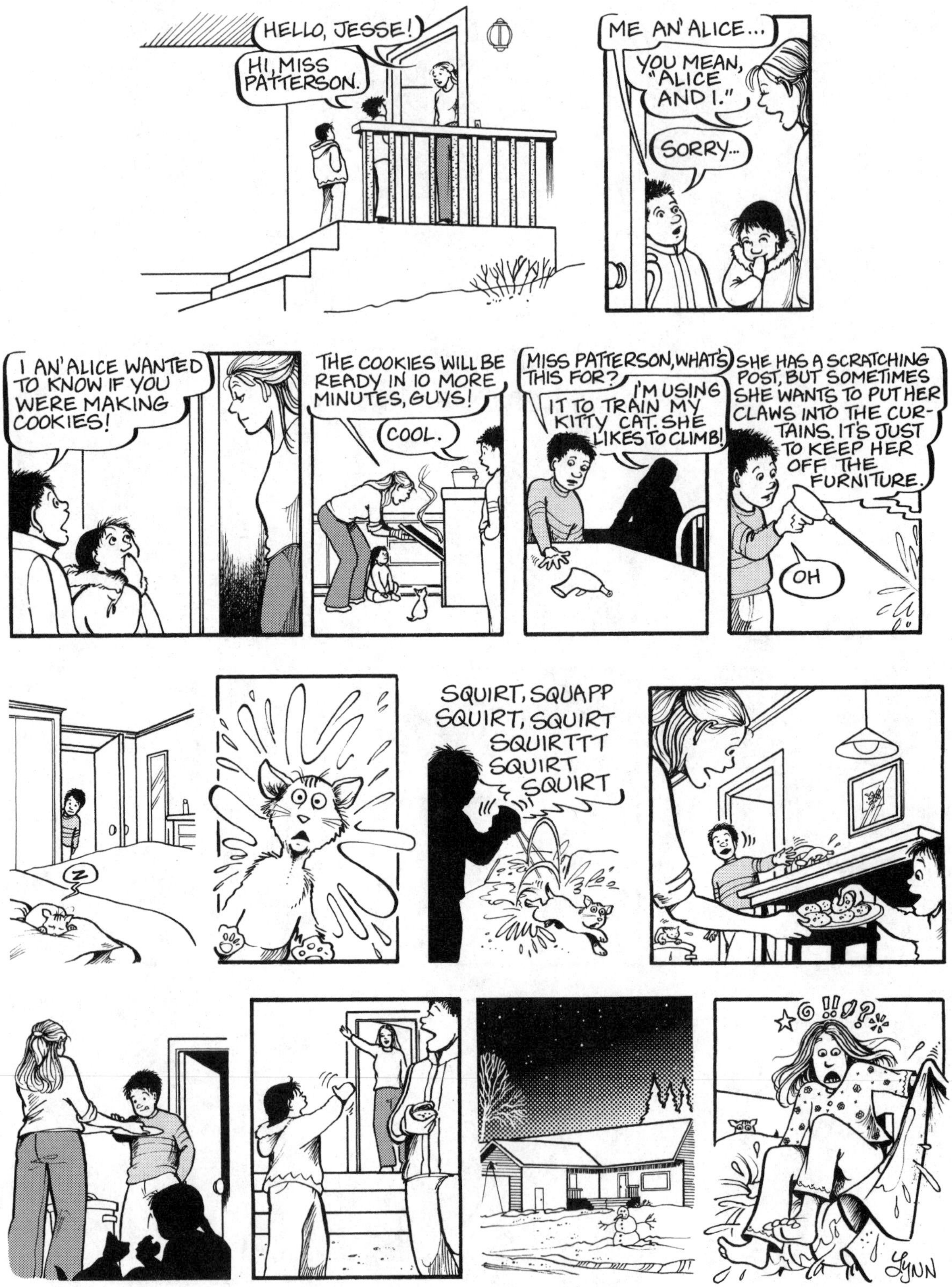
HELLO, JESSE!
HI, MISS PATTERSON.
ME AN' ALICE...
YOU MEAN, "ALICE AND I."
SORRY...
I AN' ALICE WANTED TO KNOW IF YOU WERE MAKING COOKIES!
THE COOKIES WILL BE READY IN 10 MORE MINUTES, GUYS!
COOL.
MISS PATTERSON, WHAT'S THIS FOR?
I'M USING IT TO TRAIN MY KITTY CAT. SHE LIKES TO CLIMB!
SHE HAS A SCRATCHING POST, BUT SOMETIMES SHE WANTS TO PUT HER CLAWS INTO THE CURTAINS. IT'S JUST TO KEEP HER OFF THE FURNITURE.
OH
Z
SQUIRT, SQUAPP
SQUIRT, SQUIRT
SQUIRTTT
SQUIRT
SQUIRT
LYNN

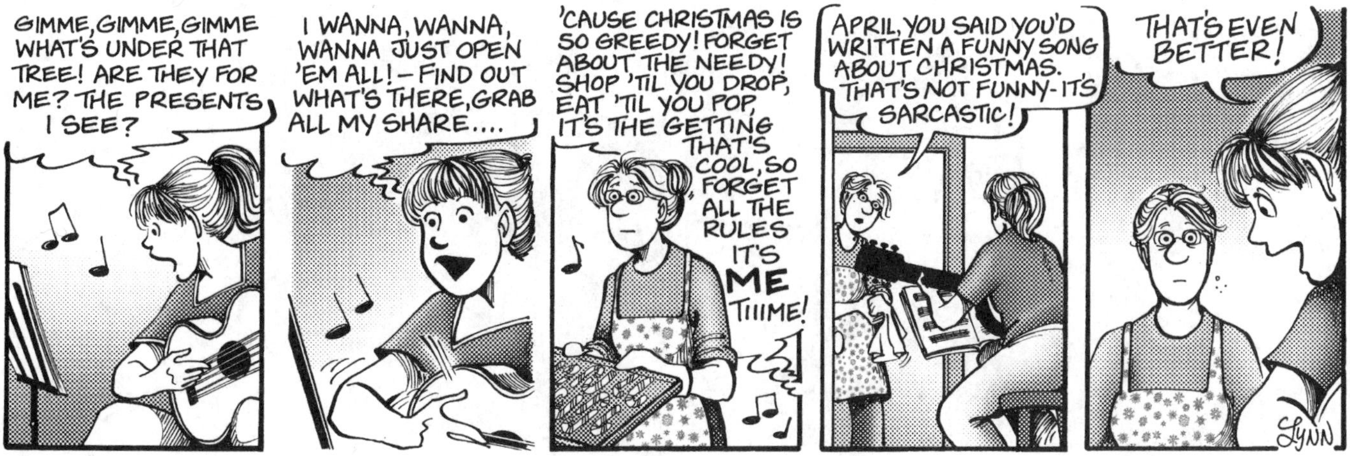
GIMME, GIMME, GIMME WHAT'S UNDER THAT TREE! ARE THEY FOR ME? THE PRESENTS I SEE?
I WANNA, WANNA, WANNA JUST OPEN 'EM ALL! – FIND OUT WHAT'S THERE, GRAB ALL MY SHARE....
'CAUSE CHRISTMAS IS SO GREEDY! FORGET ABOUT THE NEEDY! SHOP 'TIL YOU DROP, EAT 'TIL YOU POP, IT'S THE GETTING THAT'S COOL, SO FORGET ALL THE RULES IT'S ME TIIIME!
APRIL, YOU SAID YOU'D WRITTEN A FUNNY SONG ABOUT CHRISTMAS. THAT'S NOT FUNNY- IT'S SARCASTIC!
THAT'S EVEN BETTER!
LYNN

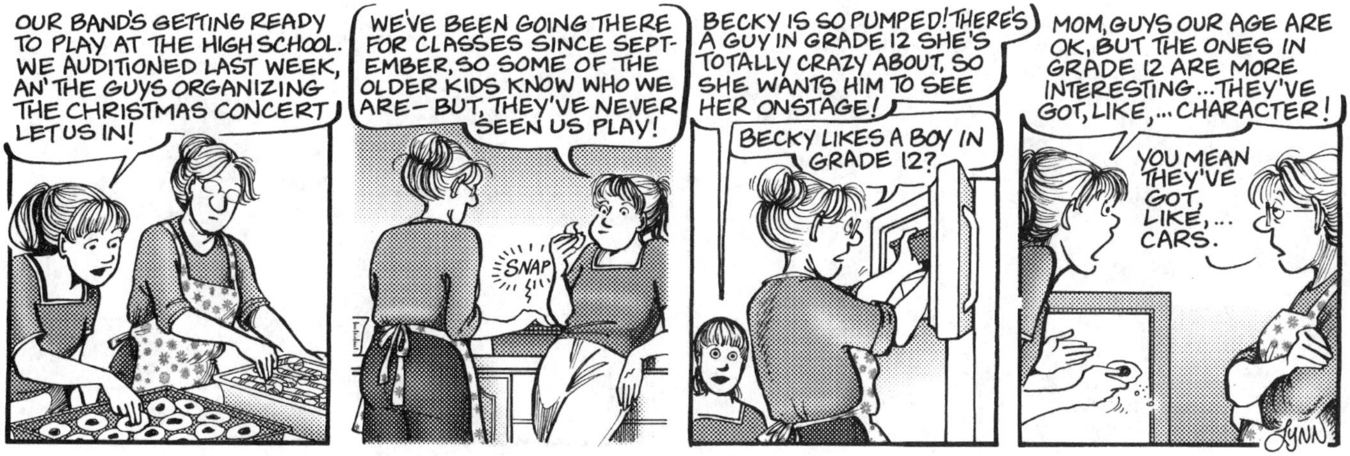
OUR BAND'S GETTING READY TO PLAY AT THE HIGH SCHOOL. WE AUDITIONED LAST WEEK, AN' THE GUYS ORGANIZING THE CHRISTMAS CONCERT LET US IN!
WE'VE BEEN GOING THERE FOR CLASSES SINCE SEPTEMBER, SO SOME OF THE OLDER KIDS KNOW WHO WE ARE – BUT, THEY'VE NEVER SEEN US PLAY!
SNAP
BECKY IS SO PUMPED! THERE'S A GUY IN GRADE 12 SHE'S TOTALLY CRAZY ABOUT, SO SHE WANTS HIM TO SEE HER ONSTAGE!
BECKY LIKES A BOY IN GRADE 12?
MOM, GUYS OUR AGE ARE OK, BUT THE ONES IN GRADE 12 ARE MORE INTERESTING... THEY'VE GOT, LIKE, ... CHARACTER!
YOU MEAN THEY'VE GOT, LIKE, ... CARS.
LYNN

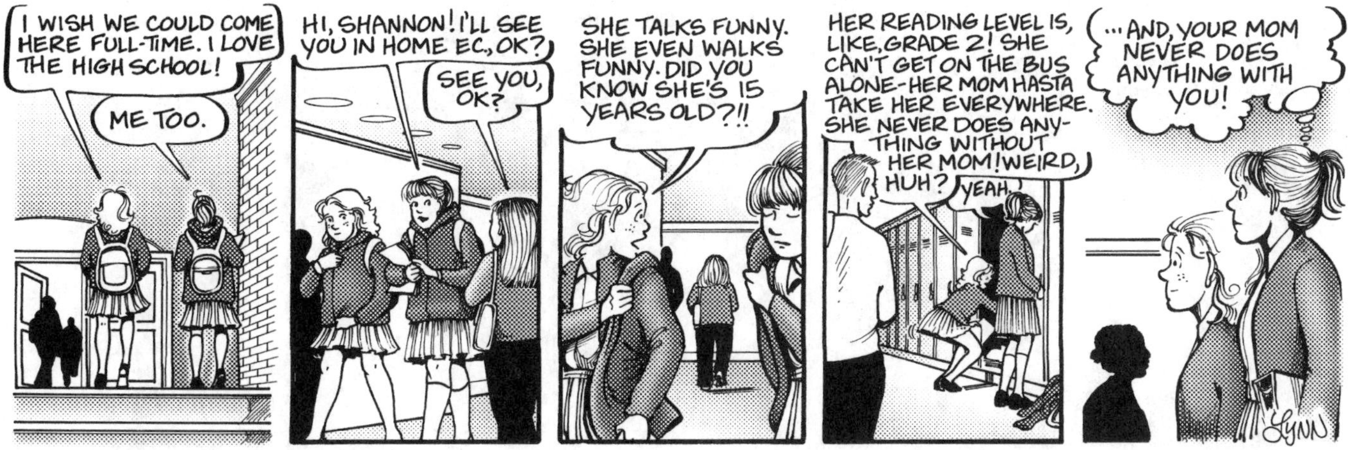
I WISH WE COULD COME HERE FULL-TIME. I LOVE THE HIGH SCHOOL!
ME TOO.
HI, SHANNON! I'LL SEE YOU IN HOME EC., OK?
SEE YOU, OK?
SHE TALKS FUNNY. SHE EVEN WALKS FUNNY. DID YOU KNOW SHE'S 15 YEARS OLD?!!
HER READING LEVEL IS, LIKE, GRADE 2! SHE CAN'T GET ON THE BUS ALONE- HER MOM HASTA TAKE HER EVERYWHERE. SHE NEVER DOES ANYTHING WITHOUT HER MOM! WEIRD, HUH?
YEAH.
...AND, YOUR MOM NEVER DOES ANYTHING WITH YOU!
LYNN

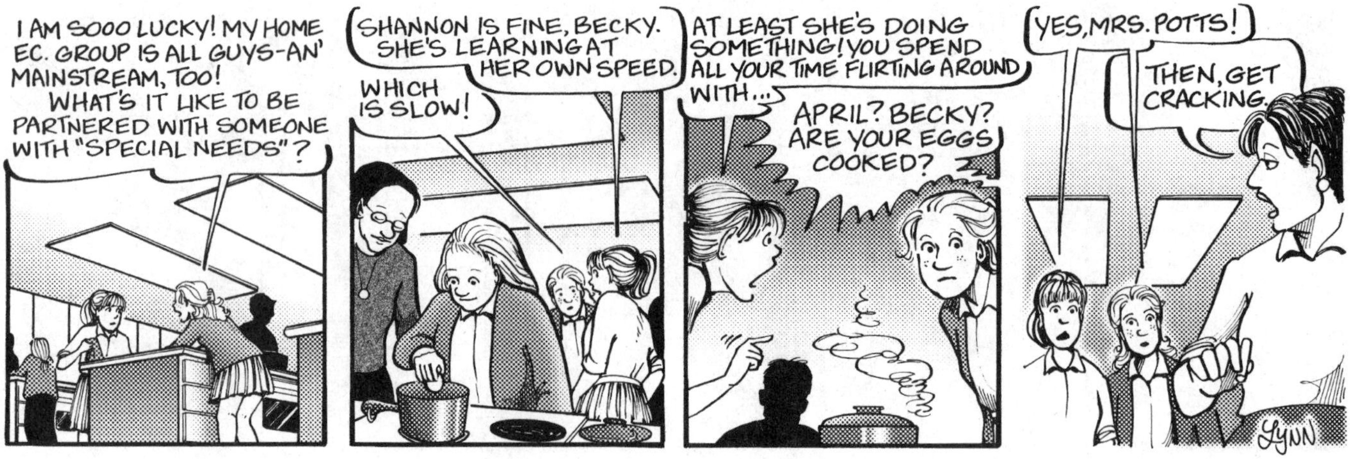
I AM SOOO LUCKY! MY HOME EC. GROUP IS ALL GUYS-AN' MAINSTREAM, TOO! WHAT'S IT LIKE TO BE PARTNERED WITH SOMEONE WITH "SPECIAL NEEDS"?
SHANNON IS FINE, BECKY. SHE'S LEARNING AT HER OWN SPEED.
WHICH IS SLOW!
AT LEAST SHE'S DOING SOMETHING! YOU SPEND ALL YOUR TIME FLIRTING AROUND WITH...
APRIL? BECKY? ARE YOUR EGGS COOKED?
YES, MRS. POTTS!
THEN, GET CRACKING.
LYNN

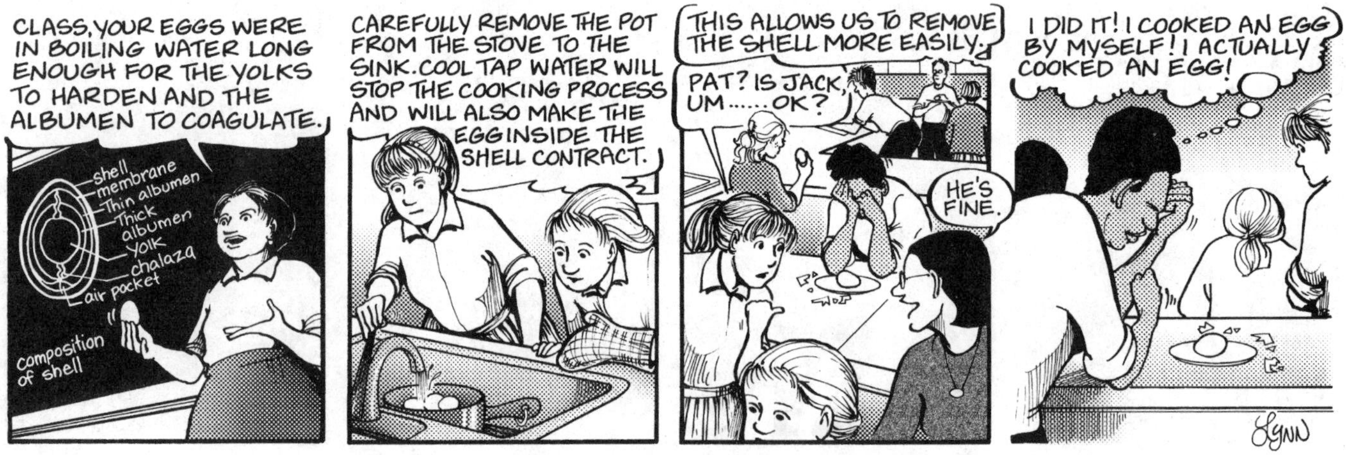
CLASS, YOUR EGGS WERE IN BOILING WATER LONG ENOUGH FOR THE YOLKS TO HARDEN AND THE ALBUMEN TO COAGULATE.
shell
membrane
Thin albumen
Thick albumen
Yolk
chalaza
air pocket
composition of shell
CAREFULLY REMOVE THE POT FROM THE STOVE TO THE SINK. COOL TAP WATER WILL STOP THE COOKING PROCESS AND WILL ALSO MAKE THE EGG INSIDE THE SHELL CONTRACT.
THIS ALLOWS US TO REMOVE THE SHELL MORE EASILY.
PAT? IS JACK, UM...... OK?
HE'S FINE.
I DID IT! I COOKED AN EGG BY MYSELF! I ACTUALLY COOKED AN EGG!
LYNN

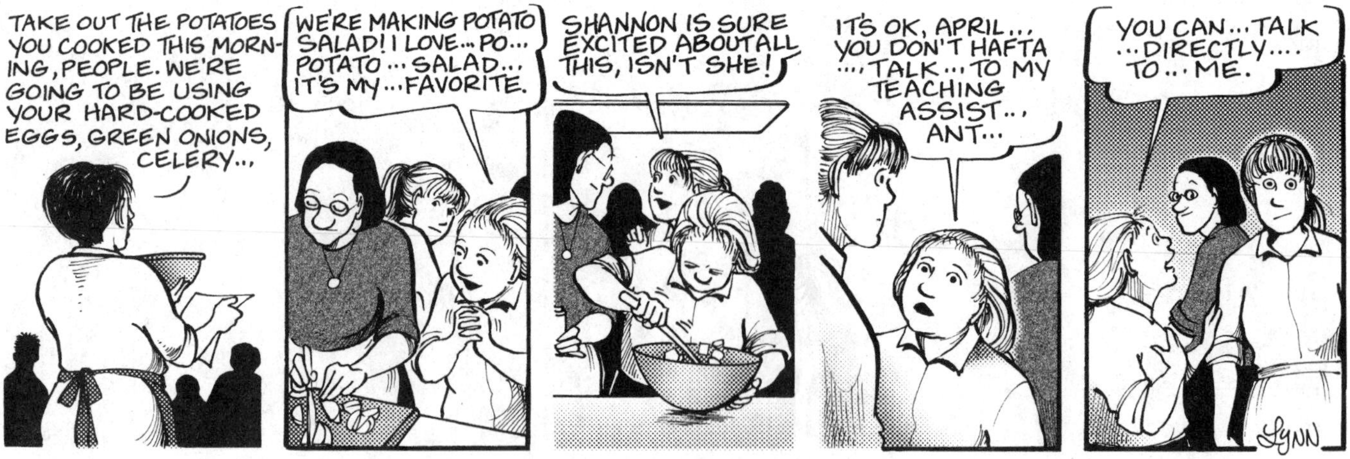
TAKE OUT THE POTATOES YOU COOKED THIS MORNING, PEOPLE. WE'RE GOING TO BE USING YOUR HARD-COOKED EGGS, GREEN ONIONS, CELERY...
WE'RE MAKING POTATO SALAD! I LOVE... PO... POTATO... SALAD... IT'S MY... FAVORITE.
SHANNON IS SURE EXCITED ABOUT ALL THIS, ISN'T SHE!
IT'S OK, APRIL... YOU DON'T HAFTA ... TALK... TO MY TEACHING ASSIST... ANT...
YOU CAN... TALK ... DIRECTLY.... TO... ME.
LYNN

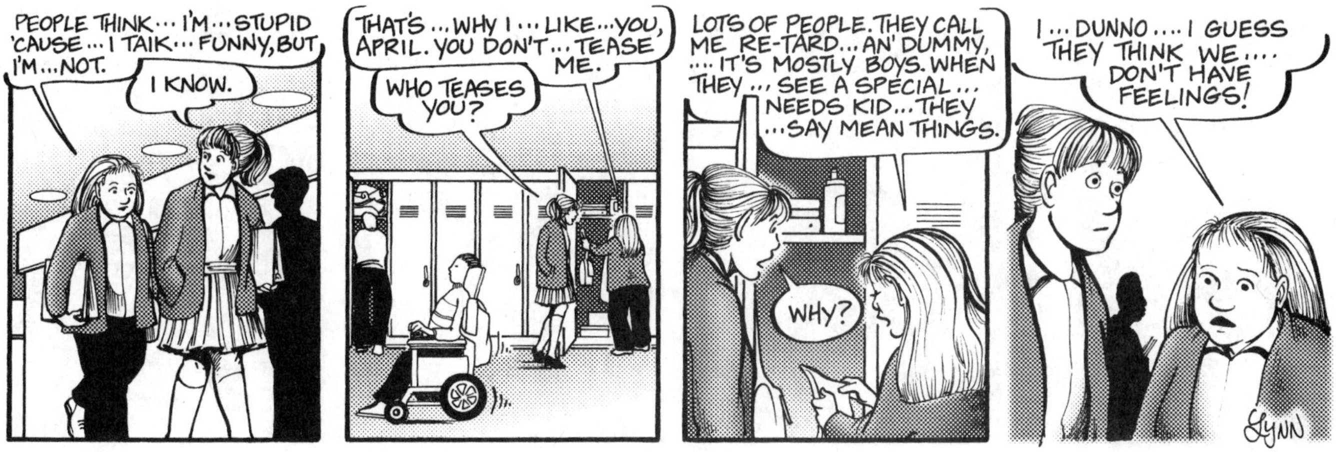
PEOPLE THINK ... I'M ... STUPID 'CAUSE ... I TALK ... FUNNY, BUT I'M ... NOT.
I KNOW.
THAT'S ... WHY I ... LIKE ... YOU, APRIL. YOU DON'T ... TEASE ME.
WHO TEASES YOU?
LOTS OF PEOPLE. THEY CALL ME RE-TARD ... AN' DUMMY, ... IT'S MOSTLY BOYS. WHEN THEY ... SEE A SPECIAL ... NEEDS KID ... THEY ... SAY MEAN THINGS.
WHY?
I ... DUNNO .... I GUESS THEY THINK WE .... DON'T HAVE FEELINGS!
LYNN

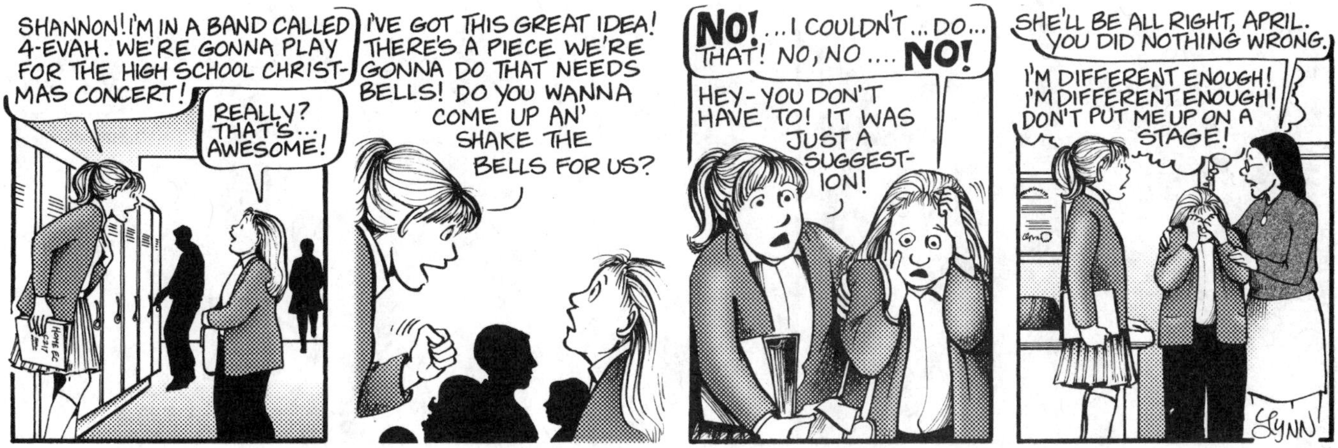
SHANNON! I'M IN A BAND CALLED 4-EVAH. WE'RE GONNA PLAY FOR THE HIGH SCHOOL CHRISTMAS CONCERT!
REALLY? THAT'S ... AWESOME!
I'VE GOT THIS GREAT IDEA! THERE'S A PIECE WE'RE GONNA DO THAT NEEDS BELLS! DO YOU WANNA COME UP AN' SHAKE THE BELLS FOR US?
NO! ... I COULDN'T ... DO ... THAT! NO, NO .... NO!
HEY- YOU DON'T HAVE TO! IT WAS JUST A SUGGESTION!
SHE'LL BE ALL RIGHT, APRIL. YOU DID NOTHING WRONG.
I'M DIFFERENT ENOUGH! I'M DIFFERENT ENOUGH! DON'T PUT ME UP ON A STAGE!
LYNN

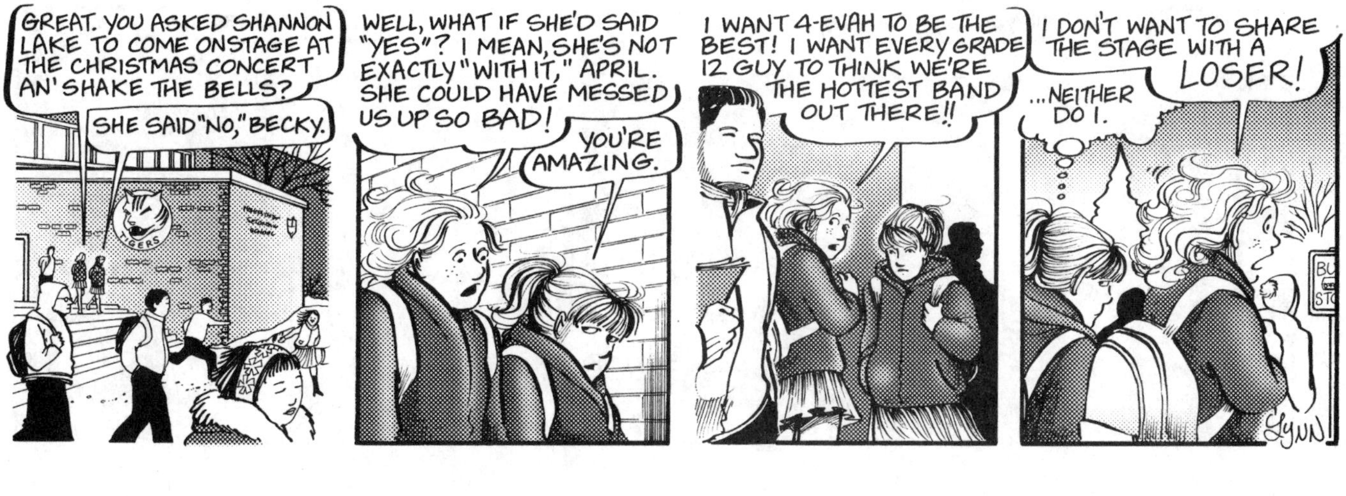
GREAT. YOU ASKED SHANNON LAKE TO COME ONSTAGE AT THE CHRISTMAS CONCERT AN' SHAKE THE BELLS?
SHE SAID "NO," BECKY.
TIGERS
WELL, WHAT IF SHE'D SAID "YES"? I MEAN, SHE'S NOT EXACTLY "WITH IT," APRIL. SHE COULD HAVE MESSED US UP SO BAD!
YOU'RE AMAZING.
I WANT 4-EVAH TO BE THE BEST! I WANT EVERY GRADE 12 GUY TO THINK WE'RE THE HOTTEST BAND OUT THERE!!
I DON'T WANT TO SHARE THE STAGE WITH A LOSER!
...NEITHER DO I.
LYNN

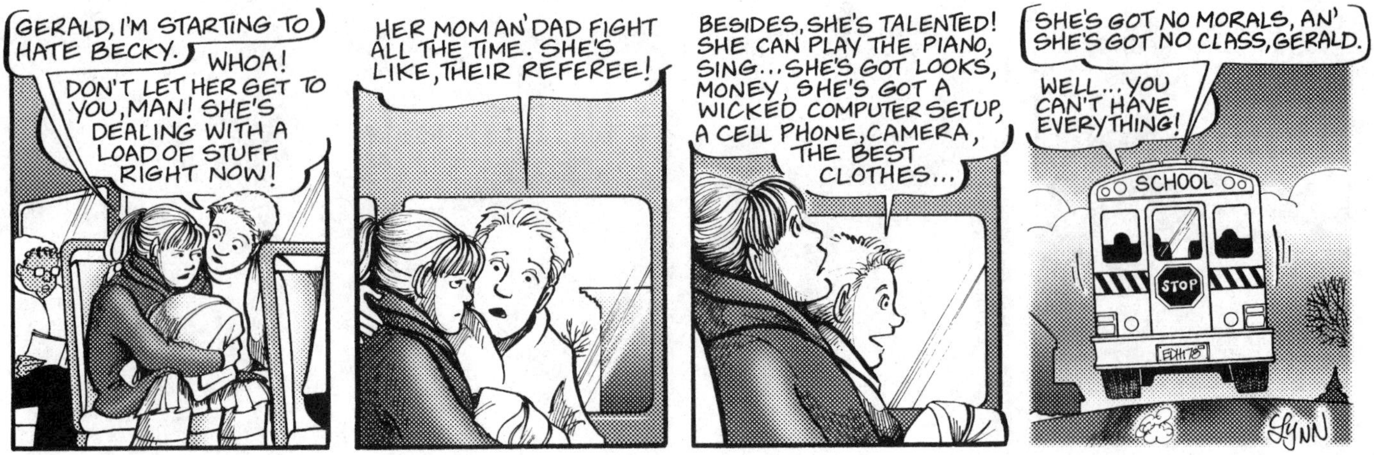
GERALD, I'M STARTING TO HATE BECKY.
WHOA! DON'T LET HER GET TO YOU, MAN! SHE'S DEALING WITH A LOAD OF STUFF RIGHT NOW!
HER MOM AN' DAD FIGHT ALL THE TIME. SHE'S LIKE, THEIR REFEREE!
BESIDES, SHE'S TALENTED! SHE CAN PLAY THE PIANO, SING... SHE'S GOT LOOKS, MONEY, SHE'S GOT A WICKED COMPUTER SETUP, A CELL PHONE, CAMERA, THE BEST CLOTHES...
SHE'S GOT NO MORALS, AN' SHE'S GOT NO CLASS, GERALD.
WELL... YOU CAN'T HAVE EVERYTHING!
SCHOOL
STOP
LYNN

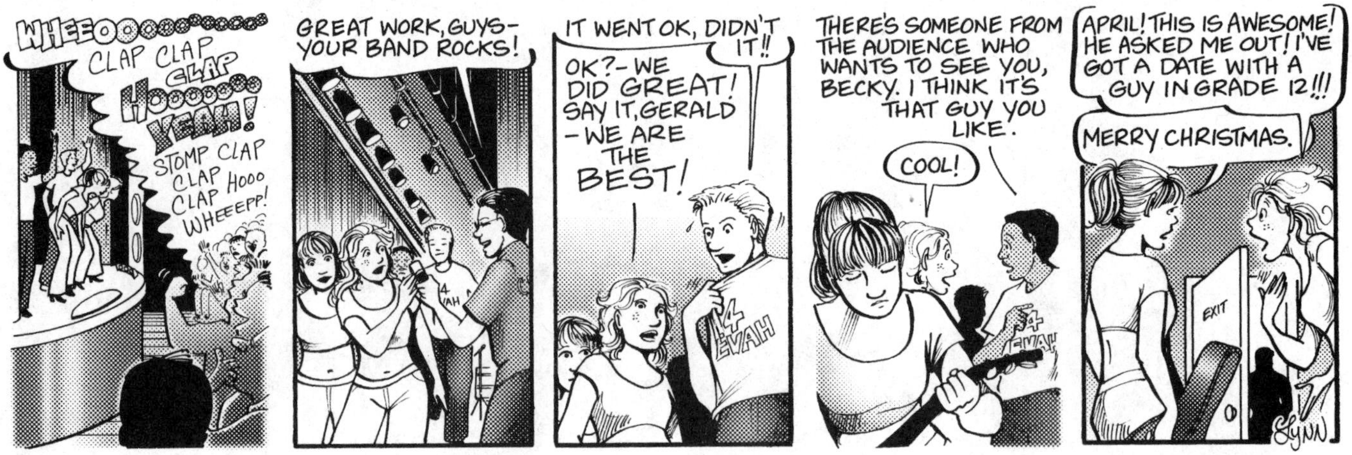
CLAP CLAP
CLAP
YEAH!
STOMP CLAP CLAP HOOO CLAP WHEEEPP!
GREAT WORK, GUYS-YOUR BAND ROCKS!
IT WENT OK, DIDN'T IT!!
OK?- WE DID GREAT! SAY IT, GERALD - WE ARE THE BEST!
THERE'S SOMEONE FROM THE AUDIENCE WHO WANTS TO SEE YOU, BECKY. I THINK IT'S THAT GUY YOU LIKE.
COOL!
APRIL! THIS IS AWESOME! HE ASKED ME OUT! I'VE GOT A DATE WITH A GUY IN GRADE 12!!!
MERRY CHRISTMAS.
EXIT
LYNN

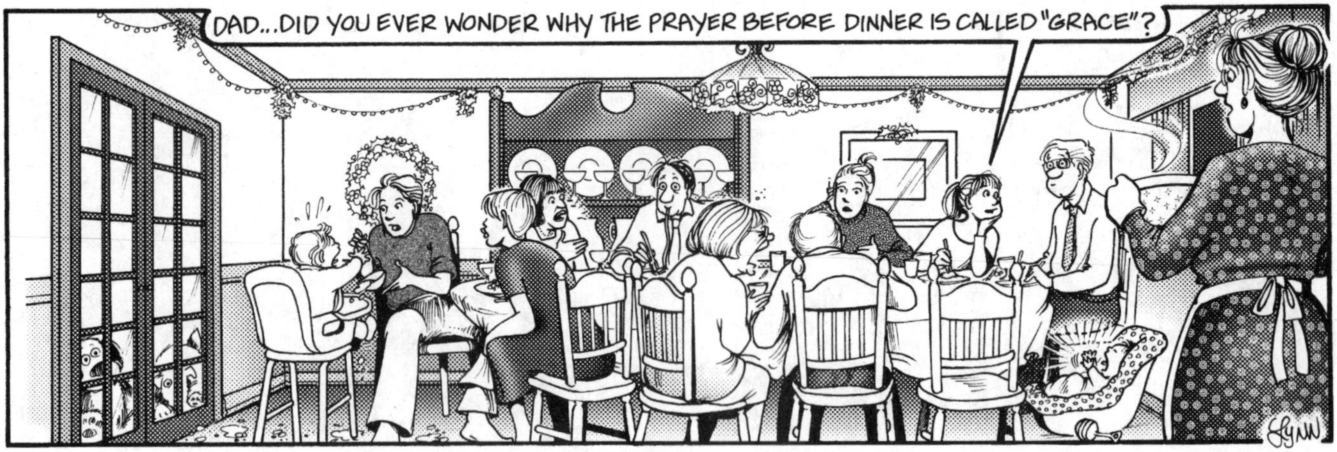
DAD...DID YOU EVER WONDER WHY THE PRAYER BEFORE DINNER IS CALLED "GRACE"?
LYNN

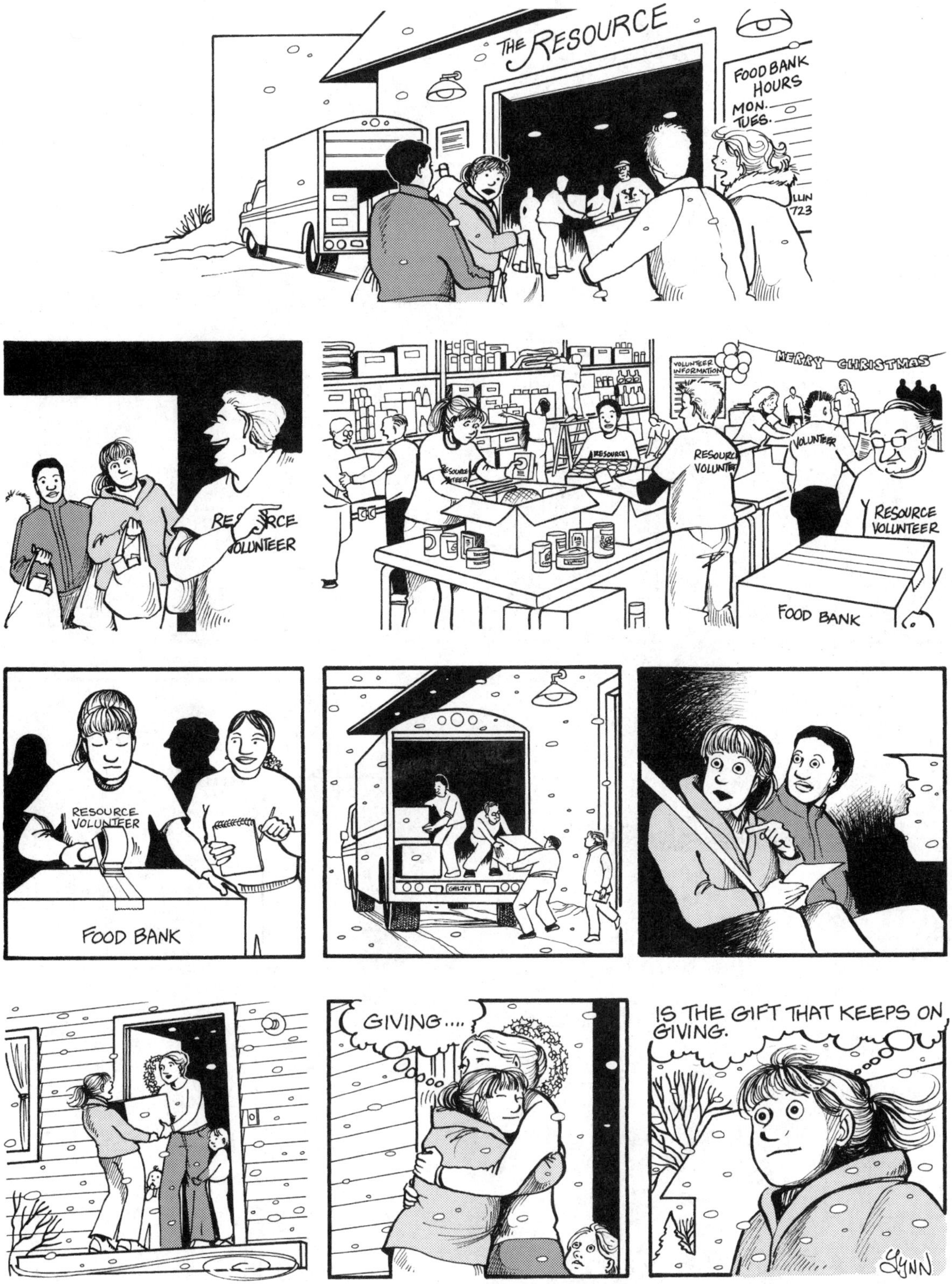
THE RESOURCE
FOOD BANK HOURS
MON.
TUES.
RESOURCE VOLUNTEER
VOLUNTEER INFORMATION
MERRY CHRISTMAS
RESOURCE
RESOURCE VOLUNTEER
VOLUNTEER
RESOURCE VOLUNTEER
FOOD BANK
RESOURCE VOLUNTEER
FOOD BANK
GIVING....
IS THE GIFT THAT KEEPS ON GIVING.
LYNN

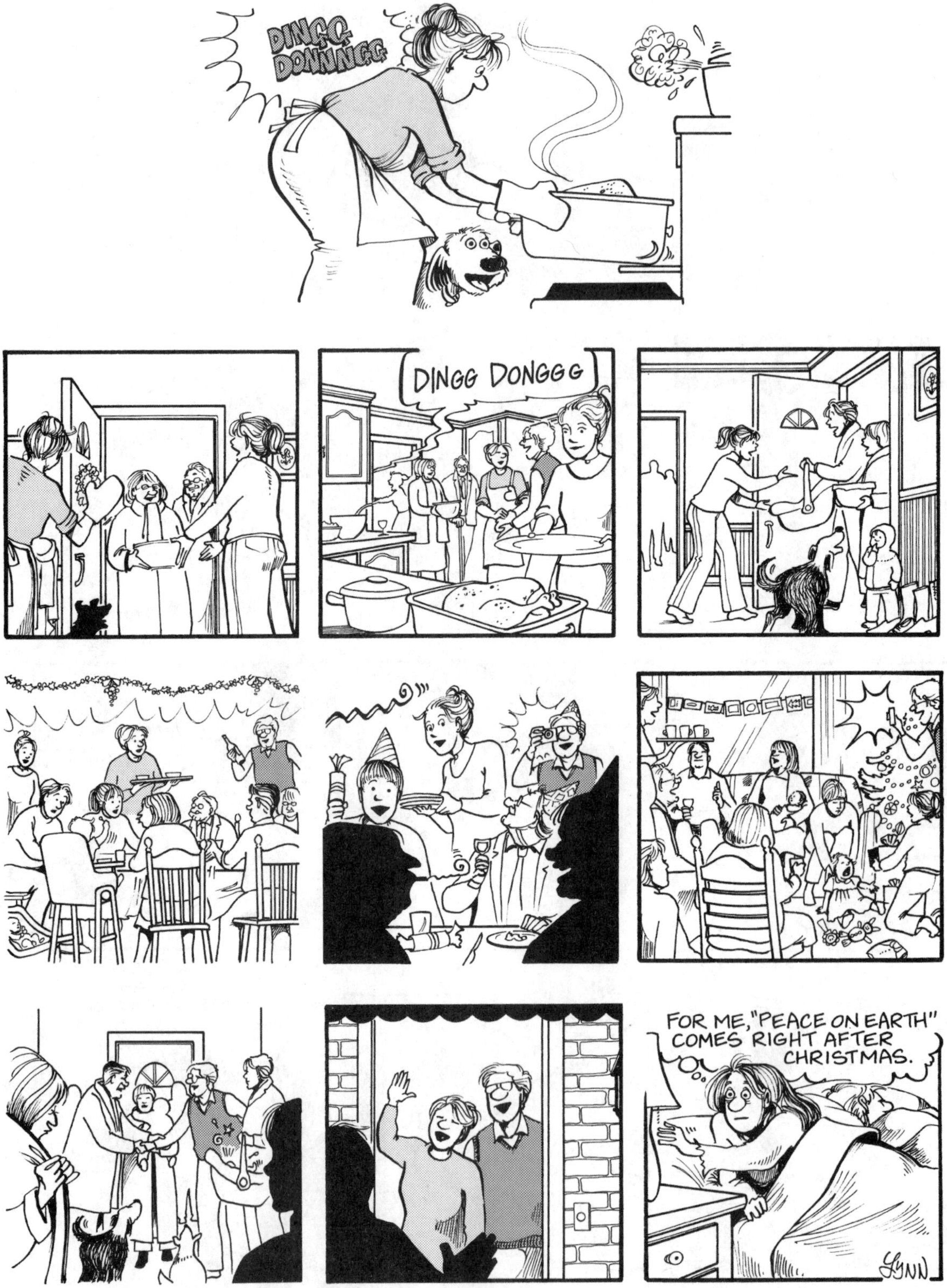
DINGG-DONNNGG
DINGG DONGGG
FOR ME, "PEACE ON EARTH" COMES RIGHT AFTER CHRISTMAS.
LYNN

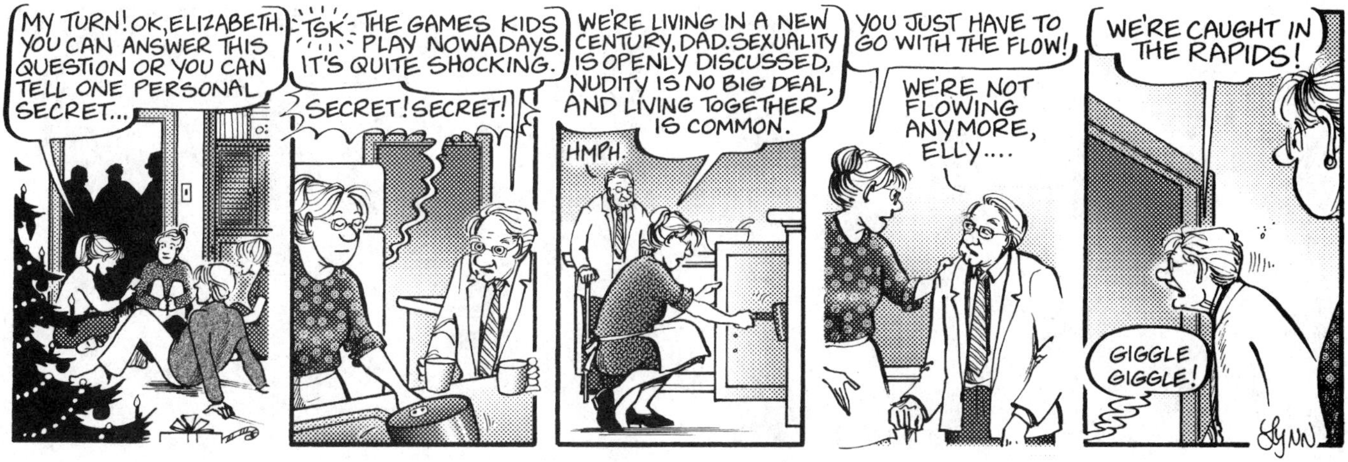
MY TURN! OK, ELIZABETH. YOU CAN ANSWER THIS QUESTION OR YOU CAN TELL ONE PERSONAL SECRET...
TSK
THE GAMES KIDS PLAY NOWADAYS. IT'S QUITE SHOCKING.
SECRET! SECRET!
WE'RE LIVING IN A NEW CENTURY, DAD. SEXUALITY IS OPENLY DISCUSSED, NUDITY IS NO BIG DEAL, AND LIVING TOGETHER IS COMMON.
HMPH.
YOU JUST HAVE TO GO WITH THE FLOW!
WE'RE NOT FLOWING ANYMORE, ELLY....
WE'RE CAUGHT IN THE RAPIDS!
GIGGLE GIGGLE!
LYNN

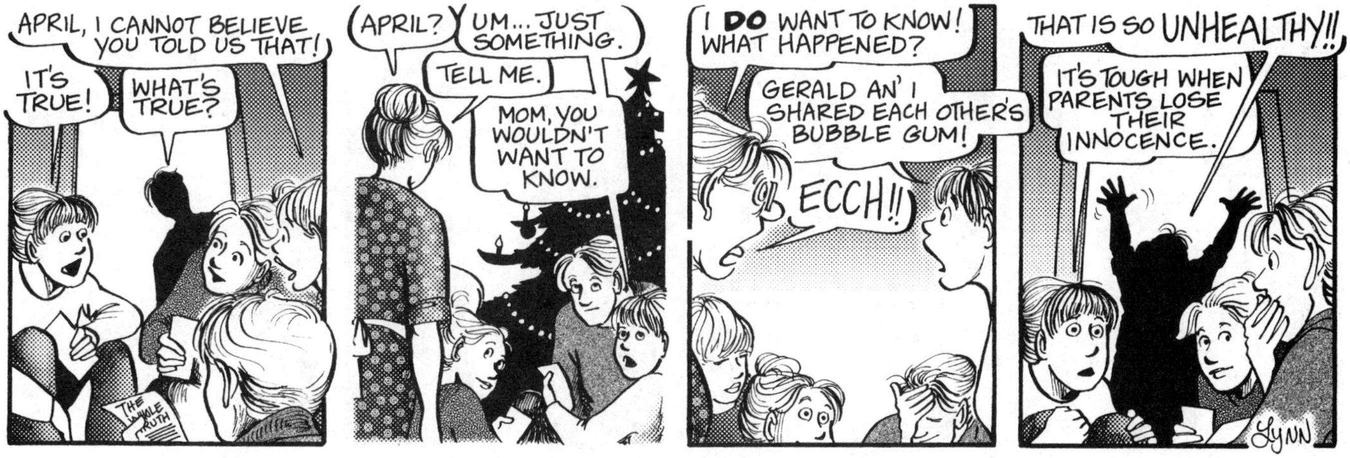
APRIL, I CANNOT BELIEVE YOU TOLD US THAT!
IT'S TRUE!
WHAT'S TRUE?
THE WHOLE TRUTH
APRIL?
UM... JUST SOMETHING.
TELL ME.
MOM, YOU WOULDN'T WANT TO KNOW.
I DO WANT TO KNOW! WHAT HAPPENED?
GERALD AN' I SHARED EACH OTHER'S BUBBLE GUM!
ECCH!!
THAT IS SO UNHEALTHY!!
IT'S TOUGH WHEN PARENTS LOSE THEIR INNOCENCE.
LYNN

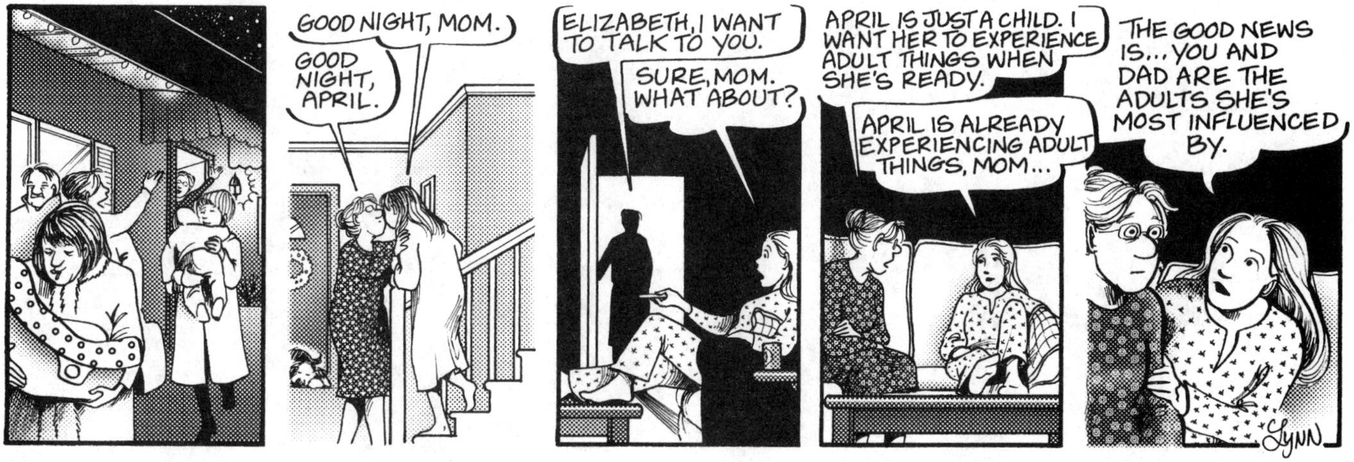
GOOD NIGHT, MOM.
GOOD NIGHT, APRIL.
ELIZABETH, I WANT TO TALK TO YOU.
SURE, MOM. WHAT ABOUT?
APRIL IS JUST A CHILD. I WANT HER TO EXPERIENCE ADULT THINGS WHEN SHE'S READY.
APRIL IS ALREADY EXPERIENCING ADULT THINGS, MOM...
THE GOOD NEWS IS... YOU AND DAD ARE THE ADULTS SHE'S MOST INFLUENCED BY.
LYNN

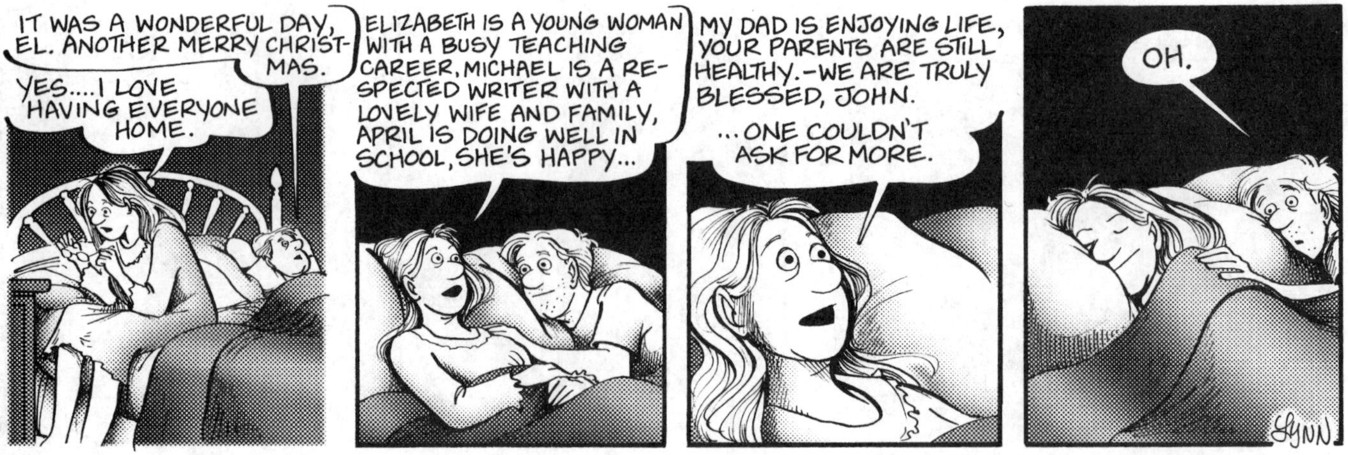
IT WAS A WONDERFUL DAY, EL. ANOTHER MERRY CHRISTMAS.
YES.... I LOVE HAVING EVERYONE HOME.
ELIZABETH IS A YOUNG WOMAN WITH A BUSY TEACHING CAREER, MICHAEL IS A RESPECTED WRITER WITH A LOVELY WIFE AND FAMILY, APRIL IS DOING WELL IN SCHOOL, SHE'S HAPPY...
MY DAD IS ENJOYING LIFE, YOUR PARENTS ARE STILL HEALTHY. - WE ARE TRULY BLESSED, JOHN.
... ONE COULDN'T ASK FOR MORE.
OH.
LYNN

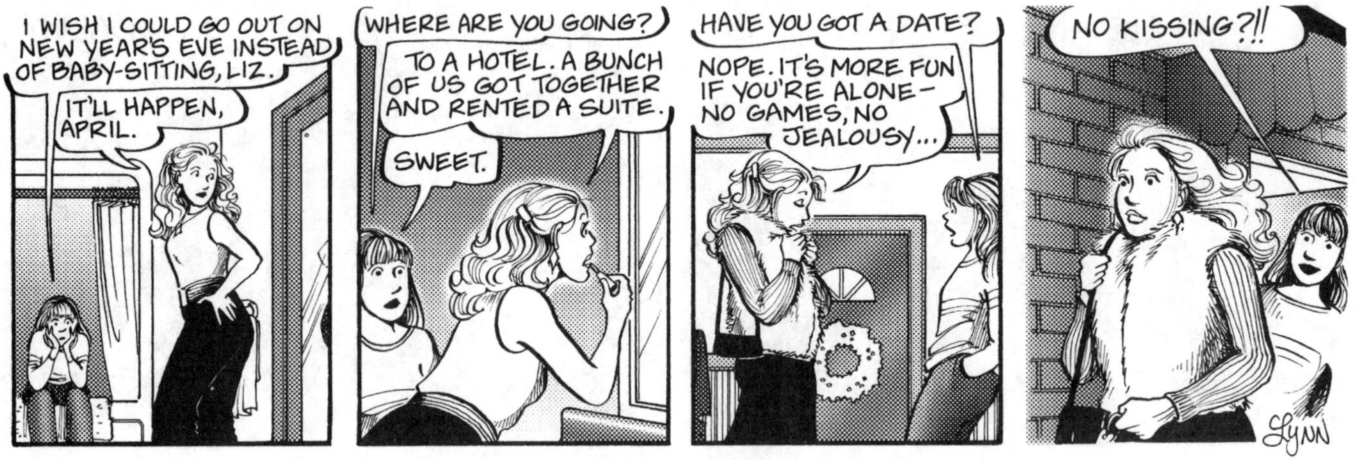
I WISH I COULD GO OUT ON NEW YEAR'S EVE INSTEAD OF BABY-SITTING, LIZ.
IT'LL HAPPEN, APRIL.
WHERE ARE YOU GOING?
TO A HOTEL. A BUNCH OF US GOT TOGETHER AND RENTED A SUITE.
SWEET.
HAVE YOU GOT A DATE?
NOPE. IT'S MORE FUN IF YOU'RE ALONE - NO GAMES, NO JEALOUSY...
NO KISSING?!!
LYNN

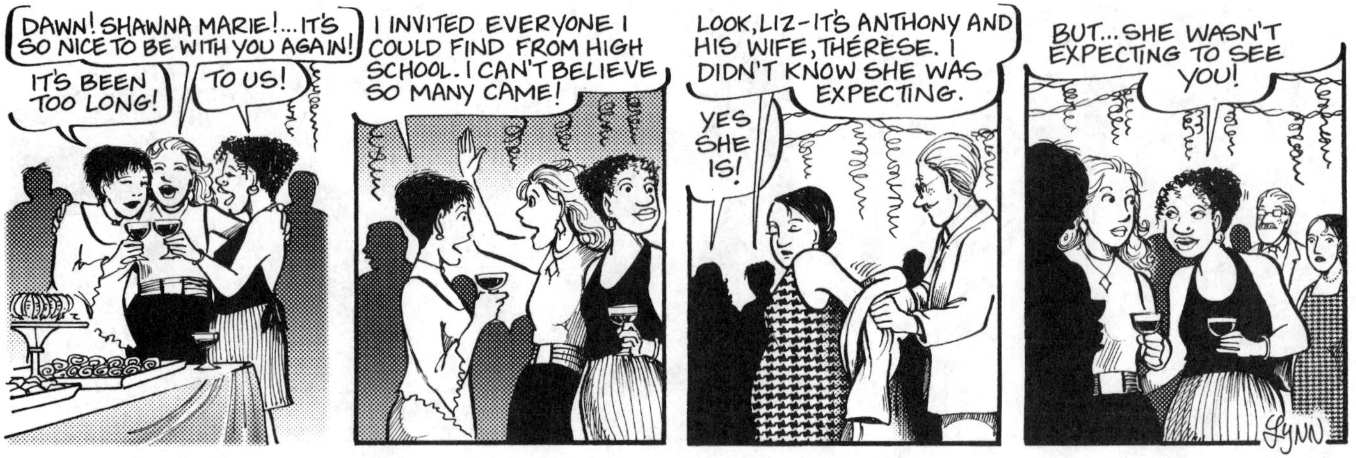
DAWN! SHAWNA MARIE!... IT'S SO NICE TO BE WITH YOU AGAIN!
IT'S BEEN TOO LONG!
TO US!
I INVITED EVERYONE I COULD FIND FROM HIGH SCHOOL. I CAN'T BELIEVE SO MANY CAME!
LOOK, LIZ - IT'S ANTHONY AND HIS WIFE, THÉRÈSE. I DIDN'T KNOW SHE WAS EXPECTING.
YES SHE IS!
BUT... SHE WASN'T EXPECTING TO SEE YOU!
LYNN

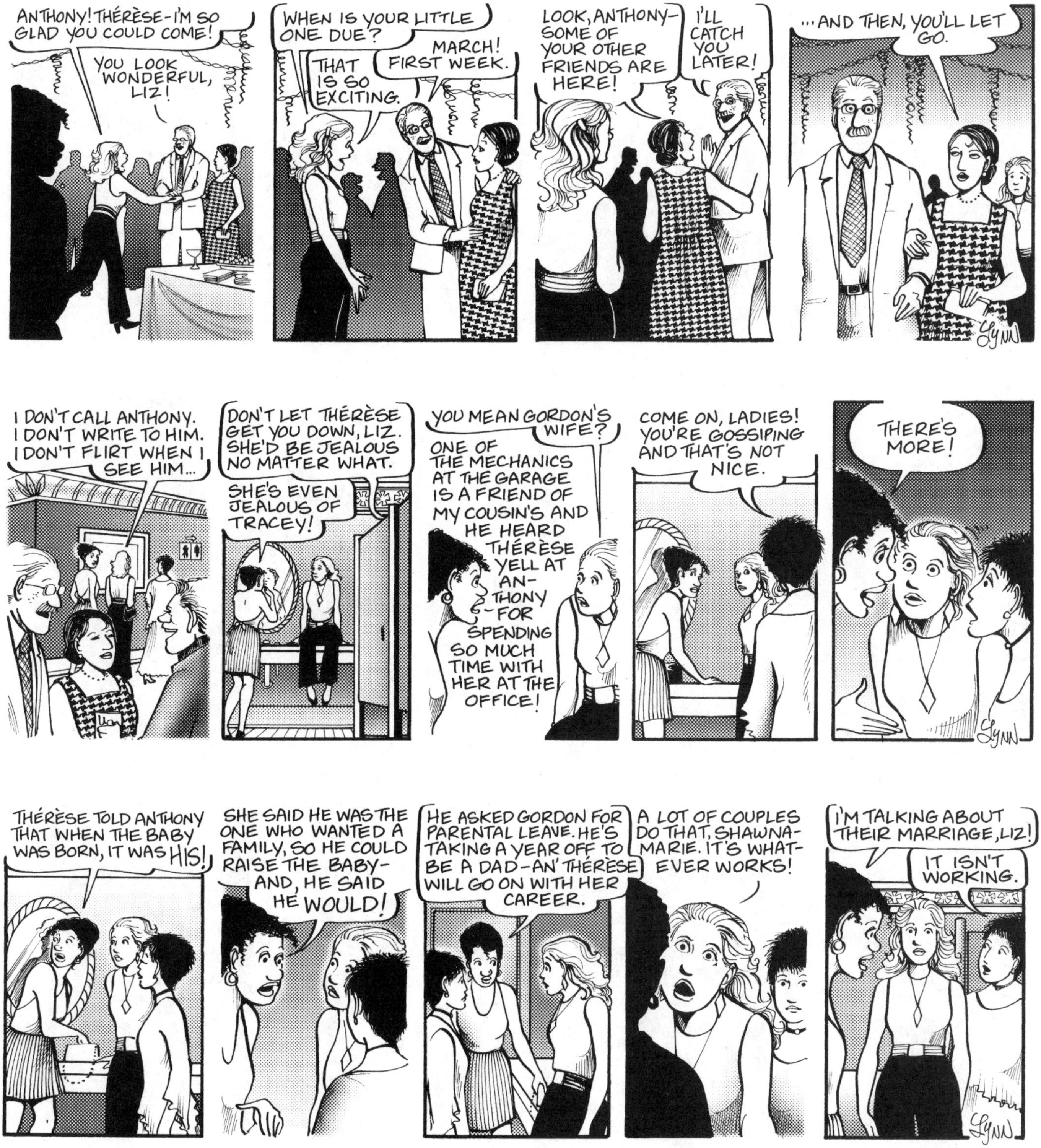
ANTHONY! THÉRÈSE-I'M SO GLAD YOU COULD COME!
YOU LOOK WONDERFUL, LIZ!
WHEN IS YOUR LITTLE ONE DUE?
MARCH! FIRST WEEK.
THAT IS SO EXCITING.
LOOK, ANTHONY-SOME OF YOUR OTHER FRIENDS ARE HERE!
I'LL CATCH YOU LATER!
...AND THEN, YOU'LL LET GO.
LYNN
I DON'T CALL ANTHONY. I DON'T WRITE TO HIM. I DON'T FLIRT WHEN I SEE HIM...
DON'T LET THÉRÈSE GET YOU DOWN, LIZ. SHE'D BE JEALOUS NO MATTER WHAT.
SHE'S EVEN JEALOUS OF TRACEY!
YOU MEAN GORDON'S WIFE?
ONE OF THE MECHANICS AT THE GARAGE IS A FRIEND OF MY COUSIN'S AND HE HEARD THÉRÈSE YELL AT ANTHONY FOR SPENDING SO MUCH TIME WITH HER AT THE OFFICE!
COME ON, LADIES! YOU'RE GOSSIPING AND THAT'S NOT NICE.
THERE'S MORE!
LYNN
THÉRÈSE TOLD ANTHONY THAT WHEN THE BABY WAS BORN, IT WAS HIS!
SHE SAID HE WAS THE ONE WHO WANTED A FAMILY, SO HE COULD RAISE THE BABY-AND, HE SAID HE WOULD!
HE ASKED GORDON FOR PARENTAL LEAVE. HE'S TAKING A YEAR OFF TO BE A DAD-AN' THÉRÈSE WILL GO ON WITH HER CAREER.
A LOT OF COUPLES DO THAT, SHAWNA-MARIE. IT'S WHATEVER WORKS!
I'M TALKING ABOUT THEIR MARRIAGE, LIZ!
IT ISN'T WORKING.
LYNN

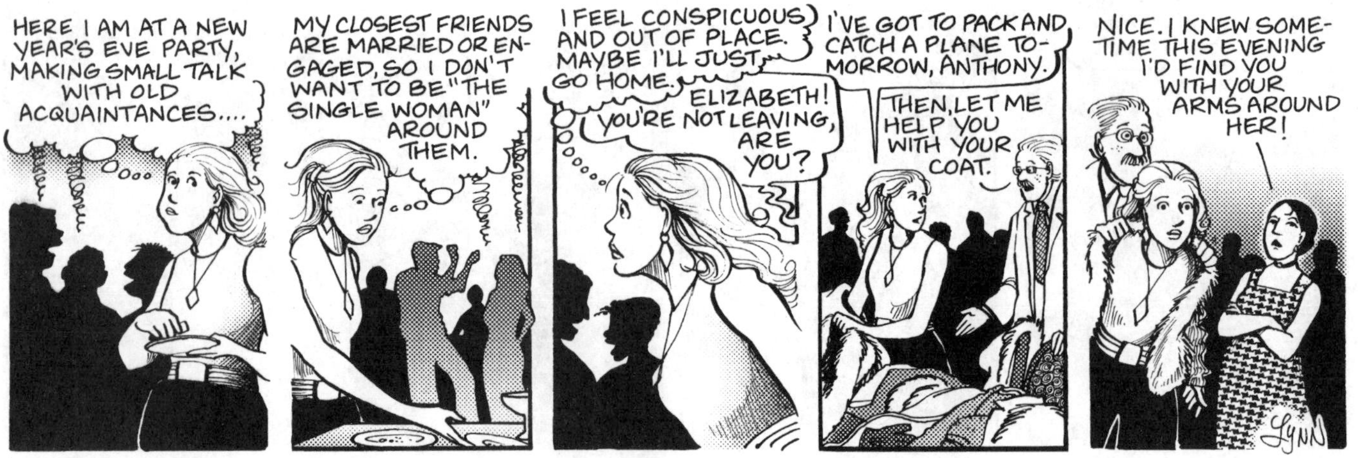
HERE I AM AT A NEW YEAR'S EVE PARTY, MAKING SMALL TALK WITH OLD ACQUAINTANCES....
MY CLOSEST FRIENDS ARE MARRIED OR ENGAGED, SO I DON'T WANT TO BE "THE SINGLE WOMAN" AROUND THEM.
I FEEL CONSPICUOUS AND OUT OF PLACE. MAYBE I'LL JUST GO HOME.
ELIZABETH! YOU'RE NOT LEAVING, ARE YOU?
I'VE GOT TO PACK AND CATCH A PLANE TOMORROW, ANTHONY.
THEN, LET ME HELP YOU WITH YOUR COAT.
NICE. I KNEW SOMETIME THIS EVENING I'D FIND YOU WITH YOUR ARMS AROUND HER!
LYNN

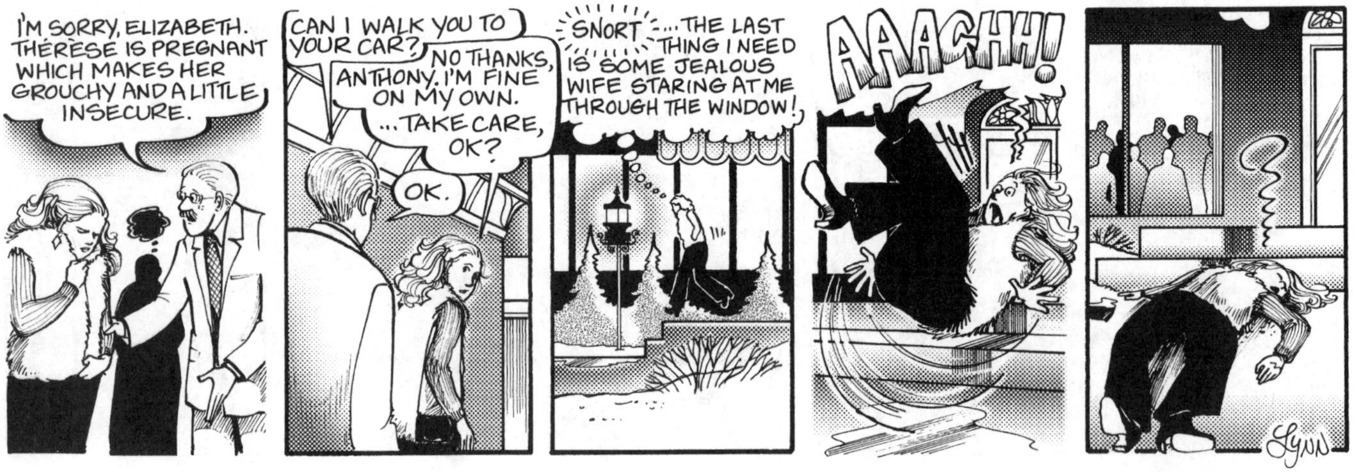
I'M SORRY, ELIZABETH. THÉRÈSE IS PREGNANT WHICH MAKES HER GROUCHY AND A LITTLE INSECURE.
CAN I WALK YOU TO YOUR CAR?
NO THANKS, ANTHONY. I'M FINE ON MY OWN.
...TAKE CARE, OK?
OK.
SNORT
...THE LAST THING I NEED IS SOME JEALOUS WIFE STARING AT ME THROUGH THE WINDOW!
AAACHH!
LYNN

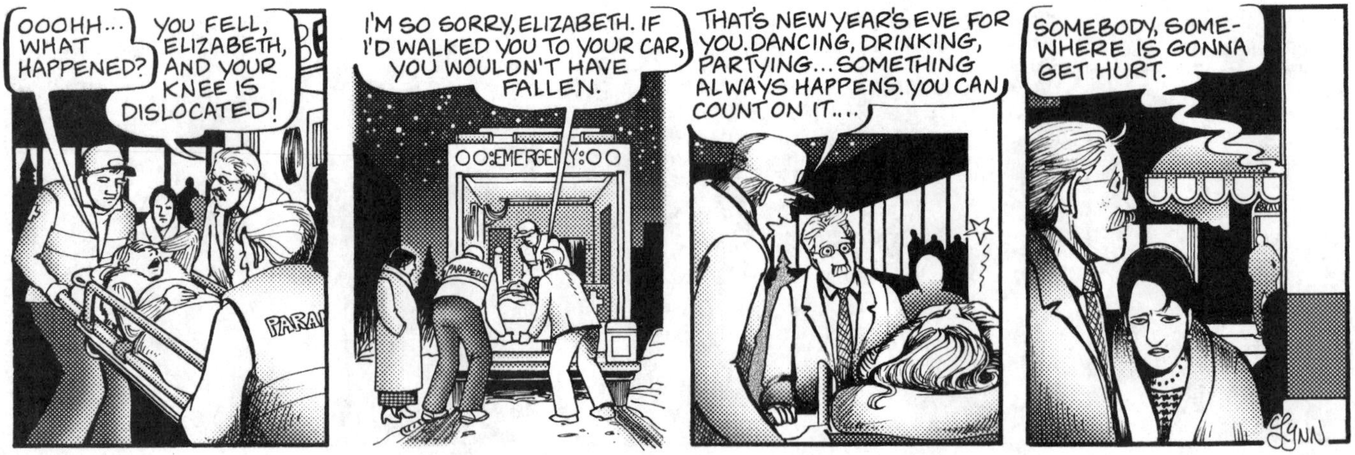
OOOHH... WHAT HAPPENED?
YOU FELL, ELIZABETH, AND YOUR KNEE IS DISLOCATED!
PARAM
I'M SO SORRY, ELIZABETH. IF I'D WALKED YOU TO YOUR CAR, YOU WOULDN'T HAVE FALLEN.
EMERGENCY
PARAMEDIC
THAT'S NEW YEAR'S EVE FOR YOU. DANCING, DRINKING, PARTYING... SOMETHING ALWAYS HAPPENS. YOU CAN COUNT ON IT....
SOMEBODY, SOMEWHERE IS GONNA GET HURT.
LYNN

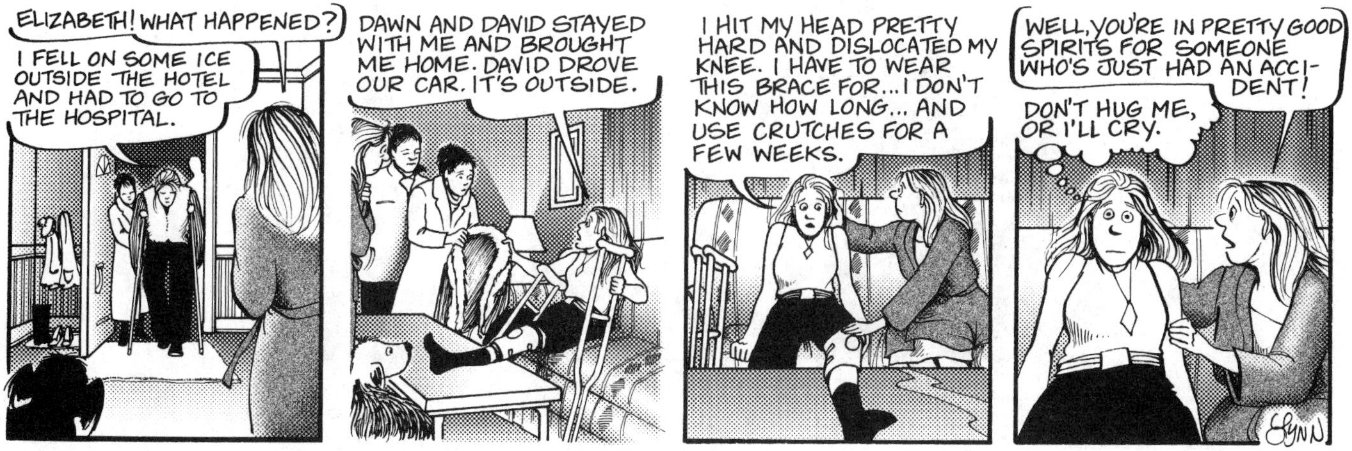
ELIZABETH! WHAT HAPPENED?
I FELL ON SOME ICE OUTSIDE THE HOTEL AND HAD TO GO TO THE HOSPITAL.
DAWN AND DAVID STAYED WITH ME AND BROUGHT ME HOME. DAVID DROVE OUR CAR. IT'S OUTSIDE.
I HIT MY HEAD PRETTY HARD AND DISLOCATED MY KNEE. I HAVE TO WEAR THIS BRACE FOR... I DON'T KNOW HOW LONG... AND USE CRUTCHES FOR A FEW WEEKS.
WELL, YOU'RE IN PRETTY GOOD SPIRITS FOR SOMEONE WHO'S JUST HAD AN ACCI-DENT!
DON'T HUG ME, OR I'LL CRY.
LYNN

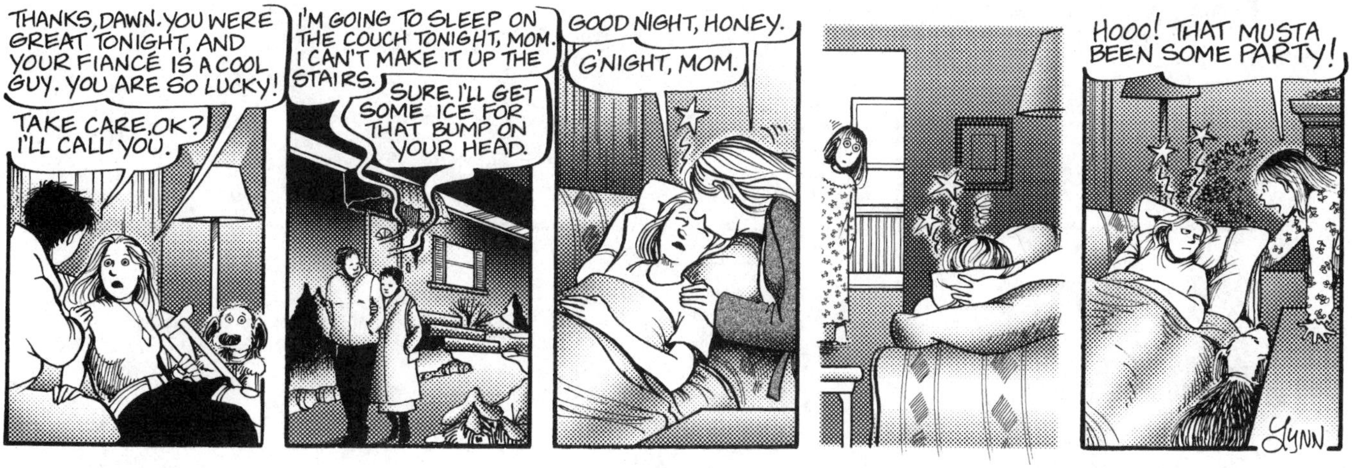
THANKS, DAWN. YOU WERE GREAT TONIGHT, AND YOUR FIANCÉ IS A COOL GUY. YOU ARE SO LUCKY!
TAKE CARE, OK? I'LL CALL YOU.
I'M GOING TO SLEEP ON THE COUCH TONIGHT, MOM. I CAN'T MAKE IT UP THE STAIRS.
SURE. I'LL GET SOME ICE FOR THAT BUMP ON YOUR HEAD.
GOOD NIGHT, HONEY.
G'NIGHT, MOM.
HOOO! THAT MUSTA BEEN SOME PARTY!
LYNN

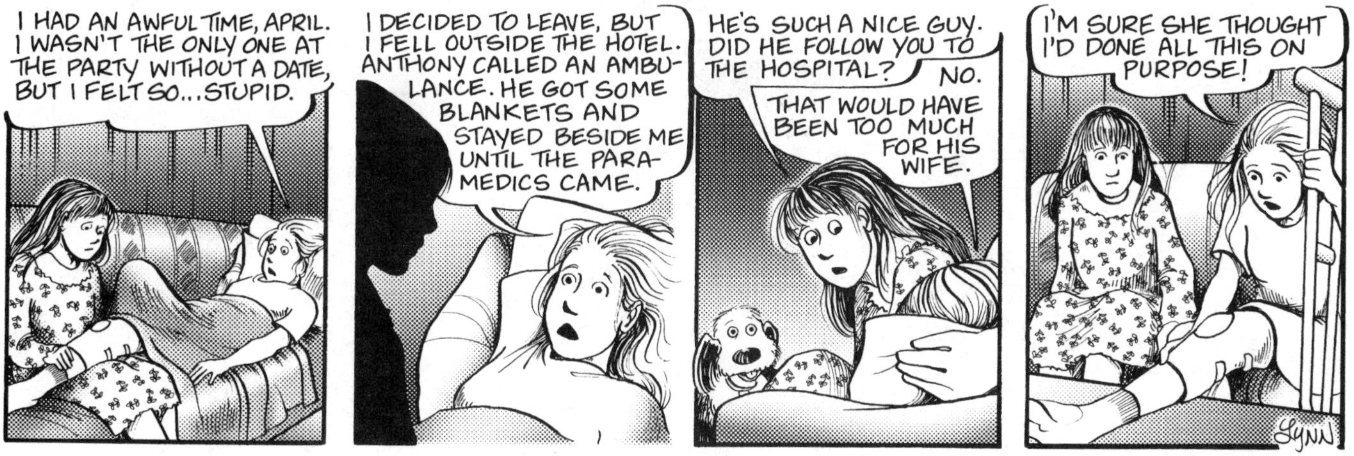
I HAD AN AWFUL TIME, APRIL. I WASN'T THE ONLY ONE AT THE PARTY WITHOUT A DATE, BUT I FELT SO... STUPID.
I DECIDED TO LEAVE, BUT I FELL OUTSIDE THE HOTEL. ANTHONY CALLED AN AMBU-LANCE. HE GOT SOME BLANKETS AND STAYED BESIDE ME UNTIL THE PARA-MEDICS CAME.
HE'S SUCH A NICE GUY. DID HE FOLLOW YOU TO THE HOSPITAL?
NO.
THAT WOULD HAVE BEEN TOO MUCH FOR HIS WIFE.
I'M SURE SHE THOUGHT I'D DONE ALL THIS ON PURPOSE!
LYNN

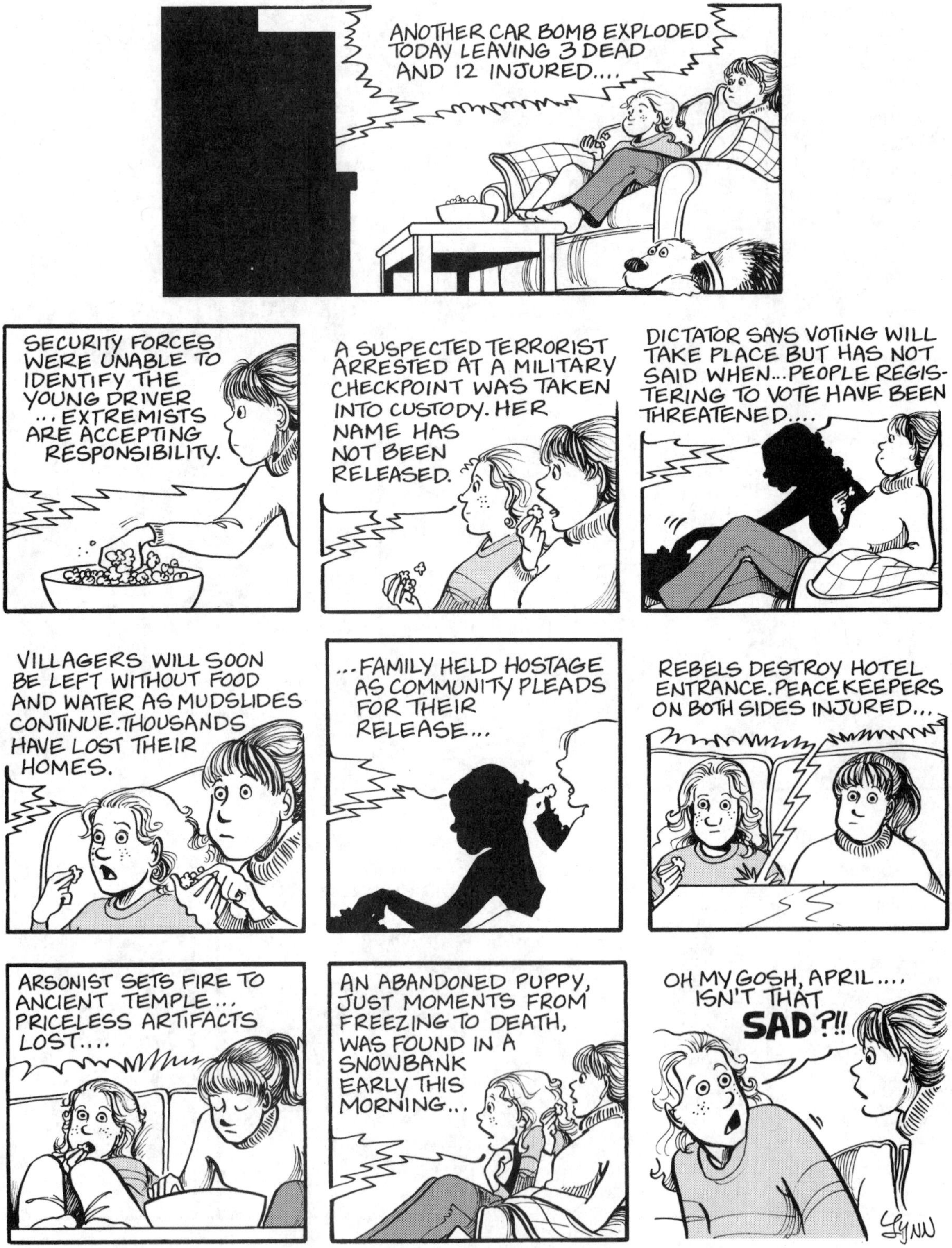
ANOTHER CAR BOMB EXPLODED TODAY LEAVING 3 DEAD AND 12 INJURED....
SECURITY FORCES WERE UNABLE TO IDENTIFY THE YOUNG DRIVER ... EXTREMISTS ARE ACCEPTING RESPONSIBILITY.
A SUSPECTED TERRORIST ARRESTED AT A MILITARY CHECKPOINT WAS TAKEN INTO CUSTODY. HER NAME HAS NOT BEEN RELEASED.
DICTATOR SAYS VOTING WILL TAKE PLACE BUT HAS NOT SAID WHEN... PEOPLE REGIS-TERING TO VOTE HAVE BEEN THREATENED....
VILLAGERS WILL SOON BE LEFT WITHOUT FOOD AND WATER AS MUDSLIDES CONTINUE. THOUSANDS HAVE LOST THEIR HOMES.
...FAMILY HELD HOSTAGE AS COMMUNITY PLEADS FOR THEIR RELEASE...
REBELS DESTROY HOTEL ENTRANCE. PEACEKEEPERS ON BOTH SIDES INJURED...
ARSONIST SETS FIRE TO ANCIENT TEMPLE... PRICELESS ARTIFACTS LOST....
AN ABANDONED PUPPY, JUST MOMENTS FROM FREEZING TO DEATH, WAS FOUND IN A SNOWBANK EARLY THIS MORNING...
OH MY GOSH, APRIL.... ISN'T THAT **SAD**?!!
LYNN

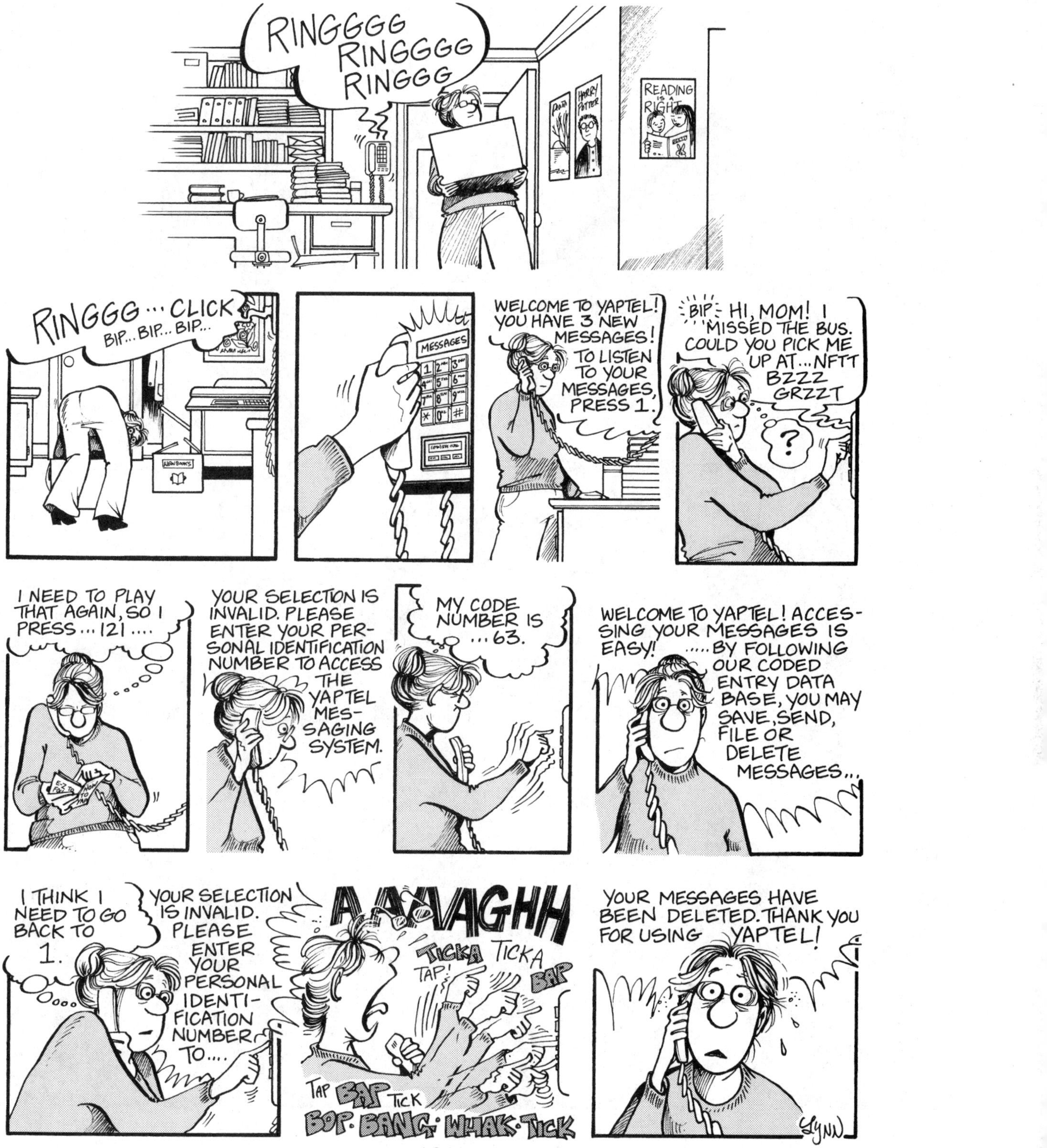
RINGGGG RINGGGG RINGGG
HARRY POTTER
READING IS A RIGHT
RINGGG... CLICK
BIP... BIP... BIP...
NEW BOOKS
MESSAGES
WELCOME TO YAPTEL! YOU HAVE 3 NEW MESSAGES! TO LISTEN TO YOUR MESSAGES, PRESS 1.
BIP - HI, MOM! I MISSED THE BUS. COULD YOU PICK ME UP AT... NFTT BZZZ GRZZT
?
I NEED TO PLAY THAT AGAIN, SO I PRESS... 121....
YOUR SELECTION IS INVALID. PLEASE ENTER YOUR PERSONAL IDENTIFICATION NUMBER TO ACCESS THE YAPTEL MESSAGING SYSTEM.
MY CODE NUMBER IS ...63.
WELCOME TO YAPTEL! ACCESSING YOUR MESSAGES IS EASY! .....BY FOLLOWING OUR CODED ENTRY DATA BASE, YOU MAY SAVE, SEND, FILE OR DELETE MESSAGES...
I THINK I NEED TO GO BACK TO 1.
YOUR SELECTION IS INVALID. PLEASE ENTER YOUR PERSONAL IDENTIFICATION NUMBER TO....
AAAAGHH
TICKA TICKA
TAP!
BAP
TAP BAP TICK
BOP. BANG. WHAK. TICK
YOUR MESSAGES HAVE BEEN DELETED. THANK YOU FOR USING YAPTEL!
LYNN

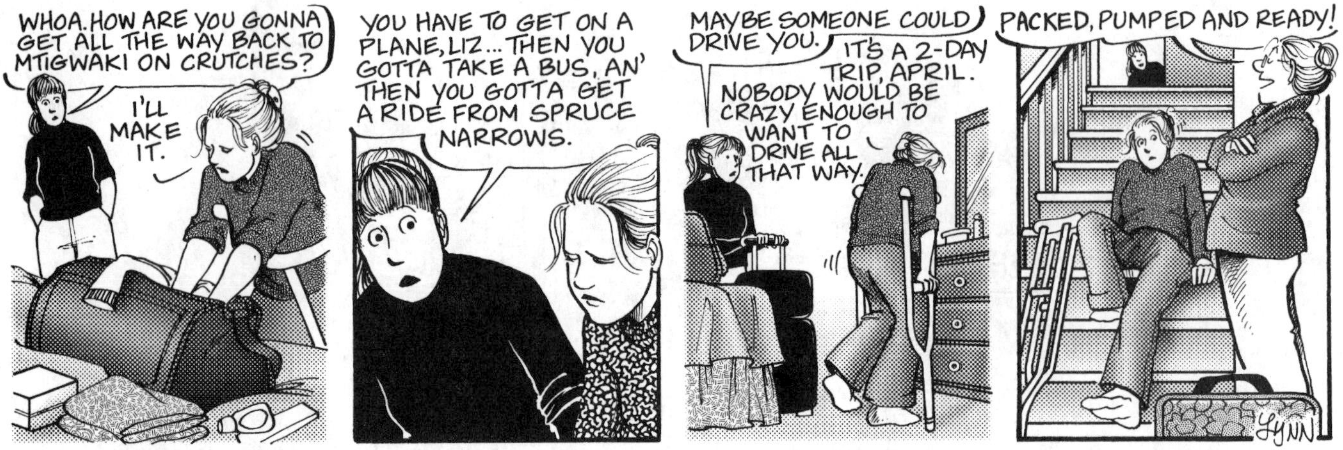
WHOA. HOW ARE YOU GONNA GET ALL THE WAY BACK TO MTIGWAKI ON CRUTCHES?
I'LL MAKE IT.
YOU HAVE TO GET ON A PLANE, LIZ... THEN YOU GOTTA TAKE A BUS, AN' THEN YOU GOTTA GET A RIDE FROM SPRUCE NARROWS.
MAYBE SOMEONE COULD DRIVE YOU.
IT'S A 2-DAY TRIP, APRIL. NOBODY WOULD BE CRAZY ENOUGH TO WANT TO DRIVE ALL THAT WAY.
PACKED, PUMPED AND READY!
LYNN

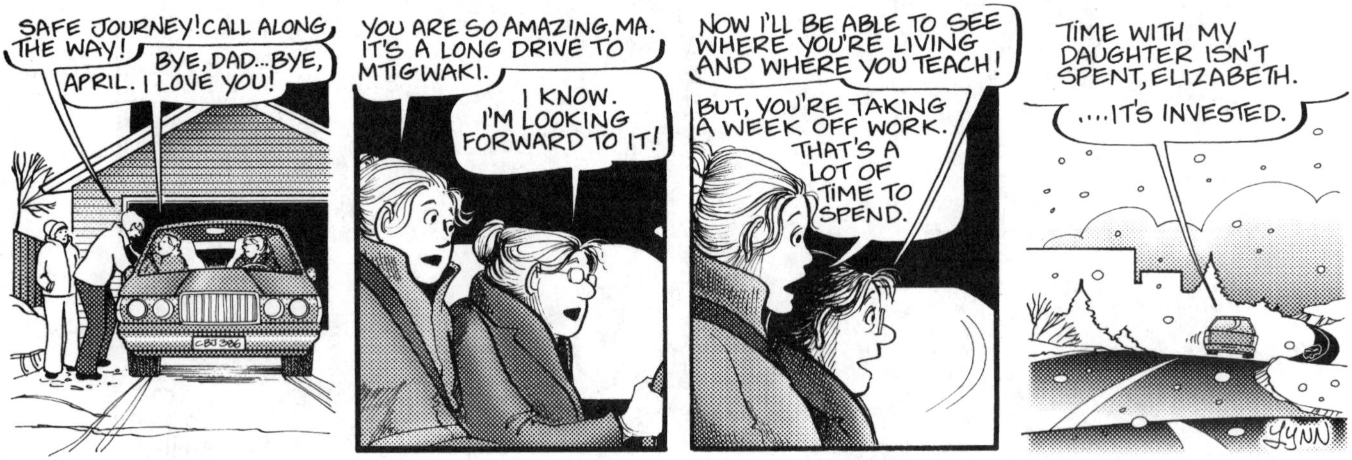
SAFE JOURNEY! CALL ALONG THE WAY!
BYE, DAD...BYE, APRIL. I LOVE YOU!
YOU ARE SO AMAZING, MA. IT'S A LONG DRIVE TO MTIGWAKI.
I KNOW. I'M LOOKING FORWARD TO IT!
NOW I'LL BE ABLE TO SEE WHERE YOU'RE LIVING AND WHERE YOU TEACH!
BUT, YOU'RE TAKING A WEEK OFF WORK. THAT'S A LOT OF TIME TO SPEND.
TIME WITH MY DAUGHTER ISN'T SPENT, ELIZABETH.
....IT'S INVESTED.
LYNN

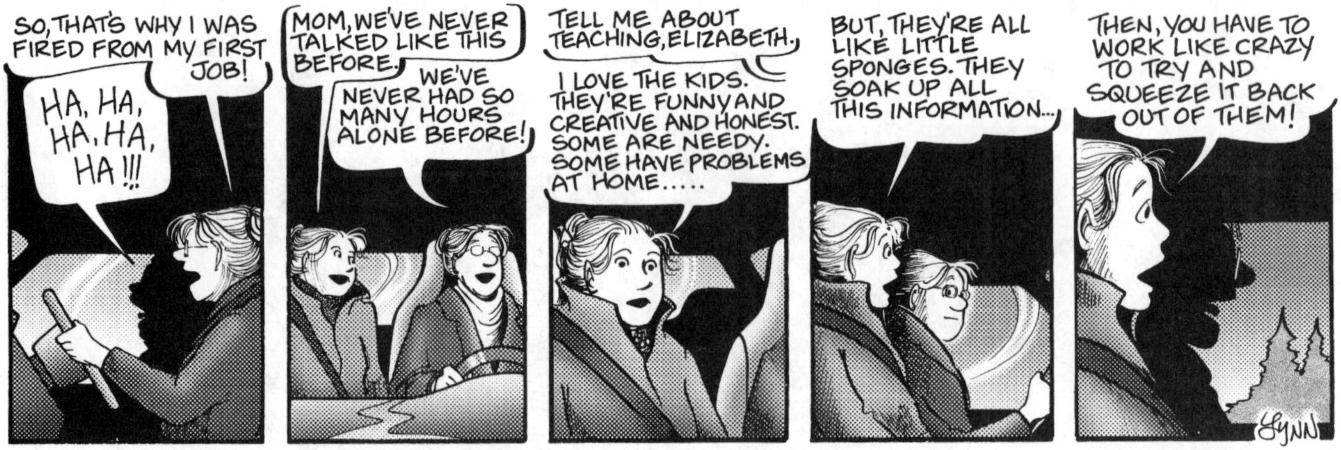
SO, THAT'S WHY I WAS FIRED FROM MY FIRST JOB!
HA, HA, HA, HA, HA !!!
MOM, WE'VE NEVER TALKED LIKE THIS BEFORE.
WE'VE NEVER HAD SO MANY HOURS ALONE BEFORE!
TELL ME ABOUT TEACHING, ELIZABETH.
I LOVE THE KIDS. THEY'RE FUNNY AND CREATIVE AND HONEST. SOME ARE NEEDY. SOME HAVE PROBLEMS AT HOME.....
BUT, THEY'RE ALL LIKE LITTLE SPONGES. THEY SOAK UP ALL THIS INFORMATION...
THEN, YOU HAVE TO WORK LIKE CRAZY TO TRY AND SQUEEZE IT BACK OUT OF THEM!
LYNN

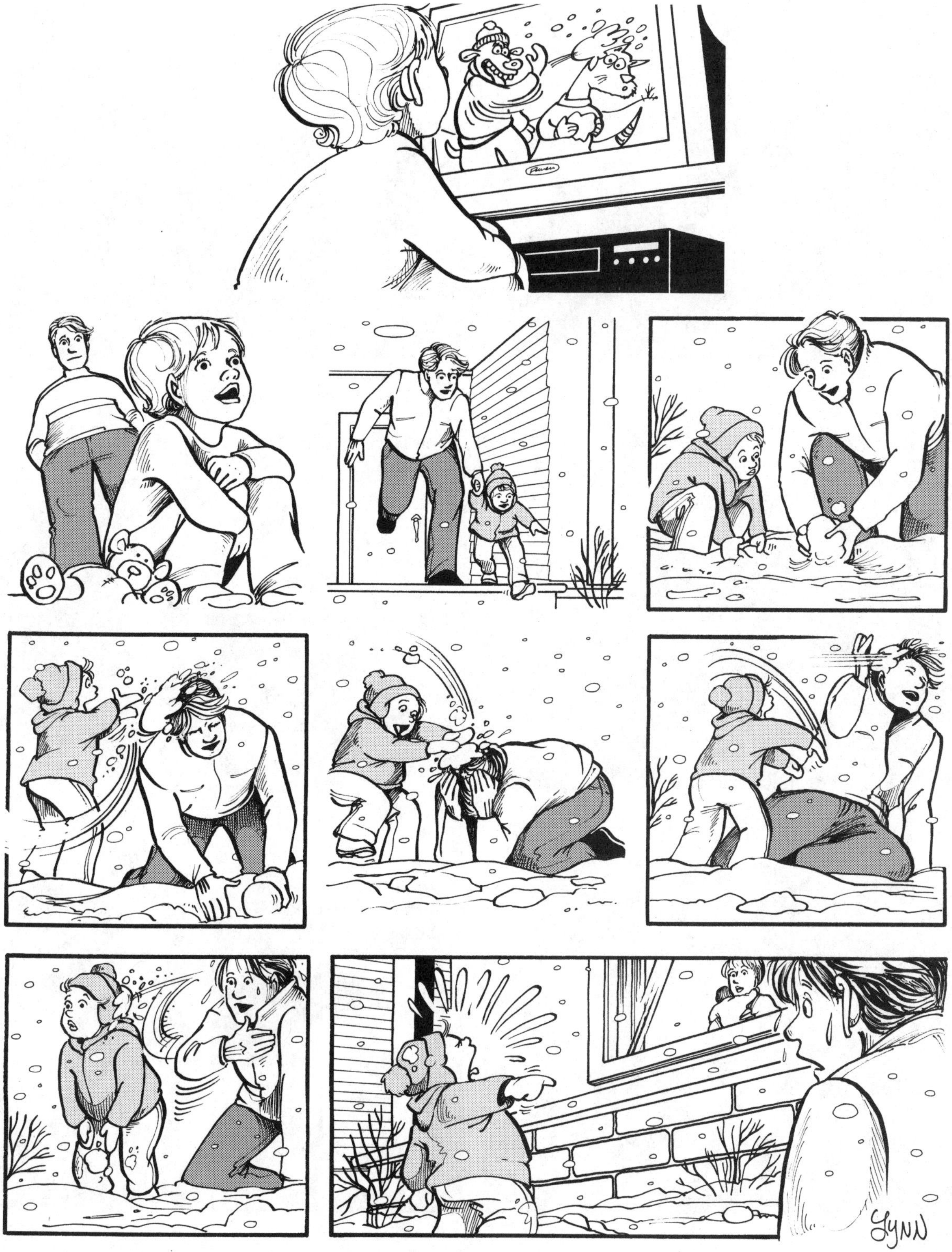
LYNN

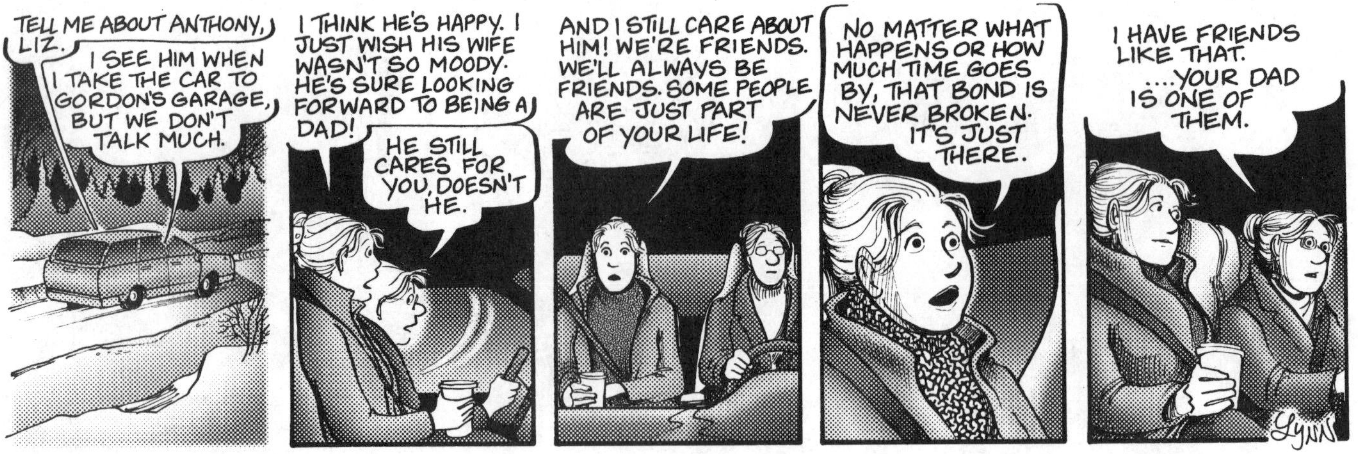
TELL ME ABOUT ANTHONY, LIZ.
I SEE HIM WHEN I TAKE THE CAR TO GORDON'S GARAGE, BUT WE DON'T TALK MUCH.
I THINK HE'S HAPPY. I JUST WISH HIS WIFE WASN'T SO MOODY. HE'S SURE LOOKING FORWARD TO BEING A DAD!
HE STILL CARES FOR YOU, DOESN'T HE.
AND I STILL CARE ABOUT HIM! WE'RE FRIENDS. WE'LL ALWAYS BE FRIENDS. SOME PEOPLE ARE JUST PART OF YOUR LIFE!
NO MATTER WHAT HAPPENS OR HOW MUCH TIME GOES BY, THAT BOND IS NEVER BROKEN. IT'S JUST THERE.
I HAVE FRIENDS LIKE THAT. ....YOUR DAD IS ONE OF THEM.
LYNN

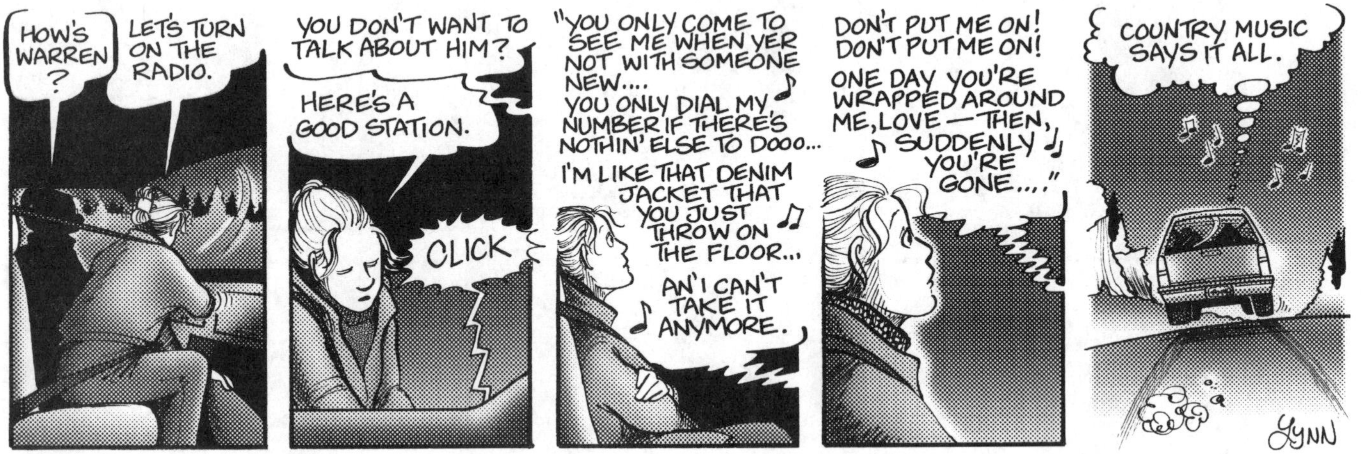
HOW'S WARREN ?
LET'S TURN ON THE RADIO.
YOU DON'T WANT TO TALK ABOUT HIM ?
HERE'S A GOOD STATION.
CLICK
"YOU ONLY COME TO SEE ME WHEN YER NOT WITH SOMEONE NEW.... YOU ONLY DIAL MY NUMBER IF THERE'S NOTHIN' ELSE TO DOOO...
I'M LIKE THAT DENIM JACKET THAT YOU JUST THROW ON THE FLOOR...
AN' I CAN'T TAKE IT ANYMORE.
DON'T PUT ME ON! DON'T PUT ME ON!
ONE DAY YOU'RE WRAPPED AROUND ME, LOVE — THEN, SUDDENLY YOU'RE GONE...."
COUNTRY MUSIC SAYS IT ALL.
LYNN

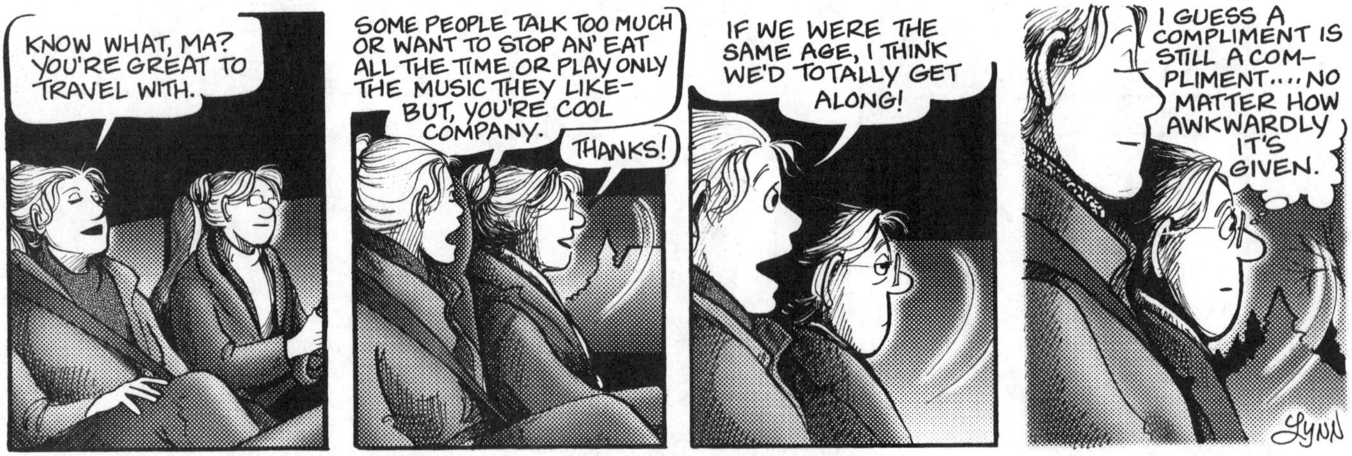
KNOW WHAT, MA? YOU'RE GREAT TO TRAVEL WITH.
SOME PEOPLE TALK TOO MUCH OR WANT TO STOP AN' EAT ALL THE TIME OR PLAY ONLY THE MUSIC THEY LIKE- BUT, YOU'RE COOL COMPANY.
THANKS!
IF WE WERE THE SAME AGE, I THINK WE'D TOTALLY GET ALONG!
I GUESS A COMPLIMENT IS STILL A COMPLIMENT.... NO MATTER HOW AWKWARDLY IT'S GIVEN.
LYNN

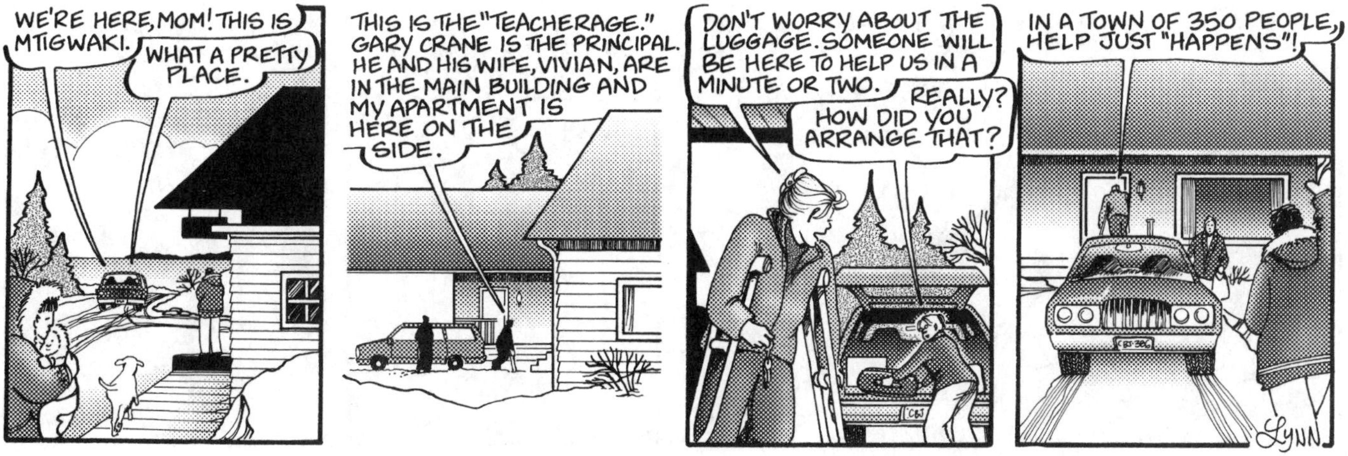
WE'RE HERE, MOM! THIS IS MTIGWAKI.
WHAT A PRETTY PLACE.
THIS IS THE "TEACHERAGE." GARY CRANE IS THE PRINCIPAL. HE AND HIS WIFE, VIVIAN, ARE IN THE MAIN BUILDING AND MY APARTMENT IS HERE ON THE SIDE.
DON'T WORRY ABOUT THE LUGGAGE. SOMEONE WILL BE HERE TO HELP US IN A MINUTE OR TWO.
REALLY? HOW DID YOU ARRANGE THAT?
IN A TOWN OF 350 PEOPLE, HELP JUST "HAPPENS"!
LYNN

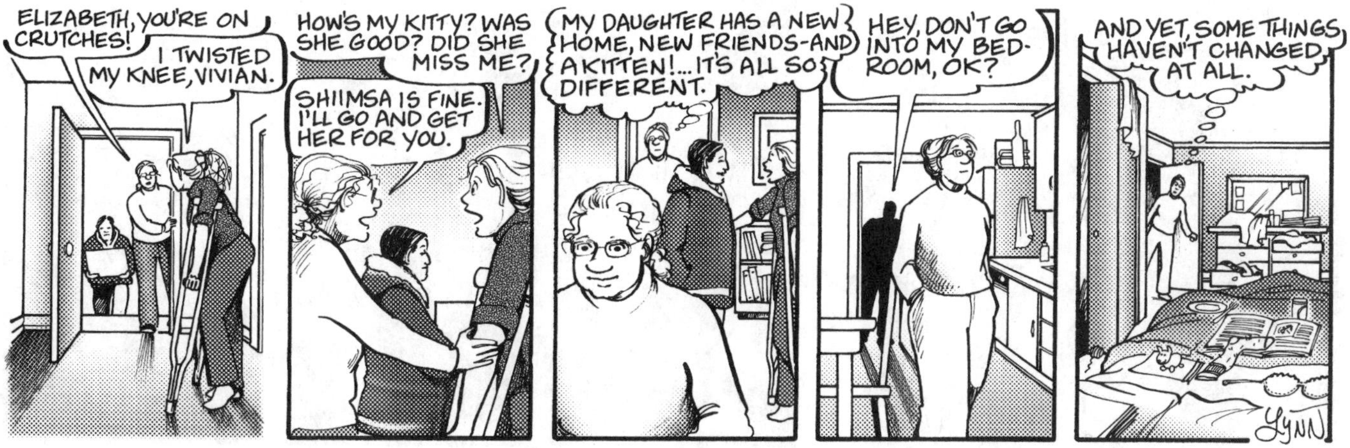
ELIZABETH, YOU'RE ON CRUTCHES!
I TWISTED MY KNEE, VIVIAN.
HOW'S MY KITTY? WAS SHE GOOD? DID SHE MISS ME?
SHIIMSA IS FINE. I'LL GO AND GET HER FOR YOU.
MY DAUGHTER HAS A NEW HOME, NEW FRIENDS-AND A KITTEN!... IT'S ALL SO DIFFERENT.
HEY, DON'T GO INTO MY BED-ROOM, OK?
AND YET, SOME THINGS HAVEN'T CHANGED AT ALL.
LYNN

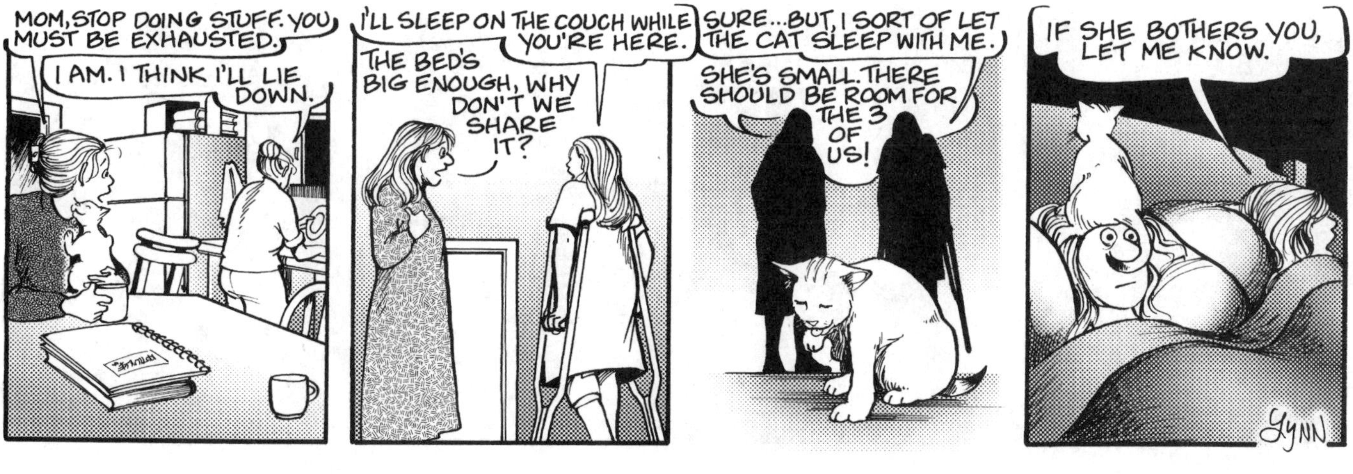
MOM, STOP DOING STUFF. YOU MUST BE EXHAUSTED.
I AM. I THINK I'LL LIE DOWN.
I'LL SLEEP ON THE COUCH WHILE YOU'RE HERE.
THE BED'S BIG ENOUGH, WHY DON'T WE SHARE IT?
SURE...BUT, I SORT OF LET THE CAT SLEEP WITH ME.
SHE'S SMALL. THERE SHOULD BE ROOM FOR THE 3 OF US!
IF SHE BOTHERS YOU, LET ME KNOW.
LYNN

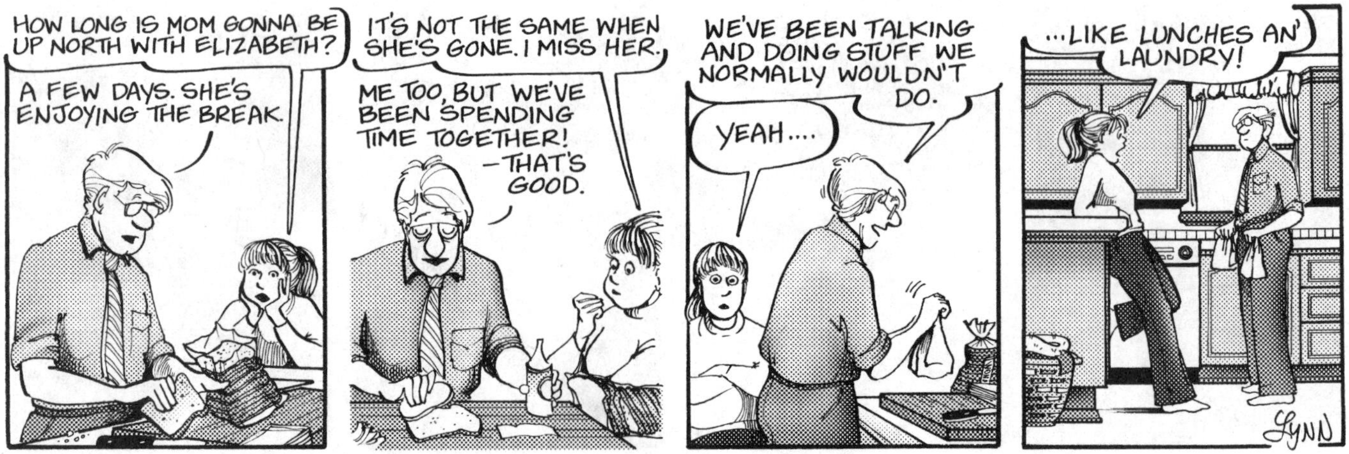
HOW LONG IS MOM GONNA BE UP NORTH WITH ELIZABETH?
A FEW DAYS. SHE'S ENJOYING THE BREAK.
IT'S NOT THE SAME WHEN SHE'S GONE. I MISS HER.
ME TOO, BUT WE'VE BEEN SPENDING TIME TOGETHER!
–THAT'S GOOD.
WE'VE BEEN TALKING AND DOING STUFF WE NORMALLY WOULDN'T DO.
YEAH....
...LIKE LUNCHES AN' LAUNDRY!
LYNN

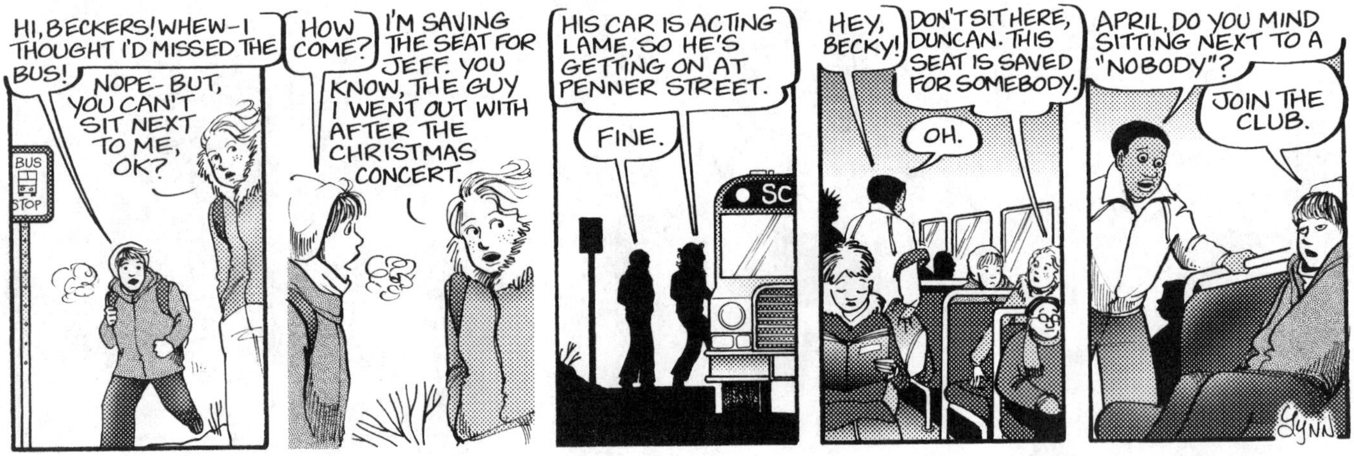
HI, BECKERS! WHEW–I THOUGHT I'D MISSED THE BUS!
NOPE–BUT, YOU CAN'T SIT NEXT TO ME, OK?
BUS STOP
HOW COME?
I'M SAVING THE SEAT FOR JEFF. YOU KNOW, THE GUY I WENT OUT WITH AFTER THE CHRISTMAS CONCERT.
HIS CAR IS ACTING LAME, SO HE'S GETTING ON AT PENNER STREET.
FINE.
SC
HEY, BECKY!
DON'T SIT HERE, DUNCAN. THIS SEAT IS SAVED FOR SOMEBODY.
OH.
APRIL, DO YOU MIND SITTING NEXT TO A "NOBODY"?
JOIN THE CLUB.
LYNN

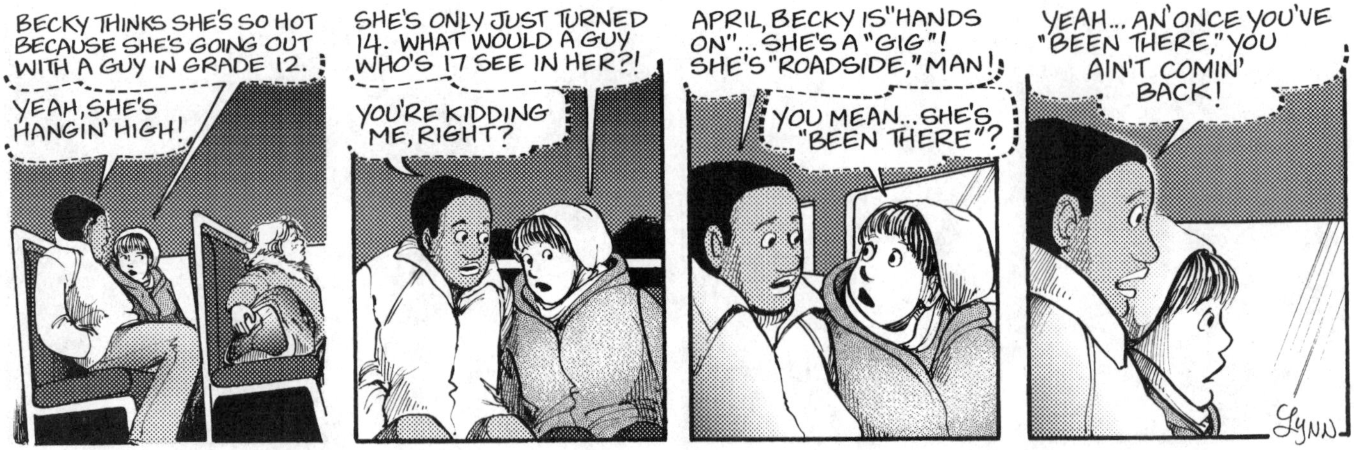
BECKY THINKS SHE'S SO HOT BECAUSE SHE'S GOING OUT WITH A GUY IN GRADE 12.
YEAH, SHE'S HANGIN' HIGH!
SHE'S ONLY JUST TURNED 14. WHAT WOULD A GUY WHO'S 17 SEE IN HER?!
YOU'RE KIDDING ME, RIGHT?
APRIL, BECKY IS "HANDS ON"... SHE'S A "GIG"! SHE'S "ROADSIDE," MAN!
YOU MEAN... SHE'S "BEEN THERE"?
YEAH... AN' ONCE YOU'VE "BEEN THERE," YOU AIN'T COMIN' BACK!
LYNN

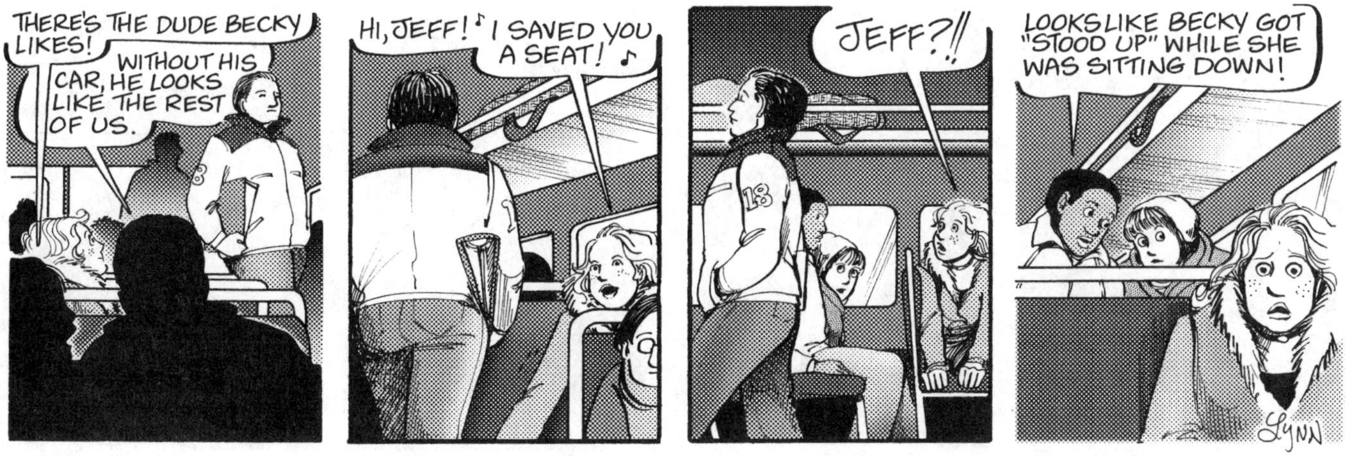
THERE'S THE DUDE BECKY LIKES!
WITHOUT HIS CAR, HE LOOKS LIKE THE REST OF US.
HI, JEFF! ♪ I SAVED YOU A SEAT! ♪
JEFF?!!
LOOKS LIKE BECKY GOT "STOOD UP" WHILE SHE WAS SITTING DOWN!
LYNN

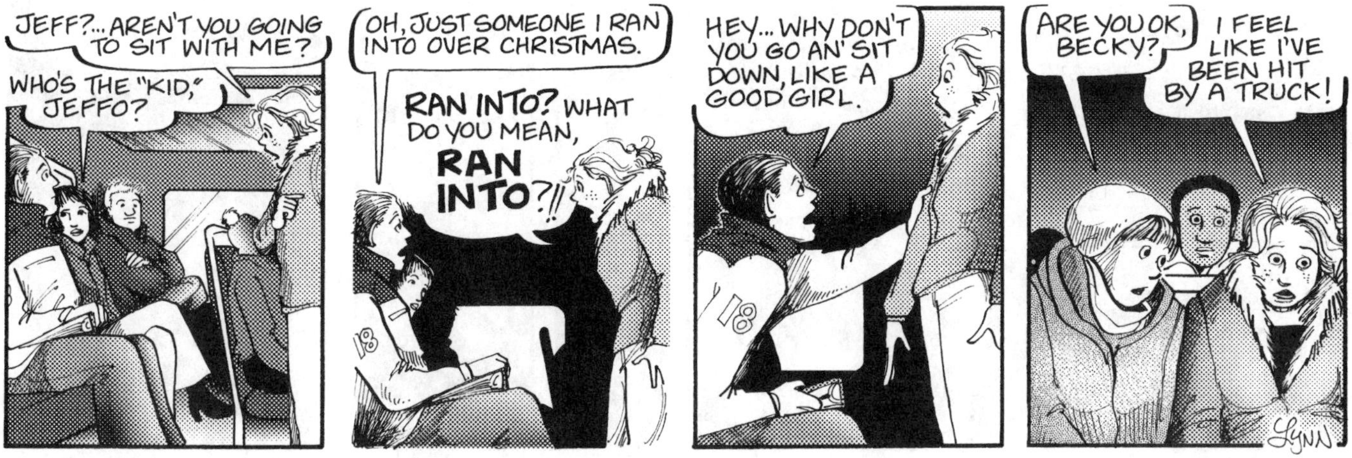
JEFF?... AREN'T YOU GOING TO SIT WITH ME?
WHO'S THE "KID," JEFFO?
OH, JUST SOMEONE I RAN INTO OVER CHRISTMAS.
RAN INTO? WHAT DO YOU MEAN, RAN INTO?!!
HEY... WHY DON'T YOU GO AN' SIT DOWN, LIKE A GOOD GIRL.
ARE YOU OK, BECKY?
I FEEL LIKE I'VE BEEN HIT BY A TRUCK!
LYNN

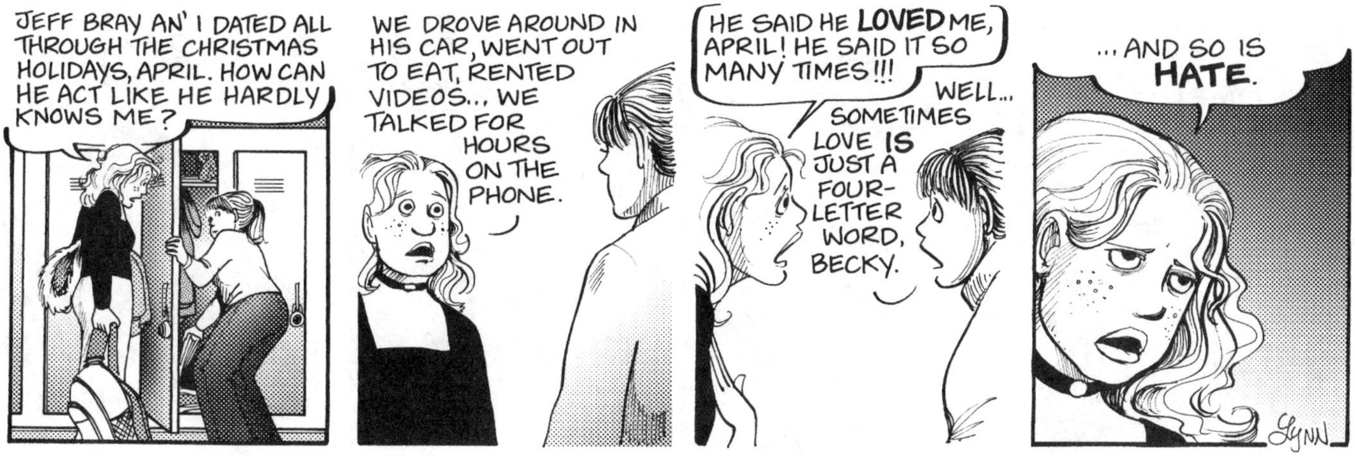
JEFF BRAY AN' I DATED ALL THROUGH THE CHRISTMAS HOLIDAYS, APRIL. HOW CAN HE ACT LIKE HE HARDLY KNOWS ME?
WE DROVE AROUND IN HIS CAR, WENT OUT TO EAT, RENTED VIDEOS... WE TALKED FOR HOURS ON THE PHONE.
HE SAID HE LOVED ME, APRIL! HE SAID IT SO MANY TIMES!!!
WELL... SOMETIMES LOVE IS JUST A FOUR-LETTER WORD, BECKY.
... AND SO IS HATE.
LYNN

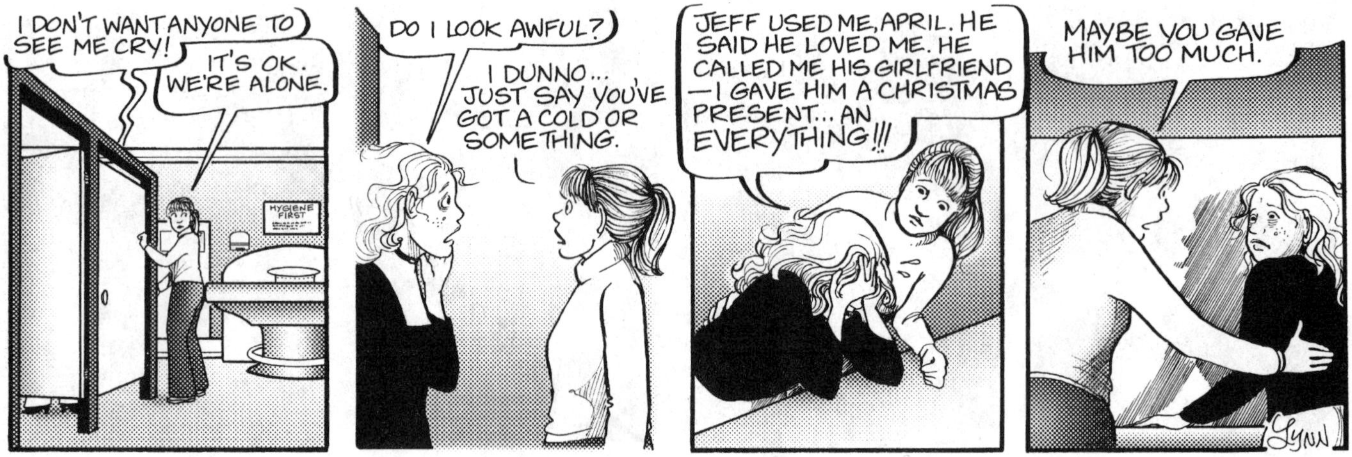
I DON'T WANT ANYONE TO SEE ME CRY!
IT'S OK. WE'RE ALONE.
HYGIENE FIRST
DO I LOOK AWFUL?
I DUNNO... JUST SAY YOU'VE GOT A COLD OR SOMETHING.
JEFF USED ME, APRIL. HE SAID HE LOVED ME. HE CALLED ME HIS GIRLFRIEND —I GAVE HIM A CHRISTMAS PRESENT... AN EVERYTHING!!!
MAYBE YOU GAVE HIM TOO MUCH.
Lynn

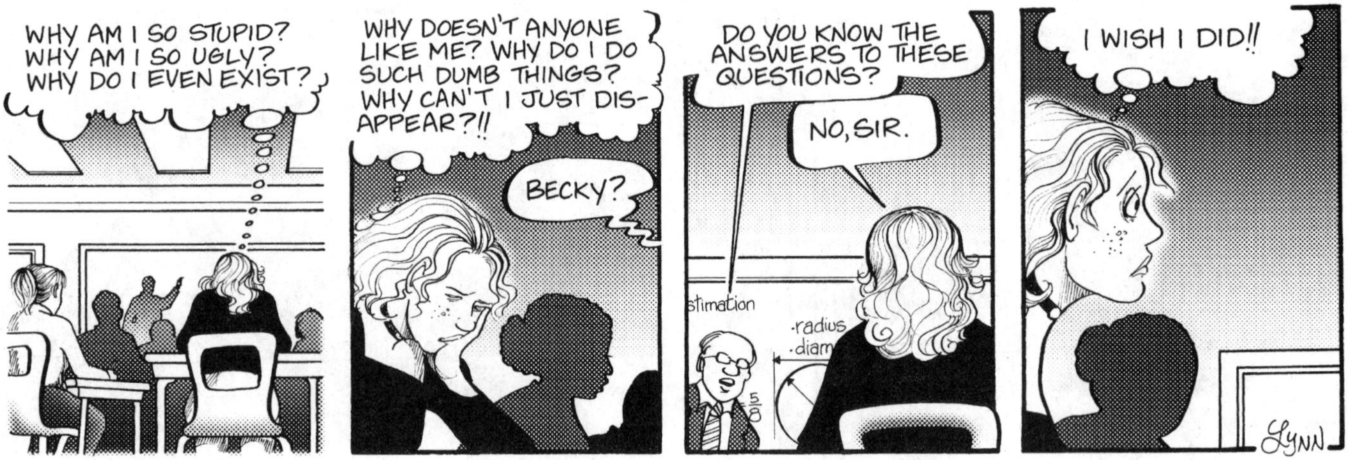
WHY AM I SO STUPID? WHY AM I SO UGLY? WHY DO I EVEN EXIST?
WHY DOESN'T ANYONE LIKE ME? WHY DO I DO SUCH DUMB THINGS? WHY CAN'T I JUST DIS-APPEAR?!!
BECKY?
DO YOU KNOW THE ANSWERS TO THESE QUESTIONS?
NO, SIR.
·radius
I WISH I DID!!
Lynn

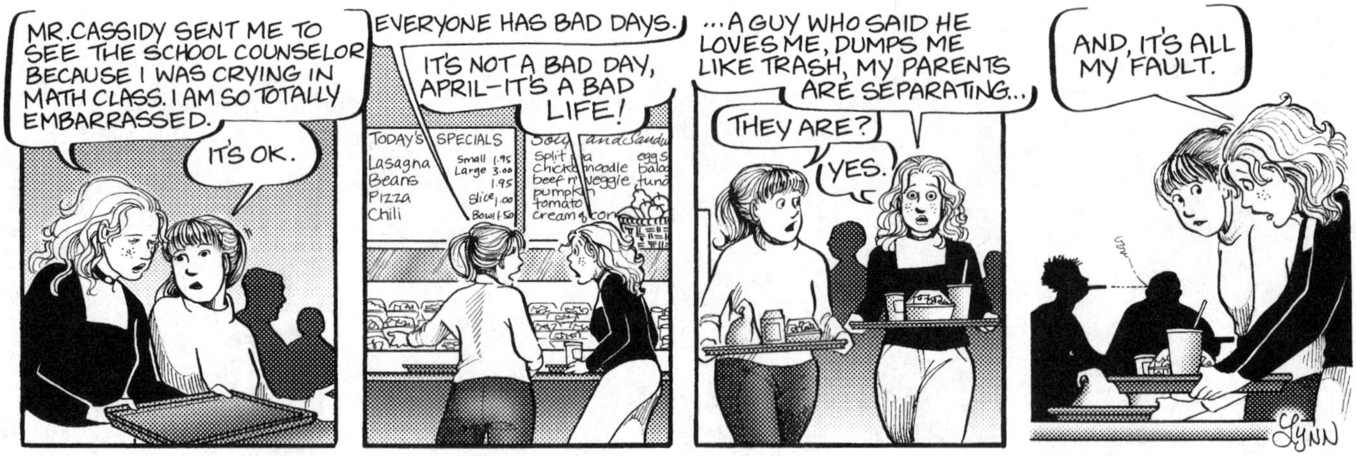
MR. CASSIDY SENT ME TO SEE THE SCHOOL COUNSELOR BECAUSE I WAS CRYING IN MATH CLASS. I AM SO TOTALLY EMBARRASSED.
IT'S OK.
EVERYONE HAS BAD DAYS.
IT'S NOT A BAD DAY, APRIL—IT'S A BAD LIFE!
TODAY'S SPECIALS
Lasagna Small 1.95 Large 3.00
Beans 1.95
Pizza Slice 1.00
Chili Bowl 1.50
...A GUY WHO SAID HE LOVES ME, DUMPS ME LIKE TRASH, MY PARENTS ARE SEPARATING...
THEY ARE?
YES.
AND, IT'S ALL MY FAULT.
Lynn

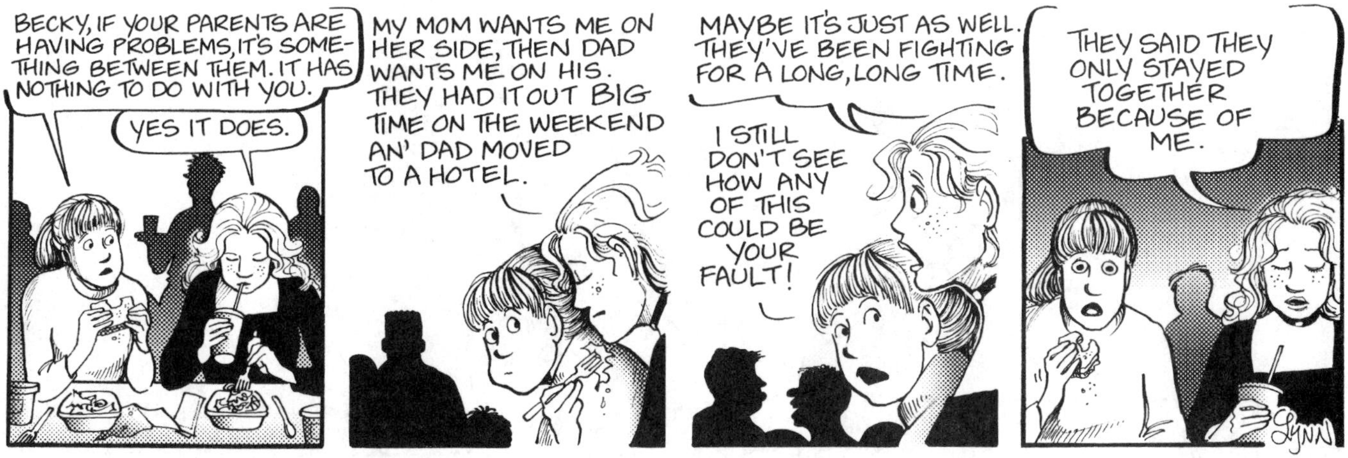
BECKY, IF YOUR PARENTS ARE HAVING PROBLEMS, IT'S SOMETHING BETWEEN THEM. IT HAS NOTHING TO DO WITH YOU.
YES IT DOES.
MY MOM WANTS ME ON HER SIDE, THEN DAD WANTS ME ON HIS. THEY HAD IT OUT BIG TIME ON THE WEEKEND AN' DAD MOVED TO A HOTEL.
MAYBE IT'S JUST AS WELL. THEY'VE BEEN FIGHTING FOR A LONG, LONG TIME.
I STILL DON'T SEE HOW ANY OF THIS COULD BE YOUR FAULT!
THEY SAID THEY ONLY STAYED TOGETHER BECAUSE OF ME.
LYNN

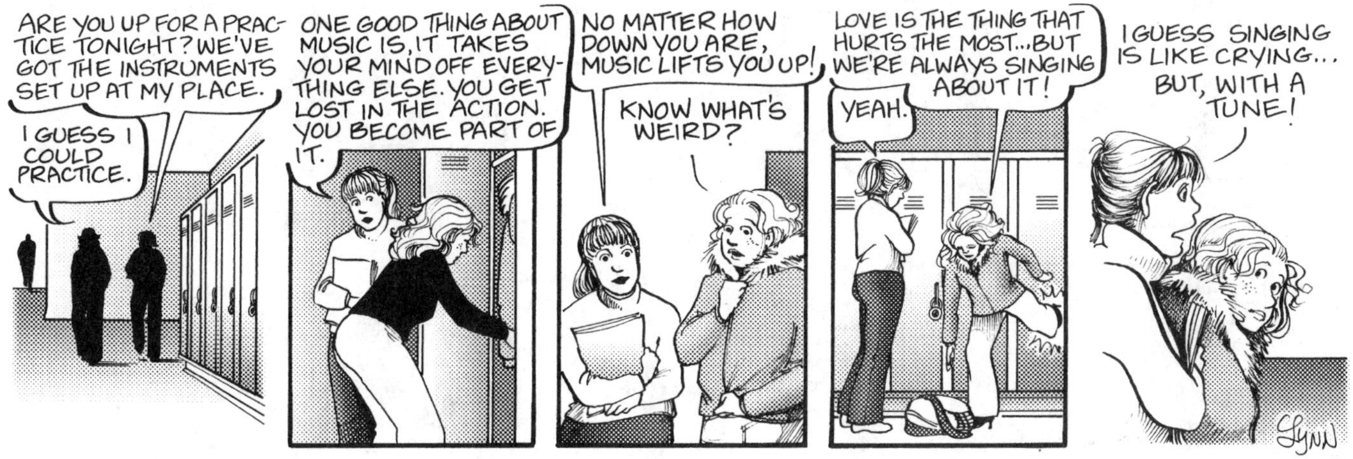
ARE YOU UP FOR A PRACTICE TONIGHT? WE'VE GOT THE INSTRUMENTS SET UP AT MY PLACE.
I GUESS I COULD PRACTICE.
ONE GOOD THING ABOUT MUSIC IS, IT TAKES YOUR MIND OFF EVERYTHING ELSE. YOU GET LOST IN THE ACTION. YOU BECOME PART OF IT.
NO MATTER HOW DOWN YOU ARE, MUSIC LIFTS YOU UP!
KNOW WHAT'S WEIRD?
LOVE IS THE THING THAT HURTS THE MOST...BUT WE'RE ALWAYS SINGING ABOUT IT!
YEAH.
I GUESS SINGING IS LIKE CRYING... BUT, WITH A TUNE!
LYNN

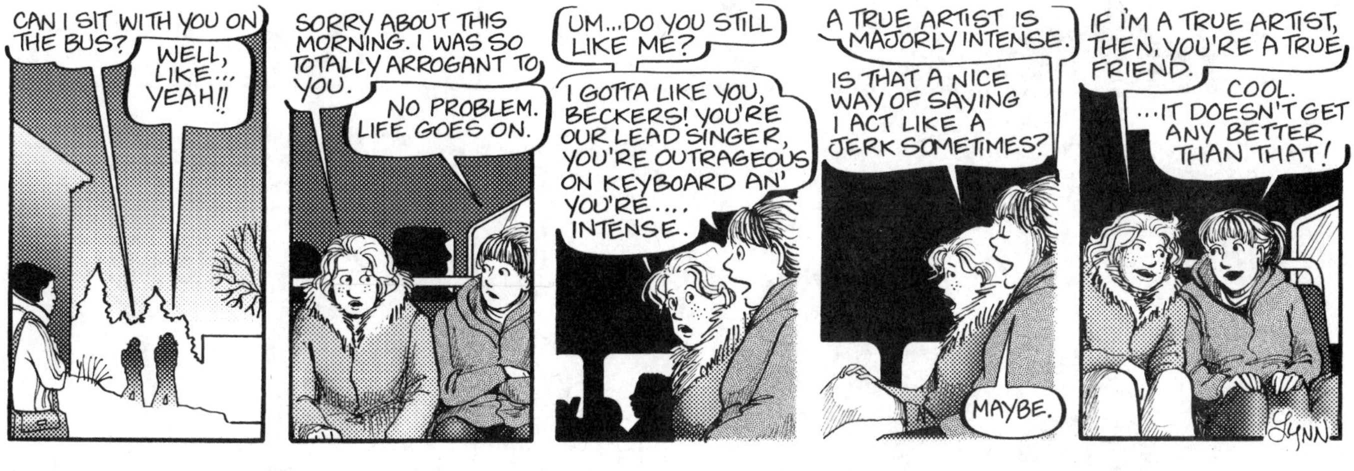
CAN I SIT WITH YOU ON THE BUS?
WELL, LIKE... YEAH!!
SORRY ABOUT THIS MORNING. I WAS SO TOTALLY ARROGANT TO YOU.
NO PROBLEM. LIFE GOES ON.
UM...DO YOU STILL LIKE ME?
I GOTTA LIKE YOU, BECKERS! YOU'RE OUR LEAD SINGER, YOU'RE OUTRAGEOUS ON KEYBOARD AN' YOU'RE.... INTENSE.
A TRUE ARTIST IS MAJORLY INTENSE.
IS THAT A NICE WAY OF SAYING I ACT LIKE A JERK SOMETIMES?
MAYBE.
IF I'M A TRUE ARTIST, THEN, YOU'RE A TRUE FRIEND.
COOL. ...IT DOESN'T GET ANY BETTER THAN THAT!
LYNN

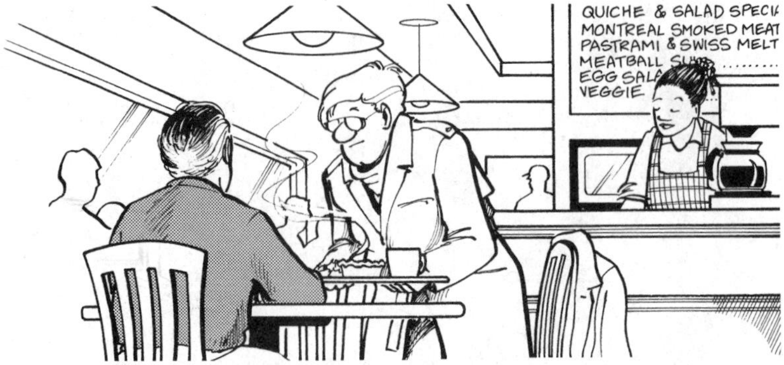
QUICHE & SALAD SPECI
MONTREAL SMOKED MEAT
PASTRAMI & SWISS MELT
MEATBALL
EGG SALA
VEGGIE

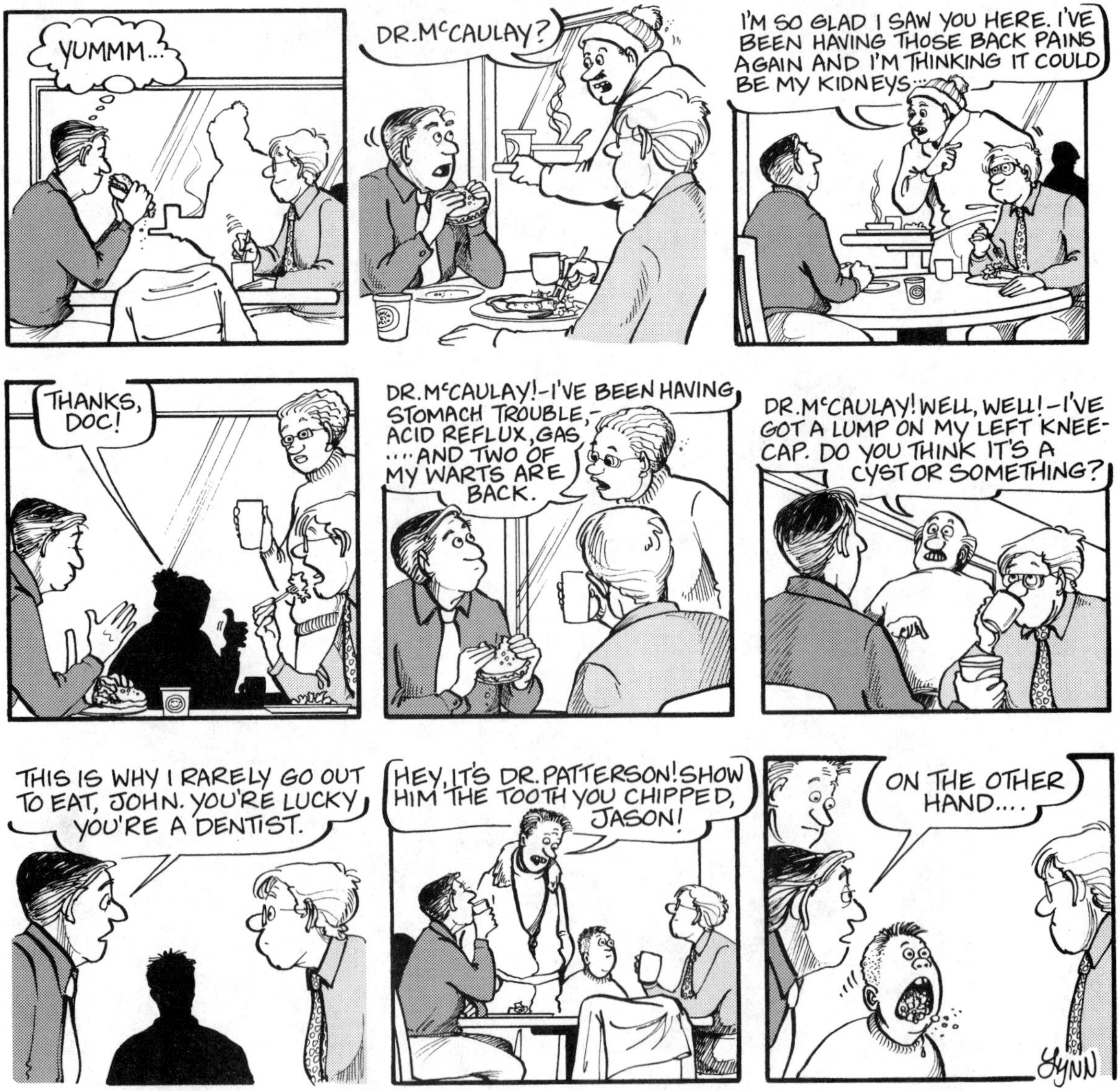
YUMMM...
DR. McCAULAY?
I'M SO GLAD I SAW YOU HERE. I'VE BEEN HAVING THOSE BACK PAINS AGAIN AND I'M THINKING IT COULD BE MY KIDNEYS....
THANKS, DOC!
DR. McCAULAY! -I'VE BEEN HAVING STOMACH TROUBLE, - ACID REFLUX, GAS ....AND TWO OF MY WARTS ARE BACK.
DR. McCAULAY! WELL, WELL! -I'VE GOT A LUMP ON MY LEFT KNEE-CAP. DO YOU THINK IT'S A CYST OR SOMETHING?
THIS IS WHY I RARELY GO OUT TO EAT, JOHN. YOU'RE LUCKY YOU'RE A DENTIST.
HEY, IT'S DR. PATTERSON! SHOW HIM THE TOOTH YOU CHIPPED, JASON!
ON THE OTHER HAND....
Lynn

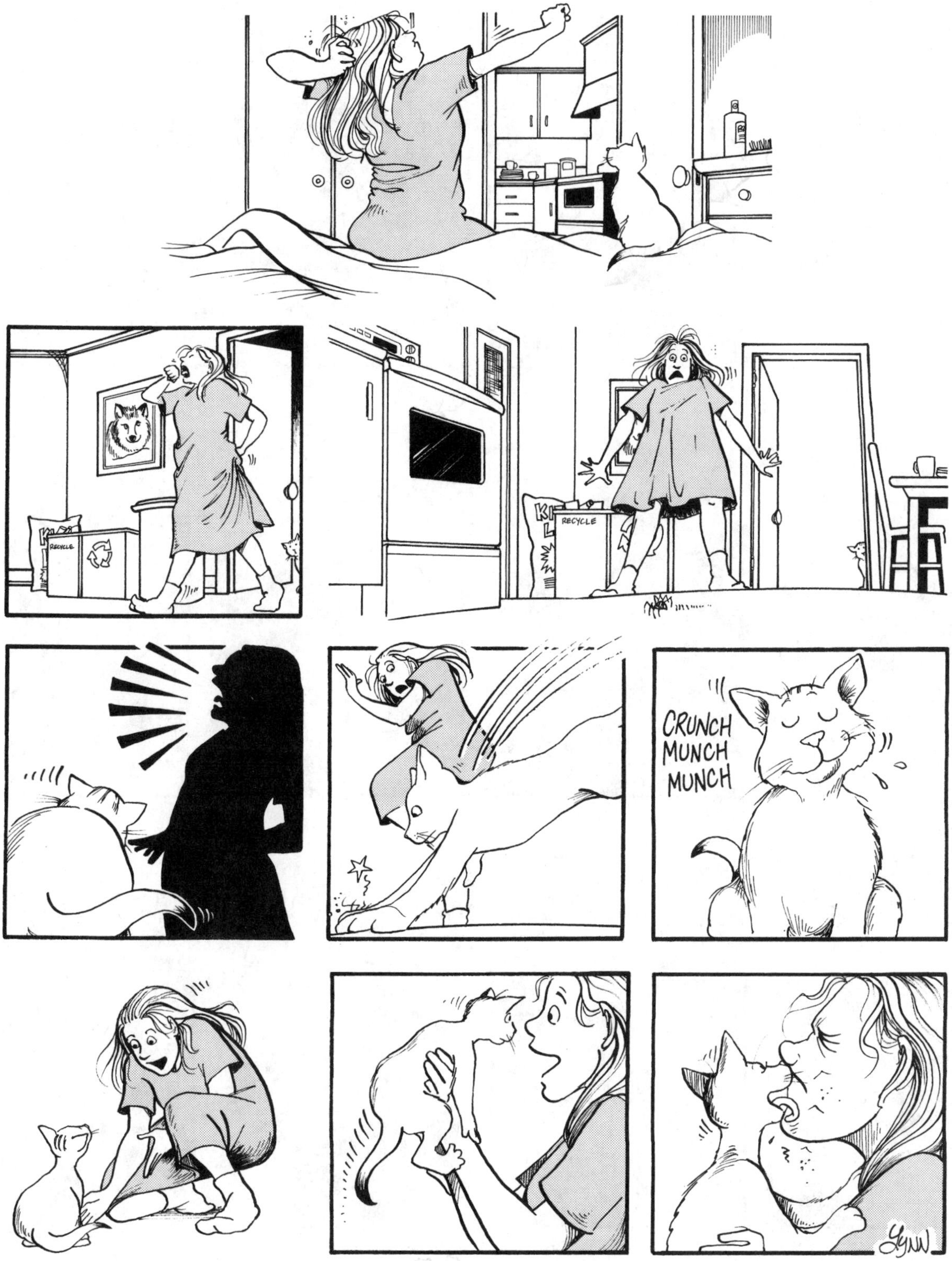
RECYCLE
RECYCLE
CRUNCH
MUNCH
MUNCH

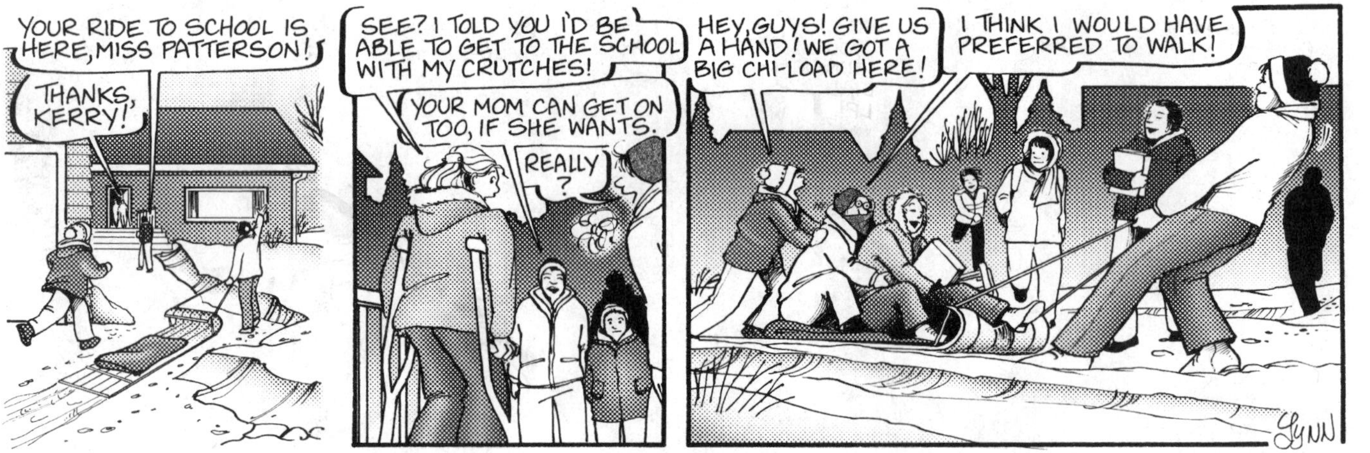
YOUR RIDE TO SCHOOL IS HERE, MISS PATTERSON!
THANKS, KERRY!
SEE? I TOLD YOU I'D BE ABLE TO GET TO THE SCHOOL WITH MY CRUTCHES!
YOUR MOM CAN GET ON TOO, IF SHE WANTS.
REALLY?
HEY, GUYS! GIVE US A HAND! WE GOT A BIG CHI-LOAD HERE!
I THINK I WOULD HAVE PREFERRED TO WALK!
LYNN

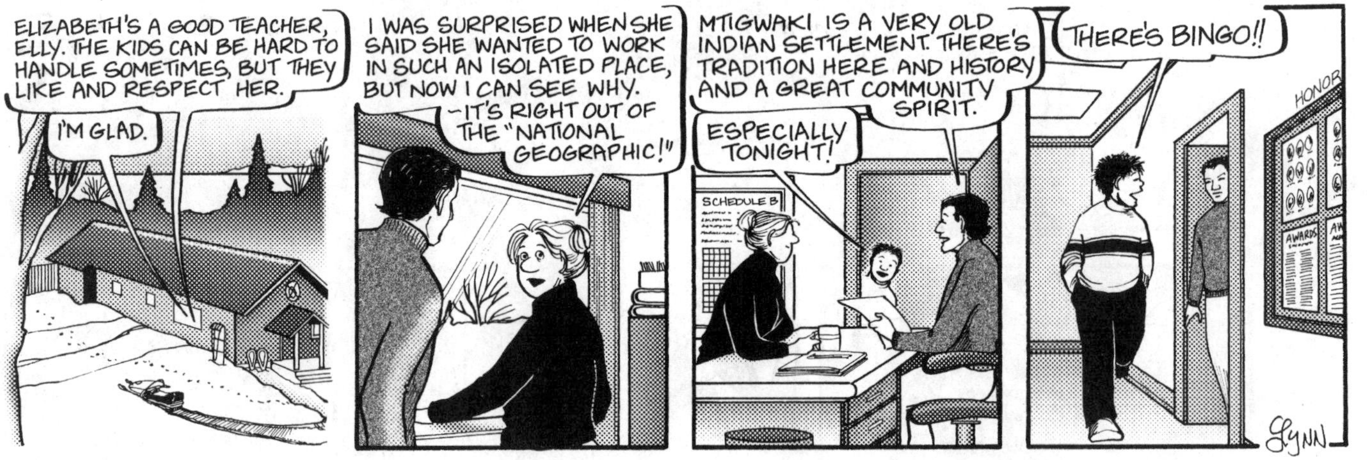
ELIZABETH'S A GOOD TEACHER, ELLY. THE KIDS CAN BE HARD TO HANDLE SOMETIMES, BUT THEY LIKE AND RESPECT HER.
I'M GLAD.
I WAS SURPRISED WHEN SHE SAID SHE WANTED TO WORK IN SUCH AN ISOLATED PLACE, BUT NOW I CAN SEE WHY.
—IT'S RIGHT OUT OF THE "NATIONAL GEOGRAPHIC!"
MTIGWAKI IS A VERY OLD INDIAN SETTLEMENT. THERE'S TRADITION HERE AND HISTORY AND A GREAT COMMUNITY SPIRIT.
ESPECIALLY TONIGHT!
SCHEDULE B
THERE'S BINGO!!
HONOR
AWARDS
LYNN

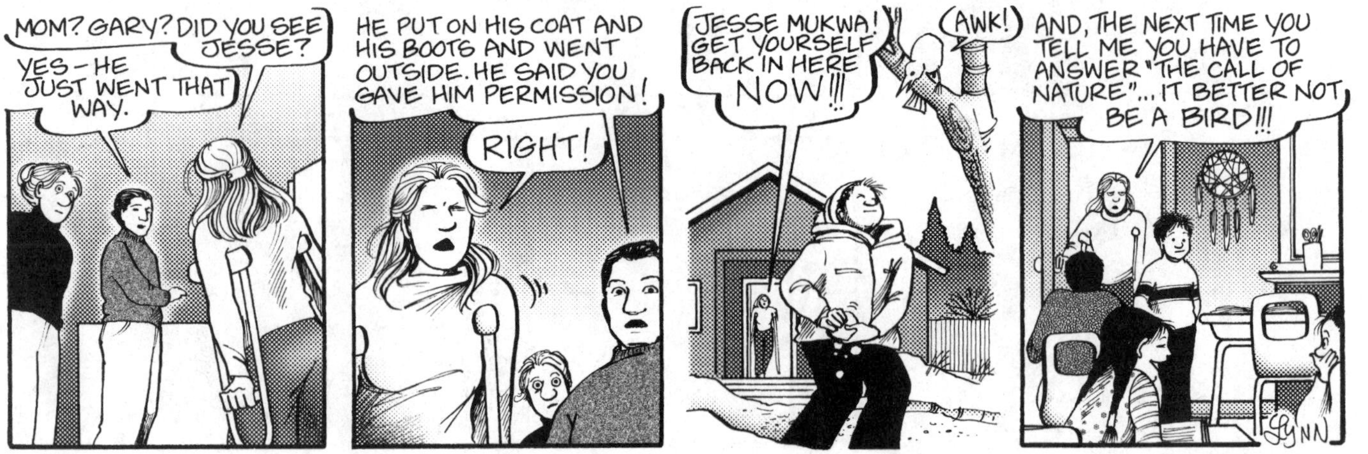
MOM? GARY? DID YOU SEE JESSE?
YES—HE JUST WENT THAT WAY.
HE PUT ON HIS COAT AND HIS BOOTS AND WENT OUTSIDE. HE SAID YOU GAVE HIM PERMISSION!
RIGHT!
JESSE MUKWA! GET YOURSELF BACK IN HERE NOW!!!
AWK!
AND, THE NEXT TIME YOU TELL ME YOU HAVE TO ANSWER "THE CALL OF NATURE"... IT BETTER NOT BE A BIRD!!!
LYNN

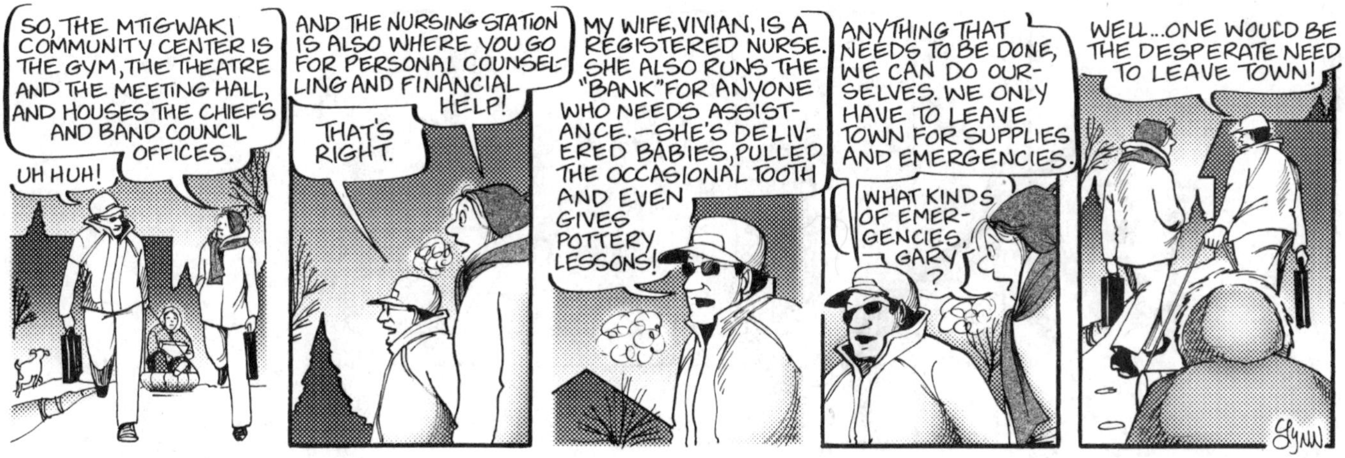
SO, THE MTIGWAKI COMMUNITY CENTER IS THE GYM, THE THEATRE AND THE MEETING HALL, AND HOUSES THE CHIEF'S AND BAND COUNCIL OFFICES.
UH HUH!
AND THE NURSING STATION IS ALSO WHERE YOU GO FOR PERSONAL COUNSELLING AND FINANCIAL HELP!
THAT'S RIGHT.
MY WIFE, VIVIAN, IS A REGISTERED NURSE. SHE ALSO RUNS THE "BANK" FOR ANYONE WHO NEEDS ASSISTANCE.—SHE'S DELIVERED BABIES, PULLED THE OCCASIONAL TOOTH AND EVEN GIVES POTTERY LESSONS!
ANYTHING THAT NEEDS TO BE DONE, WE CAN DO OURSELVES. WE ONLY HAVE TO LEAVE TOWN FOR SUPPLIES AND EMERGENCIES.
WHAT KINDS OF EMERGENCIES, GARY?
WELL...ONE WOULD BE THE DESPERATE NEED TO LEAVE TOWN!
LYNN

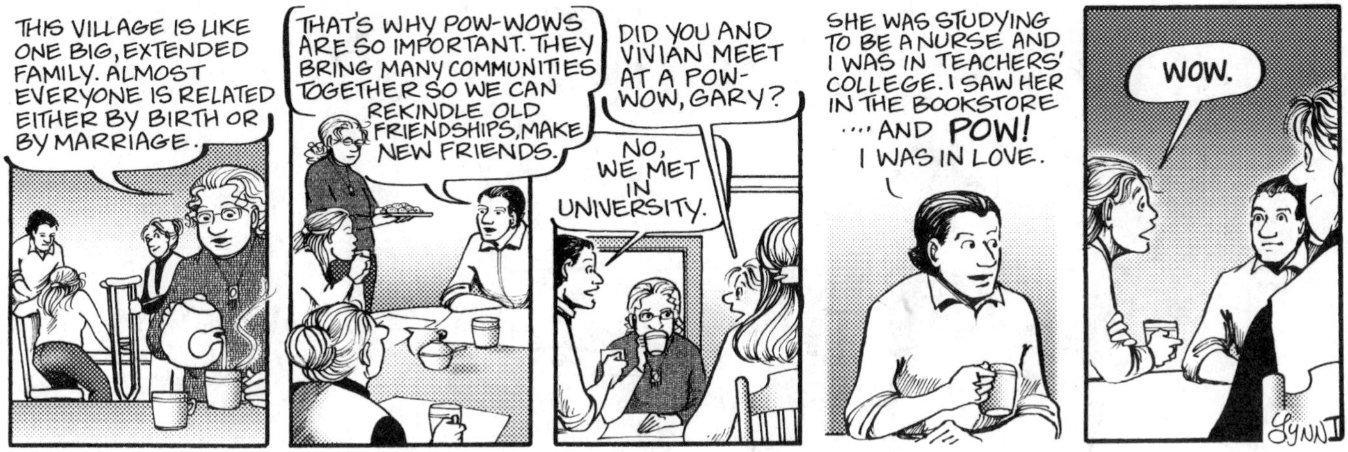
THIS VILLAGE IS LIKE ONE BIG, EXTENDED FAMILY. ALMOST EVERYONE IS RELATED EITHER BY BIRTH OR BY MARRIAGE.
THAT'S WHY POW-WOWS ARE SO IMPORTANT. THEY BRING MANY COMMUNITIES TOGETHER SO WE CAN REKINDLE OLD FRIENDSHIPS, MAKE NEW FRIENDS.
DID YOU AND VIVIAN MEET AT A POW-WOW, GARY?
NO, WE MET IN UNIVERSITY.
SHE WAS STUDYING TO BE A NURSE AND I WAS IN TEACHERS' COLLEGE. I SAW HER IN THE BOOKSTORE .... AND POW! I WAS IN LOVE.
WOW.
LYNN

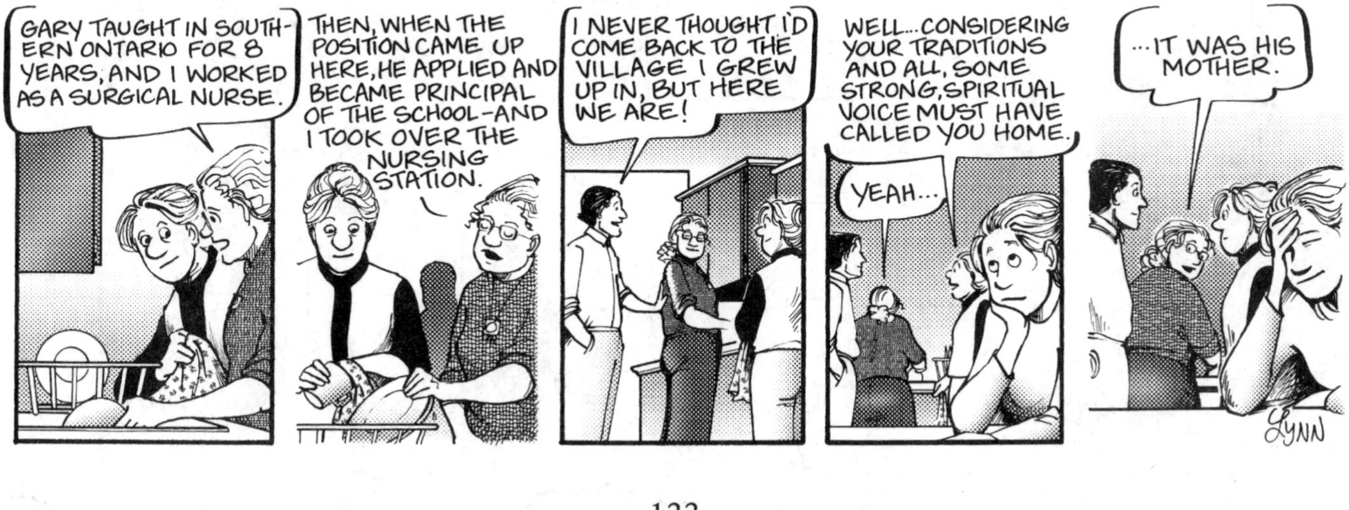
GARY TAUGHT IN SOUTHERN ONTARIO FOR 8 YEARS, AND I WORKED AS A SURGICAL NURSE.
THEN, WHEN THE POSITION CAME UP HERE, HE APPLIED AND BECAME PRINCIPAL OF THE SCHOOL—AND I TOOK OVER THE NURSING STATION.
I NEVER THOUGHT I'D COME BACK TO THE VILLAGE I GREW UP IN, BUT HERE WE ARE!
WELL...CONSIDERING YOUR TRADITIONS AND ALL, SOME STRONG, SPIRITUAL VOICE MUST HAVE CALLED YOU HOME.
YEAH...
...IT WAS HIS MOTHER.
LYNN

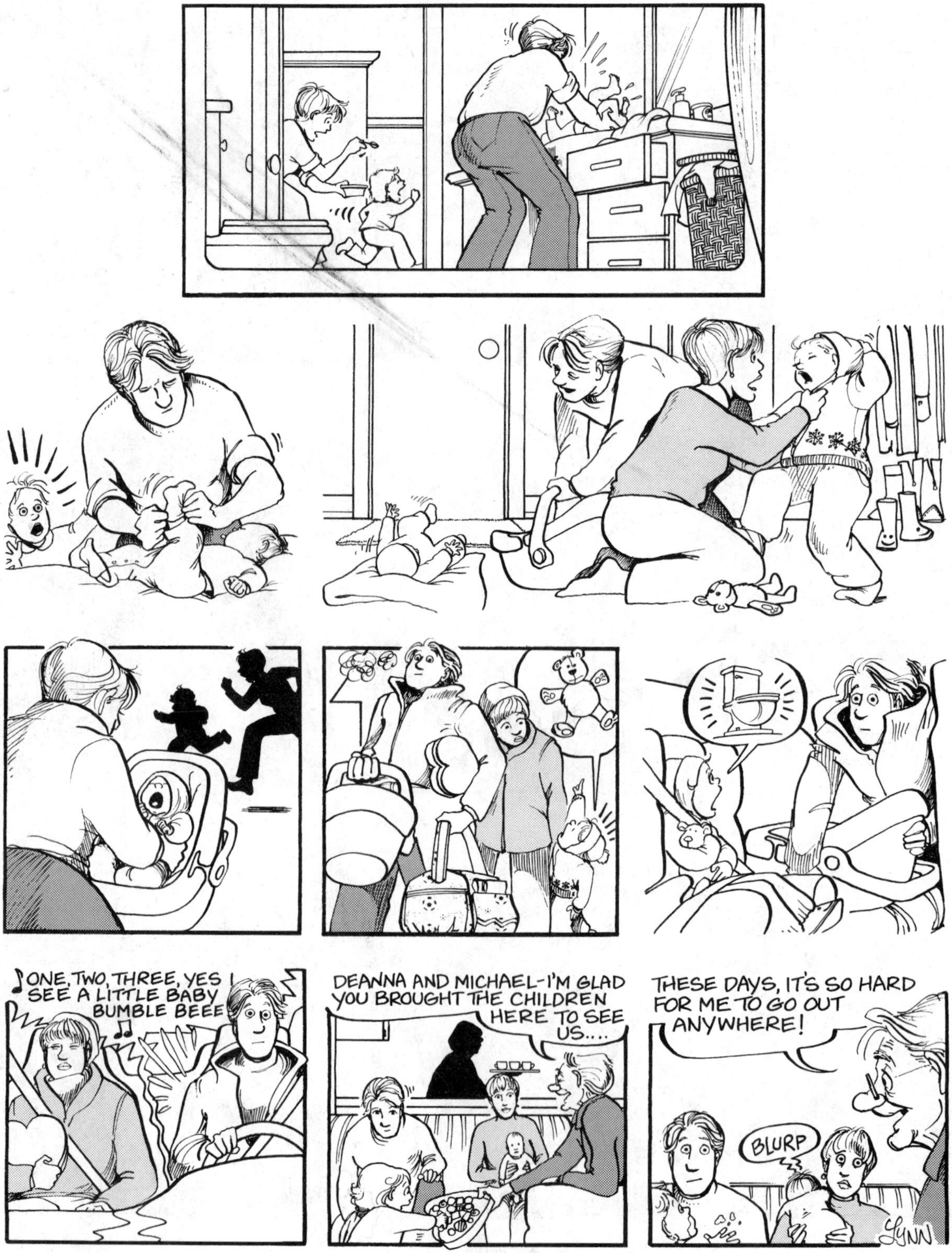
ONE, TWO, THREE, YES I SEE A LITTLE BABY BUMBLE BEEE
DEANNA AND MICHAEL-I'M GLAD YOU BROUGHT THE CHILDREN HERE TO SEE US....
THESE DAYS, IT'S SO HARD FOR ME TO GO OUT ANYWHERE!
BLURP
LYNN

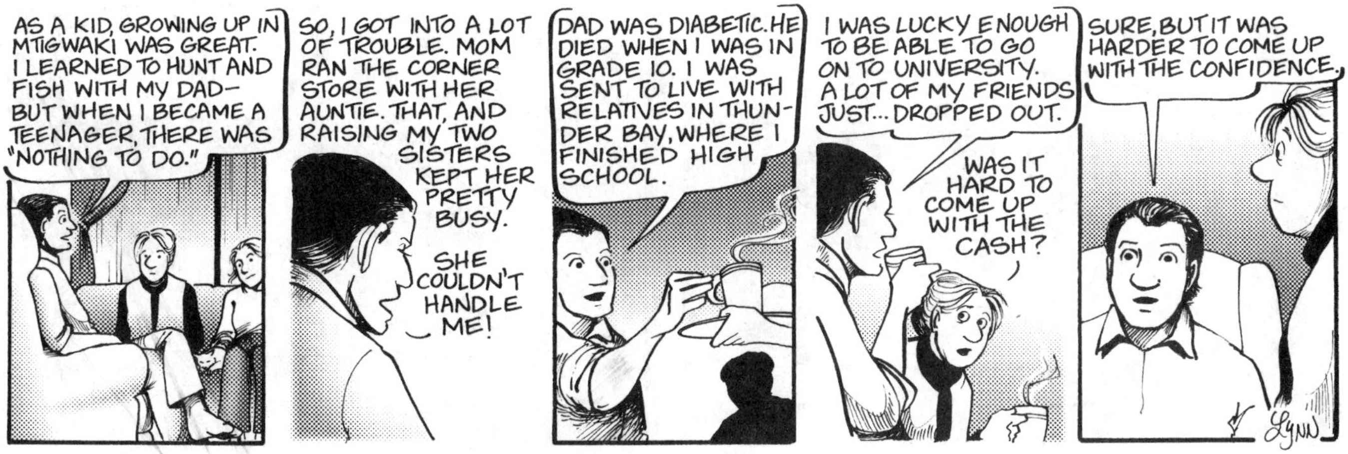
AS A KID, GROWING UP IN MTIGWAKI WAS GREAT. I LEARNED TO HUNT AND FISH WITH MY DAD– BUT WHEN I BECAME A TEENAGER, THERE WAS "NOTHING TO DO."
SO, I GOT INTO A LOT OF TROUBLE. MOM RAN THE CORNER STORE WITH HER AUNTIE. THAT, AND RAISING MY TWO SISTERS KEPT HER PRETTY BUSY.
SHE COULDN'T HANDLE ME!
DAD WAS DIABETIC. HE DIED WHEN I WAS IN GRADE 10. I WAS SENT TO LIVE WITH RELATIVES IN THUNDER BAY, WHERE I FINISHED HIGH SCHOOL.
I WAS LUCKY ENOUGH TO BE ABLE TO GO ON TO UNIVERSITY. A LOT OF MY FRIENDS JUST... DROPPED OUT.
WAS IT HARD TO COME UP WITH THE CASH?
SURE, BUT IT WAS HARDER TO COME UP WITH THE CONFIDENCE.
LYNN

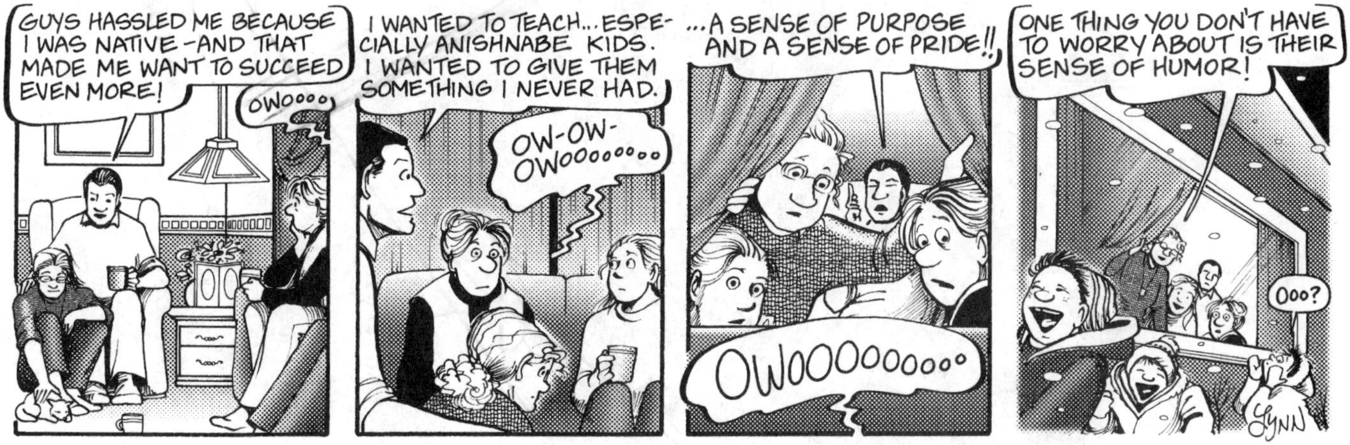
GUYS HASSLED ME BECAUSE I WAS NATIVE –AND THAT MADE ME WANT TO SUCCEED EVEN MORE!
OWOOOO
I WANTED TO TEACH... ESPECIALLY ANISHNABE KIDS. I WANTED TO GIVE THEM SOMETHING I NEVER HAD.
OW-OW-OWOOOOOOOO
...A SENSE OF PURPOSE AND A SENSE OF PRIDE!!
OWOOOOOOOOO
ONE THING YOU DON'T HAVE TO WORRY ABOUT IS THEIR SENSE OF HUMOR!
OOO?
LYNN

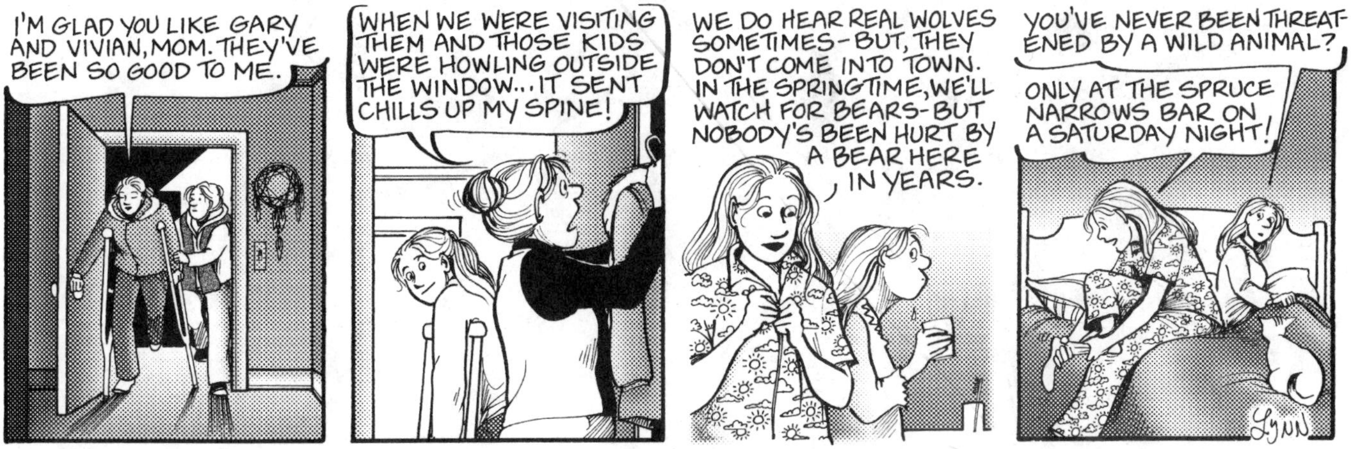
I'M GLAD YOU LIKE GARY AND VIVIAN, MOM. THEY'VE BEEN SO GOOD TO ME.
WHEN WE WERE VISITING THEM AND THOSE KIDS WERE HOWLING OUTSIDE THE WINDOW... IT SENT CHILLS UP MY SPINE!
WE DO HEAR REAL WOLVES SOMETIMES – BUT, THEY DON'T COME INTO TOWN. IN THE SPRINGTIME, WE'LL WATCH FOR BEARS– BUT NOBODY'S BEEN HURT BY A BEAR HERE IN YEARS.
YOU'VE NEVER BEEN THREATENED BY A WILD ANIMAL?
ONLY AT THE SPRUCE NARROWS BAR ON A SATURDAY NIGHT!
LYNN

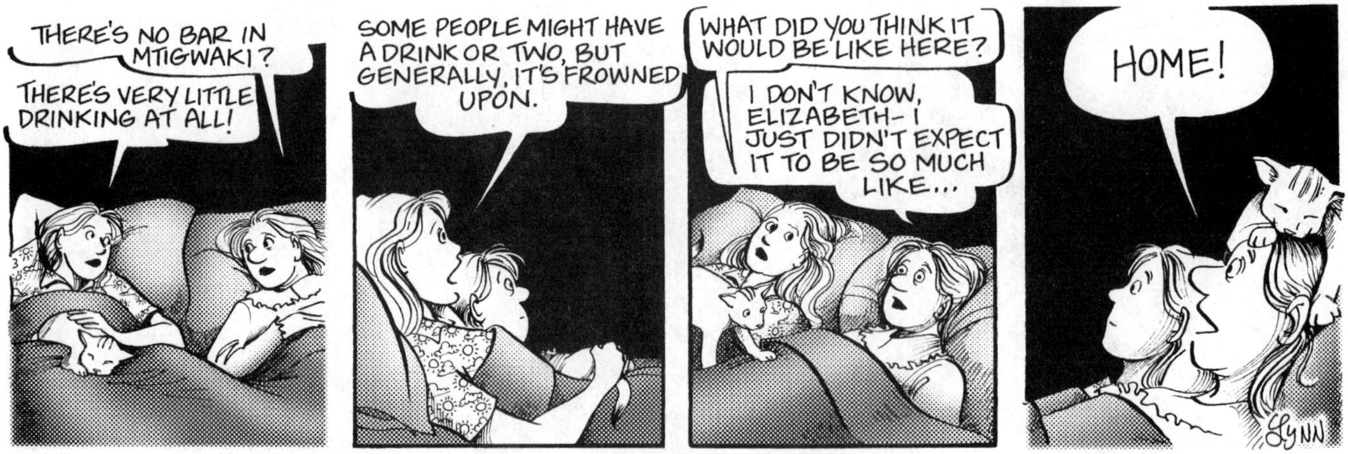
THERE'S NO BAR IN MTIGWAKI?
THERE'S VERY LITTLE DRINKING AT ALL!
SOME PEOPLE MIGHT HAVE A DRINK OR TWO, BUT GENERALLY, IT'S FROWNED UPON.
WHAT DID YOU THINK IT WOULD BE LIKE HERE?
I DON'T KNOW, ELIZABETH- I JUST DIDN'T EXPECT IT TO BE SO MUCH LIKE...
HOME!
LYNN

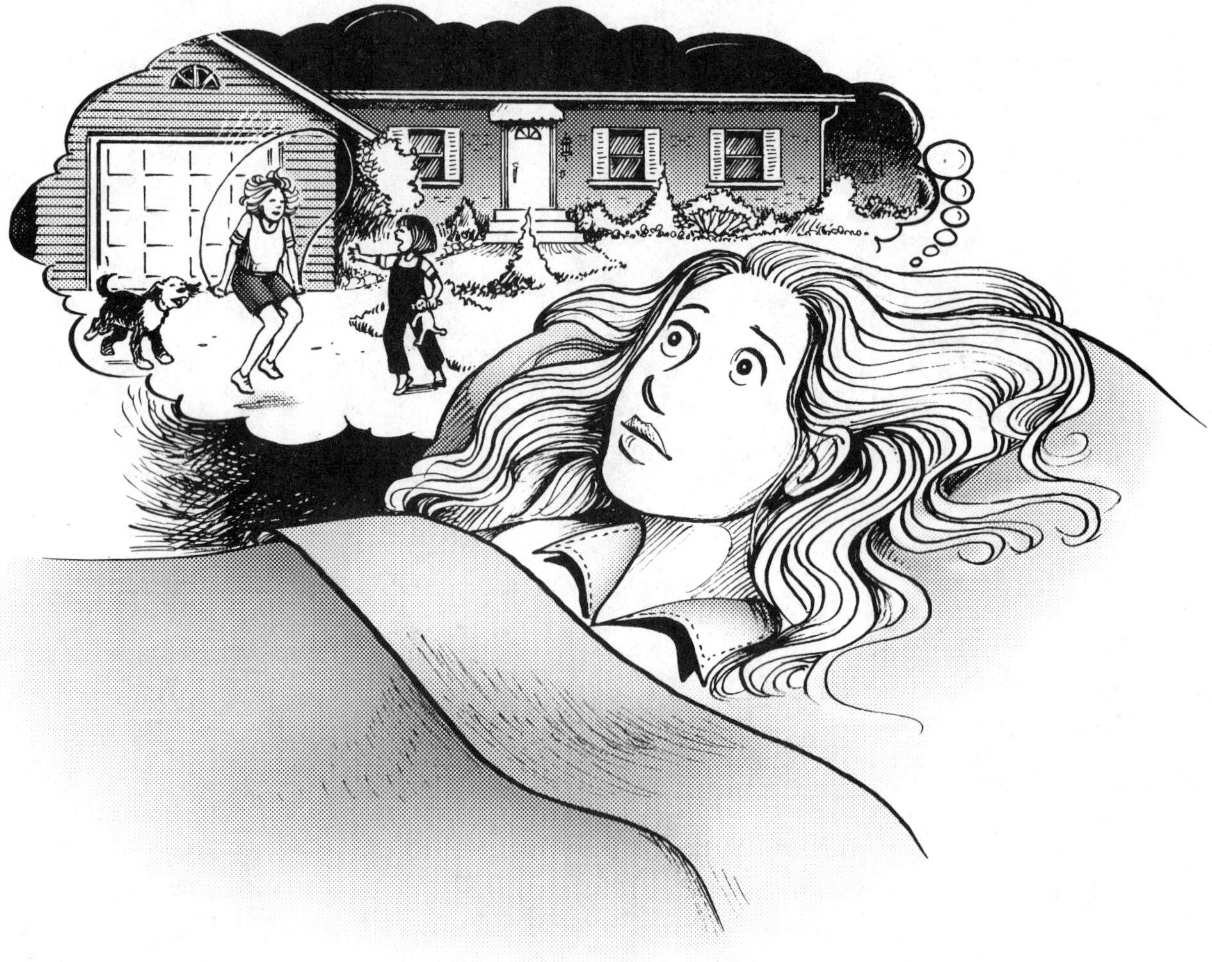